T0355371

MELODY
IN THE DARK

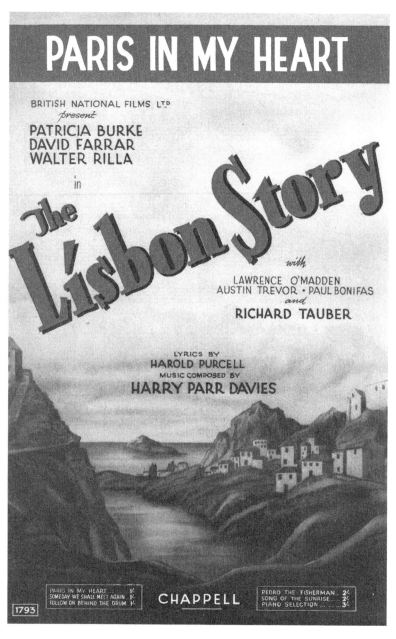

A heavyweight London stage success of 1943, Harry Parr Davies and Harold Purcell's *Lisbon Story* (1946) was directed for film by German émigré Paul L. Stein, who went on to direct his final British musical film *The Laughing Lady*, also 1946.

MELODY IN THE DARK

BRITISH MUSICAL FILMS, 1946–1972

Adrian Wright

THE BOYDELL PRESS

First published 2023
The Boydell Press, Woodbridge

ISBN 978 1 78327 749 0

The Boydell Press is an imprint of Boydell & Brewer Ltd
PO Box 9, Woodbridge, Suffolk IP12 3DF, UK
and of Boydell & Brewer Inc.
668 Mt Hope Avenue, Rochester, NY 14620–2731, USA
website: www.boydellandbrewer.com

A CIP catalogue record for this book is available
from the British Library

The publisher has no responsibility for the continued existence or accuracy of URLs for
external or third-party internet websites referred to in this book, and does not guarantee that any content on such websites is, or will remain, accurate or appropriate

This publication is printed on acid-free paper

Printed and bound in Great Britain by TJ Books Limited, Padstow, Cornwall

This book is for Roger Mellor

Contents

1968

Oliver! • A Little of What You Fancy • Chitty Chitty Bang Bang
• Mrs Brown You've Got a Lovely Daughter • Les Bicyclettes de Belsize
• Popdown   290

1969

Can Heironymus Merkin Ever Forget Mercy Humppe and Find True
Happiness? • What's Good for the Goose • Oh! What a Lovely War
• Goodbye Mr Chips   298

1970

Toomorrow • Scrooge   305

1972

The Boy Friend   310

Illustrations

All illustrations are courtesy of Paul Guinery.

Full credit details are provided in the captions to the images in the text. The author and publisher are grateful to all the institutions and individuals for permission to reproduce the materials in which they hold copyright. Every effort has been made to trace the copyright holders; apologies are offered for any omission, and the publisher will be pleased to add any necessary acknowledgement in subsequent editions.

Preface and Acknowledgements

The fortunes of the British film industry after the end of World War II were of very little significance compared with the toll that conflict had inflicted on the nation's people.

Both the coming of war and its ending were turning points for the careers of the handful of performers that we might describe as British musical film stars. Following her last major feature *Sailing Along* in 1938, Jessie Matthews made her singing and dancing farewell in the depressing circumstance of the 1944 *Candles at Nine*, reappearing only in the aptly titled short *Life Is Nothing Without Music* (1947) and, dubbed but at least in colour, in a minor role for *tom thumb* (1958). Similarly, after dominating domestic screens throughout the 1930s, Gracie Fields bid her adieu to British studios with the 1939 *Shipyard Sally*. Another casualty was diminutive Bobby Howes, ending his long run in delightfully inconsequential musical comedies of the decade with *Yes, Madam?* in 1939.

The constantly chirpy Stanley Lupino had worked consistently to cheer up British cinemagoers from the beginning of the 1930s, running out of steam in 1939 with *Lucky to Me*. The most successful husband and wife performers in British films, Jack Hulbert and Cicely Courtneidge, working separately or together, had enjoyed success since the very beginning of British musical films in 1930 with the revue extravaganza *Elstree Calling*, but faded to black with the 1940 *Under Your Hat*, Hulbert returning much diminished a decade later with *Into the Blue*, and Courtneidge waiting fifteen years before playing the title role in a cheap comedy-thriller, *Miss Tulip Stays the Night*, which involved the further indignity of her being billed below the current pneumatically splendid starlet Diana Dors. Although not in the major division, siren Frances Day was some sort of personification of British 1930s glamour until *The Girl in the Taxi* (1937), but she was largely unseen during the war years except for the 1944 *Fiddlers Three*, re-emerging eight years later in *Tread Softly*, a film that only reinforced the opinion that she had belonged to the earlier decade.

The war had been kinder to others, whose style and material may be said to have suited the country's need. At the outbreak of war, George Formby was already the most prominent male star in British pictures, and he remained for the duration, coming to a befitting end only with the 1946 *George in Civvy Street*. Jack Buchanan's gentlemanly refinement had been a constant of the 1930s, but cinematically his career quietened after 1940; it would be 1955 before he returned as a screen performer in *As Long As They're Happy* and, co-starring with Fred Astaire, Hollywood's *The Band Wagon*. Elsie and Doris Waters, the roll-up-your-sleeves and make-do-and-mend women in the British queue, made their impression with three films with a pull-yourselves-together and get-on-with-the-war attitude between 1942 and 1944. Their duty done, they did not go back to the studios. The war was even more fertile for others. The concert party mascot Arthur Askey ('Hello playmates!') was in at the beginning with his radio success *Band Waggon*, and was kept busy through the war until in 1944 he was stung by *Bees in Paradise*. It would be eleven years before he returned to the screen.

Tommy Trinder first played in 1938 with *Almost a Honeymoon* and *Save a Little Sunshine*, continuing with some notable productions of the war, among them *Champagne Charlie* and *Fiddlers Three*, and dwindling through the 1950s until the 1974 *Barry Mackenzie Holds His Own*. Bud Flanagan (notably with the Crazy Gang and stage partner Chesney Allen) remained popular through the 1930s and war, returning after the conflict with John Baxter's semi-docu-mentary *Judgment Deferred*. Frank Randle, the most disruptive comic actor of his age, threw caution to the wind in five rumbustious pictures during the war, ending with *When You Come Home*. Nobody would have been surprised if he had then fled back to the music-halls to which he belonged, but he continued to prosper in his 'Somewhere' series, clocking off in 1953 when (unlike Cicely Courtneidge in *Miss Tulip Stays the Night*) he proved he could see Diana Dors off the screen.

Anna Neagle, once Marjorie Robertson, probably deserves a paragraph of her own, and gets several of them in the ensuing pages. With her sustained commercial success over three decades, from the 1930 *Should a Doctor Tell?* through to her 1959 co-starring with popular singer Frankie Vaughan in the possibly unwisely titled *The Lady Is a Square*, she achieved a status in British cinema that few matched. The reason that she was able to sustain her career through many artistic vicissitudes is explained in two words: Herbert Wilcox. It was he who, having tried to build the now almost forgotten Chili Bouchier into a musical film star, took up Neagle, managed her career, married her, and directed her. Their first film, *Goodnight, Vienna* (1931) teamed her with Jack Buchanan. She subsequently played opposite various leading men: Fernand Graavey for *Bitter Sweet* (1933) and *The Queen's Affair* (1934); Arthur Tracy for *Limelight* (1935); Tullio Carminati for *The Three Maxims* (1936) and *London Melody* (1937). All may be said to have played second fiddle.

Wilcox then starred her in the five pictures of his 'London' series, distinc-tively located in various environs of the metropolis: Grosvenor Square, Pic-cadilly, Curzon Street, Park Lane, and Mayfair. In the enervating dullness of Britain in the 1940s, these fanciful excursions into a glamorous world through which Neagle moved with ineffable graciousness were just what Doctor Box Office wanted. By her side in all except *Piccadilly Incident* was Michael Wilding, Wilcox's third choice after Rex Harrison and John Mills; at first, 'neither Anna nor I liked the look of him at all.'[1] The effectiveness of the Neagle–Wilding partnership took the young actor by surprise. Wilcox explained that Wilding

> could not accept the fact that he personally could make an appreciable impact on cinema audiences. I told him of the mean Lowry-like houses and people in the mining districts of the North, where I served my film apprenticeship. Four walls and a roof, holes for the front door and windows, outside water closets, and not always water. I have never forgotten the grim, unglamorous existence of the people who lived in those districts. That is why I believed in glamour and that is why we were so successful.[2]

In between times, Neagle enjoyed success in a series of screen biographies: twice as Queen Victoria, as Nell Gwyn, Peg of Old Drury, aviator Amy Johnson in *They Flew Alone* (1942), a British secret agent in the 1950 *Odette* (one of her best performances), and as Florence Nightingale in *The Lady with a Lamp* (1951). In the mid-1950s, she formed an unlikely screen partnership with Hollywood's Errol Flynn in the supposedly lush *Lilacs in the Spring* and Ivor Novello's Ruritanian operetta *King's Rhapsody*, before being credited in the late 1950s as producer for popular singer Frankie Vaughan's *These Dangerous Years*, *Wonderful Things*, and *The Heart of a Man*; all these, of course, were directed by Wilcox.

The war over, it seemed there might be room for new talents to refresh the British musical film. Throughout the 1950s, despite the lack of product being produced in British studios, there was no shortage of attempts to establish various performers as primary. As in the period before and during the war and immediately after it, such talent often came from the stage, especially from what was now termed 'variety'. Enduring stardom, itself all too often the driving plot device of the British musical film, was rarely gifted, the fall from grace made vivid as a performer's name slipped into the supporting credits. It had always been thus. A lesson might be learned from Betty Balfour, immortalised through her impersonation of cockney flower-girl Squibs and voted 'Top World Star' in the 1927 *Daily Mirror* poll, from whom success fell away by the mid-1930s. She had nine years in the professional wilderness before signing up for a last project, the cut-price *29 Acacia Avenue* (1945).

Transition to the screen proved difficult for some British theatrical divas; both Mary Ellis and Evelyn Laye, distinguished in their field but less secure in studio surroundings, quickly fell away, never to be satisfactorily replaced. Frances Day, unarguably linked to the 1930s, saw her film career fade in the 1940s, although her particular skills were gloriously evident in the 1944 *Fiddlers Three*. After an eight-year absence, she returned with less glory in

---

1 Herbert Wilcox, *Twenty-Five Thousand Sunsets* (London: Bodley Head, 1967), p. 144.
2 Ibid., p. 145.

Tread Softly. Occasionally, other leading ladies of the stage were taken up by the studios, as were Jean (later Jeannie) Carson and Pat Kirkwood, although some such as Sally Gray, a perfect screen partner for Stanley Lupino, survived from the 1930s and gained a reputation as straight actresses. Rene Ray, guaranteed to brighten the lightest of confections or (as in *The Passing of the Third Floor Back*) the most portentous parable, sat out the war but returned in the 1947 *They Made Me a Fugitive*, calling it a day in 1958 with *The Strange World of Planet X*, a mild horror-flick based on her own novel.

There would always be the need for good comedians. Taking up from where George Formby had signed off, the most regular and dominantly successful of the 1950s was Norman Wisdom in a string of comedies beginning with *A Date with a Dream*. He remained a significant figure from the 1953 *Trouble in Store* until the mid-sixties. There were bursts of activity from Max Bygraves, notably in *Charley Moon* (1956), but he joined other music-hall figures such as Sid Field and Hal Monty in failing to establish himself as a major player in musical films, while the hugely successful knockabout 'Old Mother Riley' series, from the mid-1930s up to 1952, ensured Arthur Lucan's unassailable relevance as a principal cinematic clown. Throughout the 1950s, there was the suspicion that British musical films lacked a sense of direction. How, with the Depression and the war behind it, could the genre resurrect itself, be of service to its audience, have purpose and meaning?

One answer (some might suggest an easy answer) was already being tried out by the end of the fifties: product that would appeal to younger cinemagoers. The route to this El Dorado of untapped customers was 'pop', embracing leading exponents of its art, the films having been produced by the middle-aged middlemen of the British studio system. In this way, singing stars such as Frankie Vaughan and Frank Ifield were suddenly thrust into what the studios hoped would be instant and lucrative screen stardom. One of the principal artists to undergo this process from 1957 to 1968 was Tommy Steele, who was even given his very own screen biopic. In 1958, café society took on a new, 'hip', aspect with the faintly ludicrous *The Golden Disc*, its very title reminding us of that most undemanding of art forms, hand-jiving. A little (but not notably) more sophisticated than the Steele pictures, Cliff Richard in 1961 embarked on a hugely successful series with *The Young Ones*, while others joined the field. Along the way Billy Fury, sometimes identified as the British Elvis Presley, brought his pets along for the warm-hearted *I've Gotta Horse* (1965), while Mike Sarne and John Leyton cavorted around Butlin's holiday camp at Clacton for the highly enjoyable *Every Day's a Holiday* (1964). By the mid-sixties it seemed that pop-related musical films might take over the British film industry, until the advent of The Beatles marked for some the decline of such productions and performers.

Despite the many attempts to turn public taste away from the past, the ancient thrum of the supposedly dead art of music-hall and variety persisted, manifested most tellingly in John Osborne's *The Entertainer*, a play that cried out (rather like Jean Kent's *Trottie True* of 1949) to be a proper musical rather than a drama with patchwork musical items. The essence of music-hall could not be denied throughout the period, whether in Rank's disastrous *London Town* (1946), *Bless 'em All* (1949), the 1957 remake of Priestley's *The Good Companions*, *Desert Mice* (1959) inspired by the Entertainments National Service Association (ENSA), or the London travelogue of the tattered remains of music-hall in *A Little of What You Fancy* (1968).

Theatrical entertainments, often much adapted, continued to be made into films, among them *Lisbon Story* (1946), *The Dancing Years* (1950), *Where's Charley?* (1952), *King's Rhapsody* (1955), the diminutive but delightful *Five Guineas a Week* (1956), *Stop the World – I Want to Get Off* (1966), *Half a Sixpence* (1967), *Oh! What a Lovely War* (1969), and *The Boy Friend (1972)*. Even more adventurously, the studios produced musicals specifically written for the screen, as in the Hollywood-styled *London Town* (1946) and the slight but pleasing *Three Hats for Lisa* (1965), and sometimes importing a holidaying Hollywood star, as exemplified by Vera-Ellen in *Happy Go Lovely* (1951). Too often, the mere presence of a flown-across-the-Atlantic musical star failed to alter the course of the British musical film.

Those looking to British cinema to provide opera and ballet from 1946 looked to The Archers (the ground-breaking Michael Powell and Emeric Pressburger). Operating at a supposedly higher cultural level than the average British musical film, they were regarded as daring buccaneers of the British studios, distinctively inventive and liable to ravishing visuals. *The Red Shoes* (1948), Offenbach's *The Tales of Hoffmann* (1951), and *Oh ... Rosalinda!!* (1955) provide testament. To these, we might add Gene Kelly's Technicolored *Invitation to the Dance* (1956) and the 1953 straying-from-the-facts biopic *Melba*. Another musical biography concerned the persistent purveyors of light entertainments long cherished by the British middle-class and its Victorian fathers, in *The Story of Gilbert and Sullivan* (1953). William Schwenck Gilbert, despite a gallows sense of humour and an unerring adherence to British decency, was one of the neatest lyricists and librettists of any age. Arthur Sullivan was a composer whose notably conservative talents were only truly nudged towards greatness when his 'establishment' writing and oratorio-like despondency were abandoned for lighter material.

Melody in the Dark revisits the British musical film from the beginning of the end of World War II to the early 1970s and is in its way a companion volume to my earlier *Cheer Up!: British Musical Films, 1929–1945*. In its way, it is rather like settling into your cinema seat halfway through the main feature, as was often done during the period this book covers, before the fashion for separate performances. How often the whispered remark 'This is where we came in' heralded the scooping up of hats and coats ready for departure. In concert with *Cheer Up!*, *Melody in the Dark* makes no claim to be encyclopaedic in nature. Neither is it comprehensive: the films it deals with are those singled out for discussion by the author. It makes no attempt to chart technical developments in the British film industry. The films are grouped chronologically year by year and arranged month by month in the sequence established by Denis Gifford in his indispensable *British Film Catalogue*, 'chronologically in order of their initial exhibition' with the explanation that 'It is common for films to be dated by their dates of release [although] this practice has not been followed here'.

Once again, I am indebted to the film historian and biographer Roger Mellor for the advice and encouragement he has offered throughout the preparation of this book. Michael King has given invaluable assistance on technical issues. Once more, Paul Guinery has most generously allowed me to explore his extraordinary collection of sheet music, lending a flavour and atmosphere to the book that 'stills' from the various films would not have provided.

The selection and exclusion of various British musical films is the responsibility of the author. A film with scant musical content may be included when one with more substantial credentials for inclusion is disregarded. Modern technological advances have been a boon to those interested in such material as we have here, making it likely that the history of British musical films is now more accessible and viewable than ever before. Readers are likely to be well informed, and to have opinions that may not chime with those of the author. However, I think it would be a mistake to write a book that attempts to cast a critical if affectionate eye on the British musical film with the intention of always pleasing the reader. You are invited to disagree with any of the opinions expressed in the following pages. As it happens, if I sat down to watch these films again, in many cases I would probably disagree with what I have set down here. Or not. Any idiocies that remain are my own.

1945

Old Mother Riley at Home	*Here Comes the Sun*
Sweethearts for Ever	*What Do We Do Now?*

MAY

Already an experienced director of the often-shambolic Arthur Lucan comedies, with *MP* and *Overseas* behind him, Oswald Mitchell was rehired for British National's **Old Mother Riley at Home**, produced by Louis H. Jackson and filmed in December 1944. The last of the wartime series before Lucan and Kitty McShane returned four years later with *Old Mother Riley's New Venture*, Mitchell and George Cooper's screenplay, with 'original story and dialogue' by Joan Butler, made no reference to the conflict that Britain had been enduring since 1939 beyond the appearance of some land-girls turning hay as Kitty and boyfriend Bill (Willer Neal in highly unsuitable correspondent shoes) stroll through an unconvincing countryside singing Percival Mackey and Donald O'Keefe's 'Let's Pretend We're Sweethearts'. Lucan's biographer understandably labels this 'a particularly nauseating duet between the "young lovers" [...] The lovers in question were fifty-two and forty-eight years old.'[1]

Neal had previously played in *Overseas* billed as Billy Breach. The *Monthly Film Bulletin* (*MFB*) decided that Neal 'must, one feels, have been chosen for the part on the strength of a moderately tuneful singing voice rather than for any pronounced acting ability'.[2] In fact, Neal had long been Kitty's on-stage and off-stage boyfriend; the triangular relationship between Arthur, Kitty, and Neal would persist until Arthur's death. Audiences of the day would have been unaware of the performers' emotional complications; now, the complexity lends a certain prurience to what we have on screen. O'Keefe and Mackey also contribute the rousingly jolly 'Cheer Up and Smile If You're Feeling Blue', performed by Kitty with her customary blankness and total lack of cinematic technique.

NOVEMBER

To herald the dawn of a new post-war era for the British musical film, direct from the bargain basement came the 'spectacularly untalented' American writer-director Frankland Atwood Richardson, who 'perpetrated some of the most incompetent quickies of the 1930s'.[3]

Richardson was responsible for the 1932 *Don't Be a Dummy* and a steady supply of hastily assembled entertainments such as the 1945 *Cabaret*, and 1946 *Amateur Night* featuring the Borstal Boys and the grotesque gurning of comedian Ernest Sefton. Richardson's new unintentionally hilarious concoction, **Sweethearts for Ever**, marked the occasion by presenting a mercifully brief variety bill of thirty-three minutes, produced for Empire Films by Moss Goodman and Victor Cockraine Hervey.

We are present at a celebration of Ma and Pa, a pair of dodderers running a boarding-house for lodging vaudevillians who are presenting them with their very own 'Command Performance'. As portrayed here, advanced senility has already settled in as they smile mindlessly at the ghastly entertainment spread for their delight.

Retained from *Cabaret* is the supposedly Chinese danseuse Mayura in a routine more stationary than sinuous. Her enticing hand movements suggest she is drying her fingernails. Mayura almost takes a tumble when she is entangled with her unmanageable drapery, but, aware of Mr Richardson's evident distaste for retakes, she carries on regardless. Plucky soubrette Rosalind Melville tells us 'I'm Happy When I'm Singing', but might have been given a better song. She is also stuck with a puerile running joke with her 'boyfriend' impressionist Carl Carlisle, whose impersonations take a good deal of footage (his speciality is to do Flanagan and Allen at the same time).

Most extraordinary of all is the rare opportunity to see the jazz and ragtime specialist Jules Ruben (here credited as Rubens), founder of the Jules Ruben School of Modern Rhythmic Piano Playing. Explaining that 'at this time' there is 'an acute shortage of artists' (and of talent, if his fellow performers are anything to go by), he straps himself into a sort of Lazy Susan roundabout head-gear harness with revolving hats, announcing himself as 'The Utility Concert Party'. Restoring calm, Johnny Dennis beguiles juddering Ma and Pa with Irish evergreens 'Rose of Tralee' and 'Danny Boy'.

DECEMBER

The films of John Baxter bestride British cinema from 1933, the year his remarkable *Doss House* set the path to which he resolutely stuck through a long career. As Geoff Brown and Tony Aldgate wrote, 'It may not be the last word in documentary realism – too much make-up, melodrama, and the soundtrack's sentimentalized arrangements of popular tunes see to that. Yet the film pursues its usual subject [the parlous living conditions of down-and-outs] with a forth-right sense of purpose.'[4]

As much may be said of almost every picture Baxter directed, despite their evident imperfections. Throughout the 1930s his unfailing efforts to promote social cohesiveness with a sincerity and naivety rare in British film-making, in concert with his constant recall of music-hall and variety, mark him as unique. The philosophy that imbues his work is never shallow and seldom profound, but is essential not only to the finest of his non-musical films as in the seminal *Love on the Dole* and *The Common Touch* (both 1941), but to every one of his 'lighter' pictures that at some point burst into song.

Without hesitation, we look to the lovely *Say It with Flowers* (1934) with its music-hall veterans Florrie Forde, Marie Kendall, and Charles Coborn forging the (according to Baxter) indestructible link between the working man and the halls. We look to Baxter's adaptation of J. B. Priestley's *Let the People Sing* (1942) for its treatise that the ordinary person can overrule officialdom when music is the catalyst for rebellion. We look to his *Old Mother Riley in Society* (1940), the finest of all of the many Arthur Lucan comedies, because it is Baxter who underpins the comedy with a touching melancholy absent from any other of the series; Baxter restores Lucan's ability as a tragedian at a time when others threatened to turn him into a low comedian. We may also look to the partnership Baxter forged with Bud Flanagan and gentlemanly Chesney Allen, through *We'll Smile Again* (1942), *Theatre Royal* (1943), *Dreaming* (1943), and **Here Comes the Sun**, on which shooting began at Ealing on 3 April. *The Times* decided that 'If its hilarity falls a little flat, at least [it] has substance. Mr Bud Flanagan contrives a good deal of robust fun at the expense of studio manners and methods, and adopts a variety of extravagant disguises in the interests of the deliberate absurdities of his script.'[5]

In fact, Flanagan simply gets hold of the film and never lets go, barnstorming through sequences that have lost none of their edge in seventy years, batting gags more hairy than gooseberries into the ninepennies. The prison scenes are particularly well done, not least the broadcast concert performed by the inmates. 'They're all very clever, aren't they dear,' says the governor's charming wife. 'Yes, they are,' he replies. 'That's why they're here.' After *Here Comes the Sun* Baxter planned another Flanagan and Allen picture to be called *Gag Man*, but Allen's declining health scuppered the project. After a seven-year absence, Flanagan returned in Baxter's fascinating *Judgment Deferred*.

In the difficult conditions of the last days of war, in July Grand National began location filming at Collins Music Hall in Islington for its new picture, **What Do We Do Now?** Producer Maurice J. Wilson and actor Charles Hawtrey making his debut as director had to cope with clearing away the filming par-aphernalia before the live shows at Collins took over each day, boards having been set up over the auditorium on which the cameras could operate. In the circumstances, Grand National cautiously announced its plan, *Kinematograph Weekly* reporting that 'The producers do not claim to be making a masterpiece, but they have got hold of some little-known personalities who have talent and big personalities, notably Jill Summers, a gifted Lancashire comedienne.'[6] In fact, the company included several established, even notable performers, with the top-billed George Moon and Burton Brown supported by comedian Ronald Frankau, Gloria Brent, Monte Crick, and Leslie Fuller, the popular star of so many 1930s film comedies making his final appearance. Other attractions in what was a pretty impressive roll call included Edmundo Ros's Conga Band, Steffani and His Thirty Silver Songsters, and Harry Parry's Swing Band.

George A. Cooper's screenplay worked around the Skewball Hippodrome's comedians Wesley (Moon) and Lesley (Brown), who turn detective to solve the mystery of a necklace stolen from fellow artiste Birdie (Summers). The proceedings include a title song and 'What's the Use?', both written by Allan Gray and lyricist Tommie Connor, but George A. Cooper's screenplay and Hawtrey's inexperienced direction (he was never to direct again) failed to impress, with the *MFB* complaining of 'a thin story and poor dialogue' and that 'the off-stage performances of some of the music-hall artists are very amateurish.'[7] Uncharacteristically, the reviewer at *Kinematograph Weekly* was in assault mode: the film was 'crude and witless'. Here was a pathetic attempt to make a British *Hellzapoppin*. Its intentions are honourable, but wit and showmanship are completely lacking. Its laughs can be counted on a mittened-hand. We'll say no more, except to remind the provincial and industrial exhibitor that it has star values and carries the feature quota ticket.'[8]

1946

Why were aeroplanes being built in the studio where the put-upon Mr Ruggles was trying to make a major British musical film? Did the hammering never stop?

London Town

Under New Management   *Amateur Night*
Lisbon Story   *Piccadilly Incident*
George in Civvy Street   *London Town*
Gaiety George   *Spring Song*
I'll Turn to You   *The Laughing Lady*
Meet the Navy   *Walking on Air*

FEBRUARY

The generous contribution of the Mancunian Film Corporation to the nation's welfare had catapulted George Formby to prominence with two cheaply produced entertainments, *Boots! Boots!* (1934) and *Off the Dole* (1935), after which he never darkened Mancunian's doors again. Although the company would not find another performer with so much potential, Mancunian went on building modest pictures around some of the most dependable comedic artistes of the 1930s and beyond, among them Nat Jackley, Norman Evans, Sandy Powell, Betty Jumel, Douglas Wakefield, Tessie O'Shea (like Formby, an enthusiast for a ukulele), and, most prominently, the uncontrollably anarchic Frank Randle. A regular repertoire of actors peopled Mancunian's 'Somewhere' series begun in 1940 with *Somewhere in England*, followed by *Somewhere in Camp* and *Somewhere on Leave*, both in 1942, and, very much along the same lines, *Demobbed* (1942). Unashamedly offered as low comedy, the usually pantomimic proceedings were often flavoured with musical items provided by such middle-of-the-road purveyors of culture as husband-and-wife team Anne Ziegler and Webster Booth, and piano duettists Rawicz and Landauer; such acts threatened Mancunian productions with something similar to sophistication.

The first post-war product, ***Under New Management***, proved that even Mancunian could come up with a neat title that might as well describe the times, had the advantage of a well-established, tightly knit team that worked almost as a family made up of people who knew what sort of pictures its customers wanted, and knew how to make them. At the helm was the untiring John E. Blakeley, not the finest of British film-makers but certainly one of the least pretentious. Nevertheless, the young Blakeley aspired to greatness, and under the umbrella of Song Films Limited produced twelve two-reel 'Cameo Operas' in the 1920s, the bravest of enterprises before film sound had been officially invented. Boiling down Verdi's and Puccini's and other composers' work to ten minutes must have been a stretch, and the result primitive, but 'The costumes could have graced any high budgeted drama, the locations were well chosen, and the photography was visually striking. Overall, [Blakeley's version of] *La Traviata* was an excellent production and was far removed from anything to be seen in Blakeley's later work.'[1]

Made at Hammersmith's Riverside Studios, *Under New Management* wound itself around Joe Evans (Norman Evans), who inherits a run-down hotel, targeted by crooks who realise the value of the land on which it stands. The script was by Blakeley, credited on screen as Anthony Toner, and Arthur Mertz, credited as Roney Parsons; Mancunian product was nothing if not 'in house'. The musical numbers, 'A Little Bit of Shamrock' and the lively company number 'We'd Join Up Again Today' (its title itself an indication that although the war might be ended, memories lingered), had lyrics by Mertz and another Mancunian regular, composer Albert Stanbury, with a score played by Percival Mackey's Orchestra. Promoted as a 'Scream-Lined Comedy', it had the advantage of Evans as the bosomy 'Over the Garden Wall' housewife, as well as his 'Going to the Dentist's' sketch in which he plays both dentist and terrified patient, exclaiming 'Battling Fanny' (perhaps a forefather of 'Bloody Norah') when the pain gets too much, and is understandably apprehensive when informed that the dentist has 'only been at it a fortnight'.

There is also that most rubber-necked giraffe of eccentric dancers Nat Jackley, alongside many who had appeared with him and Evans in *Demobbed*: the sublimely physical comedienne Betty Jumel, Dan Young, Tony Dalton, and Marianne Lincoln, now joined by Nicolette Roeg, the singing ingénue of *Home Sweet Home*. Others involved in the musical inserts include the 'Strolling Vagabond' Cavan O'Connor, the Donovan Octette, and Mendel's Female Sextette. The film was believed lost until a copy, lacking the final reel, was found in California.

MARCH

Making films based (often, and mistakenly, loosely) on London stage musicals had been a favourite pursuit of British film-makers up to and through the war, and a policy that recommenced with one of the most stolid London stage musicals of 1943, **Lisbon Story**. For some reason, it had managed almost 550 performances in the West End. Such success may have suggested it to British National and producer Louis H. Jackson as a copper-bottomed winner. The choice of Paul Stein as director further suggested that serious work was afoot, although Stein's own critique of his previous British musical film *Waltz Time* ('it stinks') was a little worrying. The theatre version, written by Harold Purcell and composer Harry Parr Davies, whose tunes had already helped several Gracie Fields's pictures, was now adapted by Jack Whittingham. British National had signed the stage show's leading lady Patricia Burke to repeat her role of Gabrielle Girard; Stein, long associated with the famous tenor Richard Tauber and having hired him for the 1935 blockbuster *Heart's Desire*, now signed him to sing *Lisbon Story*'s big hit, 'Pedro the Fisherman'.

On screen, the work failed to excite, being denounced by *Kinematograph Weekly* as 'colourful hokum'.[2] The gap between the London staging of 1943 and the film of 1946 did not help. The international and inevitably the domestic situation had undergone tremendous upheaval. Part of the film's problem was that its very story was a leftover from the war years. There would of course be many more such leftovers among the musical films to come; well into the 1950s, remembrance of the conflict remained a significant component of the genre. Meanwhile, Lisbon's story turned out to be about a British officer (David Farrar) sent to rescue an atomic scientist from the Nazi clutches. He falls for Girard (Burke), a cabaret artiste of the Parisian Magador, who plays her part by pretending to be a collaborator. The *MFB* recognised 'nothing but Occupied Europe clichés piled high at a time when we should have learned better', complaining that 'The whole affair is geared to showmanship [...] and will greatly shock any visitor from countries which have suffered actual Occupation.'[3]

The criticism is all the more cutting because Stein was himself an émigré who had escaped Nazi Germany. His film was no better received in Australia, where, except for Tauber's appearance, it was denounced as 'tiresome [...] stodgy stuff, stodgily produced' with Burke suffering from 'bunchy dressing and make-up; and every player, from that pat-a-cake dialogue'.[4] The British *Daily Telegraph* fell into line, seeing the picture as 'neither a musical comedy nor a tragedy but a tinsel wartime drama which rarely carries any conviction'.[5] Much-needed relief was offered by Stephane Grapelly (Grapelli) and the stylish Polish dancing act of Halama and Konarski. Some of Purcell and Davies's theatre score made it to the screen ('Some Day We Shall Meet Again', 'Follow the Drum', 'Never Say Goodbye', and 'Song of the Sunrise'), with Tauber bringing in the Sérénade from Lalo's *Le Roi d'Ys*, but it was 'Pedro the Fisherman' that kept Britain whistling; at one time, the publisher of its sheet music was selling 50,000 copies a week. Davies and Purcell wrote Burke's 'Paris in My Heart' for the film.

For Tauber, *Lisbon Story* was not only his last film with Stein, but his last; he died two years later, taking with him a contribution to the British musical film that is in many ways unique. One of several 'classical' singers who left their imprint, Tauber outran the competition. He may never have been the most cinematically appealing of his type, but his pictures of the mid-1930s made with Stein, *Blossom Time*, *Heart's Desire*, and *Land without Music*, solidified his popularity with the domestic public. There would be no more musical films for Burke; today, she is remembered, if at all, as the wireless mother of 'The Clitheroe Kid' Jimmy Clitheroe. Stein's next assignment of 1946 was yet another florid operetta-styled programme filler, the irresistible *The Laughing Lady* (she was Anne Ziegler).

After the end of war, the British film industry seldom looked to British musicals for screen adaptation. Between 1946 and 1971 these comprised:

1946   *Lisbon Story* (stage version 1943)
1950   *The Dancing Years* (stage version 1939)
1953   *The Beggar's Opera* (stage version 1728)
1955   *King's Rhapsody* (stage version 1949)
1959   *Expresso Bongo* (stage version 1958)
1960   *The Entertainer* (stage version 1957)
1963   *What a Crazy World* (stage version 1962)
1966   *Stop the World – I Want to Get Off* (stage version 1961)
1967   *Half a Sixpence* (stage version 1963)
1968   *Oliver!* (stage version 1960)
1969   *Oh! What a Lovely War* (stage version 1963)
1972   *The Boy Friend* (stage version 1954)

To this, we may add the Nöel Coward 'Red Peppers' sequence comprising one-third of the dishwater-dull 1952 *Meet Me Tonight*, based on its stage version of 1936. Broadway musicals that were filmed in British studios were the 1952 *Where's Charley?* (US stage version 1948; London stage version 1958) and in 1966 *A Funny Thing Happened on the Way to the Forum* (US stage version 1962; London stage version 1963).

The last of George Formby's World War II pictures, *I Didn't Do It*, had fared less well than many of his earlier comedies. The coming of peace marked a significant change, indicated by the title of his first post-war picture with Columbia British, **George in Civvy Street**, once again produced and directed by Marcel Varnel and written by a small army comprising Howard Irving Young and Peter Fraser, with contributions from Ted Kavanagh, Max Kester, and Gale Pedrick. Their wealth of experience did little to disguise a distinct falling-off with our George now pretending (as if anyone was fooled) to be happy-go-lucky army soldier George Harper being discharged from the army. Homeward bound on ship, he hints at the high jinks to come when they get back to Britain, because 'We've Been a Long Time Gone' (a typically neat number written by Formby and his regular writing partner Fred E. Cliffe). It's a catchy enough beginning, but a poor comedy sequence with the star trying out various dialects warns us that he may not be at the top of his form. George is remarkably upbeat as he collects his demob clothes, singing Michael Carr and Jimmy Kennedy's 'I Was Christened with a Horse-Shoe' and urging the British public to buck itself up and look to the future.

Arriving home, George makes for his old local The Unicorn, now in a ruinous state. Across the way, The Lion is run by Mary Colton, played by Rosalyn Boulter, the last in the long line of Formby's on-screen girlfriends, all of whom had triumphed in BBC received pronunciation. Nevertheless, George romances her with Wallace Towers and Ian Cunningham's natty 'It Could Be'. Mary responds in the discreetly charming manner adopted by all Formby's on-screen partners, but why was he never hitched to a homely mill-girl? Most of his screen girlfriends look as if they knew shorthand, and the scripts bleach any characterisation out of them. By now, anyway, you can feel the pace of the film slipping, with poorly executed silliness (messing about in a boat and much else) instead of wit, a supporting cast going through the motions. When crooks trick him into almost losing his licence, George takes refuge in reading *Alice in Wonderland*. This is the most interesting sequence, and the daftest, as Lewis Carroll's characters come to life in sub-Tenniel designs while George, now dressed as the March Hare, gambols through another of his and Cliffe's items, but it sits uneasily in the context of the story, although Boulter makes a convincing Alice.

Back from Wonderland, we have George's army mates and the musicians of Johnny Claes and His Clay Pigeons coming *en masse* to his rescue, renovating The Unicorn and preparing for its Grand Reopening. The jealous male admirer of Mary's (more bad casting) has her imprisoned in The Lion when his gang is about to ruin The Unicorn's celebrations, but she escapes in time to warn George, who has been entertaining his customers with 'I Won't Need a Licence for That' (Formby–Cliffe). The film reaches a new low with the arrival of a trouble-making minx (Daphne Elphinstone, in her – on this evidence not surprisingly – only film role), who performs a striptease to Fred Sandford's 'You Don't Need Them' (clothes, that is) that outrages the guests and will surely close the pub. It should have; it is a depressing low point in a film that can ill afford another. The shock horror this undressing unleashes is in accordance with everything else here. George, it seems, lives in a world that is, to put it mildly, intellectually constricted. More to the point, *George in Civvy Street* assumes its audience is equally disadvantaged. With its decent, self-explanatory title in place, here was an opportunity to gather together the myriad problems faced by a man returning home after war, with all its comic and romantic possibilities, in a wittily inventive entertainment. Instead, the film sits and stares back at us, a little gormlessly.

The *MFB* thought it 'not very amusing. [Formby] will presumably please his numerous and faithful fans, though he is unlikely by this performance to win over those people who still remain unappreciative.'[6] Cinemagoers were probably unaware that their star had spent five weeks in a psychiatric hospital early in the year. It would only be with the advent of Norman Wisdom in 1953 that another British entertainer would come close to what Formby had achieved in British musical films. His retirement from the screen did not preclude further successes on stage, notably the British musical *Zip Goes a Million* in 1951, although his last years were plagued by ill-health. He died in 1961.

Gaiety George provides the ideal opportunity to celebrate yet another George, George King, sometime 'King of the Quota Quickies', with a reputation for cranking out cheap, quickly produced product and building up a fortune. His cinematic beginnings were modest but impressive: he directed his first feature *Too Many Crooks* in 1930, with a cast that included Laurence Olivier. Subsequently, King seldom worked with so distinguished a performer, in a career that was never allowed access to the First Division, but unceasingly accumulated an impressive list of credits as both producer and director. Lofty critics may have scoffed when he took up the last of the great actor-managers Tod Slaughter, whose career had been spent trudging from one dilapidated theatre to another in a catalogue of hoary melodramas, to which his portrayal of murdering villain brought a unique quality never recaptured. Search the world as we may, there is only one Tod Slaughter, once seen, never forgotten. In 1935, King filmed the great man's performance of Squire Corder in the immensely enjoyable *Maria Marten*, which was followed by several other pictures that showed Slaughter at the peak of his dastardliness, culminating in *Crimes at the Dark House*, a rollicking reworking of Wilkie Collins's *The Woman in White*.

King was not known for his musicals, which makes *Gaiety George* the more surprising. It is a work in direct line from Ealing's glorious *Champagne Charlie* (1944) and Gainsborough's *I'll Be Your Sweetheart* (1945), sturdy and well constructed. Katherine Strueby's screenplay, by no means strikingly original and in part indebted to precursors such as Butcher's Film Services' warm-hearted account of a music-hall dynasty through changing times *Variety Jubilee* (1943), had contributions and additional dialogue by Basil Woon, based on a story by Richard Fraser and Peter Creswell. The opening credits introduce a biopic 'inspired by' the Edwardian impresario George Edwardes, now represented by personable George Howard (Richard Greene), persuasively using his soft-burred Irish accent to charm the world into putting on his shows. We know that, whatever obstacles are strewn in his path, he will become the Cameron Mackintosh of his day.

Kinematograph Weekly learned that 'In making his decisions to retain or discard incidents for the script [King] ignores the fact that they are about George Edwardes, and considers if they would be entertaining and good story value if they were only about an anonymous character.'[7] *The Times*'s critic would not have had customers rushing to the Regal. It wasn't only that 'the director makes only the most tentative efforts to capture the theatrical spirit of the times. Regarded solely as fiction, *Gaiety George* is not gay or polished enough and it is yet another example of our inability to compete with Hollywood when it comes to the "musical".'[8] This archival plaint was so prevalent in critical reaction to British musical films that it hardly bears the repeating. The same argument was to be levelled at the British stage musical, almost consistently up to and beyond the arrival of Andrew Lloyd Webber, when critical judgement inexplicably warmed towards a product that suddenly seemed to be transatlantically transportable. Why would King or his team

Produced and directed by the maverick wunderkind producer and
director George King, *Gaiety George* (1946) purported to tell the
story of Irish impresario George Edwardes (now George Howard)
with considerable charm.

want to bring Hollywoodian glamour to this modest offspring of their talents?
They were perfectly at home, constricted as some of the scenes appear, in the
picture's rainy streets, the on-stage glimpses of bottom-of-the-bill music-hall
acts, and the plum-in-the-pudding extracts from the pretty musical shows that
George puts on with no more artistic wish than to please the public. In all
these, Otto Heller's crystalline photography and William C. Andrews's clever
sets know exactly what they are about.

The film begins at its end: the first night of George's new musical, *A Man and a Maid*. He is too ill to be there. We are flashbacked to when he was a hard-up young upstart about town, determined to become a great showman. He buys up the Princess Theatre, where some wine-and-spirits music-hall artists are going through their paces; fragments of the Temperance favourite 'Please Sell No More Drink to My Father', 'Molly O'Morgan', and 'They're All Very Fine and Large' are accompanied by a tin-pot pit band. It is here that he meets soubrette Kathryn Davis (Ann Todd), soon to be his ever-supportive wife. He introduces a new sort of entertainment, a musical comedy called *Tallyho Girl*, rescuing it from failure with a publicity stunt that involves horses and hounds. This provides one of the first musical sequences that hold the film together, captivatingly staged by Freddie Carpenter and including the ensemble's 'Look What Britain Can Do', and 'One Love' waltzed by Todd and Patrick Waddington. In preparation for his new production *Tomboy Princess*, he auditions Florence Stevens (Leni Lynn), who reprises 'One Love'. He buys a racing horse, calls it 'Tomboy', and enters it for the Gold Cup. It wins, handing George another publicity coup.

When the difficult leading lady (Isobel Jeans) refuses to appear on stage in her underclothes, George hires Florence. Scenes from the new show, more polished and characterful than *The Times* describes, are directed by Leontine Sagan, whose experience of musicals included the directing of several of Ivor Novello's stage successes. The generous on-stage extracts, written by Strueby, are miniature pastiches written and scored by composer George Posford and lyricist Eric Maschwitz, whose long-lasting collaboration had prospered since the early thirties.

George's shows travel the world, but in London he falls ill. Trapped in Vienna as war erupts, he is imprisoned in an internment camp until, his health and spirit broken, he is allowed to return home. He learns that his only child, 'The Nipper', has been killed in action. Although obsessed with an idea for his new production *A Man and a Maid*, he has no funds to put it on. Unknown to him, Kathryn persuades the company to work for nothing. It is his greatest success. He waits at home. Kathryn brings him the good news.

Greene is an appealingly unstuffy hero, especially moving in the last scenes, while Todd exudes a convincing loyalty. They are supported by a splendid company that has Peter Graves as a cynical critic, and Morland Graham as George's faithful assistant. Lynn sings with a metallic precision that is not easy on the ears, but *Gaiety George* is abundantly enjoyable, not least when it bursts into the period charm of its score, and Tower Bridge opens to allow passage to the *Tallyho Girl*'s paddle steamer. Such incidental pleasures did nothing to sway C. A. Lejeune's opinion that the film was like doing *Hamlet* without the Prince of Denmark. Furthermore, the two stars 'fight a losing battle with an awkward copyright situation, a wan script, the shortest musical comedy on record (one opening number), and a technical style reminiscent of 1931'.[9]

MAY

In a waiting room, you idly take up an out-of-date magazine and begin reading a story. It engrosses you, but at the bottom of the page, just as it reaches its climax, you are informed that it is 'continued on page 48'. By the time you have found the page and located the concluding half paragraph, now in tinier print, the connection is broken. The same problem inhibits Butcher's well-meaning **I'll Turn to You**, concerning the problems experienced by heroes returning home from the war. It is a theme explored in Formby's *George in Civvy Street*, in Mancunian's *When You Come Home*, and in Lance Comfort's non-singing *Great Day*, with Eric Portman as an embittered ex-serviceman driven to the brink of suicide. As the *MFB* explained, Butcher's 'timely film deals with a rehabilitation problem, and will have a special appeal for young people demobbed from the Services'.[10] In an ideal world, perhaps, although it is doubtful that *I'll Turn to You* would have got its message over to the young. Its director Geoffrey Faithfull was from 1916 one of the industry's pioneers, working as cinematographer on almost 200 pictures, but with only two credits as director, *I'll Turn to You* and the previous year's *For You Alone*. In the circumstances, we might have expected a little more imagination from him. In the lengthy musical interludes, he seems simply to have kept the camera running, while the plot goes irretrievably into the sidings.

The two films share the policy of keeping the musical sequences essentially separated from the dramatic. Indeed, *For You Alone* also featured the London Symphony Orchestra and two singers. The credits insist that *I'll Turn to You* is 'based' on the song of the same name by Howard Barnes and Louise Craven, and makes its point at once, with Sandy MacPherson seated at his organ, accompanying Sylvia Welling in the singing of it. Listening in is Aileen Meredith (Terry Randall), longing for the return of husband Roger (Don Stannard), 'one of the finest pilots in the RAF', now languishing in a military hospital. Japan surrenders, the war is done, and Roger is coming home. Aileen struggles to find accommodation but finds time to be taken to a plush tea-room by admirer Henry (the excellent Ellis Irving) where violinist Albert Sandler is playing with his Palm Court Orchestra. The plot stops for Welling to sing Ivor Novello's 'The Little Damozel'. This gentility is interrupted only by Sandler's 'little comedy number' 'Scrub Brothers Scrub' written by Onslow Boyden Waldo Warner, which by contrast seems almost revolutionary.

Faithful Henry stands by Aileen in her search for a roof over the family's head before Roger returns. Around this time, the writer Mollie Panter-Downes noted that 'the personal columns of *The Times* are full of pathetic house-hunting advertisements inserted by ex-service men – the new displaced persons, who fought for the homes they are now desperately seeking, mostly, alas, without success'.[11] So it is for Roger and Aileen, but she settles for moving into the very working-class home of Mrs Gammon (Irene Handl). For this we must be grateful, as Handl and her egg-laying milkman Mr Joy (George Merritt) are more fun than nappy-washing Aileen and morose Roger, for whom home and hearth means cramped surroundings, a crying baby, thwarted ambition when he goes back to the job he left six years before, and jealousy of good old Henry. No television for diversion, and only the BBC making the effort to stiffen Britain's backbone with programmes that sought to bring society together in the new age. In March 1946, Wilfred Pickles began travelling across the country, urging factory workers and the listening public to *Have a Go!* Prizes, scarce during the war and decidedly modest, were available. Such entertainment was unlikely to lift Roger's spirits.

The BBC had not forgotten women, but in October it was the voice of Alan Ivimey that chaired the new *Woman's Hour*. Aware that a woman's work was said to be never done, the BBC assumed her chores allowed a modest respite at two o'clock in the afternoon, by which time any self-respecting housewife had done the washing-up, and the programme was scheduled for 2 p.m. This depressing expectation can only make us more sympathetic to the cloistered existence that the Rogers and Aileens were enduring across Britain. Undeterred, the first broadcast edition of *Woman's Hour* struck an egalitarian note, with guests including Deborah Kerr and a housewife from Charlton-cum-Hardy, a Mrs Elsie Crump.

Back on screen, Roger never lapses in his devotion to Aileen as he copes with the knowledge that he can do nothing to improve their lot. He tells her what he's given her: 'scrubbing brushes, greasy water – rivers of it – miles of washing, coal-buckets, dirty grates … what I've given you with all my fine talk and will go on giving you for heaven knows how long.' They escape for a treat to a music-hall (we see them watching Slim Rhyder, bicycle-riding eccentric), but unable to cope, Roger walks out. Henry discovers him working as a bellboy in a hotel. There is a rapprochement, and Henry tells him that Aileen is still at the flat, waiting for him. Roger goes to the flat, but Aileen and her parents are at a New Queen's Hall concert, where the London Symphony Orchestra under the baton of the film's musical director Harry Bidgood rattles through the *William Tell* overture at top speed, followed by the choir of the Welsh Guards. In concert with all the musical sequences of the picture, it's unimaginatively done, but paves the way for Roger and Aileen to be reunited as John McHugh stoically faces the camera to sing 'I'll Turn to You'. The film occasionally aligns itself with the less intellectually gifted (Handl and Merritt) but seems intent on the middle-class predicament of Roger and Aileen, its accent reinforced by the slabs of parlour music and snatches from the classics, although Handl and Merritt dutifully attend the final concert.

JUNE

British National's celebration of the Royal Canadian Navy's variety show, **Meet the Navy**, begins as a naval assault. 'Try to act like professionals', the on-screen producer suggests to his cast of amateurs, but professionalism is in pretty short supply. Lester Cooper and James Seymour's lifeless screenplay, almost unintelligibly cobbled together by director Alfred Travers, celebrates the world-wide success of the outsize concert party that had played the London Hippodrome in 1945, and a Royal Command Performance. The *MFB* noted 'an uninspired script telling a confused narrative [with] many library shots which are painfully impaired by stage lighting and stage make-up.'[12] These are the least of the picture's worries.

Hordes of artistes flood the screen, drilled almost to perfection in often purely mathematical choreography. They are reminded that 'This is a script and, remember, we're going to stick to it.' 'Why?' someone asks. 'People who go to the movies like to know such things. We're telling a story of how we started, where we went and what happened to us.' Still, we may see the film more as a meandering sequence of songs to do with the sea, bits and pieces of 'Blow the Man Down' and 'What Do We Do with the Drunken Sailor?' and an inevitable hornpipe. Attempts to bring the company's individuals to life expose sexist attitudes, while the lyrics insist that 'Beauty and Duty are doing their bit.' Female nurses, relieved of their chores, sway meaninglessly in time to the music. A ludicrous Russian sequence, in a nightmarish setting by Olga Lehmann and Gilbert Wood, has the seriously stentorian Oscar Natzke 'recalling days departed' and 'Days That Can Be Mine No More', and Cossack dancing. Any 'natural shortcomings are completely offset', claimed *Kinematograph Weekly*. 'It's just the thing for the tired businessman and housewife. The kids will revel in it too.'[13]

In fact, the songs especially written for the company by P. E. Quinn and lyricist R. W. Harwood are pleasant: 'Your Little Chapeau', 'Brothers-in-Arms', 'Beauty on Duty', and 'Rockettes and the Wrens'. John Pratt at last gets the chance to sing his 'comedy' number 'You'll Get Used to It', written by Pratt with music by Freddy Grant. Although in the style of Lionel Monckton's 'I've Gotta Motta' from *The Arcadians*, it lacks that song's shine. The standout is Quinn's 'The Boy in the Bell-Bottom Trousers', offering several reasons why the audience might want to bump into a sailor.

> The boy in the bell-bottom trousers
> Is young and clean and strong
> And a ship with a salt-spray upon her
> Is where such men belong!
> On the deck when he's fighting a breeze
> When the ocean is wavy
> He's the pride of the Navy and master of the seas.
> He's the cream of the crop, people sigh,
> When the boy in the bell-bottom trousers passes by!

By now, things have brightened up considerably, with speciality (and professional) dancer Alan Lund capering through Harold Arlen and E. Y. Harburg's 'Lydia the Tattooed Lady' with attendant sailors. At such moments it seems likely that the only reason these young men joined the Navy was that they would learn to tap-dance. No doubt unintentionally, a picture that began by being merely boring turns into high camp, the 'Brothers in Arms' finale (shot in Technicolor) at last bringing the individuals into focus. Just in time, after a good deal of nonsense, we are reminded of the service and bravery at the back of it all.

JULY

Following his 1945 *Sweethearts for Ever*, writer-director Frank A. Richardson returned with the 35-minute **Amateur Night**, produced for Radnor by Moss Goodman and Victor Cockraine Hervey. When fog-bound artistes fail to turn up for a theatre show, the stage manager (Ernest Sefton) pulls in street performers who have been entertaining the waiting queues. The *MFB* reported that 'The players are not well-known, nor is any new talent evident'[14] in what *Kinematograph Weekly* described as 'a crowded, though hardly top-line, bill [and] the direction, and staging, like much of the talent, is frayed at the edges.'[15] Frank King's Orchestra supports turns that include impressionist Carl Carlisle, singer Geraldine Farrar (presumably not the Hollywood star of Cecil B. DeMille's 1915 silent *Carmen*), accordion player Lorna Martin, and The Borstal Boys.

AUGUST

I Live in Grosvenor Square, the first of the Herbert Wilcox–Anna Neagle Mayfair-based escapist romances, teamed Neagle with Rex Harrison in 1945. It paved the way for Wilcox's five-year programme of cosmopolitan epics: *Piccadilly Incident*, *The Courtneys of Curzon Street*, *Spring in Park Lane*, and *Maytime in Mayfair*, throughout which Neagle and Wilding's partnership flourished. Wilcox explained that the fledgling Wilding

> could not accept the fact that he personally could make an appreciable impact on cinema audiences. I told him of the mean Lowry-like houses and people in the mining districts of the North, where I served my film apprenticeship. Four walls and a roof, holes for the front door and windows, outside water closets, and not always water. I have never forgotten the grim, unglamorous existence of the people who lived in those. That is why I believed in glamour and that is why we were so successful.[16]

For C. A. Lejeune, **Piccadilly Incident** was one of Wilcox's films 'which, with the best intentions in the world, singularly fails to come off'.[17] *The Times* was relieved that 'At least Piccadilly Circus is real, and very nicely photographed it is too; so are the railway carriages, the stations, the taxis, all real and nicely photographed, and their solidity throws into unfortunate relief the flimsiness of the story they serve.'[18] The *New York Times* suggested that 'the British are quite as capable as the Americans of unconvincing direction, ill-considered writing and tedious acting,[19] a view not shared by the oleaginous journalist Godfrey Winn, who assured *Picturegoer* that 'In *Piccadilly Incident* is born the greatest team in British films.'[20] In this, the popular film magazines and a great number of British cinemagoers heartily agreed, despite the *New York Times* insisting that 'some wise impulse made the British hesitate to send *Piccadilly Incident* to the U.S. when it was finished in 1946.'[21] In January, Wilcox had been negotiating with three Hollywood stars to join the cast.

Florence Tranter's scant storyline was screenplayed by Wilcox's favourite screenwriter of choice Nicholas Phipps, who supplied 'the most luridly melo-dramatic of the Mayfair cycle', a work of (considering its content) inordinate length.[22] In blitzed London, a romance ensues between WREN Diana Fraser (Neagle) and dashing Captain Alan Pearson (Wilding). The lovers are parted when Diana is sent abroad and then posted to Singapore, but an enemy submarine scuppers the ship and, so far as Alan and England know, Diana is 'Missing Presumed Drowned' for the next three years. In fact, she has washed up along with some of the sailors on a desert island bearing an uncanny resem-blance to a corner of Welwyn film studios. Agreeing to dance a tango (one of Neagle's rather mechanical routines) with the sexually frustrated Bill (Michael Laurence), she spurns his advances. Rescued at last, she returns home only to discover that Alan is now married to American Joan (Frances Mercer), who has had his son. As proof of her love for Alan, Joan plays and sings Herman Hupfeld's 'As Time Goes By'. At last meeting Alan, Diana rejects his attempt to console her. Her cry of 'Don't touch me. I don't want you to touch me' is one of the film's most effective moments, to which Neagle brings conviction. During a bombing raid, Diana is fatally injured, dying as she asks Alan for a kiss. Wilcox directs the drama at a funereal pace, padded out with much pouring of drinks and lighting of cigarettes.

Musically, the film is a smorgasbord of generally undigestible elements against the background of Anthony Collins's uninspiring score. Old favour-ites are dragged in to add another layer of sentiment: Leigh Harline and Ned Washington's 'When You Wish upon a Star' courtesy of Walt Disney, Nat Ayer and Clifford Grey's 'If You Were the Only Girl in the World', and 'How Could I Know?' by Adrian Foley and Phil Park, while Diana performs her signature song of uncertain authorship 'You Are My Sunshine'. A late burst of pent-up emotion comes when Alan runs through Vivian Ellis's musical miniature 'Piccadilly 1944' on the piano. Ellis subsequently explained that 'It was while standing in Piccadilly Circus that I first had the gleam of the idea for "Piccadilly Incident", a piece of descriptive music that was ultimately performed, to my entire dissatisfaction, in an Anna Neagle film of that name.'[23]

As the *MFB* noted, 'Scenes at home remain credible, but the desert island existence of Diana and her colleagues, though done with a commendable lack of glamour, is a little harder to believe.'[24] Nevertheless, the castaways attempt to lift their spirits with that most depressing of British activities community singing, reviving (with the assistance of Leslie Dwyer's mouth-organ) 'Loch Lomond', 'Rolling Home', and 'I've Got Sixpence'. Most curious of all, long before Diana is shipwrecked, is the 'Boogie Woogie Moonshine' sequence choreographed by Wendy Toye, with Neagle and dancers involved in a shadow-play to the uneasy accompaniment of Beethoven's 'Moonlight' Sonata and 'You Are My Sunshine'. It's a peculiarity never satisfactorily explained, but offers a decent sample of Neagle's balletic abilities.

Neagle rises above such moments to cope with Phipps's dreary wittering, but the supporting cast seems remarkably unenthusiastic. There is the usual sprinkling of old codgers often shipped into Wilcox pictures, in this case the epitome of the British film old codger A. E. Matthews, alongside Edward Rigby and Reginald Owen. It is Owen as a bewigged judge who at the film's end frightens the audience out of its wits by explaining the predicament in which Alan and Joan's son finds himself. In the eyes of the law he will be forever regarded as illegitimate. This sudden outbreak of legal stricture makes an odd climax to a film with such a dodgy grasp on reality, reminding cinemagoers of a war that they probably came into the cinema hoping to forget. For some, Wilcox and Phipps's smug depiction of upper-middle Mayfair society may sit uncomfortably alongside the more truthful picture of immediately post-war Britain portrayed by Ealing's determinedly gloomy *It Always Rains on Sunday* in 1947.

For Roger Mellor, there is no denying that

> Anna Neagle proved once and for all to any doubters that she could really act, ranging from conventional glamour in the early scenes, sexual tension in the scenes with Bill, shed of all glamour in the island rescue, and the real electric charge of the final encounter [...] It is not surprising that this emotional roller-coaster of a film led to queues round the block at ABC cinemas in 1946 and led to audience awards from both the *Daily Mail* (1946) and *Picturegoer* (1947).[25]

Vivian Ellis wrote of Neagle that 'Perhaps her most effective performances were her off-stage ones in places like the Naval Hospital wards. Here, her absolute sincerity and lack of pose were seen at their best'.[26]

The most trumpeted musical film of the year, **London Town** brought one of the sternest rebukes from the *MFB*. 'Presumably if it had cost less it could have been cut by a further half-hour. An editor with authority and intelligence could still turn it into a musical of the average Hollywood standard. Ruthlessly impartial editing [...] is its chief lack'.[27] Much has been lamented regarding J. Arthur Rank's disastrous decision to make a big musical that would outdo anything Hollywood could offer, with a cast of British stars, mountains of make-up, the fuzziest Technicolor you're likely to see this side of Judy Garland's Kansas, and a script that surely originated on the back of a bus ticket? Questions are begged. Why does Sid Field go to bed with his clothes on? What has led to him being the single parent of thirteen-year-old Petula Clark (gone and never called me mother)? Why is Sonnie Hale in the role of Charlie described as 'the greatest comedian in the world'? It can only be because director Wesley Ruggles hadn't the brass neck to say, 'Mr Hale, we've decided to cut that line when you describe yourself as being the greatest comedian in the world.' It is certainly a line lacking in conviction, especially with one of Britain's most legendary comics, Sid Field, close by.

Why does the Cameron Mackintosh of the film Mrs Barry (unconvincingly played by Greta Gynt) live in a flat that looks like the ground floor of Versailles? Why, if Sid Field's sketches are supposed to be taking place on stage in front of an audience, is there no laughter? It may be because some of them are no longer as funny as they once seemed; after all, it's not a first house Monday night at Glasgow Empire. Why are the backstage dressing-rooms as big as aircraft hangars and decked out like a florist's van? Surely the real dressing-rooms in the West End of 1946 were rabbit-hutch-sized and waiting to be condemned? How many severely theatrically untrained but genuine Pearly Kings and Queens were bussed in from the East End for the truly hideous cockney farrago that invades the endless finale? This wizard idea at least meant the management didn't have to provide their costumes. And why did 'The 'Ampstead Way' never catch on as a new dance craze? Perhaps because it's idiotic. Jimmy Van Heusen and Johnny Burke's songs are attractive enough to keep us amused for a few minutes, but they are thinly spread, with two numbers, 'My Heart Goes Crazy' and 'So Would I', making return visits.

What state of mind was the great American choreographer Agnes de Mille in when she dreamed up the frankly daft Daffodil Ballet, musically arranged by Toots Camarata? It resembles a voodoo session following electric shock treatment after a pandemic of St Vitus Dance, involving Tessie O'Shea as a severely vibrating London flower-girl. Why did de Mille's fellow choreographer Freddie Carpenter, faced with impossible odds, not throw in the sponge when the ''Ampstead' number erupted and the studio was invaded by coachloads of Pearly Kings and Queens who seem not to have mastered the choreography (basically moving up and down and backwards and forwards and hoping for the best), and who confirm once and for all the shocking state of British dentistry in post-war Britain as they continue to jump up and down through a medley of genuine music-hall songs, among them Albert Chevalier's time-worn 'Wot Cher!', Harry Champion's signature anthem 'Any Old Iron', and Marie Lloyd's 'Don't Dilly Dally'? As if this isn't enough to persuade us we are witnessing an East End knees-up, an unidentified Pearlie gets the biggest close-up of the film to sing 'Give Me an Old Fashioned Pub'. It is mercifully brief.

The questions continue. Why did J. Arthur Rank hire colour-blind American director Wesley Ruggles to superintend a Technicolor movie? In 1930s Hollywood Ruggles had enjoyed success working alongside major stars including Mae West, Clark Gable, and Carole Lombard, but washed-up by the

London Town (1946) was the clumsy first post-war attempt by a British studio to manufacture a Hollywood-styled musical film. The response was, to put it kindly, muted. It squandered the talents of its cast, including the great British comedian Sid Field.

mid-1940s, he was given this last hurrah by Rank. Apparently, Field insisted that the director must be American. Why was the responsibility of the most expensive film any British studio had yet mounted given to writers Elliot Paul and Sig Herzig, based on a story 'and production' by Ruggles, with additional dialogue by Val Guest? Why is choreographer Joan Davis credited for 'second Trafalgar'? What, indeed, *is* 'second Trafalgar'? Why does the film, luxuriously dressed as it strives to be, look washed-out, dun-coloured, soupy, and is it true that the post-war shortage of fabrics meant costumier Honoria Plesch had to make do with remnants and the rags and tatters of redundant military uniforms? Didn't J. Arthur Rank have enough clothes coupons? Why did designer Ernst Fegté design sets that proved unsuitable for Shepperton? Why were aeroplanes being built in the studio where the put-upon Mr Ruggles was trying to make a major British musical film? Did the hammering never stop? Why when Ruggles takes the company out on a Bank Holiday boating spree do the interpolated studio shots look so inappropriate, and why does Mary Clare become hysterical when she breaks into the chorus of 'Any Way the Wind Blows'? Why did so glorious an artist as Tessie O'Shea agree to be tossed from a great height into the studio's water tank? Who, indeed, thought the stunt up? Will some thesis of the future reveal details of the 'additional dialogue by Val Guest', or why it wouldn't have been possible for Field to play the sketches in front of a live audience rather than wading through them to complete silence (except for the hammering of the aeroplane makers) as if at a rehearsal?

Whatever innovations were introduced by Rank's *London Town* nevertheless offered a storyline of unremitting immaturity, set in that backstage-on-stage world of showbusiness into which steps a chancer who, before the final credits roll, becomes a star. The script is distinguished only by its reluctance to deliver any shred of wit or reality, with characters about whom we cannot care. Provincial comic Jerry Sanford (Sid Field) goes to London with his daughter Peggy (an excellent Petula Clark) to break into the big time via impresario Mrs Barry (Greta Gynt). She already has her star comedian, Charlie (Sonnie Hale), but Peggy naughtily causes Charlie to miss curtain-up, and Jerry goes on as a stand-in and comes off as a star. This encapsulates everything to do with plot, in a film that relapses into a series of meaningless song and dance sequences, and re-creation of four of the star's stage sketches.

The supporting performances (excusing Miss Clark and the impeccable Jerry Desmonde) are without exception feeble. The resulting gloom (despite desperate efforts to cheer the place up with excessively colourful settings) is accentuated by a peculiarly downbeat number, 'If Spring Were Only Here to Stay' arranged by Robert Farnon. This is lugubriously performed by Marion Saunders and a huddle of starveling children in what appears to be a bomb-damaged building filmed in a blackout through pea-soup fog: a genuine London not so Particular. Like so much of what is happening on screen, it has nothing to do with anything else, merely casting a deep depression over proceedings that have long outlived their necessary span. There was praise from *Kinematograph*

Weekly placing it 'indubitably and triumphantly in the category of "mammoth" musical', with Field 'a comedian of genius whose diverting antics I watched with tears of laughter streaming down my cheeks'.[28]

However, *The Times* put *London Town* 'well below the present standard of British films', for in American cinema

> their choruses are as rhythmical in movement as they are decorative in looks; their leading ladies are truly stars, even if the firmament is tinsel; they have life, speed, and agility; and, above all, the makers of them know how to cut and how to stop. They are the products of technical authority, and on all these counts this British film has a negative report to offer.[29]

In every sense, this is a tasteless film. Sidney Gilliat decided that '*London Town* did not prove that we could not make musicals, but instead proved that you don't use old hacks to make them'.[30] It was clear to Peter Noble that 'when we have attempted to make films in the Hollywood idiom, we have failed'.[31] The problem here was exacerbated by the fact that its star was a major British comedian of the time, trapped in a musical that

> deserved instant oblivion; as a comedy, on the strength of those sketches alone, no English film has a greater right to be revived. It is impossible as one watches Field to disassociate his performance from a ghostly one-man parade of modern comedians. Field's own comment today would probably be no different to his analysis of his own quality at the time of his success: 'I suppose I'm just peculiar altogether'.[32]

The *Observer* wasted no sympathy.

> One would have imagined that if all that was thought necessary was to stage a revue and photograph it, someone who knew a revue when he saw one would have been called in to supervise, if nothing more, what is a very specialised art [...] Presumably no one thought it specialised, difficult or even an art.[33]

In America, *Variety* was no less scathing.

> Treatment of the film is thoroughly American, facing the question why it should have been made in Britain at all. In every respect it apes the American model, and London, as the London *Times* points out, becomes a suburb of Hollywood. Most surprising of all is the quality of the musical items, which fail every time to stun the ear with haunting hits and lack good voices throughout.[34]

Nevertheless, *London Town* remains our only solid evidence of Sid Field's pre-eminence as a comedic performer, but outside of the sketches he really has nothing of note to do either dramatically or musically; the songwriters provide him only with the opening number 'You Can't Keep a Good Dreamer Down', sung as he tucks his daughter into bed. The best the studios came up with as a follow-up was the dreary 1948 *Cardboard Cavalier*. The sketches in *London Town* at least archive those he performed with such distinction on stage, in concert with his immaculate straight man, the consistently under-valued Jerry Desmonde, whose skills should surely be remembered alongside those of Field and who subsequently became Norman Wisdom's filmic straight man. Best among the sketches are the delightful 'Tubular Bells', the cavorting of the classic spiv Slasher Green with his vaudeville number 'You Ought to See Me on Saturday Night' by Walter Ridley and Sid Colin, and Field's wonderfully camp photographer. The golfing sketch is much less successful, laboriously played out by Field and Desmonde clearly in want of an audience to make it work, but on screen it is Field's photographer who seems to have attracted most attention. Such a protracted and patently 'gay' performance of a character had never before (and has seldom since) been offered to a British or American audience. Rank's nervousness was obvious. As the film ends with Field and Kendall climbing the staircase in 'The 'Ampstead Way', and just as the audience are putting on their hats and gloves for the homeward journey, Kendall emerges from the curtains, announcing that 'Sid wants me to tell you that in the photographer's sketch he was only acting.' Such prurience on the part of the management merely counts as another black mark against an already unlucky picture, whose vulgarity (a supreme example is the elongated piano sequence, with a whole row of madly thumping pianists recalling the more modest but much more charming piano pyramid in John Baxter's *Stepping Toes* of 1938, and the army of violinists) is fully exposed.

Today, viewing the film may be overshadowed by our knowledge that its star was already unwell, spending five weeks in a psychiatric ward in early 1946. Substantial periods of ill-health culminated in Field's death in 1950.

NOVEMBER

C. A. Lejeune welcomed a new operetta from the British studios, 'a film which allows Carol Raye to gambol and twitter, and positively encourages Leni Lynn to let off high-powered renderings of Paul Rubens' "I Love The Moon" and "Little Grey Home In The West", [in] a musical novelette about the Cad and the Chorus Girl'.[35] The slight plot centres on a brooch, around which romance blossoms despite the hero (well-reviewed Peter Graves) being shipped to America. Based on a story by Lore and Maurice Cowan, the British National picture was produced at Elstree by Louis H. Jackson and directed by Montgomery Tully, who co-wrote the screenplay with James Seymour. It marked the end of a busy period for Hans May of composing operetta scores at the close of war, with *Waltz Time* (1945) followed by three more in 1946: *Lisbon Story*, *The Laughing Lady*, and now **Spring Song**. Everything was in May's usual competent, agreeable but unremarkable manner, with lyrics by Alan Stranks and attractively lush arrangements by Wilfred Burns.

With its workmanlike score from the prolific Hans May and lyricist Alan Stranks, *Spring Song* (1946) was considerably brightened by Carol Raye and Jack Billings's dancing and its jogging-through- the-countryside title song.

Released in the States as *Springtime*, the picture was boosted as a 'Brand New Musical Dance-Sing-Sensation'. One suspects that American customers may have been disappointed at its gentility, but in British cinemas it seemed more like one of the last gasps of operetta, concocted at a very substantial distance from the likes of Franz Lehár or Emmerich Kálmán. *Kinematograph Weekly* contained its excitement: 'The picture is told in flashback, is built entirely upon clichés, but, all the same, it has a healthy nostalgic glow [...] a safe rather than subtle mixture of ancient and modern.'[36]

Despite complimenting British National for making a picture on such a meagre budget, *Variety* considered that '*Spring Song* could easily have been elevated in nostalgic charm like that of *Meet Me in St Louis*, but conventional handling has robbed the original story of any individuality.' It also forecast that Raye would be 'a big topliner. Hollywood is certain to take more note of her than British producers have so far,'[37] but it was not to be; she is probably best remembered today for the ridiculously supernatural *While I Live* (1948), a film distinguished only by its brilliant Charles Williams's piano theme 'The Dream of Olwen'. On the evidence of *Spring Song*, Raye was a vivid screen presence distinguished in dance, whom an imaginative British film industry might have put to better use.

Despite the spotlight falling on third-billed American Leni Lynn for her singing appearances and 'We Must All Pull Together', *Spring Song* was British National's final attempt to endear her to the British public in a role that unarguably did her no favours and ended her film career. The lion's share of numbers went to Raye: the zippy 'You Must Jitterbug' with the dancers; May and Stranks's ballads 'Somewhere in This Great Big World' and 'Love Again'; the wittily staged 'I Can't Make Up My Mind' with its dancing stage-door Johnnies, and Hermann Löhr's Victorian favourite 'My Little Grey Home in the West'. She also leads Graves and a gaggle of young men out for a spree in the joggingly delightful title song as they trot through English countryside past chorus-singing yokels. There remains the highlight of Raye's stunning *pas de deux* choreographed by and danced with Jack Billings, 'Give Me a Chance to Dance'.

Singing the praises of Peter Graves's performance as heroic Tony Winster, the *MFB* discovered 'a stereotyped story told, mainly, in an unambitious way, although with some moments of charm and freshness'.[38] Despite complimenting British National for making a picture on such a meagre budget, *Variety*'s American critic reported that '*Spring Song* could easily have been elevated in nostalgic charm like that of *Meet Me in St Louis*, but conventional handling has robbed the original story of any individuality'.[39]

After long service, flitting in and out of British musical films as guest artistes, duetting Webster Booth and Anne Ziegler at last made top billing in British National's Technicolor romance of the French Revolution, written by Jack Whittingham from a play by Ingram D'Abbes and produced at Elstree by Louis H. Jackson. Its émigré director Paul L. Stein, whose success in British musical films peaked in the mid-1930s with Richard Tauber's *Blossom Time* and *Heart's Desire*, had returned to operetta in the final phase of his career in British studios, with *Waltz Time* (1945), *The Lisbon Story* (1946), and, finally, ***The Laughing Lady***. The kindly response of the *MFB* was carefully modulated.

> Anne Ziegler and Webster Booth are both thoroughly at home in the period costumes ['stock' supplied by Nathan's, theatrical costumier] and settings [R. Holmes Paul], and from the point of view of the music [Hans May] at least no better choice could have been made for the leading roles. The film is full of tuneful romantic melodies and there is a strong supporting cast. Direction makes the most of the luxurious settings, which compare favourably with American productions of the same type.[40]

The stars had been travelling troubadours in *Waltz Time*; now, they were 1790 star-crossed lovers aristocratic Andre (Booth) and Denise (Ziegler). Hoping to save his mother from the guillotine, Andre is sent to England to retrieve Marie Antoinette's priceless necklace 'The Pearls of Sorrow'. Whittingham's story swims around a startlingly slim Prince of Wales (Peter Graves) and Denise's astonishingly obese father (Francis L. Sullivan), hijacked by Andre as a highwayman, although he's officially an artist commissioned to paint Denise. Their infatuation finds its natural response in a series of duets, as in the attractive 'Laugh at Life' and 'Love Is the Key', with Denise's philosophical belief that 'Wisdom is so unromantic!' In song, she expounds her theory that 'In an Old Chateau, There Lived the Echo of a Half-Remembered Chanson', but Pa wants her married to dreary old snob Mountroyal (punctiliously enunciating Felix Aylmer), who shows her the space left in his gallery of family portraits for a future wife. His attitude to marriage is somewhat old-school: 'I've never waited for a woman yet and I don't intend to start now.'

Andre's departure for France provides May and his librettist Alan Stranks with the film's most dramatic musical sequence, 'Magical Moonlight', as Denise clambers over sea-tossed rocks for a final embrace. It's the most gripping image: Denise swathed in her midnight-blue cape, Andre jumping from the boat to duet, the sailors looking on in wonderment as the luscious orchestrations fill the air. The story rolls along muddled lines, with Denise providing a cabaret turn at a grand Brighton Royal Pavilion ball with 'I'll Change My Heart', followed by a stately gavotte choreographed by Eileen Baker. Back in France, Andre and his rollicking comrades extol the pleasure of 'Wine, Wonderful Wine' before he is reunited with Denise. The music remains unoffensive throughout.

Stein's aptitude for such material, the clever settings of R. Holmes Paul, and the sterling company including Paul Dupuis as Andre's faithful companion and Charles Goldner's Robespierre add weight to what is one of

Well-deserved, popular, and refined duettists Anne Ziegler and Webster Booth at last had their cinematic starring roles in Paul L. Stein's unlikely costume operetta *The Laughing Lady* (1946).

the very last extravagant gasps of British operetta on film. What matter that neither Booth nor Ziegler is especially cinematic? After long duty done, they deserve to be up there, and for the most part *The Laughing Lady* is a vehicle worthy of them.

The musical numbers featured in **Walking on Air** were judged 'exceptionally shrewd and showman-like' in *Kinematograph Weekly*,[41] but in the time-worn format of variety turns carelessly strung together in an unconvincing scenario. Directed by Aveling Ginever, who co-wrote the screenplay with Johnny Worthy and Val Guest, Susan Shaw is a skater who wants to be a ballerina but has to do with being the back legs of an ice-show pantomime horse. A situation that might have developed along surrealist lines is the excuse for showcasing some interesting black musicians. At Marylebone Studios, Piccadilly Cinematograph Productions' producers Michael H. Goodman and Joseph G. Frankel assembled an impressive company.

Acting as compere, Worthy, teamed with Bertie Jarrett (the two sometimes billed as 'America's Dark Gentlemen'), heads a programme that includes Lauderic Caton and His Rhythm Swingtette, Jamaican acoustic double bass player Coleridge Goode, African-American drummer Freddie Crump, and Ray Ellington. Along with various standards including 'Honeysuckle Rose' sung by Jill Allen, W. C. Handy's 'St Louis Blues' and 'Jack Street Blues', the score features Peter Noble's 'I Just Don't Know How to Swing'. A Welsh comedienne sings a comedy number, the Skating Avalons bedazzle, and Worthy wrote the title song and 'Harlem Jamboree'. The *MFB* lamented the 'somewhat negligible material of this new musical' and 'discrepancies [problems with continuity and synchronisation] which can hardly be overlooked in this curiously ill-assembled production'.[42]

1947

The actors, try as they may, never seem 'quite', but behave rather in the manner in which those of lower status imagine the upper-class to behave

The Courtneys of Curzon Street

When You Come Home   *Holiday Camp*
Life Is Nothing Without Music   *The Hills of Donegal*
The Courtneys of Curzon Street   *Comin' thro' the Rye*

MARCH

The films of Frank Randle resonated throughout the northern film industry between 1940 and 1953, beloved of what trade journals considered 'industrial' audiences, but less revered by critics and rarely exhibited down south. The fact that Randle was so blatant a comic genius left the major studios unmoved, perhaps fearing the physical damage he might inflict on not only the premises but the staff. When he was unleashed, there was no guarantee what might happen; scriptwriters resigned themselves to what he did with their words, directors threw up their hands when the cameras rolled. One cannot imagine Randle at the mercy of Columbia British, or any stifling interloper between him and his public in the dark.

Nevertheless, Randle moved from Mancunian, where he had the benefit of John E. Blakeley's affectionate understanding, to Butcher's Film Services for the fascinating *When You Come Home*, produced and directed by that most unsung of British directors John Baxter. Baxter was without doubt the best director Randle ever had, and there is an argument for claiming the partnership was made in heaven. For a start, both men were steeped in the music-hall tradition, but opinion is divided as to how well their partnership worked. The writer John Montgomery, who handled the film's publicity, had made up his mind:

> I'm afraid it was *not* a good film, because the script [ostensibly by David Evans and Geoffrey Orme, with 'additional scenes and comedy material' by Randle] was so muddled. The director John Baxter was absolutely lost. The film cost twice as much as it should have – six times as much as any other Randle film, but I think it made less money than any of them. [Randle] really wasn't funny in the film; the script crippled him, and John Baxter was such a quiet, charming man that Randle [...] was completely out of his element.[1]

Perhaps, although Baxter would have known very well what he was taking on with Randle as his star; after all, he had already directed three Old Mother Riley films with Arthur Lucan and Kitty McShane, enough to test anyone's mettle. There can be no doubt that Baxter sometimes lets his star's antics go on too long, as in a shaving scene, but Baxter imposes enough of his trademark touches to move the picture into another category, one removed from Randle's other work. *When You Come Home* (a title that underlines the basic domesticity of the piece) fully exploits Randle's famous characterisation of a decrepit, toothless old man, beginning and ending the film in the setting of home and hearth peopled by an extraordinary collection of ancients. Now, he is Grandpa, the odd-job man at the Empire music-hall, about to celebrate his birthday in the bosom of his family. His memories take him back to earlier days as we flashback to the refrain of 'When You Come Home' as sung on stage by Linda Parker. The fusty and (as Montgomery was right to say) 'muddled' plot concerns the efforts of villainous fake hypnotist Franklin (Jack Melford) to take over the Empire, a ruse that involves his vampish assistant trying to seduce Grandpa. 'Oh dear mother,' he cries, 'Burn my clothes!'

Musically thin as it is, the film yields considerable pleasure. Its juvenile couple, under-used Diana Decker and Fred Conyngham (looking like a young Nöel Coward), share the delightful 'Take a Step' (lyric by Bruce Sievier and music by the film's musical director Percival Mackey) as they negotiate a staircase before they segue on to the Empire's stage to continue their routine choreographed by Conyngham and Hazel Gee. A second duet, 'Take It from Me', is over almost before it's begun. Those refugees from concert party Leslie Sarony and Leslie Holmes get to perform their underwhelming party piece 'Fill 'em Up Again', but it is the melancholy title song that underpins the story's sentiment, its melody building to a crescendo as Grandpa, enjoying the satisfaction of complete contentment among his old and young family, at last goes berserk as he recalls his experiences at the Battle of Balaclava, and without realising it destroys his birthday cake before climbing the stairs to bed.

Incidental pleasures include Olive Sloane, briefly seen as a barmaid; Gus Aubrey, the 'camp' member of Randle's on-stage troupe of supporting performers; monumental Lily Lapidus; and Hilda Bayley as gracious Lady Langfield, happy to confess that she was once a chorus girl. Of course, the film would be nothing without Randle. The *MFB* considered that it 'would be vastly improved by the omission of numerous ramifications of plot and superfluous turns which merely hold up the action without contributing to the furtherance of the story'.[2] Succinctly, David Parkinson finds Randle 'a colossal bore' experiencing 'his cinematic nadir with this desperate flashback comedy'.[3] In one of its more acute notices, *Kinematograph Weekly* found that 'The plot is very loosely knit and the artless by-play, instead of strengthening its modest pattern, keeps causing it to drop a stitch', and Randle could not 'eradicate its many flatspots'. Ultimately, the picture was 'an artless alternation of Pinocchio-like whimsy and old-time villainy, slapstick and sing-song [...] It is at its best when the star is left to his own resources.'[4]

Patrons may have noted that Randle makes a special concession for the great ballroom scene as the film closes: he has put his teeth in. In case the audience has missed them, he explains, 'Even these teeth don't belong to me.' There is nothing unusual here. As John Fisher tells us, when on stage it was 'More than likely than not that he had taken his dentures out at the beginning of his act and thrown them in the stalls.'[5]

APRIL

Horace Shepherd's dogged determination to keep on making featurettes with his Inspiration Films continued with **Life Is Nothing Without Music**, a sort of picture postcard from Devon sent by Jessie Matthews, whose duties included singing the title song by Fred Hartley. These were shoddy surroundings for the British cinematic idol, 'the Dancing Divinity' of the 1930s. What was it about Shepherd's proposal that had lured her from her domestic retirement at Farnham? Previously seen in the dreary *Candles at Nine* (1944), this latest outing, filmed at Kensington's Viking Film Studios, only emphasised her decline. The 35-minuter involved BBC radio announcer Alvar Lidell and Matthews's pianist Bob Busby, but proved 'a very unflattering medium' for its star. The *MFB* commented on her 'unbecoming clothes' (a regular criticism throughout her 1930s career) and the 'tendency towards exaggerated and stagey gestures [that] detract from the star's appeal', finding the photography 'lifeless and unimaginative', with Lidell and Busby camera-conscious and 'quite embarrassing to watch'.[6] Many years would pass before Matthews's final film, *tom thumb*.

MAY

In a year that offered British cinemagoers Alberto Cavalcanti's adaptation of Charles Dickens's *Nicholas Nickleby*, John Boulting's brilliant *Brighton Rock*, Michael Powell and Emeric Pressburger's *Black Narcissus*, Charles Crichton's *Hue and Cry*, Robert Hamer's gritty *It Always Rains on Sunday*, and Carol Reed's *Odd Man Out*, the biggest box-office success was Herbert Wilcox's **The Courtneys of Curzon Street**. Of all the directors listed above, he is the least likely to ever be given a retrospective at the British Film Institute. With Wilcox, the difference between critical and popular success is laid bare, as evidenced in this soggy tale of the supposedly elysian Mayfair. Ever the showman, Wilcox instigated a formidable marketing campaign, which stretched as far as Luton, a world away from that supposedly inhabited by Messrs Neagle and Wilding. The management of the Savoy Cinema had two female staff members dress up as 'two ladies from Curzon Street', who paraded through shopping centres and streets, closely followed by a car that carried advertising for the film. Deals were made with local cycle shops, furnishers, dress-shops, and music, radio, and electrical dealers.

With gentlemanly restraint, *The Times* declared the picture was 'proof, if proof were needed, that when we make films which do not altogether succeed in their pretensions, we make them more pleasantly than Hollywood.'[7] C. A. Lejeune thought it 'bosh of the highest order, but if my livelihood depended on booking the right film into the average cinema, this is one I wouldn't dare to miss.'[8] In 1990, the *Guardian* suggested that 'Home fires are kept burning, but hardly passion, in a tepid romantic saga typical of its stiff-necked time and producer-director Herbert Wilcox.'[9]

This is not to say that Wilcox's collection of cabinet photographs of an upper-class English family (they live in Curzon Street, after all) is either dull or unentertaining. For those prepared to sit through a series of totally predictable events, the picture is highly watchable, although the actors, try as they may, never seem 'quite', but behave rather in the manner in which those of lower status imagine the upper-class to behave. In this, they have the full cooperation of the story invented by Florence Tranter (although there is not a hint of originality in it) and a similarly obliging screenplay by Wilcox favourite Nicholas Phipps.

At neither extreme of her dynastic progress from chirpy maid of 1899 to elderly grand old lady of 1945 is Neagle convincing. We meet her first at the Courtneys' New Year's ball for their servants (of whom there appear to be battalions) as the new century dawns. It must be a big 'do': cook has used twenty-four eggs in the soufflé (a feat presumably listed in the *Guinness Book of Records*). As a party piece, lady's maid Kate (Neagle) recalls the Emerald Isle by singing 'A Place o' Me Own'. The heir to the Courtney fortune, Edward (Michael Wilding), enraptured by her winsomeness, means to marry her against the wish of his mother, for whom Kate is 'not quite'. 'Family and background are very strong things,' she tells him, 'and even if you push them away, sooner or later they'll come back and insist on being recognised.' Nevertheless, Kate and Edward marry, and Kate gets a lady's maid of her own and is put through a sort of Eliza Doolittle test at a Royal Command classical concert. She invites more censure by joining Edward in the wicked polka, danced by Edward weighed down by ceremonial braid. Supper will be at Romano's (where else?). The gossips wag on: will he have to resign his commission because he has stooped to marrying a maid? Unable to cope, Kate has Edward's son and leaves Curzon Street, finding success on the stage as May Lynton. We see her starring in *The Runaway Girl*, singing 'The Soldiers in the Park'. Without benefit of microphones, we may wonder if May's timid vocalising will reach beyond the front row of the stalls. The Great War breaks out, and Kate is reunited with Edward at an army concert where she sings Haydn Wood's 'Roses of Picardy', although once again Neagle's thin piping hardly seems what to give the troops.

Son Edward, a patriotic chip off his father's block, wants to be a soldier too, and recites a bit of Rupert Brooke to show he's thought about it. In France, father Edward is in the trenches. At home, son Edward plans to wed a girl from the lower class; what irony (the only shred of it that inhabits Phipps's script) that it is *her* family that objects to moving up the social ladder.

The war tidied away, father Edward goes into the City. The pursuit of money consumes him, and we at once doubt the wisdom of such an adventure. Son Edward is in the army, fighting in the desert. At home, his young wife is pregnant. With immaculate timing, the Curzon Street butler brings in a telegram (the one we've been expecting) from the War Office. 'Killed!' she cries. 'That means I won't see him any more.' With this profound statement she collapses, gives birth to a son, and dies.

Kate sees that Edward has changed. From here on, Wilding gives us *stooped* acting. Wall Street panics, the Stock Exchange implodes, and if only the windows at Curzon Street were higher from the ground he might have ended things there and then. The house, and everything, is lost, but Kate refuses to sell, returns to the theatre, and reprises 'Roses of Picardy'. World War II erupts, with Edward insisting, 'Darling, I have to take my turn.' Fire breaks out when Kate is performing on stage. She saves a girl from the burning building, but Edward is badly hurt. At this moment the picture moves us into the sympathetic 'They'll never be the same again' phase. An advanced old age creeps on them with surprising speed, and – with symbolic snow on the ground – their grandson arrives with the girl he wishes to marry. More irony: she is a munition factory worker! In one of the most startling moments of Phipps's fast-evolving saga, the now creaking and silver-haired Kate declares, 'Thank goodness there's none of that stupid class prejudice now.' 'No,' agrees Edward, 'Thank goodness for that.' It is perhaps appropriate that the picture ends on this blithe example of wishful thinking.

AUGUST

August! A perfect month for our trip to **Holiday Camp**, a site of enforced enjoyment. Do not expect to bump into the Courtneys, but most of the rest of humankind turns up in Gainsborough's irresistibly enjoyable compendium, written with a sure understanding of the matter in hand by director Sydney and Muriel Box, with additional dialogue by the crowd-pleasing Denis Constanduros and Ted Willis, names that induce a homeliness exemplified in the true stars of the film, the emblematic family of Huggett. It's a fascinating snapshot of the mass hysteria manifested in the holiday havens of Billy Butlin. The first of his staycation getaways had opened at Skegness three years before the start of war, followed by Clacton in 1938. Gainsborough's portmanteau collection of vignettes, with its numberless unpaid extras (Mr Butlin's guests), paints an extraordinary picture. Mass Observation observer

Gladys Longford thought it 'one of the funniest films I ever saw [it is unclear if Gladys meant funny as in comic or funny as in very peculiar]; if this be a real picture of a holiday camp, God forbid I should visit one'.[10] It was Godfrey Winn, that obliging behemoth of English literature, who had come up with the idea after popping into the Butlin's at Filey for a quick peep; we can only imagine the twists and turns that his original scheme went through to produce the strangely unconvincing mélange that landed up on screen.

> Significantly, [Winn] depicted the holiday camp as a social melting-pot, where the different classes could come together – on the face of it a fanciful notion, yet it seems that for several years after the war the clientele were as much middle-class as working-class. That did not stop the camps acquiring, in some eyes, a reputation as little better than concentration camps for the proletariat.[11]

We meet this disparate cross-section of the holidaying British as the coaches spill out countless numbers of new arrivals, greeted with the loud-speaker announcement that they will be 'ready for the cup of tea that's waiting for you in the reception hall'. They could probably do with a strong brew, ready for the journey into the unknown that awaits them, especially when singles are expected to share their charmless chalets with total strangers (of the same sex, naturally). The many questions arising from this arrangement have not occurred to the writers. The couplings can be quite bizarre: well-educated, quietly sophisticated spinster Esther Harman (Flora Robson) has to bed down alongside pathetic little man-mad dizzy Elsie Dawson (the brilliantly squeaking Esma Cannon), who turns out to be the truly tragic figure of the piece. Decent young Jimmy Gardner (decent but perennially middle-aged Jimmy Hanley) shares his chalet with sadistic, murderous con-man Hardwick (Dennis Price, smooth as ever, in a character study that seems to reference the notorious Neville Heath murder case of 1946).

The most dramatic sequence has Esther breaking the camp's regulations by climbing the stairs (George Provis's set suddenly suggesting German Expressionism) to the unexpectedly high-res studio from where the blind announcer (Esmond Knight) constantly delivers his endless messages to the listening crowds. The quality of his messages ('Hello campers! *Still* enjoying your dinner?' he asks, probably just as their dish of semolina pudding arrives) verges on the mischievous. Perhaps in a 1947 holiday camp context, this would be considered wit. In fact, the announcer seems quite the wrong man for the job. He is as sophisticated and well-educated as Esther, who thinks she recognises his voice as that of the man she had once hoped to marry. He thinks of the camp as 'one of the strangest sights of the twentieth century, a great mass of people, all fighting for the one thing, the frantic search for pleasures, each one of them tired and dispirited, eager for peace yet frightened to be alone'.

Unknowingly, Elsie admits to Esther, 'That voice does something to you, doesn't it?', but Esther leaves the announcer's eyrie after learning that he is married. As for the tragedy of Esther's disappointment, it is in stark contrast to the hedonistic opportunities for romancing that the camp provides, and that mostly goes on outside, between couples leaning against the chalet doors. The leaning position is probably necessary to avoid the accusation that the film slyly suggests the possibility of pre-marital sex. For the Huggetts, the camp is a prospect of Elysian delight, a well-earned break from the daily round endured by solid working-class Joe (solid Jack Warner) and meek and mild and wholly commendable Ethel (who else but Kathleen Harrison?), the personification of a woman who knows her place in society and will probably even have a kind word to say about Mr Butlin's semolina. The public's affectionate response to the Huggetts was so encouraging that they went on to more filmic adventures in *Here Come the Huggetts* (1948) and *Vote for Huggett* and *The Huggetts Abroad* (both 1949), and were revivified as the Knowles family for *Home and Away* (1956).

The obligatory joy of being on site and (basic though it may be) *en suite* is noticeable, although the only conveniences we see are public, conveniences designated 'Lads' and 'Lasses'. Communal participation is at the film's core, best expressed in four brief musical moments: a choral outburst of the 'Hokey Cokey', the nineteenth-century campfire song 'Knees Up Mother Brown', and 'Cheerful' Charlie Chester getting the camp theatre's audience going with the vulgar traditional folk-song 'The Farmer and His Pigs' and that most embarrassing of physical exercises that accompanies Worton David and Norman Reeve's 1899 'Bobbing Up and Down Like This'.

SEPTEMBER

There is something reassuring in the fact that, two years after the end of war, Butcher's Film Services was still putting its faith in pictures that might as well have been made a decade earlier. Its very title, **The Hills of Donegal**, conjures visions of Ireland's mystical landscapes, but John Dryden's screenplay is doggedly studio-bound, its fervent Irishness produced and directed by John Argyle and courtesy of the Nettlefold Studios in Walton-on-Thames. Predictable, melodramatic, hugely sentimental, and bursting with its passion for the Emerald Isle, Dryden's story brings in several issues, among them alcoholism, domestic and sexual abuse, and racist attitudes to gypsies. The *MFB* complained that 'So many side issues [...] make for disjointedness, whatever they may lend to local colour.'[12] Perhaps, but Argyle and his capable cast give it all they've got, not least John Bentley in his first feature and James Etherington in his last (he died the following year). There was a qualified welcome from *Kinematograph Weekly*: 'Expressly made for the provincial ninepennies, it definitely puts Butcher's back on the beam' in 'a sound example of the popular species'.[13] The review nevertheless praised the film's efforts to 'provide music to meet the demands of even the most exacting patrons'.[14]

Opera singer Eileen Hannay (Dinah Sheridan) turns her back on her career as a prima donna (in rather shabby productions, from the evidence on screen), parting from her adoring leading man Michael O'Keefe (Etherington) to marry his ne'er-do-well cousin Terry (Bentley). At her farewell performance, Eileen and Michael sing F. N. Crouch's 'Eileen Mavourneen'. They duet in Wilfred Sanderson and P. J. O'Reilly's 'The Hills of Donegal'. The newlyweds move to Ireland to Eileen's ancestral home Curraghmore, but her parents are long dead and the property uninhabitable. They move into the farmhouse of curmudgeonly but lovable housekeeper Hannah (Maire O'Neill) and befriend curmudgeonly but lovable Old Jake (Moore Marriott) and lovably cute adolescent Paddy (Brendan Clagg), but Terry's past sexual and financial association with another singer, Carole Wells (Tamara Desni), threatens to ruin him. He demands that Eileen sells Curraghmore, she refuses, he reaches for the bottle.

Mystery surrounds the death of Eileen's parents, legends of the family's inheritance hidden at Curraghmore, and the curse that will befall those who disturb it. Terry is angry when Eileen strikes up a friendship with swarthy gypsy Daniel (Robert Arden). Far away, Michael and Carole are rehearsing the 'Brindisi' in *La Traviata*. At the gypsy encampment, the Romany way of life as imagined by British musical films offers us the Irish Gaelic Dancers, and David Java and His Gypsy Orchestra, the hectic gypsy choreography of Margherita Stanley (moving around open fires), old women smoking pipes, Daniel playing a melancholy tune on his fiddle, and very possibly several hedgehogs awaiting roasting.

Michael's feelings for Eileen never weaken ('Believe Me, If All Those Endearing Young Charms'). A drunken Terry assaults Eileen, but Eileen stands by him, and is heartened by the arrival of Mrs McTavish (Irene Handl) via Old Jake's pony cart ('The Low Back'd Car'). But justice will out: Terry goes to the theatre where Carole is appearing in Smetana's *The Bartered Bride*. He assaults her, and during a struggle high above the stage she falls to her death. At Curraghmore, the family fortune is at last discovered, but Terry shoots Daniel (now revealed as Eileen's half-brother). With his last breath, Daniel kills Terry.

DECEMBER

A documentary on the life of the peasant poet Robert Burns, **Comin' thro' the Rye** is so suffused with song that it can justly claim to be a British (or Scottish) musical film. One of only four pictures directed by Walter C. Mycroft, it was based on a scenario by Gilbert McAllister and produced by Arthur Dent at the Kay Carlton Hill Film Studios. Distinguished by the photography of Cedric Williams and Frank McLachlan and the art direction of Victor Hembrow, it balances a narrated programme of the life and loves of Burns (played, silently, by Terence Alexander) with a score presided over by W. L. Trytel, the frequently overlooked favourite composer of Twickenham studios. The film is crafted in bucolic and literary affection, with crystalline photography of landscape and skilfully directed musical sequences. In domestic setting, we have the fine Welsh tenor Trefor Jones, frequently featured in Ivor Novello's stage musicals and Mary Ellis's singing partner for the 1937 film of *Glamorous Night*. Musical highlights include 'Green Grow the Rushes-O', 'Oh Whistle and I'll Come', and Jones's singing of 'My Love Is Like a Red Red Rose'. Everything combines to stir the emotions 'till all the seas gang dry', in a little gem that tastefully and passionately reminds us of what we may long have forgotten.

1948

We've all been so busy praising *Hamlet* and *Henry V* that we have not understood that the factory workers and their wives much prefer to go to the pictures to see Frank Randle.

Holidays with Pay

Nightbeat	*Holidays with Pay*
One Night with You	*The Red Shoes*
Spring in Park Lane	*Date with a Dream*
A Song for Tomorrow	*Here Come the Huggetts*
Cup-Tie Honeymoon	*The Brass Monkey*

FEBRUARY

British Lion went into full *film noir* mode with **Nightbeat**, a tale of dodgy spivs, racketeers, and seedy nightclubs, produced and directed at Isleworth by Harold Huth (replacing the originally intended director Brian Desmond Hurst) and shot in fifty-six days. Guy Morgan and T. J. Morrison's screenplay had 'new scenes and story editing' by Roland Pertwee. Perhaps Mr Pertwee was responsible for the gloomier scenes stuffed with hard-bitten dialogue and suggestions of sexual abuse. Accusing Jackie of being a 'two-faced dame', Rocky (Nicholas Stuart) reminds her to 'Remember the last time I beat you up'. At least its leading man Maxwell Reed had some sort of animal attraction, a rare quality in British film actors of his period. The sunken depths of its story seem no place for the well-brought-up Anne Crawford, whose presence is eclipsed by the clearly dangerous villainess, nightclub singer Jackie, played by Christine Norden ('of whom much is expected'[1]) making her film debut.

The claustrophobic sexual relationships and fistfights and a night-time dockside chase are skilfully managed in a film that at times seems to point forward to *The Blue Lamp* of 1950, as well as pinpointing the difficulties that faced ex-servicemen after the war: will they go to the good or the bad? The film's general murkiness includes two nightclub numbers by its composer Benjamin Frankel and lyricist Harold Purcell, 'I'm Not in Love' and 'When You Smile', sung by Norden. Neither is remarkable, although the *MFB* considered that 'Once again Benjamin Frankel offers a score that is well-constructed and subtly shaded. Its integration with the dialogue is quite exceptionally successful'.[2] Sidney James is remarkably good as an exhausted pianist, and in the closing scenes Norden goes to pot splendidly.

APRIL

'We were doing much better work than this in the days of the early British talkies', wrote C. A. Lejeune after sitting through **One Night with You**, 'and I would gladly exchange the whole of [it] for a reel of *City of Song, Evergreen, Evensong, Bitter Sweet* or *Sunshine Susie*. Those old films, besides being infinitely more tuneful, had a natural lightness and buoyancy that is wholly missing from the present production'.[3]

There is no denying that *One Night with You* seems to have boomeranged back from a pre-war era, perhaps because the Two Cities' film was a sort of remake of Frank Capra's 1934 *It Happened One Night* which also had the considerable advantage of Clark Gable and Claudette Colbert as the nocturnally stranded lovers, while Josef Somlo's version made do with Patricia Roc ('a disinterested, completely characterless performance' according to the *MFB*) and imported tenor Nino Martini, who had a 'fine tenor voice' but whose singing 'is frequently interrupted', and whose performance was 'parrot-like and unimaginative'.[4] There was general disappointment, with the American press complaining of 'a limp, tedious and transparent farce hardly worth all the strenuous histrionics and singing'.[5]

Perhaps Martini suffers from being at the end of a line of good foreign tenors lured into a British studio, predecessors who had been handed better material and enjoyed very considerable success: the virile Jan Kiepura (the sort of heart-throb that Martini had no chance of becoming), the delightfully self-effacing Josef Schmidt, and, triumphing above them all, the far from cinematically compelling Richard Tauber. Making his only appearance in a British film, his Hollywood credits in *Here's to Romance* (1935) and *The Gay Desperado* (1936) long behind him, Martini never takes fire in a plot that seems little more than an adjunct to the continuing dilemma faced by the film's creators, although he 'sings admirably; he also shows considerable tact in fitting himself into the meshes of a commonplace but perfectly harmless musical comedy'.[6]

Like Schmidt's 1936 *A Star Fell from Heaven, One Night with You* is basically a satire on film-making, and more specifically on the art of making a British musical film. Based on a story by Carlo Ludovico Bragaglia, the 'adaptation and dialogue' is from the intellectual pens of Caryl Brahms and S. J. Simon, collaborative authors of many entertaining literary novels. They provide a screenplay that, if not brilliant, is persistently wordy, and in this regard stands above many of its type. It may be that their witty caricature sometimes seems too supercilious about the very sort of picture they had now been hired to write. There is much discussion between the emotionally wrought director (excellent Charles Goldner, stretching every sinew) and his creative team.

What they need, of course, is 'a beautiful, simple, cheap, idea' with 'A song at the beginning, a song in the middle and a song at the end.' As for the intended hero, 'You know what a tenor does? He sings and sings and sings,' preferably without being as frequently interrupted as Martini's unfortunate tenor Giulio Moris is. His fate here is to spend an uncomfortable night, due to train timetable muddles, on railway stations and in prison, with pretty Mary (Roc).

'The music throughout is pleasant', conceded the *MFB*, 'but the comedy is stodgy and dismally slow'.[7] The judgement is fair enough. The several subtleties of the dialogue are there for those who recognise them, but the balance of music and comedy (best when the wordless Stanley Holloway is involved) is miscalculated, the bursts of melody – as in the forgettable 'Pathway to Heaven' (there is also a 'Path through the Forest') and title song – never distinguishable or memorable, with no visual supplements to enhance them. To what extent this deficiency is the responsibility of the directors or writers is unclear, but for long stretches Brahms and Simon seem intent on pursuing a comedy of manners involving a cosmopolitan argument that surely had little appeal to the general cinemagoer wanting to get out of the rain. As we are assured, the film audience expects 'A song at the beginning, a song in the middle and a song at the end', preferably without interruption. Perhaps the 'film within a film' concept is worked to death, when a more musically accented approach (and a great deal more vim in the sedentary numbers) would work better. As the *Guardian* tactfully warned, 'Those will get the most fun out of it who go to see it with the least expectancy.'[8]

Happily, *One Night with You* has an absolutely bullseye moment. It is its last, when, watching the film that Moris has made, Mary walks from her seat in the cinema not only up to the screen, but *into* it. For some, this fusion of the film's disparate elements may be magic enough. Or not.

Some summaries persist in suggesting that **Spring in Park Lane** is a musical film. Essentially, it is not, beyond its deft background score by Robert Farnon, and the use of Manning Sherwin and lyricist Harold Purcell's delightful 'The Moment I Saw You', originally written for Cicely Courtneidge in Arthur Macrae's runaway musical comedy success of 1945 *Under the Counter*. Nevertheless, Nicholas Phipps's screenplay totters on the edge of wanting to *be* a musical, but all we get is a dream-like dance sequence (a gentle choreography by Philip and Betty Buchel) beguilingly performed by Anna Neagle and co-star Michael Wilding. The twenty-first of Neagle's films to be directed by Herbert Wilcox, it was also the fourth and penultimate of their 'Mayfair' series.

C. A. Lejeune suggested that most of the Wilcox–Neagle films 'are frank novelettes, and yet there is something in their unaffected delight in the simpler clichés of popular fiction that endears them to people not generally addicted to this form of entertainment'.[9] This was fare that 'can be recommended unreservedly to the serious-minded. They at least will find in it the pure essence of escapism which the season and the weather and the state of the world demand'.[10] It's a generous assessment. Following on the recent release of Rank's enjoyably overblown *Good Time Girl* (1948), with pouting Jean Kent as a woman 'no better than she should be', Wilcox made his distaste for such cinematic aberrations quite clear, hoping that producers would make 'what one might call open pictures, happy, unclouded pictures. We do not want sadism, abnormality and psychoanalysis. That sort of thing is no good for the average audience – they do not understand it and in most cases do not want to understand it.' This, despite the fact that Miss Kent had set the box-office tills happily ringing.[11] The *News of the World*, too, regretted British cinema's rush to portray reality; after seeing Cavalcanti's *They Made Me a Fugitive* (1947), its critic 'sought escape into the sunshine, desperately longing to encounter again the simple sentimentalities of *The Courtneys of Curzon Street*'.[12]

Commercially, *Spring in Park Lane* was the most successful British film of its year, and remains one of the most seen of all time. Few of its patrons would have known its history. Alice Duer Miller's play *Come Out of the Kitchen* had already been filmed as a silent directed by John S. Robertson in 1919, again as the 1930 multi-lingual *Honey* directed by Wesley Ruggles, and with Jack Buchanan in the 1935 *Come Out of the Pantry*, directed by Jack Raymond, whose *Splinters* (1929) can lay claim to being the first of the British musical films proper.

The familiar theme of class distinction is never far from the Wilcox thesis, and Park Lane has plenty of it. Wealthy Judy Howard (Neagle), under the patronage of Wilcox favourite Tom Walls as a sort of Uncle Avuncular giving one of his apparently lazy performances, is amused to discover that their new footman Richard (he's really a Lord in disguise) knows about the Pre-Raphaelites, just as in *The Lady Is a Square* Neagle is amused to discover that another new footman (this time it's Frankie Vaughan) has heard of Mahler and Tchaikovsky. Meanwhile, the light banter is just what the 1948 doctor ordered, along with some clumsy Wilcox/Phipps in-jokes, with Peter Graves taking a good look at the new footman and observing, 'You're not unlike Michael Wilding.' This is Wilcoxian wit.

The British cinemagoer could have wanted for no less demanding fare. Astonishingly, the film's success led Alexander Korda to offer Neagle the title role in his projected film *Mary Poppins*, to be directed by either himself or Wilcox, but as Wilcox explained, 'She agreed entirely with me that to go from *Spring in Park Lane* to *Mary Poppins* would be fatal [...] In my hands it would have been a Yorkshire pudding.'[13]

JUNE

The musical oddity *A Song for Tomorrow* was the cinematic debut of the prolific director Terence Fisher, summarily dismissed by the *MFB*'s announcement that its 'script [by William Fairchild], production and acting are shoddy and insignificant'.[14] Its 'only redeeming feature' was its star Evelyn McCabe, a performer who seems to have immediately evaporated into cinema history. Produced by Ralph Nunn-May via J. Arthur Rank Production facilities at Highbury Studios (the home of the Rank Charm School), this faltering nonsense finds Flight Lieutenant Derek Wardell (Shaun Noble) awaiting an operation in a military hospital. As he drifts into anaesthetic unconsciousness, he hears the voice of a contralto singer. It is Helen Maxwell (McCabe). The ensuing romantic entanglements, with Wardell and his doctor Roger Stanton (Ralph Michael) vying for her attentions, are dealt a serious blow by neither McCabe nor Noble showing any acting ability. In these plodding circumstances, McCabe's singing comes as blessed relief. Just as well: Stanton explains, 'Your voice forms a bridge in his mind.' Wardell is already engaged to a girl he no longer remembers, but is fascinated by Helen's voice. Convinced that a recreation of the operation may restore his memory, he is back on the operating table, but finally takes himself off to the country, returning only to say goodbye to Helen as she is about to go on stage at Covent Garden in *Samson and Delilah*.

Understandably, McCabe's performance of 'Softly Awakes My Heart' is tearful. Her welcome interpolations, accompanied by the London Symphony Orchestra under Muir Mathieson, include an 'aria' by William Blezard (now best remembered for his musical association with Joyce Grenfell), the 'Londonderry Air', Arthur Young's 'Philomel' to Shakespeare's lyric, 'Believe Me, If All Those Endearing Young Charms', and Henry F. Lyte's 'Abide with Me'.

Mancunian's 'musical comedy burlesque' **Cup-Tie Honeymoon** lived in hope of fulfilling its publicity machine's declaration that 'Millions of Football Fans will want to see this excellent Musical Comedy' with three musical numbers by Mancunian's resident composer A. W. (Albert) Stanbury, musically directed by Fred Harris, whose day job was as musical director at Manchester's Palace Theatre: 'Evening Star', 'Goodnight – Sweet Dreams', and 'Let's Make a Go of It'. Only the latter is on show in the only available print, sung by the film's star Sandy Powell ('Can you hear me, mother?') and bouncing Betty Jumel, along with an uncredited song about football, slim pickings compared with the musical content of many Mancunian productions. The credits attribute the screenplay to Anthony Toner (the director John E. Blakeley) and Roney Parsons (Arthur Mertz), and in fact it was completed by Harry Jacobson after Mertz died during filming. It provides an excuse for much broad comedy from Powell in a migraine-inducing overcoat, Jumel, and 'toff' comedian Dan Young in a drawn-out slapstick kitchen routine. Pat McGrath is the bright, breezy but uninteresting hero Eric, picked to play for England but embroiled in a crooked financial deal when he is not involved in a remarkably insipid romantic complication. We must be grateful for Jumel's contribution that incorporates her trademark pratfalls. She also has a way with a line: 'My second husband was a real football fan. I was a real football Fanny.' Young, too, gets away with material that may have slipped past the censor, mentioning his visit to a nudist camp: 'I was frozen stiff.'

Patricia Phoenix, who would go on to legendary fame as Elsie Tanner in the television soap opera *Coronation Street*, made her screen debut after Blakeley had seen her perform in repertory at Chorlton. On screen, she and Powell share a sketch in which her soldier husband returns home after five years of war. 'Love's a wonderful thing,' he tells her. 'Starts in heaven and ends in the *News of the World*.'

Even the most inquisitive of cineastes might blench at sitting through Mancunian's almost two-hour-long **Holidays with Pay**. Its very title tilts a hat at the working-class audience. Mancunian's supremo, the irrepressible John E. Blakeley, unashamedly admitted that the quick, cheap pictures he made in Manchester were not, never had been, and never would be intended for the 'La-di-da' (his own phrase) cinemagoers in London. The journalist Ross Shepherd railed at the vast sums of money recently spent by Rank: 'You've got it all wrong, Mr Rank – they want Randle not Shakespeare.' He continued, 'We've all been so busy praising *Hamlet* and *Henry V* that we have not understood that the factory workers and their wives much prefer to go to the pictures to see Frank Randle.' Shepherd suggested that Rank and his like 'should slip quietly away from the Dorchester Hotel and have a chat with the queues outside his cinemas in Preston and Pudsey. I am quite sure he would come back and fire all his scriptwriters who live in Kensington Gore.'[15]

At least Blakeley's new film offered a northern alternative to the Dorchester: a 17/6d a night bed and breakfast in Blackpool. *Holidays with Pay* proved that Blakeley's post-war commitment to Randle comedies was unshaken, following the 1945 *Home Sweet Home*. Although Mancunian had sparked George Formby's stellar career with *Boots! Boots!* (1934) and *Off the Dole* (1935), catapulting him into the first division, no such transfer was available to Randle, whose reputation resided with what the trade papers considered 'industrial' audiences. *Holidays with Pay* 'was recognising the fact that at this period the British workforces were for the first time enjoying their own holidays with pay'. As such, this was a film with a purpose, and it seems entirely appropriate that Harry Jackson and Mavis Compston's screenplay, based on a story by Anthony Toner, should despatch the Rogers family to Blackpool, where Randle was already a God-like comedic icon. Sadly, the film was not to be one of his best; perseverance is required if one is to appreciate its worth.

Randle is fortunate to have 'Two Ton' Tessie O'Shea playing his wife, Pansy. Miss O'Shea submits to every indignity inflicted upon her, sparing nothing in a zestful participation in the shambles. Her energy levels are off the scale, whether struggling with the broken-down motor in which they travel, their stay in a surprisingly prim guest-house, or a long-drawn-out sequence in a supposedly haunted house. At one moment Randle presents her with a present: a small brassiere. Her reaction – 'What am I supposed to do with this?' – appears unrehearsed, and she quickly leaves the scene. Was this perhaps another of Randle's unscripted attempts to undermine the script?

Whatever the truth, O'Shea's complicity with the ongoing muddle continues, with one scene springing up a possible answer to another question: had she *really* leapt into that water tank in *London Town* or was it done by a double? *Holidays with Pay* suggests otherwise, for now she is indeed all at sea in a boat, trying to cross to another, when she falls in, not a double in sight. One wonders if there was any other actress prepared to do such stuff for the sake of a quick burst of laughter from an audience. This is surely a plucky, tireless woman, exuding a natural warmth. Away from the Randle-dominated scenes, the writers have clumsily interpolated a crime element and a romantic element in the tepid romance for the Rogers' daughter Pam (Sally Barnes) to little effect.

JULY

There will be some, among them perhaps your author, who will smart at the inclusion of **The Red Shoes**, a film steeped in accolade, sandwiched, squeezed, between one of Frank Randle's knockabout Mancunian outings and a cheaply made comedy that wasted Jean Carson, one of the many girls that British films forgot.

We walk on hallowed ground as we approach and regard Michael Powell and Emeric Pressburger's ballet-drama, with its screenplay by Pressburger and Keith Wilbur based on a dark story by Hans Christian Andersen. Its reputation comes down to us, heavily laden with Oscars, garnered with pontificating opinion. We disregard the possibly discouraging fact that it lasts over two hours. Luminaries are involved: for the Terpsichorean sequences one of Diaghilev's favourites Leonid Massine, the actor and dancer Robert Helpmann, and Moira Shearer as Vicky Page, a reincarnation of Andersen's tragic heroine. Who will dare to question the passionate authority of Sir Thomas Beecham's conducting of Brian Easdale's score? Criticism is left open-mouthed by the enormity of Hein Heckroth's production designs, perplexed by the intellectual interplay between its components, the artistic and emotional tussle that pervades those two long hours. At the centre is Anton Walbrook's Boris Lermontov, created by an actor for whom no amount of waxing eloquence would be sufficient. What else, when Dilys Powell wrote that 'in this matter of enjoyed authority and daring, Powell and Pressburger have in my opinion no rival anywhere, either in

America or in Europe. And in them we see a producer-director team who, even when their basic story is banal, are not afraid of imaginative decoration.'[16] As Ian Christie points out, both those red shoes and the tales of Hoffmann posed a 'critical dilemma: could they be judged merely as films, in view of their large dance and music content?'[17]

OCTOBER

The first production of Tempean Films, formed by Robert S. Baker and Monty Berman, was the 55-minute **Date with a Dream**. Directed by Dicky Leeman and written by Carl Nystrom from an original story by Leeman, Baker and Berman, it has a poverty-stricken air that is immediately apparent. The plot barely exists, beyond the fact that a gang of army mates demobbed after the war in the desert reconvene to put on a show back in Blighty. Throughout, there is some pleasure gained from Vic Lewis and His Orchestra, formed two years earlier and making Big Band sounds in constrained circumstances, invading the artistes' lodgings to do a big orchestral number. Berman was not speaking of *Date with a Dream* when he explained 'The fact was that with our budget we couldn't afford to build the sets that the films required',[18] but might as well have been.

The gap-toothed *éminence grise* and chief comedian of the reconstituted troupe is Terry (Terry-Thomas) who ploughs on regardless through some lamentably unfunny stand-up routines and impressions (an awful Maurice Chevalier, for one) and yodelling, these sequences made the more ridiculous because the added canned laughter is so ineptly introduced. Len and Bill Lowe, a popular variety cross-talk duo, were clearly progenitors of Morecambe and Wise, but their skills are all but crushed here. For some reason, space is made for the guitar-playing troubadour Elton Hayes, one of the least offensive of balladeers and surely one of the most insipid as he sings 'Sombrero'. There is also a fleeting glimpse of Norman Wisdom (his first on film) in his boxing-ring knockabout sketch.

Leading lady Jean (eventually to become 'Jeannie') Carson bears much of the responsibility of propelling the action and putting over Vic Lewis's songs, 'Unlucky', 'Let Me Dream', and, with the Lowes, 'How about Me for You?' and 'Now Is the Time for Love'. Also heard are 'Here Comes the Show', 'You Made Me Mad', and Ken Thorne's 'Whose Turn Now?' Meagre as these items are, it is interesting to see Carson in embryo, before she found stage success in the American-British musical *Love from Judy* (1952). Contractually trapped into its long run, when the show closed she escaped to America, where she became the star she might have become at home. The British studios failed to find a decent vehicle for her talents, which were wittered away in such trifles as *An Alligator Named Daisy* (1955). Perhaps chastened by her experiences in Britain, Carson had a reputation for saying 'no', turning down Lerner and

Loewe's invitation to be the original Eliza Doolittle in their *My Fair Lady*. By the time she returned to London in the sixties for the musical *Strike a Light!*, Britain had forgotten her all over again.

Adding to the air of muddling along, Terry-Thomas's wife Ida Patlansky cuts a strange figure as a theatrical landlady, as does Julia Lang (best remembered for her association with the BBC's *Listen with Mother*) as Madam Docherty. Baker and Berman went on to substantial successes with films and such television series as *Randall and Hopkirk*, *The Saint*, and the excellent crime series *Gideon's Way*.

NOVEMBER

Gainsborough's delectably enjoyable *Holiday Camp* (1947) first introduced the Huggett family to the British public. **Here Come the Huggetts** announced their return, now slightly re-formed and with the welcome addition of young Petula Clark as their youngest, Pet, 'father' Joe and 'mother' Ethel (impeccably cast Jack Warner and Kathleen Harrison) were joined by Susan (Susan Shaw) and Jane (Jane Hylton). Even the *MFB* was pleased to see them back: 'Though the story is negligible, most of the characters are so natural and human that we seem causally to be sharing the emotions of a real, typically English family.'[19]

As a snapshot of suburban lower-middle-class life in the aftermath of war, it is inestimably in debt to its surprisingly deft, witty screenplay by Mabel and Denis Constanduros and Peter Rogers. The arrival of flashy young teenage relative Diana (Diana Dors) sends shock waves through the family; Susan, after all, is a fine example of post-war social mobility, with a job at that thoroughly respectable bastion of culture Boots Subscription Library. Diana makes even more of a workhouse donkey of poor Ethel. As Pet explains about her mother, 'She's awfully simple. She doesn't know much about the world.' The thrilling expectation of catching sight of the impending royal wedding ends in disappointment, courtesy of ever-complaining Grandma (Amy Veness, often the first choice for cinematic grumpy relatives), but what *Meet the Huggetts* does so simply and cleverly is to look compassionately on the humdrum.

Produced by Betty E. Box and directed in sure style by Ken Annakin, the film makes space for Edmundo Ros and His Orchestra to play 'Samba 34a', for Ros to sing Peggy Lee and Dave Barbour's 'Mañana', and for Clark to sing Jack Fishman and Peter Hart's 'Walking Backwards'. A burst of community singing of music-hall song at the film's end consolidates the friendly comradeship at the heart of the piece, using Albert Chevalier's 'My Old Dutch' and Vesta Victoria's no-show-nuptial 'Waiting at the Church'. The public's approval of this first Huggett family biopic encouraged two follow-ups in 1949, *Vote for Huggett* and *The Huggetts Abroad*.

DECEMBER

Three of Carroll Levis's earlier discoveries, 'The Two Laundry Men from Peckham' and Bernard Flynn 'The Singing Gas Collector from Whitechapel', are sadly absent from **The Brass Monkey** (also known as *Lucky Mascot*), produced for Diadem by N. A. Bronsten and David Coplan. Built as it is around Levis's reputation for bringing amateur talent to the attention of the some-times unsophisticated British public, the amount of literary talent employed to very little effect seems a trifle excessive. The combined efforts of Alec Coppel and director Thornton Freeland's original story, and additional dialogue by William Freshman, Vernon Sylvaine, and Robert Buckland, barely justified this muddled mystery, which is distinguished only by the surprising appearance of Ernest Thesiger alongside an amateur night out of variety turns. On this occasion, even so notable an artist as Terry-Thomas is as amateur as the rest, singing the excruciatingly embarrassing 'Somebody Blew My Bluebird's Egg' (music by Pat Quinn, lyric by no less than Noel Langley). He also heads up Gaby Rogers's number 'It's the Greatest Business in the World', choreographed by the renowned Buddy Bradley on what was obviously not one of his good days. T-T suffers, too, from an absurdly inappropriate dubbed voice.

Sid Colin and Steve Race's dismal 'Home Sweet Home' is thrashed to death by Avril Angers's sub-Betty Hutton performance. Saddled with irritating and unfunny malapropisms, she manages to be consistently unamusing. Even the velvet darkness of Hutch's voice (Leslie Hutchinson) in Colin Campbell's 'To-morrow's Rainbow' fails to impress. Meanwhile, the background score 'written and composed by Dr. Bernard Grun' trundles on, leaving us to wonder if the doctor was writing for an entirely different picture.

It is good to see non-professionals taking their chance, not least young Winnie from Yorkshire, who with commendable assurance informs Levis that her real career (as if Levis would be in the least interested) is as a painter. Here, of course, she is more fodder for Levis's battle-cry that 'The new and unknown artists of today are truly the stars of tomorrow' and shows how well she can play 'The Flight of the Bumble Bee' on her accordion. The Ward Brothers chip in with a musical act apparently inspired by Heath Robinson.

In the manner of Wilfred Pickles in his radio series *Have a Go!*, Levis relishes in soliciting personal information from his fame-seekers. Witness Fred, a very elderly 69-year-old with thirty-two grandchildren and four great-grandchil-dren. Never missing an opportunity, Levis jumps in with 'Little man, you've had a busy day', another example of the script's scintillating ripostes. Fred is still fit enough to essay 'Endearing Young Charms' on his musical saw.

No actor or distinct personality, Levis is at least on home territory, with not one of the featured amateurs threatening a challenge. He was a survivor. He enjoyed enduring popularity from 1936 via his talent-spotting programmes on Radio Luxembourg's 'Quaker [Oats] Quarter Hour', and had already been head-hunted by British film studios for the 1939 *Discoveries*. His career carried through to the 1950s, sponsored by Bird's Custard on Luxembourg and touring British theatres. It was reported that before filming *The Brass Monkey* he had suffered a breakdown.

His leading lady is Carole Landis, slumming it before returning to America to resume her career in Hollywood, but this was to be her last film. She sings Ross Parker's melancholic 'I Know Myself Too Well (to Admit That It's Over)', a lyric that would prove tragically prescient. She died from a barbiturate overdose in July 1948. She had once written, 'I have no intention of ending my career in a rooming house, with full scrapbooks and an empty stomach.'

1949

Where else can you learn to write music for nude women?

Murder at the Windmill

Vote for Huggett
Somewhere in Politics
Bless 'em All
Melody in the Dark
The Huggetts Abroad
It's a Wonderful Day
Murder at the Windmill

Maytime in Mayfair
Old Mother Riley's New Venture
Trottie True
What a Carry On!
Skimpy in the Navy
High Jinks in Society

FEBRUARY

Vote for Huggett was the second of Gainsborough's adventures for what was one of Britain's best-known families. The new episode reassembled much of the original creative team responsible for the previous year's *Here Come the Huggetts*, producer Betty E. Box, director Ken Annakin, and sure-handed writers in Mabel and Denis Constanduros in collaboration with Allan Mackinnon. The opportunity for a mild satire on local politics was skilfully exploited. Four years after the end of a devastating war, regeneration of housing for the working and middle classes was of prime importance in council chambers debating town planning. Now, it hurtled dependable, decent, honest-as-the-day Joe Huggett (Jack Warner) into the maelstrom of warring municipals with its tin-pot politicians. Ethel Huggett (Kathleen Harrison) is terrified by the prospect of becoming a public figure, goaded by the appalling wife of a local official, Mrs Hall, played up to the hilt by Adrianne Allen. Amy Veness's Grandma Huggett is usually somewhere about, ready to douse enjoyment, and there are three delightfully dotty old ladies to add to the general merriment.

Petula Clark entertains at a fete with Egbert Van Alstyne and Harry Williams's luscious 'In the Shade of the Old Apple Tree', telling her audience that 'I think the old songs are sometimes the best'. Gainsborough's final outing for the Huggetts, *The Huggetts Abroad*, followed.

Mancunian's **Somewhere in Politics** (its working title was *That's My Man*) demands a place in any account of British musical films, but its originally released print (a generous 108 minutes) is believed lost, the only remaining fragment of eighteen minutes having no musical content. It is unfortunate. The full version included Josef Locke at his most vigorous (and seemingly fresh after long hours of drinking and carousing with his co-star Frank Randle) performing Dermot Macmurrough and Josephine V. Rowe's evergreen ballad 'Macushla', John Stevenson's setting of 'Oft in the Stilly Night', and Othmar Klose and Rudi Lukesch's 'Hear My Song, Violetta', with its English lyric by Harry S. Pepper. We also regret the lack of Tessie O'Shea's contribution, 'Spade and Bucket'. The film was produced and directed for Mancunian by John E. Blakeley; the script (highly liable for alteration by the unpredictable Randle) was credited to Randle, Harry Jackson, and Arthur Mertz, and gave opportunities for the double-act of Syd and Max Harrison to preserve some of their fast-talking routines. Fortunately, the eighteen surviving minutes show Randle and O'Shea on top form.

MARCH

The Glaswegian comedian Hal Monty has gone missing, unremembered by such chroniclers of comedy as John Montgomery, John Fisher, and Leslie Halliwell, despite his bill matter of 'Laugh and be Happy' being immortalised in two cheaply made movies of 1949. **Bless 'em All**, produced by Arthur Dent and directed by Robert Jordan Hill for Advance Films at Southall Studios, Middlesex, resembles an after-birth of the recent war, a backward picture of British army life four years after the end of conflict; indeed, a celebration of it.

The screenplay, which often recedes as the film spontaneously flies off in different directions, was by Aileen Burke and Leone Stewart with additional dialogue by C. Boganny and (no surprise) Monty, all based on a story by Dent. Its Poverty Row provenance is obvious, but Monty's apparent insistence that he uses the opportunity as a showcase will either repulse or cajole the viewer. He may have been a second-drawer comic, this ex-balloon sculptor whose real name was Albert Sutan, and who subsequently changed his name to Albert Sutton and worked as one half of a male dance duo, before becoming Eddie May and finally transmogrifying into Hal Monty, under which flag he toured in variety in the 1950s. No doubt some of the tried and tested material in *Bless 'em All* was still on parade when he starred in 'the new, screamingly funny army revue' *Monty's Army* twice nightly at the Windmill Theatre, Yarmouth.

On screen, Monty became Skimpy Carter, the rawest and most disobedient of recruits, flanked by his mates Peterson (Max Bygraves in his film debut) and Jock (Jack Milroy). They make a happy trio, almost charming in their innocence. Although Bygraves has yet to find his acting feet, we see his potential when he tries a stand-up comedy routine and when he sings 'I'm Afraid to Love You'.

Milroy is assured, at ease, meeting Monty for a cook-house scene that descends into pantomimic chaos, much of it (if we note Milroy's reactions) as unexpected as it was unscripted. Monty's third co-star is Les Ritchie as the bellowing, put-upon Sergeant Willis. It's another vibrant turn in what is basically a queue of music-hall acts, 'extremely funny in the parts which are not too-long-drawn-out' in a film that 'as a whole is amateurish and technically below average.'[1] It's no wonder that the shadow of ENSA persists throughout, with snatches of two of their makeshift revues produced for the soldiers, 'Dancing Dolls' and 'Mirth and Melody'. Knocked-up and undemanding as it is, it never flags, allowing Monty to do his 'vent' act with his doll Se*bar*stian, or letting Milroy sing and tap his way through 'Maggie Cock-a-Bendy', or Ritchie letting rip on the parade ground.

There is no shortage of music, more carefully worked into the fabric than seems likely. The songs catch the mood of the picture perfectly, both in portraying the war and in recollection of it: 'Run Rabbit Run', 'We're Going to Hang Out Our Washing on the Siegfried Line', 'Boom', 'Bless 'em All', Monty's chorus-rouser 'Hi-Di-Hi', 'All's Well Mademoiselle', Monty and Se*bar*stian's 'What More Can I Say?', and 'I'll Be Seeing You'. Professional polish may be lacking, but the energy and intention to please is not, no matter how old or obvious its wit. 'I've always wanted to meet Jane Russell,' says Bygraves, 'for two good reasons.' *Kinematograph Weekly* thought it a 'wildly incoherent but cheery low comedy musical extravaganza [...] a trifle long but funny for the most part, it's a reliable rib tickler for the industrial masses'.[2] Monty reunited with Bygraves and Ritchie later in the year for *Skimpy in the Navy*. While Monty's name slipped away, Bygraves (in Britain) and Milroy (at home in Scotland) may both be said to have acquired iconic status.

It was a busy year for Advance Films, and for Southall Studios, with its publicity department trumpeting a 'NEW LOOK Comedian with the RUBBER NECK' ('By Heck – What a Neck!') in what it named 'The Anti-Gloom Film' *Melody in the Dark*. Not Nat Jackley but Ben Wrigley, in a picture 'bound to tickle the industrial masses',[3] written and co-produced by John Guillermin, produced and directed by Robert Jordan Hill, and musically supervised by George Melachrino. Showgirl Pat Evans (Eunice Gayson) inherits her uncle's strange house (the pressbook promised a gothic house scarer 'with eerie music and spooky bedrooms and corridors'), moving her out-of-work fellow artistes in and turning it into a nightclub, only to be beset by ghostly activities enacted by crooked servants. During the proceedings, Alan Dean sang 'If I Won the Penny Pool', The Keynotes sang 'Jingle Jangle Thingamajig', Marion Saunders sang 'Our Time Is Now', Dawn Lesley sang 'My Song of Love', and the Stardusters Dance Orchestra presented 'Welcome Inn' and 'Gay Doggie'. The company included two impressionists, Carl Carlisle (late of *Sweethearts Forever*) and Maisie Weldon, and The London Lovelies. Guillermin admitted that 'This Adelphi production also riffed teasingly on the name of a slightly more recent addition to the crowded mystery-comedy, *Whistling in the Dark* (1941) starring Red Skelton', and that *Melody in the Dark* was basically 'a showcase for a succession of cheaply-booked stage performers'.[4]

MAY

The last of Gainsborough's Huggett family sagas, ***The Huggetts Abroad*** reassembled producer Betty E. Box and director Ken Annakin with a screenplay from the Constanduroses (Mabel and Denis), now collaborating with Gerard Bryant and Ted Willis, based on a story by Keith Campbell. Understandably, life in dreary Britain, 'queues, rations, the ruddy awful weather', stirs dreams of far-off foreign parts, and unlikely as it seems, the Huggetts pack up and go on safari. Far from home and hearth, they are a little out of their comfort zone in a storyline that stretches credibility, and studio-bound recreations of desert sands do nothing to sustain illusion. Petula Clark has two brief musical moments, singing Jack Fishman and Peter Hart's 'House in the Sky' and the severely whimsical 'Doodle-Oodle-Day', in which Jack Warner, Harrison, and along-for-the-ride Jimmy Hanley join. Warner and Harrison were retained for the BBC radio series *Meet the Huggetts*. It ran from 1953 until 1961, testament to the enduring popularity of what came to be known as 'Huggettry', 'a term of derision for working-class domestic comedy'.[5]

Produced, written, and directed by Hal Wilson, Knightsbridge Films' ***It's a Wonderful Day*** was fifty minutes in the company of bandleader-cum-songster John Blythe in Devon, to which he had escaped from a busy schedule. After admiring the scenery, he is joined by his colleagues, including the George Mitchell Swing Choir and the Seven Imeson Brothers. The *MFB* unenthusiastically reported that 'Blythe, who can portray "spivs" and other unpleasant characters with such telling effect, is completely wasted [...] and seems scarcely likely to achieve a resounding success as a singer'.[6]

Lovable old stage carpenter Gimpy (Eliot Makeham) welcomes us to London's Windmill Theatre, the home of 'Revudeville', the longest-running revue in theatre history, whose 60,000 performances were packed with comics (many of whom went on to become big names), musical items, and naked girls under the strict instruction of the Lord Chamberlain not to move. It so happens that this is a special occasion, for after the last show of the day (the seventh of this non-stop entertainment) the body of a man shot through the heart is discovered in the front row of the stalls. An inspector (Garry Marsh) and his over-educated sergeant (Jon Pertwee) begin their investigation by demanding that the last half hour of the show be repeated exactly as it took place earlier that evening, in a bid to establish at what point a gunshot might have been fired.

This is the perfect excuse for the generous helpings of musical numbers occupying Grand National's unmissable ***Murder at the Windmill***. Produced by Daniel Angel and Nat Cohen, and written and directed by Val Guest, it's the old trick of combining a crime story with musical items, but in this case the trick works admirably, providing not only a decent picture in its own right but an historical document of a British institution that even in the darkness of World War II kept its doors open (almost exclusively to male theatregoers), justifying subsequent use of its catchphrase 'We Never Closed.' A non-English-speaking visitor asks at the box office about the souvenir programme, in which the Windmill's girls are abundantly photographed: is the brochure available in other languages? 'Don't worry,' he's told, 'I think you'll understand the pictures all right.' Of course, it was the nudity, tastefully diluted by careful positioning and subtle lighting, and *not* the quaint musical numbers and comics that kept the box-office till ringing, but nudity on screen was out of the question; the nearest we get is a brief glimpse of the Windmill's iconic Fan Dance. The actress Judith Bruce assures me that she was dancing it at the age of sixteen and that the theatre was run by Vivian Van Damm (played here by Jack Livesey) 'like a convent.' Van Damm's daughter Sheila records how

> Jimmy Edwards did his comedy turn, as Jimmy Edwards, and Johnnie Gale, who had become our stage director, went along to Nettlefold Studios to play himself. Twelve of our forty-two girls went along too. The entire stage and auditorium of the Windmill was reproduced at Nettlefold faithfully, and with zealous attention to authenticity. Father, having given permission for anything to be borrowed from his office if necessary, was astounded to arrive at the theatre one morning and walk into a bare, empty room. A studio lorry had called, taken him at his word, and gutted it.[7]

The show-within-the-show items are done with real charm, with the genuine Windmill personnel adding authenticity. Ex-Windmill girl Diana Decker is a little over-bright as the show's leading lady; the *real* Windmill girls on view act more naturally. So, with occasional detours into the murder mystery, the musical numbers, orchestrated for the film by Ronald Hanmer and directed by the prolific Philip Martell, reveal themselves as the invaluable archival documents they are. Guest contributes two items: 'Two Little Dogs' performed by Donald Clive, Jill Anstey, and the girls, with Robin Richmond seated at an electronic organ and pulled on stage, and 'I'll Settle for You' for Diana Decker, Donald Clive and the girls, with clothed female tableaux and a male impressionist. Pertwee appears as a manic Danny Kaye. The dancers perform Charles Rose and Ronald Bridges's 'Mexico'. Rose was the Windmill's 'regular' composer for thirty years. He once asked, 'Where else can you learn to write music for nude women?' We also see Rose's 'King's Night Out' (co-written with Reginald Bristow) and 'Life Should Go with a Swing' (co-written with Ronald Bridges). Bill Currie's 'A Modern Romeo' features Decker in a routine involving a 'shotgun wedding', and shots are heard. For some reason, neither the inspector nor sergeant takes any notice of this. The corps of dancers is un-identified, but one must be the Windmill's choreographer Jack Billings, whose out-of-house credits included arranging dances for *Spring Song* (1946) and *Happy Go Lovely* (1951). At the close of the number the girls shoot off blanks into the air. The riches continue with Edwards's solo act with his trombone as Marsh and Pertwee look on stony-faced. They seem more attentive when Christine Welsford does the Fan Dance.

When Clive absconds from the theatre, he's accused of being the murderer, but he's too self-conscious and pleasing to be the culprit. When the real murderer is caught, the company have to start work again immediately on the next seven shows. The Windmill must never cancel a performance! 'We've never closed yet and we certainly aren't going to close now,' insists Van Damm. The sting in the tail is Gimpy's goodbye to us. The fact that he's been explaining things to 'the padre' suggests he may be facing a curtain rather more final than any that ever fell on stage at his beloved Windmill. In 1966, Stanley Long and Arnold Louis Miller's *Secrets of a Windmill Girl* gave the theatre the X-rated certificate that Van Damm had for so long assiduously avoided.

JUNE

Following on from Herbert Wilcox's *I Live in Grosvenor Square, Piccadilly Incident, The Courtneys of Curzon Street*, and *Spring in Park Lane*, his 'London' series of romantic entertainments built around Anna Neagle reached a terminus with the Imperadio–British Lion **Maytime in Mayfair**. Once again, cosmopolitan sophistication is in the air, if not so obvious on screen. On this occasion Michael Wilding's Michael Gore-Brown (presumably not related to the Gore-Blimeys) inherits a prominent London fashion house run by exqui-sitely turned-out Eileen Grahame (Neagle). No paper is too thin to inscribe the events that ensue, dreamed up by Nicholas Phipps who had already written the others in the series.

The arch historical references to Mayfair that act as a sort of introduction must have been a total mystery to most of its suburban audience, and just as baffling to many Mayfairians. From here on in, the fact that we are in Mayfair is more or less disregarded. The performances of all concerned come dangerous-ly close to 'play-acting'; there is a difference (more subtle than realised here) between characterisation and pretending. It is one of the unsettling flaws in a picture that sets itself apart from anything like real life, but hasn't the wit or skill to convince us of its authenticity, as some of Wilcox's old guard come back on parade, among them Phipps (having written himself into it), suave Peter Graves, and veteran Tom Walls making what the credits coyly describe as a 'courtesy appearance'.

Here and there the picture rouses itself for a set piece such as the mannequin parade of ladies of a certain age, showcasing the latest costumery invented by Molyneux, Hardy Amies, Norman Hartnell, *et al.* Are we to assume that Wilcox had latched onto product placement, or did he advertise these fashionistas out of the goodness of his heart? Certainly, none of the creations seem wearable by people obliged to travel by public transport. Our attention returns for a dream sequence, experienced by Wilding in his pyjamas and enhanced by William C. Andrews's setting, the crystalline Technicolor photography of Max Greene, and choreography of Philip and Betty Buchel. Such incidentals are plums in a decidedly stodgy pudding.

The most explosive moments come fast on each other's heels whenever Neagle appears in yet another unlikely get-up designed by Kitty Francis, whose vivid imagination is not even eclipsed by Hartnell's Fairy Queen wedding dress. Reducing the star to a revolving clothes-horse does her no favours, startling as these fabrics may be. At one point, Miss Neagle appears in several shades of raspberry. Whatever her outfit, she is as restless as ever, forever dabbing at her hair like a pantomime dame and manoeuvring out-of-control fox furs, or ramming on long gloves even if she's only going down to the corner shop for a pint of milk. For a supposedly brilliant and successful businesswoman, she has a totally inappropriate daintiness about her, and no actress deserves to have the camera watching her eat a messy dessert. Above all, there is an insufferable air of clubbishness about the whole affair, further aggravated by the tiresome in-jokes: the Michael Wilding Fan Club is mentioned, and we are informed that Eileen 'looks like Anna Neagle'. This is footling self-indulgence.

Musically, it is an undistinguished occasion, buttressed by Robert Farnon's rather anonymous score. At various moments the lounge-lizardly Graves smoothly breaks into Gabriel Ruiz and Ricardo Lopez's 'Amor' in its British lyric by Sunny Skylar, and there is considerable use of Fred Prisker and lyricist Kermit Goell's 'I'm Not Going Home' and Bruno Bidoli and lyricist David Heneker's 'Do I Love You?' Farnon's arrangement for the prolonged fashion parade is worked up from this and his 'Journey into Melody'.

The *MFB* was discouraging. 'The whole tone of the film is meant to be light and gay, but its purpose is defeated by the dialogue [and] Anna Neagle's performance is painstakingly refined.'[8] Halliwell dismisses it as 'a witless comedy fit to set one's teeth on edge, with over-acting and poor musical numbers'.[9] In a comment on Neagle's next film performance in *Odette*, the *MFB* suggested that 'good intentions are not enough [...] tact and sympathy cannot make up for a fundamental defect in imagination'.[10] The verdict might as well stand for *Maytime in Mayfair*. One can't imagine that Mayfair folk would have (a) recognised it or (b) been seduced by its complacent exclusiveness, so patently is it a film made for gawping at by those existing beyond its privileged boundaries. Meanwhile, the *Guardian* was under the impression that it was watching an earlier film all over again, for 'the same formula [as for *Spring in Park Lane*] has been followed remorselessly. It has inevitably not come alive a second time.'[11]

JULY

The Old Mother Riley series of Arthur Lucan comedies had continued to thrive, commercially if not artistically, from the mid-1930s. A natural pause came with the end of the war, marked by *Old Mother Riley at Home* (1945). If the old Irish washerwoman was to be got ready for the approaching decade, she needed a leg up, as did the production values. To what extent this was achieved by **Old Mother Riley's New Venture** is questionable, but her latest adventure, produced by Harry Reynolds and directed by John Harlow, had a West End showing. Con West and Jackie Marks's screenplay, with additional material by Harlow, moved at speed, with Lucan in invigo-rating form, bouncing through the script and giving a thoroughly rounded impression as the Old Mother and flighty daughter Kitty (Kitty McShane) move from their humble Ration Row home (singing a snatch of 'Oh Patrick Mind the Baby' as they leave) into a grand London hotel of which she has been given charge by a weary manager who decides to hand management over to the first person who comes through his door. On cue, Mother Riley comes somersaulting in.

> 'You'll have to excuse me barging in like this, sir,' she explains, 'but I can show you a perfect alibi.'
> 'Alibi?'
> 'The alibi in which I came in by.'

There is excellent play between Lucan and McShane but she, beset by weight problems and the 'boiled' look that overcame her features, fills her role uncomfortably. For her cabaret scene cameo, the giant ribbon that crowns her inappropriate costume suggests an ageing overfed Shirley Temple. Romance springs between Kitty and David (Willer Neal) as the hotel's preparations for a St Patrick's Day party unroll. Hotel guests watch as David, dapper in riding breeches, boots, cravat, and trilby, sings Thomas P. Westendorf's 'I'll Take You Home, Kathleen'. This is cabaret at its most ghastly. His throaty rendition is topped by Kitty's 'Galway Bay', a haunting ballad that seems traditional but was in fact composed in 1947 by Arthur Colahan. Puff-sleeved, be-cloaked, and be-ribboned, she entrances her audience.

Second cousin to *Champagne Charlie* (1944) and *Gaiety George* (1946), Rank's Two Cities' **Trottie True** still yields considerable pleasure despite what we may see as its principal fault: it is not the full-blown musical it shows signs of yearning to be. Rather, we must put up with its occasional outbursts of music-hall interruptions, while being grateful for the elegant background score by Benjamin Frankel, not least for its typically Frankelian 'trotting' melody. We are thankful, too, for the superb settings by Ralph Brinton, the period splendour of Beatrice Dawson's costumes, and Harry Waxman's brilliant exploitation of Technicolor. Above all, we have Jean Kent in what she considered her favourite film.

Its critical reception was reserved. *The Times* thought it 'less concerned with what goes on on the stage than with the means and methods by which the chorus marries into the peerage', and considered it a pity that '*Trottie True* has not the courage and ambition to be more than it is.'[12] The *MFB* reported:

> The film hovers on the edge of a charm, humour and style which it never quite achieves [...] it is never funny enough, and the colour and designs are pretty and ornate but not really stylish. Brian Desmond Hurst has handled some rather thin material smoothly, but without visual wit or sufficient variation of pace. Fundamentally, what is missing is a star with real personality.[13]

The *New York Times* saw 'something less than original and rarely sprightly. *Trottie True*'s tale is an old one and it hasn't worn well with the years.'[14]

C. Denis Freeman's screenplay was based on the 'literary' novel of Caryl Brahms and S. J. Simon, basically the life and loves of a George Edwardes Gaiety Girl. When we first see Trottie, she is already the Duchess of Wellwater, taking the air in her open carriage as her old friend and admirer, music-hall performer Joe (Bill Owen), observes, 'She looks a little sad.' On a visit to female friends, she breaks away from their social chatter when she hears a barrel-organ in the street and moves to the window, recalling, 'I've had so many exciting moments. So many exciting moments', as the film flashbacks to her childhood. This particular moment, with Waxman closing in on Kent's face, is an abiding image that impresses itself into our memory, the camera so intimate that we can smell the face powder. In its way, this is the equal of cinematographer Glen MacWilliams's abiding close-up of Jessie Matthews in *Evergreen* (1934). We will never be closer to the essentially melancholic Trottie than at this moment.

Her fascination with the stage begins in childhood, when Pa takes her to the music-hall. Enraptured, she leans over the balcony to watch another child protégée, 'The Great Little Tessie', perform Dent and Goldburn's 1913 hit 'Never Mind', made popular by Clarice Mayne and Gertie Gitana. Trottie makes her debut singing Frankel's 'The Kid from Camden Town'. She's still singing it as a young woman, as well as winning over the audience with 'White Wings' (its authorship is disputed; possibly Joseph Gulick, perhaps Banks Winter), a song that became the anthem of the Young Women's Christian Association.

Her rise to fame follows conventional lines, from music-hall to more sedate musical comedy, although it's a little odd that an Edwardes production would include Trottie's music-hall item 'I Was a Good Little Girl till I Met You', written by F. C. Harris and James W. Tate and made popular by Clarice Mayne. The impetus of the film changes gear when Trottie acquires a little army of admirers: dependable Joe, Scots balloonist Sid Skinner (Andrew Crawford), calculating romancer Maurice Beckenham (Hugh Sinclair), a wealthy theatrical 'angel', and, at last, the aristocratic Lord Digby Landon, impeccably played by James Donald. The film takes a turn for the better as soon as he appears; this

The closest that Jean Kent ever got to a genuine musical film was her performance in the title role of *Trottie True* (1949) based on one of Caryl Brahms and S. J. Simon's literary novels. It longed to be a full-blown musical.

is a sensitive and refined actor, who even manages to make Digby's sub-Wildean pronouncements ('Art is an inspiration, but life is a fact. They should be kept each in their clearly defined water-tight compartments far apart') contemplatable.

Nevertheless, the film centres on Trottie. Kent uses every trick in her considerable armoury, evident in the wonderfully disparate collection of characterisations she attempts in one of her most enjoyable films, the 1949 *The Woman in Question*. The question apropos her impersonation of Trottie True is how she manages to balance the dramatic with the comedy scenes. Her transition from singing music-hall artist to Digby's wife is subtle and convincing, although Kent plays the comedy very broadly, when a more nuanced approach might have worked more effectively. Her dual personalities are emphasised at a grand ball. Digby's mother, unconvinced that Trottie will be a 'suitable' daughter-in-law, unsmilingly confronts her as she enlivens the guests (and the servants) with a waltz song and A. J. Mills and Bennett Scott's 'When I Take My Morning Promenade'. The Duchess unsmilingly challenges Trottie to 'Give us another of your *music-hall* songs'. Trottie sings 'White Wings'. Her transmogrification to being socially acceptable is confirmed when the Duchess turns to her husband. 'You know,' she tells him, 'she'll do.'

Once married, Trottie becomes involved in an innocent sexual imbroglio that seems to spell disaster for her relationship with Digby. The rounding-up of procedures is unsatisfactory, possibly because we have never felt especially involved with the heroine's emotions. The spectre of the critically disastrous *London Town* may, even three years on, have constricted the development of Trottie's story into something more affecting. Even so, admire her as we do, one wonders if Miss Kent could have sustained a full-blown musical. On stage she appeared in two, *She Smiled at Me* and the Scots romance *Marigold*. Neither had encouraging reviews, and they did not long detain her.

SEPTEMBER

Squarely directed at those 'industrial masses', well beyond the sophisticated cineaste, product continued to pour from John E. Blakeley's Mancunian Film Corporation's studio in Dickenson Road, Ausholme. Filming for *Somewhere on Parade* was completed by May 1949, 'produced with the sole intention of providing burlesque comedy entertainment, and is not meant in any way to be derogatory to any of the [national] services'. Perhaps in an attempt to distance itself from Mancunian's preceding 'Somewhere' films, the new vehicle for comedy duo Jimmy Jewel and Ben Warriss (two of the most successful precursors to Morecambe and Wise) was retitled **What a Carry On!**, and was briskly dismissed by the *MFB* as 'Vulgar slapstick'.[15] Jewel and Warriss were already settled into their long-running radio series *Up the Pole* (1947–52) and cartooned in *Film Fun*, but Jewel felt corseted by Blakeley's attitudes to comedy.

'When we arrived at the studio we had our own thoughts of how things would be [but] John Blakeley had his own way of working and we had our own ideas, and we often disagreed. We would have liked it if he'd done things our way, but he never gave in.'[16]

Harry Jackson had saddled Jewel and Warriss with a screenplay based on Anthony Toner's insubstantial story, a ruse to allow the comedians to use material from their stage act running alongside an absurdly 'serious' but subservient narrative. The tired army-life knockabout routines, achingly familiar and visually repugnant to those familiar with Blakeley's work, seemed outworn and fustian as they looked back to the war. As long-suffering Sergeant Locke, 'Britain's Greatest Tenor' Josef Locke provided occasional respite by performing 'Ave Maria' and 'Abide with Me'. What did it matter that Mr Locke's reputation as a heavy drinker and notorious womaniser did not altogether chime with the air of religiosity? In fact, those items are missing from the surviving, shortened print, leaving only Locke's singing of Georges Kroger and Charles Helmer's bombastic 'La Rêve Passe' ('The Soldier's Dream'). Technically questionable as his performance may be, there is no doubting the communicative skill with which he roaringly entertains.

NOVEMBER

Following *Bless 'em All*, **Skimpy in the Navy** reunited Hal Monty (all but forgotten today, but then billed as 'Britain's newest comedian') with Max Bygraves in a nautical lark concocted by Monty, Aileen Burke, and Leone Stewart. It followed the adventures of Skimpy Carter (Monty), Tommy Anderson (Bygraves), and Jack (Bob Trent), sailors three who join the Navy and go treasure-hunting on the island of Sorrento. Hastily made at Southall Studios by David Dent's Advance Films, it was directed by Stafford Dickens. Dent's achievement in securing a London release on the Granada circuit was encouraging for such a minor company, and box-office records were broken at the Empire, Long Eaton. The industry's press appreciated the success: 'This is certainly a feather in the cap of Arthur Dent, who has consistently argued that there is a huge market for the unsophisticated comedy type of film.'[17]

Comedienne Avril Angers and Susan Raye assisted, with the comedy adagio act Billy Rhodes (he had been a Munchkin in Hollywood's *The Wizard of Oz*) and Chika Laine ('Comedy Dancing Racketeers'), supported by the Cabaret Orchestra under the general musical direction of veteran W. L. Trytel. The musical numbers included Bygraves singing 'Opportunity' and the traditional 'She Was Poor but She Was Honest', first heard in the year of Queen Victoria's death, but certainly not intended as a biographical comment on her passing. Also included were Angers's 'That Dusty Western Trail' and 'Hibernian Lament', and Monty in 'Bell-Bottom Trousers' and 'Capito'.

DECEMBER

Advance followed up with a second vehicle for Wrigley – yet another product of Southall Studios, *High Jinks in Society* – after which the Hull-born comedian moved to America, where his film credits were less prominent, playing a costermonger in *My Fair Lady*, a workman in *Bedknobs and Broomsticks*, and a grave-robber in the television movie *Mystery in Dracula's Castle*. Hopefully, he recalled the *MFB*'s recognition that in *Melody in the Dark* he 'is comical and raises many laughs, and without him the film would be more uninteresting than it is'.[18]

By May 1947 Hull-born performer Ben Wrigley (bill-boarded as 'A grand new comic you will like') was touring in a twice-nightly 'nude' revue *Naughty Girls of 1947*; two years later, his first film *Melody in the Dark* marked the beginning of a screen career. As a follow-up at Southall Studios, Robert Jordan Hill and director John Guillermin created the vehicular *High Jinks in Society*, with rubber-necked Wrigley as a window-cleaner hired by Lady Barr-Nun to protect her jewellery from thieves. The star's striking physical features were happily exploited with him in drag (posing as a duchess), creating havoc at a crooked séance, and nailing the villains, in what David Quinlan described as 'clean, crazy, modestly inventive fun',[19] and what Chibnall sees as 'a comedy involving jewel thieves in the grand tradition of the quota quickie'.[20] As Chibnall notes, like John Blakeley at Mancunian, Arthur Dent 'understood that many "industrial audiences", particularly in the north of England, wanted to relax with undemanding comedies that could be made very cheaply and yet still play as first features, providing popular music-hall comics occupied the starring roles'.[21] *Today's Cinema* concurred, pronouncing the film 'Adroitly designed for the delight of the masses who will react joyfully to the Wrigley gags and sallies, and respond audibly to the engaging inanities of Moore Marriott [in another of his 'old gentlemen' parts].'[22]

Music was provided by Arthur Wilkinson, with additional musical entertainment by The Squadronaires and the Radio Revellers ('The BBC Masters of Melody'). Unexpectedly, Wrigley relocated to the USA, and was next seen on screen as a Covent Garden costermonger chum to Julie Andrews in the 1964 *My Fair Lady*, a workman in *Bedknobs and Broomsticks*, and a graverobber in the television movie *Mystery in Dracula's Castle*. Hopefully, he recalled the *MFB*'s recognition that in *Melody in the Dark* he 'is comical and raises many laughs, and without him the film would be more uninteresting than it is'.[23] Back home, the *Daily Renter* cut to the chase by regarding Mr Wrigley's high jinks as frankly unsophisticated.

1950

For some reason, admirers of Novello have never been able to rouse his ghost for the public benefit

The Dancing Years

The Dancing Years	*A Ray of Sunshine*
Old Mother Riley Headmistress	*Soho Conspiracy*
The Lady Craved Excitement	*Lilli Marlene*

APRIL

Ivor Novello is the only British composer of our period to have had three of his stage musicals filmed: *Glamorous Night* in 1937 and *King's Rhapsody* in 1955 sandwiching **The Dancing Years**. Generally considered Novello's most popular work, the Viennese romance had opened in London at Drury Lane in 1939, closed because of the war, then toured before returning to London for a triumphant run. Just as *The Maid of the Mountains* was the standout operetta of the West End during World War I, Novello's lush entertainment was the standout of World War II. Inspiration came when Novello saw MGM's *The Great Waltz* of 1938 starring Militza Korjus, and wondered if Roma Beaumont (who had been a hit in Novello's previous musical *Perchance to Dream*) could get away with playing a young girl on stage. In 1950, only one member of the original cast made it on screen for *The Dancing Years*, the Welsh Clara Butt-cloned, stentorian-voiced close friend and semi-housekeeper for Novello, Olive Gilbert. Now, a mercifully unsinging Dennis Price played young Viennese composer Rudi Kleiber, with Gisèle Préville as the operatic diva Maria Zeitler and Patricia Dainton in the Roma Beaumont role of young Grete. Associated British Picture Corporation believed that 'this picture will answer the question as to whether British studios can make a successful full-length musical'.[1]

Novello considered this his most 'serious' operetta, as Richard Traubner explains.

> The original intention was to set the play within the framework of invaded Vienna, the old hero-composer having been condemned to death for his help in aiding Jews to escape from Austria. The romance which followed this opening prologue was to have been a flashback. In the final version, watered

down by the timid Drury Lane management, the prologue appeared at the end of the play, and overt references to Hitler were cut out.[2]

Here was to be a musical play of at least some substance, with some historical context, at a time of great international unrest, not least the rise of the Nazis and reign of the Third Reich. We may understand Drury Lane's reluctance to emphasise the dark truths that were playing on the world stage in 1939. It is more difficult to understand why, five years after the end of World War II, the Nazi element that underpinned the story is totally disregarded. This undercut

Dennis Price was never going to be an adequate stand-in for
Ivor Novello in *The Dancing Years* (1950), but the score at least
reminded cinemagoers of one of Novello's most sumptuous arias,
'My Life Belongs to You'.

the words that Novello had written for Rudi, in what Tony Staveacre describes as 'the nearest [Novello] ever came to making a political statement'.

> We shall see great changes and feel it here – times of unrest and anger and hatred in the world – and these things are strong. We shall almost forget to laugh and make music, but we shan't quite forget, and some day we'll wake up, as from an evil dream, and the world will smile again and forget to hate, and the sweetness of music and friendliness will once more be important.[3]

It's an emotional outburst that might presage some reasonable philosophical argument, but Novello's work is notable for its complete lack of profundity; this, indeed, is one of its most appealing traits. Thus, what we have does not really happen in Austria; we are not at the Golden Apple Inn in the Vienna Woods but in John Howell's highly coloured version of them in 1910, now and again erupting with yodelling and modelling of Lederhosen. Frank Staff's choreography veers from the quite dreadful to the effective, in routines featuring two distinctive British dancers, Moyra Fraser and the extraordinary Pamela Foster (whose life deserves a biography), but something essential is lacking: as one character insists, 'What Vienna needs is a new composer.'

Rudi (Price) is that person, overheard by Maria when singing one of his compositions. As little Grete foresees, 'One day the whole world will listen to his music.' *The Dancing Years* is fairly stuffed with sweeping statements in the true Novello manner. Robert Farnon's luxurious orchestrations replace the theatrical originals by Harry Acres and are conducted by Louis Levy, underlining the gentlemanly romantic misunderstandings. The impossibility of Price's task is brought home at almost every point. When he confesses, 'I should like to catch this moment in mid-air and say "This is for always!"', we know that only one man could have got away with such a line, and that man is not to be found here. Préville is a credible Maria, and Dainton an appealing Grete. The sole survivor from the stage production is Olive Gilbert, who perhaps understandably performs a little self-consciously (she is no actress). How often she must have thought, 'Of course, on stage we did it differently.'

The Times was unimpressed, announcing that Novello's stage play 'has been made into a British Technicolor film, and that is really all that can profitably be said'. The plot 'presumes at moments to take itself seriously' [...] "Music" "Spectacle" "Romance" "Colour" proclaims the programme and here, after a deplorable fashion, they are.'[4] The *MFB* seemed unexcited, finding 'All the familiar stage ingredients literally transferred to the screen [...] with heavy sentiment as the keynote.'[5] On the whole the *Observer* 'thoroughly enjoyed it, though I'm afraid Dennis Price, in the Novello role, is no Novello.'[6] *Kinematograph Weekly* agreed that in a picture of 'unadulterated Ivor Novello', Price 'is no Ivor Novello but everything considered he does a good job.'[7]

He could hardly be considered a satisfactory substitute for the great Ivor, but neither was Barry MacKay in *Glamorous Night* or Errol Flynn in *King's Rhapsody*. There could be none; plucked from the stage, none of these operettas survived transition to the screen. The absence of the writer-composer as the star of his own works crippled them from the start, just as the very few (and unsuccessful) attempts to revive Novello's stage musicals since his death in 1951 have failed. It has unjustly been almost forgotten that he was, in several regards, the Andrew Lloyd Webber of his day, a comparison that might have appalled Novello and one that does little credit to Novello's extraordinary place in British theatrical history as film and stage actor, playwright, and composer. Today, the works of Noël Coward, whose career ran in parallel with Novello's through the first half of the twentieth century, are revived and critically discussed, while Novello's work, including his many light comedies that have never been revisited, languishes. Interest in Coward has been maintained by what at times has seemed a Coward-obsessed mafia of writers, actors, and critics for whom 'The Master' can do very little artistic wrong. For some reason, admirers of Novello have never been able to rouse his ghost for the public benefit. There are times when Novello's name seems only to live on via the 'Ivor Novello Awards' made in recognition of 'creative excellence in songwriting and screen composition'. Novello was a generous soul, however, and might well have approved of the styles of music that receive his awards. It is unlikely that recipients of Novello Awards have the slightest idea of who he was.[8]

Associated British Picture Corporation's *The Dancing Years* was produced at Elstree by Warwick Ward, 'written' (after Novello) by Ward and Jack Whittingham, and directed by Harold French. Novello's lyricist Christopher Hassall is uncredited. Happily, the film retains most of the original Novello–Hassall stage score, including a sequence from the 'opera within the musical' *Lorelei*. The male chorus relish the fact that they are in 'Uniform', but otherwise the score is mostly in the hands of Préville with 'Waltz of My Heart', 'I Can Give You the Starlight', 'The Wings of Sleep' (duetted with Olive Gilbert), the dramatic 'My Life Belongs to You' (with Martin Ross), and 'My Dearest Dear'. Dainton is suitably coy in the trippingly Edwardian pastiche 'Primrose', and Gilbert is allowed to join Préville for 'The Wings of Sleep', the duet that Gilbert had originally sung on stage with Mary Ellis. It had a tremendous ovation at the Drury Lane premiere. Happily, the film also retains some extracts from the 'opera within the opera' 'Lorelei', with Préville centre-stage. The on-stage mother of 'Lorelei' is dubbed by Gilbert. We also have the 'Leap Year Waltz' sequence, a superb example of Novello's incidental dance music.

King's Rhapsody, the third and last Novello musical to be filmed, opened in London in September 1949 and had the misfortune to be turned into a Herbert Wilcox extravaganza in 1955. Its star, Anna Neagle, remembered it as 'a headache from the beginning'.[9]

MAY

A late entry in the 'Old Mother Riley' series of Arthur Lucan and Kitty McShane comedies, Renown's **Old Mother Riley Headmistress** sagged in parts. At moments, Lucan seems to be gazing vacantly, almost removed from the elements that make up this hotch-potch of a picture. There are moments, as during the long-shots of the audience at the concert, when he sems light years away, and he never looks comfortable in his schoolgirl's guise, an ancient refugee from St Trinian's. He may be excused not only when we consider John Harlow's rudimentary direction, which represented a falling-off even from the unspectacular achievements of the previous *Old Mother Riley's New Venture*, but when we understand the worsening state of his marriage to McShane, still playing the Old Mother's daughter, some explanation may be found.

We look to 'Kitty' to provide the musical content as music mistress at St Mildred's School for Young Ladies. At a shambolic Sports Day, she guides her young pupils through Richard Morgan and Edith Temple's 1946 hit 'Count Your Blessings'. All in white, adorned with her favourite puff-sleeves, Kitty appears as soloist with the choir in 'Till All Our Dreams Come True'. The screenplay by Harlow and Ted Kavanagh is based on a storyline by Jack Marks and veteran Riley-writer Con West in her last assignment for the series. It has been said that relationships between Lucan and McShane had so deteriorated by the time filming closed down that for their next feature, *Old Mother Riley's Jungle Treasure* (1951), they refused to appear together, their separate contributions being cobbled together at editing. This seems unlikely, although there is no doubt that in the final adventure of 1952, *Mother Riley Meets the Vampire* (i.e. a broken-down Bela Lugosi still trading on his Dracula reputation), Kitty is nowhere to be seen. Her last years were troubled. After Lucan's bankruptcy and death in the wings of the Tivoli Theatre, Hull, in 1952, Kitty attempted a comeback, but managements, despite the fact that technically speaking she had been one of Britain's most successful film stars, were uninterested. The film editor Ken Behrens was one of the few who kept in touch and put up with her.

> She often used to invite me home for dinner with her man friend [Willer Neal, who often played her boyfriend both on stage and film] that she had been living with for some years. But somehow it always ended in disaster, there were always fights, and one day she threw a leg of lamb at me. I ducked and it went out of the window into the street. The neighbours got quite used to these events. On one occasion I found Kitty in a dustbin outside the post office, she had left the pub and feeling a little unsteady she sat on the side of the bin and fell in. As she was stuck I had to roll her home. Fortunately, it was a Sunday when no one was around.

When her friend Danny [Neal] died [during a long drinking session] Kitty and I became much closer. As she got older I think she regretted some of the nasty things she had done, not only to Arthur Lucan but to other people. Sadly, she died completely unloved and unwanted. Lucan once lifted her up from nothing and made her a star, she showed her gratitude by destroying him.[10]

She was sixty-six. At her inquest the cause of death was recorded as excessive alcoholism. Her estate came to £530.

AUGUST

In August 1949 the *Radio Times* enticingly announced the beginning of a new 'adventure serial' on the BBC Home Service, starring Peggy Hassard and Robin Bailey. Written by Edward J. Mason, the programme was in direct line from his still-remembered radio serial of 1946 *Dick Barton Special Agent*. Hammer's three-film series of Dick's cases began in 1948, and in 1950 Hammer (as Exclusive Films) took up Mason's new crowd-pleaser, filming ***The Lady Craved Excitement*** at its Oakley Court premises in Windsor. Anthony Hinds produced the screenplay, which was co-written by Mason, John Gilling, and director Francis Searle. It was excellently cast, with incisive Hy Hazell and perky Michael Medwin as cabaret artistes Pat and Johnny. The musical sequences, filmed at Bray's Hotel de Paris, comprise two numbers for Hazell by George Melachrino and lyricist James Dyrenforth, 'Ladies of the Gaiety' and the bright title song, neither distinguished, with light-touch choreography by Leslie Roberts.

Set among sticks of lush furnishings that might have been leftovers from *Spring in Park Lane*, the film showed little attempt to disguise its general shoddiness, but the cast move through it with commendable *esprit*: Sidney James (although largely incomprehensible as the Italian nightclub owner), Danny Green (ever the cuddly crook), the British quota quickie's miniature mascot Ian Wilson as the wonderfully seedy Mugsy, and Thelma Grigg as a vamping villainess. Much changed from the radio storyline, the picture has Andrew Keir as a deranged artist obsessed with having Pat as the perfect model for his painting of Anne Boleyn's execution: 'I cannot begin to tell you how closely you resemble her,' he insists. 'Before or after?' asks Johnny.

Kinematograph Weekly welcomed 'Amiable nonsense, appropriately interleaved with tuneful songs [and] it earns full marks for making it snappy.'[11] while the *MFB* recommended 'A light crime-comedy with some impossible and quite amusing situations; suitable entertainment for the young.'[12]

Those in search of 'An Irresponsible Medley of Song and Dance' may have been satisfied by the 55-minute concoction *A Ray of Sunshine*, a variety revue headed by comedian Ted Ray. An Adelphi film directed by Horace Shepherd, written and compiled by Gordon Duncalf, it was made at Kensington's Viking Film Studios. The 'Star Bright Sparkling Show' presented 'America's Latest Dancing Thrill' Armand and Anita; Wilson and Keppel (complete with Betty) enduring 'Cleopatra's Nightmare'; 'The Girl of Many Voices' Janet Brown with imperson-ations of Marie Lloyd, Jessie Matthews, Gracie Fields, and Kathleen Harrison; Morton Fraser's Harmonica Gang; Ivy Benson and Her Girls' Band; showy pianist Freddie Bamberger assisted by Pam; Lucille Gaye; and Roberta and Her Feathered Friends (dancing with ostrich fans).

OCTOBER

Soho Conspiracy might have been yet another quickly cobbled-together crime thriller. Those lured into the auditorium by its promised hint of thuggery had been deceived by film-maker E. J. (Edwin) Fancey, his prodigious output evidence of 'a willingness to exploit the topical and the mildly salacious that was at odds with attempts to promote British cinema's claims to seriousness, quality and wholesomeness'. As directed by Cecil H. Williamson and written by Williamson (also credited with 'décor') and Ralph Dawson, DUK Films' production was based on material by Steno and M. Monicelli. Such credits were designed to hide the fact that much of the content had been burgled from an Italian film, *Follie per l'Opera*. The title of *Soho Conspiracy* suggested

> a late contribution to the post-war spiv cycle, but it was nothing so predict-able. Instead, it recycled footage of Italian opera singers from Continental films and grafted on a story of a young man's attempt to stage a benefit concert for a Soho church rebuilding fund. It was not hard to see the joins in the footage, especially when the audience is asked to believe that a London gymnasium could be transformed for the concert into something that looks suspiciously like La Scala or La Fenice.[13]

Notable singers Tito Gobbi, Beniamino Gigli, Tito Schipa, and Gino Bechi (unaware of being regurgitated) even made way for the comedy dou-ble-act of Syd and Max Harrison in a roughly performed slapstick decorating routine. Somehow, Fancey inveigled the always impressive Peter Gawthorne into playing Father Shaney, a charmer of an old Irish priest, in which role Gawthorne brings some much-needed skill into focus. The proceedings are frequently incomprehensible. At this distance of time, we may almost admire Mr Fancey's barefaced cheek and take a dubious pleasure in what he has produced for our delight, not least the performances of David Hurst (also seen in the unmissable *Mother Riley Meets the Vampire*) as the waiter Franco, and Annette Simmonds as the film's villainess Margaret Draper.

DECEMBER

'No doubt you are the young lady who inspired a song that lives in the heart of every German soldier?' asks a menacing Nazi officer of Lilli Marlene, the subject of two fanciful biopics directed by Arthur Crabtree. The first was *Lilli Marlene*, produced by William J. Gell for Monarch Films and made at the Gate Studios, Elstree. *Kinematograph Weekly* sighed with relief that 'The film is not a critic's picture, and thank heavens for that! [...] it clearly proves that simplicity is the key to box-office success [...] Every exhibitor who knows what's good for him will give *Lilli Marlene* the glad-eye.'[14] An innocent young woman working in her uncle's café in North Africa, she is indeed the inspiration for a song that the Third Reich believes will make her 'The Pin-Up Girl of the German army'. She refuses to sing it for the Nazis 'in the language of the fatherland', until they persuade her that 'we have ways and means' of forcing her, threatening that her uncle and aunt will be shot.

On the Western Front, boys of the Desert Rats, well represented here by a gang that includes Leslie Dwyer, Stanley Baker, and the ever-ebullient John Blythe (especially touching in his death scene: 'Payday's come'), tidy up a bombed town hall in readiness for an ENSA concert. When the performers do not reach the Front, the boys get up their own show – 'a sort of sing-song' – as the Entertainments Officer (Richard Murdoch) puts it, with Lilli (as of yet not in the Nazi clutch) centre-stage, singing 'Bless 'em All' and in chorus with the boys 'Let's Have Another One' and 'a song that breathes of home' (and quite strongly of Vera Lynn), 'We'll Meet Again'.

Lilli is abducted by the Germans and removed to Cairo, where she becomes a star, frequently breaking out into *that* song. She broadcasts alongside Estelle, played by Estelle Brody, a rare appearance for the delightful ingénue of the 1925 London musical *The Blue Kitten*. It does not seem in the least appropriate that Brody should sing 'Mademoiselle from Armentieres'. Meanwhile, the romance between Lilli and the army broadcaster Steve (Hugh McDermott) never dwindles.

Leslie Wood's skittering screenplay has yet more vicissitudes in store for Lilli, played by 'new star' Lisa Daniely.[15] Once again nabbed by the Nazis, this time in the form of the totally miscast Michael Ward, that most naturally fey of all character actors, Lilli is tortured ('I wonder how she can take it!') and forced to work for them. Their efforts to give her 'a brand new German mind' seem to have succeeded. Not so. At the end of war, Lilli moves to London, where she is the idol of the returning Desert Rats. In fact, her broadcasts sent from the Nazis had contained coded messages fed to her by British intelligence.

'The film steers its way unevenly through a variety of implausible situations', reported the *MFB*, 'but with the title song persuasively sung by Lisa Daniely and liberal doses of army humour, makes agreeable enough entertainment'.[16] Stay-at-home Britons may well have come to know this heroine through the gramophone recordings of Marlene Dietrich (playing for the Germans) and Anne Shelton.

Lisa Daniely was British films' Lilli, forever remembered as waiting 'underneath the lantern by the barrack gate' in the 1950 *Lilli Marlene*. In time, Daniely reprised her role for *The Wedding of Lilli Marlene* (1953).

1951

The whole affair, indeed, is so middle-aged and fustian that a general torpor overcomes all

Happy Go Lovely

Happy Go Lovely   *Lady Godiva Rides Again*
The Tales of Hoffmann   *London Entertains*

MARCH

The often-vaunted special relationship between Britain and the USA might have guaranteed a friendlier critical response to Associated British Picture Corporation's **Happy Go Lovely**, produced by Marcel Hellman and directed at Elstree by Bruce Humberstone, who stood by his assertion that 'there is no reason why typical American musicals cannot be made in England'; indeed, he was proud of 'a musical in colour to challenge Hollywood'. *Kinematograph*

Neither Hollywood's swirling Vera-Ellen or the suavity of David Niven could do much to rescue *Happy Go Lovely* (1951), intended as a semi-official contribution to the Festival of Britain celebrations.

Weekly played along, proclaiming it a 'platinum-plated light entertainment, with a fascinating tartan finish [that] clearly outpoints the Yanks at their own particular game. No praise can be too high.'[1] This, of course, is nonsense, but also begs the question: why would a British studio *want* to make a musical that looked like an American musical? This seems to have been a long-ignored problem. Mr Humberstone explained that 'my intention was to have a maximum of four musical numbers designed for simplicity with a Continental flavour. I believe large choruses have been overdone and, generally speaking, I think that the public is tired of them.'[2]

The screenplay by Val Guest and experienced writer of intimate revue material Arthur Macrae, based on the 'film story' of F. Dammann and Dr H. Rosenfeld, could hardly have been less original, or indeed less appropriate for a film that would be coinciding with the Festival of Britain. For the *MFB*, 'the story dwindles to a tedious backstage affair, eked out with corny lines and corny jokes'. Even the Hollywood-type set piece 'Piccadilly Fantasy' (a sort of British equivalent of Hollywood's 'Slaughter on Tenth Avenue') was 'enclosed within the conventional framework and pseudo-American, synthetic in style, lacking a spontaneous flavour'.[3] As David Shipman recognised, the dancing star imported to head up this enterprise 'took a risk and did a British musical [...] dancing round a painted Piccadilly with young men in bowler hats (it was all on that level)'.[4]

Nevertheless, Humberstone and his colleagues clearly hoped to turn a corner while being chronically hampered by the tiredest of plots about theatrical misunderstandings, a heroine longing for stardom, and a very so-so score from Mischa Spoliansky, with sparse musical numbers arranged by Angela Morley. Humberstone regretted that he had been unable to find any 'experienced motion picture director in London', but finally lighted on Pauline Grant and Jack Billings. All very well, but did he have no ability to bring over a notable American choreographer?

He did, however, have top-billed David Niven as super-rich but untutored-in-love B. G. Bruno, and Vera-Ellen, one of Hollywood's most brilliant dancers, with Cesar Romero as the frustrated theatre director Frost, working to unravel a plot that held little interest and was peppered with several unsensational performances from such as Joan Heal, lumbered with what must be one of the worst opening numbers of any British musical film, 'MacIntosh's Wedding' (lyric by Barbara Gordon), the much-diminished 1930s puckish star Bobby Howes, and other refugees from that era, Wylie Watson, Joyce Carey, Billy Milton, and Diane Hart. Whatever else Humberstone brought to the plate to reinvigorate the British musical film, youth was not invited to the party. The whole affair, indeed, is so middle-aged and fustian that a general torpor overcomes all. Spoliansky's 'One-Two-Three', and 'Would You – Could You?', with its Jack Fishman lyric, make no attempt to rise to the occasion, and surely the film's title might have inspired a decent song?

Vera-Ellen is absurdly overdressed by Anna Duse, and would be absurdly overdressed all over again for her next British visit, *Let's Be Happy*. For the present, her presence in Britain inspired the film's publicity machine to mount a nation-wide competition to 'find the local Vera-Ellen'. As for the real thing, Halliwell recalled 'a lamentably unspontaneous musical with no use of cinema techniques or natural locales. Even allowing for the flat handling, it is tedious.'[5]

MAY

As early as 1923, those tales of Hoffmann had been translated into (silent) film by the Granger-Vita Film Company, on which occasion the *Evening Standard* declared the result 'remarkably clever'.[6] The *Daily Graphic* applauded the Austrian production, which 'will come like fresh rain after long drought to the filmgoer wearied of interminable artificialities'.[7]

The more sympathetic of readers may understand the various difficulties faced by an author obliged to comment, as informatively and entertainingly as possible, on a very great number of British musical films seen by cinemagoers between the end of World World II and the beginning of the 1970s. The hill has sometimes loomed steep before him, and, on one or two occasions, he has baulked at the prospect of finding anything original, worthwhile, quirky enough, to say. It is as if, on a long journey, there is always the road that has not been taken, the path that has been avoided, where decisions as to how to deal with a film have, frankly, been waived. There have been three notable baulks; Michael Powell and Emeric Pressburger are responsible for all of them. The impenetrable forest of words, praise or condemnation, behind which lurk three of their principal works, is territory so well trodden by critical reassessment that only the bravest should plunge into it with confidence. Those works are *The Red Shoes* (1948), *The Tales of Hoffmann* (1951), and *Oh ... Rosalinda!!* (1955).

Born of an idea by Sir Thomas Beecham, who recorded the soundtrack before filming began, Powell and Pressburger's film of **The Tales of Hoffmann**, Offenbach's most 'serious' opera first performed in 1881 and still in the repertoire of many opera houses, began to be shot at Shepperton from July 1950. In fact, this film and *The Red Shoes* are widely separated not so much by their content as by their design. *The Red Shoes* does not have the benefit of Hein Heckroth's lush, incandescent brushstrokes, without which *The Tales of Hoffmann* would be a beast of very different colours. Of course, ballet remains a vital ingredient of the *Tales*, in which The Archers have melded Heckroth's visionary design with dance and its poor cousin, mime, with opera. Heckroth's name gives it away; what we are seeing must at the very least be a distant cousin to Germanic Expressionism, slackened from the rein, on holiday, AWOL, given *carte blanche* to impregnate every corner of the film.

What is in any way British about this? Perhaps, more than one might at first acknowledge, The Archers' sense of neo-romanticism is roused. There is about Heckroth's contribution elements of John Minton, of Keith Vaughan, of John Piper, set in rocky outcrops reminiscent of the strange paintings of Evan Charlton. In this, the film seems for most of its length to belong entirely and exclusively to itself. It is Heckroth alone who defies comparison with any other film. It is the visual elements that fix us, the luxuriousness of their invention and integrity. The service done is not especially to Offenbach's opera, perhaps less digestible than it would be in the opera house, where spirits might be revived between the segments by a well-deserved interval gin-and-tonic. On film, the piece becomes what it cannot escape becoming, a portmanteau picture of different parts with little discernible connection.

Here are three of Hoffmann's tales: 'The Tale of Olympia' involving three luminaries of the dance world, Moira Shearer, Robert Helpmann, and Léonide Massine; 'The Tale of Giulietta' involving Ludmilla Tchérina, Helpmann, and Massine; and 'The Tale of Antonia' involving Helpmann, Massine, and Ann Ayars. Notable opera singers dub much of the performance, although Robert Rounseville as Hoffmann sings his own role, as does Ayars. The operatic film is a troublesome beast at the best of times, and in many ways Powell and Pressburger have produced one that could in many ways not be bettered, although, in pieces as it is, it is difficult for the film to build up a head of steam, no matter how glorious the photography, how skittish and brilliant the ideas.

In a highly critical assessment, Gavin Lambert criticised the film's strongly Teutonic tone, claiming that 'there is no unity of style anywhere' and that 'behind all the effects, the strivings, the opulence and the apparatus, there seems no clear sense of direction, no single purpose at all', merely 'a welter of aimless ingenuity'.[8] Ian Christie recognises 'not only a unique artistic landmark in British cinema – the absolute antithesis of realism – but a virtual anthology of the Hoffmannesque themes underlying their work as a whole'.[9]

NOVEMBER

Beyond William Alwyn's orchestral score (not our concern) there are two brief bursts of song in London Films' **Lady Godiva Rides Again**, outbursts so brief that they would not have earned their place here were it not for director Frank Launder and Val Valentine's screenplay, at which we may pause to consider the state of the nation in a year of official celebration. The Sidney Gilliat and Frank Launder production has many of the hallmarks of their highly significant contribution to British films, in a catalogue of works imbued with their sympathetic wit. After all, Launder and Gilliat wrote the screenplays for Hitchcock's timelessly sublime *The Lady Vanishes* (1938) and Carol Reed's *Night Train to Munich* (1940), and wrote and directed one of the seminal films of the war in *Millions Like Us* (1943). Launder and Gilliat also co-produced the 1948 adaptation of Norman Collins's bestseller *London Belongs to Me*, with the screenplay written by Gilliat (who also directed) and

J. B. Williams. Working together and separately, Launder and Gilliat made a contribution to British film that holds a special, often underestimated, place in history. Who has not at some time been seduced by the sheer silliness of *The Happiest Days of Your Life* (1950), a film that glorified the talents of Alastair Sim and Margaret Rutherford? Among this portfolio, *Lady Godiva Rides Again* serves as a reflection of how British life was lived, and perceived, six years after the end of war.

Given the opportunity to make a film of its own time, Launder and Gilliat might have sharpened its satirical edge. Perhaps it's the constant air of kindliness that softens the barbs. On the face of it, the story is nothing out of the normal (as normal as anything was in British films), about an ordinary young woman from a working-class family wanting to escape the daily grind and dullness in a grey, war-scarred landscape. Bruce Babington describes 'the opening montage of a claustrophobic, cultureless British life enclosed by the horrors of a wet old-style British Sunday'.[10] We 'get the picture' immediately: it's raining, and doesn't look like stopping. We are in rain-soaked suburbia, where it's bucketing down as virulently as it did throughout Ealing's *It Always Rains on Sunday* (1947). Britain would be just as soggy at the beginning of the 1955 *Value for Money*, and things had not improved by 1958 when Tony Hancock suffered his 'Sunday Afternoon at Home' on the BBC Home Service. It is from such a stultifying torporific atmosphere that *Lady Godiva Rides Again* emerges. When Marjorie Clark (Pauline Stroud) is persuaded to enter a beauty competition that promises a prize of £1,000, a mink coat and a continuous supply of Fascination Soap, her route to success seems clear. As a talent scout tells her father:

> There are three million girls in this country between the ages of seventeen and twenty-three, hurling themselves down the same blind alleys: dances, speedways, films, worshipping at the altar of Jean Simmons and Betty Grable, living by proxy, with what at the end of it? Marriage, to some factory worker or counter-hand. Seven years to live and then the kitchen sink. I'm offering your daughter a chance of escape.

Ultimately, Launder and Gilliat's concern is with delusion. It's there in the meeting between a disappointed Marjorie, whose fame soon resides in strip shows, and elderly washed-up film director Murington (Alastair Sim).

> Murington: Surely you have heard of the British film crisis?
>
> Marjorie: I thought it was over.
>
> Murington: My dear girl, what with television to the left of us, Hollywood to the right of us, and the government behind us, our industry – laughable term – is forever on the brink.

DECEMBER

In August 1951 the *Eastbourne Herald Chronicle* broke the news that the Eastbourne Girls' Choir was to appear in a musical film produced by the New Realm Film Company. The choir's founder Miss Edith Pearson explained 'The film is planned for approximately ninety minutes' and that 'several scenes are to be taken in Switzerland'. By the time *Kinematograph Weekly* saw **London Entertains**, it was 'a kaleidoscope musical featurette' lasting forty-eight minutes, with no glimpse of Switzerland. This cut-price offering was inevitable, being a product of E. J. Fancey.

Edwin John Fancey, whose directorial credits pepper any history of British films, was patriarch of a family that thrived in the lower reaches of British film-making. During the war, he had produced two musical films starring Ethel Revnell and Gracie West, *The Balloon Goes Up* and *Up with the Lark*. His tawdry *London Entertains* was 'the sort of theme that Fancey would exploit rather more pruriently in later years, but in this "U" film it provided a way of linking a travelogue and a string of night-club acts' into a sort of celebration of the Festival of Britain.[11] In fact, Fancey doesn't even bother with the nightclub turns, being content to let his sleepy camera gaze on the unconvincing expressions of those exposed to them.

As it happened, the British film industry had already organised its own contribution to the Festival in its biopic of William Friese-Green *The Magic Box*, which seemed to suggest that it was he who invented moving pictures. He didn't. A depressing catalogue of commercial and personal failure, *The Magic Box* was an oddly downbeat offering at a time of patriotic whooping, but the fact that Laurence Olivier was persuaded to briefly appear as a London bobby on the beat who becomes the first person to see a moving picture was proof enough of its importance. Those wanting a conducted tour of the festival, with decent commentary, could turn to Philip Leacock's documentary *Festival in London*, produced for the Crown Film Unit. William Alwyn wrote the score for this, as he had for *The Magic Box*.

Meanwhile, *London Entertains* had 'script, lyrics and additional dialogue' by Jimmy Grafton. We follow a group of girls at an exclusive Swiss finishing school (taught as much 'sheing' as skiing) about to be finished, although to judge from what we see on screen the girls have long outstayed their welcome. As if attracted to the Festival of Britain – such a remote fascination for those so far away – their wish to see the phallic wonder of the Skylon for themselves send them back to Britain. What more sensible than that they should start up their own escort business, 'At Your Service'. Contrary to any misunderstanding, the girls will merely accompany visitors (mostly males, but the occasional Indian prince and princess come in handy) to the sights of London at this time of nationalistic pride; as Reg Pickard's anthem explains, 'We'll All Meet Down at the Fair'.

What follows is of little historical interest. For no apparent reason we see Gloria Swanson hobbling around the Festival's building site on the South Bank, a mere snippet of the yards of stock footage Fancey has up his sleeve. That reliable chronicler for Mass Observation Gladys Langford saw it as 'Hideous buildings in a sea of mud'.[12] The girls' fortunes take a turn with the arrival of Irish television personality Eamonn Andrews in what can only be described as a non-acting capacity. Unconvincingly, his presence is enough to send the girls into a swoon. Meanwhile, a scholarly tone is attempted when books 'now reposing in the British Museum' are mentioned. This seems to have the cultural aspects pretty well covered. The Indian royalty is much more entertained by a visit to the Aeolian Hall, where radio producer Dennis Main Wilson is trying to organise The Goons, a comedy grouping of Harry Secombe, Peter Sellers, Michael Bentine, and Spike Milligan. Each has distinct qualities that would develop in time, and admirers of The Goons will celebrate the collaboration. Variety is introduced via scenes with comedian Joe Baker and actor Vincent Ball, while the comedy duo Tony Fayne and David Evans add to the attempted jollity.

Musical relief is at hand when the one-time American boy soprano Bobby Breen joins the girls (who seem to have been dressed in the dark) in Eros Sciorilli's 'Tinker Tailor'. Back at the Festival Hall, the main attraction is the Eastbourne Girls' Choir singing George Dyson's 'Song for a Festival' and Montague Phillips's 'Sing Joyous Bird' before they parade in printed frocks through Battersea Gardens, whose gimcrack fairground looks as if it is already awaiting demolition. Sadly, the bottom falls out of Andrews's business when all the girls get engaged, presumably gaining the escorts they had always required. To its shame, there is not even a mention of the Festival's most magical artefact, Lewitt-Him's Guinness Clock in the Pleasure Gardens at Battersea.

1952

It's the final recognition of Baxter as British cinema's Henry Mayhew

Judgment Deferred

Song of Paris	*Mother Riley Meets the Vampire*
Sing Along with Me	*Meet Me Tonight*
Judgment Deferred	*Down among the Z Men*
Where's Charley?	*Tread Softly*

FEBRUARY

Alternately romantic and farcical, played at speed with attractive musical sequences, ***Song of Paris*** is an effective exemplar of international relations enacted by its three leads: French Anne Vernon as cabaret star Clementine, Dennis Price as stiff-necked Matthew Ibbetson, head of Ibbetson's Stomach Pills dynasty, and Russian Mischa Auer as Marcel, con-man pretender to the title of Comte de Sarliac. An Adelphi production filmed at Nettlefold Studios (budgetary restrictions prohibited a visit to Paris), the light-headed comedy, based on a story by William Rose, was produced by Roger Proudlock and written by Allan Mackinnon with additional material by Frank Muir and Denis Norden. The results have a fresh sense of fun about them, as when Mrs Ibbetson receives a bunch of flowers from an admirer: 'Take off your things and I'll put them in water.' Its director John Guillermin pronounced it 'a piece of nonsense'.[1]

Romance between Matthew and Clementine blooms with her recommendation 'Let's Stay Home' by Francis Lopez, but a well-constructed development gathers its skirts for a very funny finale when Marcel challenges Matthew to a duel. Jean Dréjac's 'Chanson de Paris' evokes a Parisian atmosphere that finds perfect expression in Vernon's lively, warm characterisation. The *MFB* judged that 'Though it comes close to buffoonery at times [it does, wonderfully], both characters and presentation have life.' Curiously, it also pigeon-holed it as 'a comedy in the Wilcox–Neagle tradition', which some may have taken as a negative comment.[2] Viewers can be assured that its air of mischievousness is far removed from any Wilcox production.

Under the thumb of his disapproving, dominating mother (Hermione Baddeley on top form), Matthew is obliged to go to visit Paris, under strict instructions from mother that he will remember he is visiting a 'sink of iniquity' and must not stay the night. He does, after seeing Clementine beguile her audience with Rudolf Goer's 'Just a Song of Paris'. Almost at once, Matthew relaxes. Clementine follows him to London with Marcel, who means to marry her, and Matthew passes them off to his mother as aristocrats. Along the way, there are diverting vignettes from Kynaston Reeves's vicar, hypnotised by Clementine performing Hans May and Sonny Miller's 'Mademoiselle Après-Midi', and Richard Wattis as a stuffy official from the Board of Trade.

British cinemas moved heaven and (literally) earth to lure audiences to performances. At Norwich's Haymarket, trainee manager A. G. Amies was praised for his publicity campaign:

> The kinema cashier attractively attired in a pretty dress and picture hat, was driven on a wide tour of the town and surrounding districts, where she distributed small nosegays of flowers attached to a neat label. The flowers were given free by various donors, including the staff. The doorman, C. Yallop, even cycled to a local wood where he picked large quantities of lilies of the valley.[3]

Today, staff of your local kinema are rarely (if ever) sent out to denude the countryside to promote the current film, although such careless frolicking strikes the right note for something so silly as *Song of Paris.* It is the happiest of occasions, with few dull patches, accurately hailed by *Kinematograph Weekly* as 'an infallible blues-chaser'.[4]

Sing Along with Me is a simple story, simply told: singing Welsh grocer David Parry (Donald Peers) wins a talent competition and moves to London to seek fame as a songwriter and performer, only to be disappointed and misused until success reunites him with hometown sweetheart Gwynneth Evans (Dodo Watts). The plot must have resonated with the crooning Peers, whose career had been kick-started by the Carroll Levis or Hughie Green of the time Fred Karno, whose 'army' became a synonym for disorganised amateurism. In his autobiography, Peers confesses to a 'deep and secret longing to be an out-and-out actor'.[5] He could never have imagined that his mild, inoffensive way with a song, or his mild, inoffensive appearance, would see him become an idol of the recently discovered rock'n'roll generation. Legend has it that he may well have been the first British performer to set those frenzied teenagers screaming at his appearance, although his signature number 'In a Shady Nook by a Babbling Brook' seemed more suitable for inhabitants of retirement homes. By 1948, Peers was said to be receiving sacks of fan letters a week, and as late as 1969 he was seen in the BBC's *Top of the Pops*, singing 'Please Don't Go', a cheeky steal from Offenbach's 'Barcarolle'. Astonishingly, this reached no. 3 in the British charts, an impressive achievement in the age of The Beatles for a singer

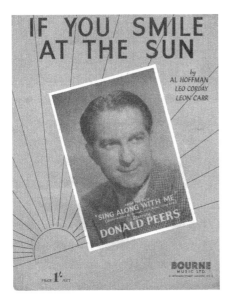

Even popular balladeer Donald 'By a Babbling Brook' Peers got to star in his very own musical film, the invitingly titled *Sing Along with Me* (1952).

described by Tony Palmer as 'The Ancient Briton of Song', who could justifiably claim to have survived the rise and fall of hand-jiving.

Harold Huth Films' *Sing Along with Me*, produced by John Croydon and directed by Peter Graham Scott, who co-wrote with actor Dennis Vance, no doubt found its audience, among whom we would probably not find Michael Kilgarriff – who found Peers's voice 'Scratchy and toneless' and his manner 'over-wheeningly schmaltzy, a deeply resistible combination'.[6] *Kinematograph Weekly* welcomed a 'Happy-go-lucky musicale [sic], presenting Donald Peers, ace music-hall, gramophone, radio and TV crooner and idol of all bobby-sox fans'.[7] The *MFB* was less enthusiastic, noting 'a trivial plot [...] and, as with other British productions of this type, an unconvincing and embarrassing romantic interest'.[8] It decided that the songs ('Take My Heart', 'If You Smile at the Sun', 'Down at the Old Village Hall', 'I Left My Heart in a Valley in Wales', and 'Hoop Diddle-i-do-ra-li-ay') were 'pleasant but unmemorable' and that the whole thing might have worked better on television.

When remembering John Baxter's **Judgment Deferred** it is inevitable that we should look for a balanced opinion in Geoff Brown and Tony Aldgate's admirable survey of this director's work *The Common Touch*, named after Baxter's British National picture of 1941. We find it in the assertion that

> *Judgment Deferred* is a defiantly weird concoction [...] One would be tempted to call the film artificial and unreal, were it not for the human heart patently beating within. As almost always with Baxter, his sincerity comes bounding through the naïve characterisations and awkward twists of plot. The broad strokes give *Judgment Deferred* the contours of a moral fable – something rarely encountered in British cinemas.[9]

This was the first project to be produced by Group 3, namely Baxter, John Grierson, and Michael Balcon, with the intention of harnessing the talents of established film-makers to bring fresh blood into the industry. Reviewing the film in the *MFB*, Gavin Lambert complained that it seems odd [...] that such an old-fashioned piece of box-office formula should inaugurate the schedule [with] a concoction of contrived melodrama and irrelevant detail, and the characterisation is lifeless. All this, combined with the artificial sets and lighting, reminds one of the lower grade British pictures of the 30s.[10]

As early as 1937, Grierson had identified Baxter's films as 'sentimental to the point of embarrassment; but they happen to be about real people's sentimentalities'. The passage of time has not always brought about a revaluation of Group 3's debut picture, more recently passed over as 'a muddled, maudlin melodrama that feels like substandard Frank Capra done by amateur theatricals',[11] but for Brown and Aldgate *Judgment Deferred* 'provided his last major opportunity to delve into favourite themes: doss house life; the virtues of Christian compassion and good fellowship; the importance of fighting for social justice and democracy'.[12]

The importance of comradeship between the working and lower classes and the middle to upper classes, and the comradeship between non-performers and music-hall performers (not a few of whom emerged from the unprivileged), is evident throughout *Judgment Deferred*, with Baxter once again the mouthpiece of the sub-cultured, the confirmation of the British way of life expressed by foreigners such as Professor Kronak in *Let the People Sing* (1942), the all-but-Dickensian sinking into abject poverty as suffered by the old washerwoman of *Old Mother Riley in Society* (1940), the spontaneous camaraderie enjoyed by off-duty soldiers with Ida Barr and Wally Patch in 'Growing Old Together', one of Kennedy Russell's blissfully nonchalant songs in Baxter's 1940 *Laugh It Off*. No matter how apparently slight the context, Baxter's message, consistent and seemingly organic, evinces the simple religiosity of his philosophy. As in Fritz Lang's 1931 *M*, the trial of Coxon (Elwyn Brook-Jones) in *Judgment Deferred* pins the parable to Christianity. However clumsy its structure, technique, or argument, *Judgment Deferred* remains a direct descendant of Baxter's 1933 *Doss House*.

In March of that year, Baxter took journalist Ernest Betts to visit some of those London dormitories, depositories of the forsaken unemployed, insect-infested dens already chronicled that year by George Orwell's *Down and Out in Paris and London*. Betts told readers of 'the interesting collection of doss-house types', describing how

> A man in a bowler hat, with a stub pipe, was reading a thriller at the table. Some were playing cards. There were very old men, still and thoughtful, and young bloods in caps and pullovers, reading the betting news. Mr Baxter viewed this new kind of 'glamour' with pleasure. I could see the camera angles racing in his mind.[13]

Kinematograph Weekly, too, recognised what Baxter was still about two decades later, welcoming a 'Quixotic comedy crime melodrama, liberally laced

with music and songs. Story slightly dishevelled and overlong, but characters neatly drawn and deployed, sentiment popular, musical asides shrewdly
handled and staging effective.' Readers were also warned that 'The ending
contains stern symbolism'.[14]

Symbolism? A rare quality in the long history of the British musical film,
and provided here by one of the least critically regarded directors of the first
half of the twentieth century, a director now and then obliged to submit to
directing Old Mother Riley. Anything approaching an award never even manifested itself as a far-off-dream for Baxter. With what dread he must often have
read the reviews of his work in the *MFB*, and read again in the reference to
Judgment Deferred's 'amateur theatricals'. The condescending tone of critical
attention (or lack of it) he suffered throughout his career seems sadly lacking
in any understanding of what the man was about. There can be no argument:
he was not a director to be spoken of in the same breath as Alfred Hitchcock
or Carol Reed. Barely a note of acclamation remains.

Baxter never had the financial wherewithal to dress his pictures well. In
and outside of war, there is clear evidence of making do and mending. Forever
budget-worried, he worked largely bereft of star names, preferring (and being
obliged to hire) names that meant less to the general public and that now are
generally forgotten. With the exception of casting star-in-the-making Joan
Collins in her screen debut as Lil Carter, Baxter relied instead on a revolving
repertory of actors capable of projecting their working-class characterisations
through the screen, without any hint of condescension. Look to the men as
they watch Marie Kendall singing 'Just Like the Ivy' in *Say It with Flowers* –
these are actors in complete accord with Baxter's philosophy. We have no understanding of how he was able to communicate this to them, but the sheer
realness of companionship is there, still to see, in film after film.

In this final phase of Baxter's career, he chooses to return to the theme, the
obsession, that eighteen years earlier had permeated his seminal *Doss House*:
the story of the cast-off, the homeless, the derelict. Re-dressed, he returned
to the subject rehearsed in *Hearts of Humanity* (1936), *The Common Touch*
(1941), and, at last, *Judgment Deferred*, effectively *Doss House* reformed by
screenwriters Geoffrey Orme, Barbara K. Emary, and Walter Meade. Journalist David Kennedy (Hugh Sinclair) is investigating a drug ring operated by
Coxon (Brook-Jones at his usual most sinister). He discovers the hiding place
of a collection of human flotsam and jetsam in the bombed ruins of a church.
Immediately, the concept of spiritual sanctuary confirms Baxter's influence.
As Geoff Brown and Tony Aldgate have it, here is Baxter's 'last major opportunity to delve into familiar themes: doss house life, the virtues of Christian
compassion and good fellowship; the importance of fighting for social justice
and democracy'.[15]

It's the final recognition of Baxter as British cinema's Henry Mayhew, the
ennoblement of street-life that would flourish decades later under directors
who basically shared Baxter's savouring of social fairness, whose cameras

lingered on faces of those brought in from the cold, from the margins: think of Terence Davies's *Distant Voices, Still Lives* (1988), and the spirit of Baxter's passion persists. Like Davies, Baxter provides the fable, peopling it with his little repertoire of the pathetic and those deserving of a better life (slim hope). Here, they include Haycoft ('The Chancellor'), played by Abraham Sofaer, to whom his fellow refugees in the crypt turn for advice; Dad (Edwardian star Bransby Williams); Blackie (a regular of Baxter's films and one of the stars of *Doss House*, Edgar Driver) reduced to picking up the remains of cigars from the gutter; Harry Welchman's dilapidated 'Doc'; and M. Martin Harvey as Martin, emotionally scarred by the war, who sees the death of Coxon (killed when the crypt's arches collapse) as judgment (or judgement) deferred. 'Let justice be done,' he proclaims, 'though the heavens fall.'

Music, as it almost always did with Baxter, has its parts to play, so that Bud Flanagan's singing of Kennedy Russell's 'Gratitude' hits the emotional mark. In nightclub scenes, Edmundo Ros and His Latin American Orchestra lighten the mood with Ros's 'No, No, My Sweet Lolita', 'With a Kiss and a Sigh', and 'My Favourite Samba' by Stanley Laudan and Ros.

JULY

For *The Times*, the star of **Where's Charley?** 'tries hard, but commits the grave sin of being unremarkable', although it admitted 'a certain unexpected fascination'.[16] *Kinematograph Weekly*'s response was lukewarm, reporting, 'No sustained riot of fun, but good, clean fun, set in a correct environment, it should tickle the masses and family'.[17] In a glowing review, the *New York Times* (possibly eager to commend a musical film that, although made in Britain, was essentially American) assured its readers that the original Broadway version was here 'repeated with all the gay abandon and sweep of burlesque that it had on the stage'[18]. Although it praised Ray Bolger, the *MFB* expressed disappointment that it contained 'some of the best elements of the American-location musical with some of the worst features of British musical comedy'; 'the songs are uninspired and the orchestration rather dull'.[19]

Clive Hirschhorn decided that 'the best reason' for seeing the film version of this 'rather tired and tiresome Victorian farce [...] was the sheer outrageousness of its star' in a 'galvanic performance'.[20] Hirschhorn has it right; the 44-year-old Bolger may not be the most convincing of Oxford students, but literally throws himself into the role, tumbling and accelerating the plot, using the experience gained from the long Broadway run of the original stage production.

In a way, the *MFB's* criticism hits the spot: this adaptation of Brandon Thomas's 1892 very British farce *Charley's Aunt* had originally been refashioned in 1948 into a highly successful Broadway stage musical by librettist George Abbott and composer Frank Loesser, with Bolger as Charley Wykeham. Ten years later, the role was taken by Norman Wisdom for a year-long London run.

Frank Loesser's American musical film *Where's Charley?* (in its way a perfectly formed *British* musical) was based on Brandon Thomas's 1892 farce *Charley's Aunt.* Ray Bolger delivered a glimmer of Broadway with his 'Once in Love with Amy' routine in the 1952 film version.

Warner Brothers' film version, filmed at Teddington with location shooting in Oxford, had a screenplay by John Monks based on Abbott's original. Most of the theatre score was retained, although 'Spettigue's Lament' is abridged, and 'The Gossips', originally vocal, is reduced to background music. The only major loss was the gorgeous 'Lovelier than Ever', a duet for the *real* Charley's Aunt, Donna Lucia d'Alvadorez, and Sir Francis Chesney, although we hear its strains. It is, however, difficult to imagine the film's Donna Lucia (stately Margaretta Scott) and Chesney (staunch Howard Marion Crawford) miming it. The song is, anyway, perfectly un-American, although it has a quality that Jerome Kern would surely have appreciated, not least in its lyrical sweep: 'Springtime, you're being devastatingly *clever*, And lovelier than *ever* before.' It is the most majestic of numbers, lusciously constructed. Amy's delightful point number, 'The Woman in His Room', is the only other major omission in what is a fine and tasteful score, always in period but never losing a contemporary relevance, with 'My Darling, My Darling' having its own success. By now, of course, Loesser had scored an even bigger hit with *Guys and Dolls* with its clutch of numbers destined to be standards. As the critic Caryl Brahms wrote:

> We know them all, of course, or most of them – musicianly popular songs, that extend our understanding of the singer or the situation. Songs with feeling and with thought at the back of them. Songs that make no twin-kle-twee concessions to the Victorian manner but belong wholly to our own day. We learned to hum them from the film *Where's Charley?* and the smash hit 'My Darling, My Darling' is currently receiving the full treatment from the song pluggers. And the amazing thing is that the lack of compromise in the lyrics and music works in the same way that good furniture of different periods can sometimes make a satisfactory whole.[21]

Despite two revivals in New York, *Where's Charley?* has never been revived in London, and thus has been denied the currency of some of Loesser's subsequent works, but its theatrical charm has not diminished in its transition into film; indeed, the fact that its theatrical efficaciousness has been retained helps to maintain the piece. Among the supporting players, Horace Cooper stands out as one of the fruitiest Stephen Spettigue's imaginable, although the pairing of Robert Shackleton and Mary Germaine as the young lovers might have been more memorable, and somehow Allyn Ann McLerie's Amy lacks colour (the retention of her solo 'The Woman in His Room' might have strengthened her characterisation). Anyway, this is indubitably Bolger's film. At forty-four, he may look a little long in the tooth to be studying at Oxford, but his frenzied acrobatics and endless transvestite costume changes keep the farce going.

Then, of course, there is *that* number with which Bolger will be forever associated, 'Once in Love with Amy'. Perhaps we are uncertain about whose choreography has helped him to achieve this enchantment; after all, on Broadway the choreographer was George Balanchine, on film Michael Kidd, but Bolger's input must have been crucial. Wherever the routine came from, it's a superbly relaxed outburst, witty and utterly beguiling, not least when Bolger invites the cinema audience to join in the reprise. It's far from certain that self-conscious British audiences would have taken up the offer, but it's another example of *Where's Charley?*'s homeliness.

There is much else to admire in Loesser's bountiful score, from the opening with its cry of 'Where's Charley?' and the male students contemplating 'All the Years Before Us' before the brisk quartet 'Better Get Out of Here' by Bolger, McLerie, Shackleton, and Germaine. The brilliant 'New Ashmolean Marching Society and Student Conservatory Band' is surely echoed in Leonard Bernstein and Alan Jay Lerner's 's glorious 'The President Jefferson Sunday Luncheon March' heard in their 1976 musical *1600 Pennsylvania Avenue*. Loesser has more delights, not least two brilliant duets, 'Make a Miracle' for Bolger and McLerie, and for Shackleton and Germaine 'My Darling, My Darling' with its casual fluency. The big dance number 'Pernambuco' brings a dash of foreign exoticism, before the lovers unite with the stately splendour of the waltzing 'At the Red Rose Cotillion'.

The last of Arthur Lucan's 'Old Mother Riley' films, **Mother Riley Meets the Vampire** (at her advanced age the 'Old' was dropped), is also the most curious because it involved Hollywood's Count Dracula. Bela Lugosi was stranded in Britain when a touring version of his gothic blood-fest collapsed, leaving its star marooned and jobless. The American film distributor Richard Gordon devised a rescue plan, persuading George Minter, who was preparing a new Lucan film, to co-star him with Lugosi. In effect, Lucan's wife and co-star Kitty McShane, now separated from him, was being replaced by a worn-out Hollywood horror star. Fernwood Films began the four-week shoot at Nettlefold Studios, produced and directed by John Gilling, in November 1951. Gordon recalled that

> Arthur Lucan behaved on the set exactly like he behaved in the film. He became Old Mother Riley and never stepped out of character. It was rather like Dr Jekyll when he turned into Mr Hyde. Arthur Lucan had the habit of ad-libbing and throwing extra things into the script, extra situations. This very much confused Lugosi, because Lugosi belonged to that era of professional actors who knew their script word-by-word before they appeared on the set [...] And he also felt that the Old Mother Riley character made him in the film more ridiculous than he would have liked to appear, by all the extra schtick that Arthur Lucan put into it.[22]

Furthermore,

> Lugosi of course had some trouble adjusting to Old Mother Riley. On the first day, I think he had trouble making up his mind whether he was talking to a man or a woman, because as usual Arthur Lucan showed up in full makeup at the studio. He was known for the fact that he never appeared in

public except in his Old Mother Riley garb – he would arrive at the studio fully made-up as Old Mother Riley, and when he left the studio in the evening, he would go home fully made-up as Mother Riley.[23]

The master touch of the publicity campaign that hoped to entice audiences to see Lucan and Lugosi's double-act by giving them the shudders included the dangling of cotton threads in cinema foyers to brush the faces of patrons, but *Kinematograph Weekly* declared that 'its dizzy tale of espionage is no master-piece of wit or horror'.[24] 'If we're in for a comedy-thriller cycle let's hope that those to come are more efficiently put together than this lumbering collection of badly timed chestnuts', suggested *Picturegoer,* while the *MFB* went for the jugular: 'stupid, humourless and repulsive'.[25]

Val Valentine's screenplay is a crude *mélange* of rowdy horseplay and milk-and-water horror spoof, coarsely directed. Now, the absence of McShane alters the balance that had been observed throughout the series. Some of us may even long for her return, albeit in one of her excruciating musical outbursts. We must make do with Lucan for no discernible reason breaking into Leslie Sarony's irritating anthem 'I Lift Up My Finger and I Say Tweet Tweet' in the (Old) Mother's knockabout shop with Dandy Nichols and Hattie Jacques as nosy customers who turn into very ill-drilled chorus girls. This absurd sequence is unquestionably the highlight of the picture. Lucan appears to have little idea as to where he should 'place' the number, mostly staring directly into the camera, while Cyril Smith's money collector joins him for a linked-arms knees-up. Close observation of Misses Nichols and Jacques is necessary, and hugely rewarding. Nichols has only the vaguest idea of what she is supposed to be doing and Jacques, suppressing giggles and trying to control Nichols, tries to steer her through what must be the worst example of choreography seen in British films, period.

SEPTEMBER

Energetic performances from Ted Ray and Kay Walsh are the most in-vigorating reasons to seek out Rank's **Meet Me Tonight**, produced by Anthony Havelock-Allan and directed by Anthony Pelissier. The compen-dium collects three playlets from Noël Coward's theatrical series of one-act dramas presented as *Tonight at 8.30,* with additional dialogue by George Barraud: 'Fumed Oak', Coward's self-confessed 'Unpleasant Comedy' about a henpecked worm of a husband who turns, 'Ways and Means' (the drea-riest of the adaptations), and the liveliest of the three, 'Red Peppers'. The film was greeted with little enthusiasm. Between them, the one-acters 'have little action and have been largely left in their theatrical form'; having been 'intended as little more than revue sketches, they fail to fill the bill'.[26] The *Observer* thought the film as a whole 'a blunt disappointment [...] Its pitch is apt to be monotonous and strident; its tone is often brutal, it constantly substitutes slapstick for intellectual argument, and it funks any conclusion that might upset the stricter moralists.'[27]

George and Lily Pepper provide the tired music-hall act going through stale routines on the stage of a provincial variety theatre; a tired entertainment but 'All clean stuff – Bring the kiddies!' These sorts of performers, like the theatres themselves, were already an endangered species by 1952. Coward's fondness for the tatty world that contained them is obvious, with the vignettes of the elderly melodramatic actress Mabel Grace, who thinks herself above it all (Martita Hunt), and sozzled musical director (Bill Fraser). The Peppers are pure Coward, hardly surprising when we know that he and Gertrude Lawrence created the roles on stage. The constant uproar of bickering that keeps their relationship going at the bottom of the bill (just above the 'Wines and Spirits') is given full rein. It hardly seems significant that Coward's dialogue is stilted and conventional; in their private moments, between turns, the Peppers thrive on an off-stage continuation of their cross-talking act. It is, however, brightened by two numbers, 'Men about Town' and 'Has Anybody Seen Our Ship?', with choreography by Freddie Carpenter, done here with appropriate artificial brio. The three plays do not sit comfortably together, and the presentation is brash, but the 'Red Peppers' segment retains its appeal.

OCTOBER

It was in 1951 that The Goons, a comedy team variously composed of Spike Milligan, Peter Sellers, Harry Secombe, and (briefly) Michael Bentine, were first heard on radio in the experimental series *Crazy People*, soon finding fame in the BBC's *The Goon Show*, first broadcast January 1952. With an alacrity available only to film companies outside the mainstream, Edwin J. Fancey wasted no time in filming their routines at the Kay Carlton Hill Film Studios for what *Kinematograph Weekly* guardedly considered 'Acceptable comedy quota for the industrial and provincial masses, and the sticks.'[28] Director Maclean Rogers's eightieth film, ***Down among the Z Men*** resurfaces from the bargain basement with Jimmy Grafton and Francis Charles's script based on the fate of a secret atomic formula at a research station. Its only relevance here is that songstress Carole Carr breaks into the comic capers, not only singing but accompanying herself for Grafton and Jack Jordan's 'If This Is Love', with a last-minute harmonisation from Harry Secombe. There is a title song sung by Carr at an army concert, and dancing from choreographer Leslie Roberts's Twelve Toppers. The *MFB*'s laconic response was that 'The producers of this film say they "have the misfortune to inflict The Goons" upon us, and this statement, like the rest of the film, is chiefly intended to be funny.'[29]

DECEMBER

Kinematograph Weekly was particularly dismissive of Albany Film Productions' admittedly drably presented **Tread Softly**:

> The picture, a sort of poor man's *Murder at the Windmill*, has a promising central idea, but uneven acting – only Patricia Dainton and John Bentley get by [...], and indifferent direction soon takes the edge off it. Attempts to create essential macabre atmosphere are offset by bizarre dance ensembles, featuring some appalling 'cissies', and more damage is done by shoddy camera work. Its poor comparison with its slick American counterpart may not, however, prevent it from registering with the *hoi polloi*.[30]

Notwithstanding, *Tread Softly* rewards attention. Produced by Vivian Cox and Donald Ginsberg, who also contributed additional dialogue to the screenplay by Gerald Verner based on his radio serial *The Show Must Go On*, it was directed by David Macdonald. Verner's crime serial, with 'interpolated numbers' by composer Basil Hempseed and lyricist Edward J. Mason (one of the creators of the 'Dick Barton' series), had broadcast on the BBC's Light Programme in 1948, with John Bentley as writer-composer Keith Gilbert, and Olaf Olsen as scheming impresario Philip Defoe; both repeated their roles on screen.

A new musical revue is to star Madeleine Peters (Frances Day), who performs the title song with her uniquely sinuous sexuality. Unhappy with tempo provided by piano-playing Gilbert, she walks out, leaving the show with no leading lady. Plucky and able, young inexperienced Tangye Ward (Patricia Dainton) replaces her. Peter's walk-out has been stage-managed by Defoe, who wants to wreck Gilbert's production. Gilbert moves the show into the broken-backed Regency Theatre, owned by elderly Shakespearean actress Isobel Mayne (Nora Nicholson) and her son Alex (Michael Ward). She warns Gilbert that no good will come of it. Alex is found murdered there. When a dressing-room, sealed for forty years, is broken into, it contains the remains of her long-decomposed husband. She explains, 'That dressing-room was his coffin.' In her first film since the 1944 *Fiddlers Three*, we find Day in obviously reduced circumstances in a smallish role without any set-piece number worthy of her status. Despite the obstacles, she is a sleek, vivid presence.

Considering the modest pretensions of the picture, Hempseed and Mason's score is sprightly, tuneful, and well performed, not least by Dainton, impressive in her 'End of the Day' with the dancers (among them an uncredited Kenneth Macmillan), and – once more joined by those 'cissies' – 'Don't Break the Spell', and duetting with affable Bentley in 'You're Lovely'. Elasticated Colin Croft has his moment in a tap routine and one of Hempseed and Mason's neatest numbers, 'You're Just Right As You Are'. Croft would later embed himself into our memory in the (supposedly) first ever British rock'n'roll film *Rock You Sinners* (1957).

The acting plaudits go to the generally under-rated, non-singing Nicholson, an actress who 'specialized in eccentric or slightly dotty roles,'[31] who steals the picture as the slightly more than dotty old actress who has not only kept her husband's body for forty years, but made sure he has fresh flowers every day. Her faithful old retainer understates the situation by explaining, 'She's never been as bad as this before.' In these segments, and with Nicholson's touching death scene, *Tread Softly* moves, unexpectedly and entertainingly, into Grand Guignol.

And then there is Day, the 'Delightful, Delicious, De-Lovely' icon of 1930s British cinema, at the end of her professional tether, looking older than her years and with a new-found steeliness that threatens Joan Crawford, and not even staying around for the film's end. There would be one more film, *There's Always a Thursday* (1957), but the game was well over by then. Inexplicably, in 1955 she recorded 'Why Did the Chicken Cross the Road?' Even more inexplicably, in 1956 she changed her name to Gale Warning to record Elvis Presley's 'Heartbreak Hotel', a grotesque footnote at the end of her career. George Bernard Shaw is said to have written his final play for her. Eleanor Roosevelt was one of her eminent admirers, assuring her, 'I find I am quite unable to resist your extraordinary and tempestuous magnetism.'

Renamed Frankie Day, she made her final theatre appearance in December 1965 in a play, *The Gulls*, at the Jeanetta Cochrane Theatre. The comedian Bob Monkhouse was delighted to be one of the company, and at the first rehearsal told her how much he had always admired her work. 'I'm afraid you are mistaken,' she told him. 'Frances Day was my mother.' She subsequently changed her name to Samta Young Johnson and drifted into obscurity. Her will instructed that there be no public announcement of her death: 'Any persons, private or press, you shall simply say that I am no longer at this address. Gone away. Destination unknown, and that is the truth.' Another truth is that she was one of the most ethereal spirits ever to illuminate the British musical film. It is no surprise that in *Tread Softly* she comes with an atmosphere of ghostliness. One of her most famous numbers, Vivian Ellis's 'Dancing with a Ghost', perhaps sums up her especial qualities.

1953

There may be no *more* musical post-war musical film than Launder and Gilliat's

The Story of Gilbert and Sullivan

Valley of Song	*Laughing Anne*
The Wedding of Lilli Marlene	*Forces' Sweetheart*
The Story of Gilbert and Sullivan	*The Limping Man*
The Beggar's Opera	*It's a Grand Life*
Always a Bride	*Trouble in Store*
Melba	

FEBRUARY

Associated British Picture Corporation's **Valley of Song** began as a radio play by Cliff Gordon, a self-styled 'storm in a Welsh tea-cup', broadcast on the BBC Home Service in 1946 with no less than Ivor Novello (himself a Welshman) as 'Llewellyn the Choir'. A BBC Television production with a 'television script' by Gordon and Michael Mills followed two years later, without Novello but with Rachel Thomas repeating her radio performance as the redoubtable Mrs Lloyd, around whom this gentle comedy revolves.

The problem erupts when one of the favourite but long-absent sons of Cwmpant returns to the village. Geraint Llewellyn's reappearance is timely: the community's choir master has just died, and Geraint (Clifford Evans) is unanimously applauded as his successor, preparing the choir's annual performance of Handel's *Messiah* for the national eisteddfod. All is set fair until he selects Mrs Davies (Betty Cooper) for the contralto solo. Unknown to him, that role has always been taken by Mrs Mair Lloyd, wife of the undertaker. Affronted and hurt to have been replaced, she walks out of the choir practice, and the battle lines between the Davies and Lloyd families (and so between factions in the village) are drawn. This is particularly difficult for young Cliff Lloyd (John Fraser) and Olwn Davies (Maureen Swanson), in love and wanting to marry.

As *Kinematograph Weekly* percipiently understood, the film 'provides much genuine amusement without a hint of malice'.[1] It's a total delight, produced by Vaughan N. Dean and directed with obvious affection and an eye to every nuance by Gilbert Gunn. Much of its charm is due to its utter Welshness and the exhilarating comedy from such as Rachel Roberts as Bessie the Milk, an almost Wagnerian Boudicca of the dairy, hilariously roaring from house to house in her milk-float chariot as she dispenses village gossip; John Glyn-Jones as bed-ridden Ebenezer Davies, avid for his space-age comic; Madoline Thomas never missing a chance as muddlesome Auntie Mary. To add gravitas, there is always Mervyn Johns, repeating his radio role of Revd Idris Griffiths. There is not a false note sounded, spoken, or sung by the London Welsh Association Choral Society.

Gordon and Phil Park's screenplay effortlessly opens up the confinement of the radio original, with enough location shots (often involving the troubled lovers) to emphasise its authenticity. Ultimately, we cannot fail to be moved by its final moments when Rachel Thomas perfectly recaptures herself by giving way to friendship and goodwill, restoring harmony between the factions and freeing Cliff and Olwn to marry:

> It's ashamed you're making me, ashamed of making so much trouble, all over a bit of old singing. But none of you could ever know what it meant to me to sing that part. All year round, it's cooking and washing and mending I am, but once a year when *Messiah* came round, I stopped being Mrs Lloyd Undertaker. I was Madam Mair Lloyd, contralto.

The *MFB* was content that 'The slender story is treated with a light hand and the direction is swift and neat, the result being both refreshing and pleasing [with] no suggestion of the music-hall conception of the Welsh.'[2] All are happy with Griffiths's suggestion that the role should now be shared between the two women, 'and the valley shall sing again'. Hallelujah!

MARCH

How exciting is an invitation to attend *The Wedding of Lilli Marlene*, Monarch Films' sequel to their 1950 *Lilli Marlene*, again directed by Arthur Crabtree with Lisa Daniely reprising the title role and Hugh McDermott returning as boyfriend Steve? The commitment of Monarch's producer William J. Gell to Lilli's story was commendable. Modest and long-drawn as it is, John Baines's screenplay is not without interest, but this went unnoticed by the *MFB*'s cold-water comment that 'Although Daniely has a pleasant voice, the ineffective musical numbers do not help to enliven this tedious picture of show business in London.'[3] The premise is unlikely: innocent Lilli Marlene, one of the few things on which the British and Germans could agree on during World War II, is rescued from a post-war domestic life of oblivion among pots and pans to become a West End star. The poor woman has been dragged into that mire of backstage complication and misunderstanding that had underpinned the British musical film from the beginnings of sound.

We meet Lilli again, eight years after the war that made her name, her innate simplicity exemplified in Daniely's rather dainty impersonation, apparently unchanged by her experiences at the hands of the Nazis. Her 1950 reincarnation already seemed to belong to an earlier epoch; three years on, the resurrection of this heroine, buttressed by a widely known popular song, strikes us as a curious event. One thing is certain, at least. Lilli is still beloved of the Desert Rats, and will rise to stardom in a musical comedy of uncertain quality. She also sings. She is especially prone to breaking into the doleful 'Why Did You Say Goodbye?' Surprisingly, very little is made of the title song, written by Tommie Connor and Johnny Reine.

> There were tears in the crowded congregation
> There were hearts that have loved but all in vain
> 'Twas goodbye to the sweetheart of the nation
> At the wedding of Lilli Marlene.

For obvious reasons, this highlight (represented as part of a stage production) is reserved for the film's closing moments.

It must be said that Lilli's personality is not of the scintillating variety, but there is ample diversion along the way in a supporting company that includes Dandy Nichols as a slatternly char, Wally Patch, Joan Heal, Sidney James as a theatrical impresario (he plays the role commendably straight), and, bouncy as ever, John Blythe. Gabrielle Brune is particularly welcome as mature, catty leading lady Maggie Lennox, but her mischievous presence only accentuates the colourlessness of Lilli's characterisation, stealing the film from its supposed star. Other amusements include a scene between Lilli and her unidentifiably foreign dresser (Irene Handl) in which their dialogue turns into linguistic soup. Handl and Daniely share the unintentionally hilarious moment when Lilli is about to go on stage dressed as a gun-slinging Ado Annie.

In the circumstances, the musical sequences come as something of a relief, being choreographed by Canadian dancer Jack Billings, already notable for his astonishing dance routine with Carol Raye in *Spring Song* (1946). Now, he presents a sub-*Slaughter on Tenth Avenue* ballet, the film's only attempt at an up-to-date Hollywood-type number (the boys even wear jeans). Another set piece is the voodoo-like jungle-inspired routine featuring a half-naked male drummer surrounded by writhing chorines. The stilted on-stage finale in which Lilli, hooped into a vast crinoline, picks her way down a staircase seems as absurd as it is anticlimactic. One suspects that the Dresden-like prettiness is there because Monarch Films already had the costumes. Nothing has changed in a scena that might as well have featured Anne Ziegler and Webster Booth in the mid-1930s.

For reasons unexplained from what we have seen, Lilli receives the sort of opening night ovation known only to actresses who have already played such roles in British musical films. We can at least sympathise with her decision to announce her immediate retirement from the stage, into the arms of Steve. Maggie Lennox will take over. We suspect that this will at least be more fun.

MAY

It's a matter of harmony and disharmony. To date, there has been no national census to decide to what extent the British public of today approve or disapprove of Gilbert and Sullivan's operas – or are they operettas? Both terms are used when referring to them; at once, we see part of the dilemma that clouds their reputation. In a desperate effort to win the devotees of Andrew Lloyd Webber to their cause, in more recent years these operas/operettas have even been presented by managements as 'musicals'. Gilbert and Sullivan divide us, a Marmite situation, but even their stoutest advocates could not deny the homage paid them by the performer Anna Russell's definition of the Gilbert and Sullivan phenomenon. Just as Rodgers and Hammerstein worked to a formula, their Victorian counterparts' trick was to work from a template that had proved commercially and theatrically effective since the days of *H.M.S. Pinafore*.

> You need a handsome young couple whose voices are supple
> And charming and just a bit sickly
> A chorus to prance through the same kind of dance
> And do everything terribly quickly.
> You need a small skinny guy who's amazingly spry
> With a voice like a vegetable grater,
> A tremendous old crone with a strange vocal tone
> Like her mouth is as full of potater
> These operas have got an identical plot, so the narrative
> doesn't much matter
> But it's great to poke fun at most everyone with your typical
> topical patter.

There is a telling scene in London Films' biopic of one of the most famous artistic collaborations of the nineteenth century. Arthur Sullivan is under pressure to finish the score of his forthcoming grandiloquent cantata *The Golden Legend* at the 1886 Leeds Music Festival. His librettist, prudish music critic Joseph Bennett, watches over the exhausted composer as he struggles to complete the work; it's a case of perspiration, not inspiration. It comes as no surprise that Bennett himself dozes off; perhaps he has already heard enough of Sullivan's worthy but patently uninspired score. As Bennett drifts into the land of Nod, Sullivan, like a naughty schoolboy hiding a rude comic inside a dreary textbook, puts *The Golden Legend* aside and resumes work on his music for W. S. Gilbert's *The Mikado*. In just such a manner, in the years after Sullivan's death, the British public lost its fondness for his oratorios (the brief snatches we have of them on screen seem perilously workmanlike), and they were no longer heard in concert halls.

This was ever Sullivan's dilemma – was he to be known as Sullivan, Britain's greatest 'classical' composer, or be shackled to his association with Gilbert? This was an artistic conflict that had no resolution; was he the servant of Gilbert's fripperies or the composer of his age? Was he japing or portentous? In a way, he was both, which makes the problem unsolvable, especially when Sullivan's lightest confections outshone those ponderous, religiously conformist works written for the great Victorian choruses and orchestras and planned to fill the Albert Hall. The conflict is skilfully explained from the beginning of **The Story of Gilbert and Sullivan** when Grace, the prissy girl with whom the young composer (although always middle-aged as played by Maurice Evans) is besotted, expresses her disapproval of his theatrical frolicking with Gilbert. Oddly, the scene is played as parodic comedy, but this is the only glimpse we get of Sullivan's private or emotional life, which is never again referred to. As Grace's father, clubbable Wilfrid Hyde-White, explains to lovelorn Sullivan, 'I suppose she wanted a Bach and found he was only an Offenbach.' It's a good line (there is a profusion of them) but perhaps not accurate, for Sullivan's music written in response to W. S. Gilbert's librettos has nothing of the Frenchman's disrespectfulness or voluptuousness. Neither has Sullivan's music the great bursts of passion or unexpected heights of emotion that arrive in plenty throughout the operas of Lehár or Kálmán. There is something kept back, emotion denied, corseted. It is perhaps just as well that Gilbert's writing, witty, deft, scrupulously literate, also denies it. Offenbach's idea of letting his hair down is the Can-Can of *Orpheus in the Underworld*; for Sullivan it's the Cacucha from *The Gondoliers*, when even a glimpse of ankle might be taboo. There are times when G and S reinforce our suspicions that Victorians really did cover up the legs of their pianos in an effort to avoid any hint of indecency. Time and again in his 'lighter' moments, Sullivan provides what Gilbert might have recognised as 'modified rapture'.[4]

We see how poor young middle-aged Sullivan scrapes a living selling pot-boilers to Chappell, but yearns to be England's greatest 'serious' composer. At the time, he was indubitably the most famous, but fate's trick has remembered him for the Savoy operas he wrote with Gilbert. Sullivan was not blind to the discrepancy. He is reputed to have said after listening to his only so-called 'grand' opera *Ivanhoe*, 'A cobbler should stick to his last.' On one occasion he presented the composer Ethel Smyth with a score of his cantata *The Prodigal Son*, telling her that he thought it his finest work. Ethel, well known for speaking her mind, told him his best work was *The Mikado*. Sullivan laughed it off, and said, 'You wretch!' but Ethel could see he was disappointed. We see in Launder and Gilliat's film how thrilled he was when Queen Victoria requested a Command Performance of one of his works, and how crestfallen he was when she asked for *The Gondoliers*.

As frequently collaborating film-makers, Frank Launder (now producing) and Sidney Gilliat (directing) well understood the complexities involved in shared effort. Their deep appreciation of their subject leaves us in no doubt that Sullivan's life was, in its way, a tragedy. The once well-thumbed vocal scores of his 'serious' works such as *The Martyr of Antioch*, of which he had such hope, now lie dust-encrusted in the lumber-rooms of philharmonic societies. It may be, too, that a lack of intellectual curiosity limited Sullivan in what he might achieve. He seems to have taken little notice of what other composers of his day were producing. If we are to accept Launder and Gilliat's portrait, Gilbert, truculent and non-musical as he was ('I once succeeded in distinguishing "Pop Goes the Weasel" from "God Save the Queen"'), was the happier partner, content in what we see as an apparently satisfactory marriage to his wife (Isabel Dean).

Cinemagoers would have to wait until Mike Leigh's *Topsy-Turvy* (1999) to learn more of Sullivan's personal life. Remarkably, rather than trying to outdate Launder and Gilliat's film, Leigh follows in its path, picks up the innate sadness, and intensifies our scrutiny. In *Topsy-Turvy*, the demons of unhappiness as suggested by the 1953 film are fully exposed. We have only to see how Leigh depicts broken George Grossmith (his vulnerability only hinted at in 1953), or how a D'Oyly Carte soprano imbues 'The Sun Whose Rays Are All Ablaze' with a terrifyingly frigid coldness. Extraordinarily, the two films belong together in a harmony that would surely have astonished their subjects.

There may be no *more* musical post-war musical film than Launder and Gilliat's, which is cleverly managed in the screenplay by Gilliat and the G & S specialist Leslie Baily, with contributions from London Films' supremo Vincent Korda. The credits acknowledge 'advice and assistance' from Richard D'Oyly Carte's daughter Bridget. This was necessary, for after her father's death she retained a rigid control of the franchise, the copyright on the operas only expiring in 1961, after which G & S became public property. Although the company continued without interruption year by year, a decline was inevitable; it wound up in 1982. But the film was not a D'Oyly Carte affair, and we can presume that Bridget saw the necessity of this. Nevertheless, the presentation of the musical numbers in no way departs from the company's hardened stylistic manner, and a few of its players are involved, notably its once principal comedian Martyn Green, who had left the company two years earlier, and the splendidly clarion tenor Thomas Round. Still to come, D'Oyly Carte's 1967 film of its *Mikado*, played by the artists who were currently performing it on stage, was unremarkable.

Musical director Isidore Godfrey had joined in 1926 and was to retire in 1955 after thirty-nine years in post. He is justly famed for his astonishing ability to bring up every performance as fresh as paint, which seems especially miraculous when you consider that D'Oyly Carte had no full permanent orchestra; Godfrey was obliged to pick up orchestral players at every theatre the company played. For the film, Sir Malcolm Sargent conducted the London Symphony Orchestra. Although his subsequent 'Glyndebourne' recordings of the Savoy operas suggest he had no natural flair for Sullivan's music, he takes everything at a brisk lick which Godfrey may not have found too disappointing.

Throughout, the incorporation of the musical extracts is well judged, and always with Gilliat's eye for detail and inflection. The music is never alone; it operates alongside the screenplay, never merely as plums in the pudding.

Gilliat is lucky, too, in his players, who are superbly in tune with the film's tone: Robert Morley's musically illiterate Gilbert is perfectly matched with Maurice Evans's Sullivan ('From now on I'm determined to devote myself to serious music'). As the D'Oyly Cartes, Peter Finch and Eileen Herlie are steadying hands, offering portraits of discreet refinement, as does Michael Ripper in a role of very few words as Sullivan's faithful servant Louis.

While criticising the characterisations of Gilbert and Sullivan, *The Times* nevertheless agreed that the film 'has vitality, even if that vitality carries a suspicion of St. Vitus's dance, and, although it is a partial failure, it contains more joy, colour, and the ingredients that make for pleasure than a hundred others with fewer charges against them'.[5] Even the usually forgiving *Kinematograph Weekly* suggested that 'the picture is not faultlessly acted, Robert Morley fails to submerge his own personality, as Gilbert, and Maurice Evans occasionally lacks colour, as Sullivan' in 'a film that is truly British in character, theme and presentation and contains neither a dull nor a cheap moment.'[6]

An unappreciative *MFB* went further, lamenting a 'frightfully proper account' of the famous partnership, in line with 'the respectfully dull costume drama productions of the Korda group since 1947', and 'it is never easy to distinguish between operetta and real-life narrative'. This is surely incorrect; if true, it would negate some of the most effective cinematic moments (Gilbert's Thames-side walks on opening nights, and Gilbert leaving the theatre when he hears of Sullivan's death) or the on-stage bickering of 'In a Contemplative Fashion', which chimes with the notorious Sullivan–Gilbert–Carte quarrel. It sounds as if the *MFB* critic should have been paying more attention, but a note of anti-Savoyard feeling creeps into his review with his parting shot: 'All will probably be bored for at least some of the time.'[7]

To all this Technicolor splendour, we add the film's overall design by Hein Heckroth, who was also responsible, with Elizabeth Haffenden, for the costumes. Two years earlier, Michael Powell and Emeric Pressburger's *The Tales of Hoffmann* had been a triumph for Heckroth, stretching British cinematic design to its limit. At times, his contribution threatened to overcome Hoffmann's tales; this does not happen here. Unaccustomed as they are to films of this type, Launder and Gilliat balance the components, period and taste, music and dialogue, all the while keeping Heckroth's painterly canvas in proportion, delighting the eye at every turn. When Sullivan lifts his baton to conduct the ladies' choir at Leeds for *The Prodigal Son*, director and designer contrive to turn them into limitless ranks of white swans, but everything here throws up another subtle frame: Gilbert's first-night rambles through London streets, Sullivan's rare burst of abandoned happiness during 'The Flowers That Bloom in the Spring', Gilbert side-stepping the expensive new carpet at the Savoy, the camera finding the flickering pages of Sullivan's last diary entry of 'A lovely day. A pity to leave such a lovely day.'

Historians have wondered if Sullivan meant to put a full stop after 'to leave', in the belief that this punctuational nicety might have shed light on his state of mind at the last. It matters nothing. We already know, from the way Louis brings news of his master's fatal collapse to Gilbert and the Carte's, that their lives have been changed for ever, that Sullivan's life has in its way been a tragedy. This scene is played alongside Jack Point's apparent death in the finale of *The Yeomen of the Guard*. We leave the film with Gilbert, alone and Sullivan-less and no less grumpy than before, receiving his knighthood, as the orchestra swells with 'He Is an Englishman'. Of that, as we know from Gilbert and Sullivan, there is no possible doubt whatever.

Despite the various indignities inflicted on their work since their deaths, not least by the gallant amateur operatic societies who for years have kept the operas alive throughout Britain, the very initials 'G and S' remain an albatross around the neck of our musical heritage. Today, a weariness seems to have clouded their achievements, perhaps already thriving in 1953 in Philip Hope-Wallace's comment that the film 'will please the unexacting, and does no harm [...] It might have been more interesting as a film if the backstage story could have been seen with a little more realism [...] not mere musical comedy tiffs and tears.'[8]

JULY

With its ill-concealed elephantine pretensions, Peter Brook's debut as a film director bore the troublesome label of 'opera', a handicap it shared with Powell and Pressburger's two operatic excursions, *The Tales of Hoffmann* (1951) and *Oh ... Rosalinda!!* (1955). Now, the unlikely alliance of Laurence Olivier and Herbert Wilcox as producers and the dangerously experimental Brook as director of **The Beggar's Opera** undoubtedly played its part in the film's coming to grief. As *Variety* summed it up, the result was 'a bold experiment which does not come off [...] an example of the uneasy partnership between screen and opera'.[9] Critical disappointment and public repulsion awaited a project of which Wilcox boasted, 'We were embarking on what must emerge as the outstanding British musical of all time',[10] but one cinema manager told him, 'They didn't even come in on Monday to tell their friends not to come in on Tuesday.'[11] *The Beggar's Opera* was taken off after its first night of a circuit booking.

The *MFB* let loose with a review that claimed that 'The basic flaw lies in the handling itself, which shows little aptitude for the cinema', and that 'Throughout many of the numbers one has a feeling that the camera is an encumbrance.' Furthermore, there was 'the failure to convey any feeling of a Hogarthian London, or any acceptable formalisation of it; the lack of robustness, of breadth, in the whole thing; and its faltering, confused de-velopment as a piece of narrative'.[12] When we look at the film seventy years on, this judgement seems not only severe but undeserved in a work full of vigour and movement, a piece that moves apace and seamlessly melds sung balladry with dialogue. Still, we come back to Wilcox's opinion that 'Larry and I were in complete harmony, but we could not get to first base with Peter' in what became 'a chronic headache'.[13] Yet Brook's film is filmic; it moves. We may imagine the pressure Brook was under, his first film (and in every way a major one) made with the dead hand of Wilcox's reputation at his back. Wilcox could never have achieved what we see on screen; Wilcox never concerns himself with complexity, Brook seems almost obsessed by it. For C. A. Lejeune the composition of the scenes was 'remarkably fine and full of character'.[14] As *Kinematograph Weekly* admitted, 'Pictorially, it's truly Hogar-thian'.[15] There is no doubt that in this the film's designer William C. Andrews, so long associated with Wilcox, excelled himself, as did Georges Wakhévitch, credited with 'opera sets and costumes'.

No other British musical film reaches so far back. In 1716, Jonathan Swift asked Alexander Pope, 'What think you of a Newgate Pastoral, among the Whores and Thieves there?' John Gay wrote it. The first performance at John Rich's theatre in Lincoln's Inn Fields in 1728 began the play's enduring popu-larity through numberless adaptations and reinterpretations. In 1968 it resur-faced as a West End musical with Peter Gilmore as the dashing, disreputable Captain Macheath, confirming Dennis Arundell's description of the play as 'really no opera but rather what the earlier twentieth century might have called a satirical revue, but in the form of a play with songs'.[16] Such a form suggested difficulties in transposing it to film, and we cannot doubt that Wilcox would have been incapable of making it work.

The quality of the adaptation by Denis Cannan, with additional dialogue and lyrics by no less than Christopher Fry, lends distinction, as does the score composed and arranged (from the original and subsequent sources) by Arthur Bliss, although the *MFB* complained that his incidental music 'adopts an in-congruous modern idiom', 'nor do his arrangements of some of the songs seem an improvement'.[17] In fact, Bliss's score, sympathetic to every mood, is in itself a considerable achievement, bursting with nuance.

Brook is fortunate, too, in the distinguished British singers brought in to dub the actors, among them Adele Leigh, Jennifer Vyvyan, Edith Coates, Joan Cross, Bruce Boyce, and John Cameron. Only Stanley Holloway as Mr Peachum and Olivier as Macheath sing their own numbers, Holloway being the more successful. Olivier's insistence that he should not be dubbed is commendable; the performance is made the more complete, even if vocally inadequate. The casting is brilliant, with outstanding performances.

AUGUST

With a reasonable quota of gentle wit, Clarion's one-song *Always a Bride* was produced by Robert Garrett, directed by Ralph Smart, written by Smart and Peter Jones, and delivered by a strong cast. Father and daughter Victor and Clare Hemsley (Ronald Squire and Peggy Cummins) pose as husband and wife to con their way through life, until British Treasury official Terence Winch (Terence Morgan) upsets the arrangement by falling for Clare. The *MFB* found it 'Pleasant entertainment, but quickly forgotten afterwards',[18] with *Kinematograph Weekly* reporting that 'Neither the story nor the dialogue is particularly snappy, but all the same, the principal players and the direction succeed in giving the elegant, if slightly stagey, set-up agreeable veneer.'[19] A delightfully disapproving trio of elderly players (Marie Löhr, Mary Hinton, and Eliot Makeham) bring a dash of stylish comedy. In a cabaret appearance, popular singer Jill Day sings Benjamin Frankel's 'Love Me Little Love Me Long', not to be confused by another song of the same name from Vivian Ellis's musical *And So to Bed*. It is followed by one of Frankel's delightful trademark jogging melodies.

For lovers of the human voice, the Australian prima donna of the New York Metropolitan, Dame Nellie Melba, lives on in ancient gramophone records. In culinary circles, she lives on as the inspiration for a sickly dessert comprising raspberries, peaches, and ice cream; a brittle sort of toast; a chicken dish involving mushroom and truffle (Melba garniture); and a sauce whipped up from redcurrant and raspberry. She is immortalised by Patrice Munsel, an Australian soprano, in a biopic of cringing embarrassment, *Melba*. We can only hope that Madame Melba's voice was a little less piercing than Miss Munsel's, a voice that may well have set chandeliers tingling when they received notice of her high notes but is equally capable of setting your teeth on edge. Filmed in a muddy Technicolor at Nettlefold and on location, Horizon Pictures' operatic treat was produced by Sam Spiegel (as S. P. Eagle), written by Harry Kurnitz, and directed by Hollywood veteran Lewis Milestone.

We first meet Nellie on Charles Armstrong's Australian farm, where her unmistakably American voice seems out of place, and to confuse us geographically even more, she sings 'Comin thro' the Rye' before turning her back on the outback and moving to Paris to seek success as a 'serious' singer, much to the disappointment of the admiring down-to-earth Armstrong (staunch John McCallum). In an early example of Kurnitz's poetically intended way with words, he tells her, 'When God gave you that golden voice, he left out your heart.' In Paris, she is heard singing in a roadside café by Eric Walton (John Justin) and sent to the terrifyingly stern singing teacher Mme Marchesi (Martita Hunt, playing up to the hilt and the best thing in the film by a good head). The old girl is retired and sickly ('It will kill her!') and impossibly demanding, putting Nellie through agonies compared with those suffered by Eliza Doolittle preceding 'The Rain in Spain': 'The high notes should be sung like the other notes, not exploded!' barks Madame; 'Up a semitone!' By now, we see that Kurnitz's dialogue is pretty well parody-proof, as it continues with such pronouncements through a biopic with barely a scintilla of truth in it.

There is brief relief in a sequence remembering the achievements of divas who have already been through it, scenes made more bearable by the sudden visual pleasure of their stage settings, but too soon we are back with Kurnitz's witless fandango, with Nellie wrecking a hotel kitchen (apparently the birth of peach Melba), swiftly followed by a mad scene from *Lucia di Lammermoor*. So deranged is Nellie after her maniacal performance that she prances through Covent Garden with the vegetable porters.

There is no shortage of male admirers, no less than the first Oscar Hammerstein (the father of Oscar Hammerstein II) and Cesar Carlton, played respectively by Robert Morley and Alec Clunes, interrupted by the arrival of Charles, who has left his sheep in Australia to pursue Nellie. She must face the dilemma that has confronted many a prima donna: marriage or career? Knowing Nellie as we do, we wonder how long it will be before Charles is sent packing. Nevertheless, she lapses into untypical sentimentality by romancing him in a carriage-ride along the prom at Cannes with Mischa Spoliansky and Norman Newell's 'Dreamtime', a song so inferior and absurdly out of kilter with everything that has gone before it that we wonder why Munsel or anyone else involved with the film sanctioned its inclusion.

Perhaps aware of this lapse, Nellie gives us long, drearily filmed extracts from several others of her successes, among them *La Traviata*, Gounod's *Romeo and Juliet* and *Faust*, and *La Fille du Regiment*. It is obvious that some trouble was taken to provide these on-stage gobbets of the repertoire, supervised by Dennis Arundell under the supervision of 'operatic advisor' Norman Peasey, but they sit, stolid, cluttered, flavourless, and uninteresting, on the screen, despite the support of the Covent Garden Orchestra and choreographer Pauline Grant. *The Marriage of Figaro*, *Tosca*, *Rigoletto*, *The Barber of Seville*: all get an airing. It's no surprise that Nellie begins to be difficult ('Madame Melba is not quite herself, gentlemen'), but what is she to do? Will she go back to Australia (as Hammerstein points out, 'To sing only to the cattle and the bush and the trees') or become a stay-at-home wife? As Hammerstein realises, 'The true answer is in her eyes.' Charles, too, is restless, understandably miffed at being known as 'Mr Melba', and leaves her, thus becoming, in a manner of speaking, Melba toast.

The film's critical reception proved that there is no accounting for taste. Caroline Lejeune's kindly review found it 'florid, ornate, rather obvious, and proliferate in montage'.[20] For *Kinematograph Weekly* (this was not, one suspects, quite its cup of tea), it was 'Lush, warm-hearted, witty and magnificently staged'.[21] The *MFB* was not persuaded: 'this might as well be any fairly silly, fairly conventional, musical [...] But for the most part the tedium of a tale told too often and not often too well is too much for the film'.[22] Bosley Crowther in the *New York*

Times considered the film 'a mere offence to the taste and credulity of an average numskull' with Munsel forced into 'acting this exceedingly silly and vapid role [...] overloaded with such obvious twaddle about ambition and success'.[23] A decade earlier, the British musical film *Evensong* was based on Beverley Nichols's novel of the same name (he had been Melba's secretary). It was another fiction-alised treatment, but in the better hands of Evelyn Laye's Nellie, especially fine in a touching death scene, and Emlyn Williams.

SEPTEMBER

A costume drama worked up by Pamela Wilcox Bower from Joseph Conrad's short story 'Because of the Dollars', Imperadio's ***Laughing Anne*** had Margaret Lockwood as the barmaid-singer of the title, miming Pierre Roche's 'I've Fallen in Deep Water' and Ted Grouya's 'All the World Is Mine on Sunday' to Lita Roza's vocals. The lyrics were by Geoffrey Parsons. Although unmentioned in Wilcox's autobiography, this was one of his more interesting projects. The *Sketch* found it 'both vivid and touching. The last two reels continue to catch the atmosphere of the steaming jungle, as well as the tension that Conrad's little story conveyed so powerfully'. The lurid quality of some of Wilcox's Technicolor films was now 'unusually restrained and fine'.[24] Bower, Wilcox's daughter, was kept in the film family, going on to provide scripts for *King's Rhapsody* (1955) and *The Lady Is a Square* and *The Heart of a Man* (both 1959).

NOVEMBER

Surely ***Forces' Sweetheart*** is a Vera Lynn film? Who else, after all, can stake the claim (at the time, some suggested Anne Shelton)? On closer inspection, it doesn't sound very appealing, a picture produced at Nettlefold by cinematic reprobate Edwin J. Fancey and directed by the workmanlike Maclean Rogers, with a screenplay by Carl Heck. Luckily, the sweetheart turns out to be cheery, gallant Hy Hazell, late of *The Lady Craved Excitement* (1950). The film turns out something of a treat, buttressed by comedy performances from Harry Secombe (as Welsh Private Llewelyn), Michael Bentine (Flight Lieutenant John Robinson RAF), and Freddie Frinton (Aloysius Dimwitty). Their determination to romance musical comedy star Judy James (Hazell) drives the snappy narra-tive, happily interrupted by a bright score by Wilfred Burns, Ralph Reader, and Manlio de Veroli.

Returning to London from entertaining the troops in Korea, Judy tries out a number from her new show, 'I'm Your Sweetheart Maybe'. A neatly done Charlie Chaplin routine in silhouette alerts us not only to Leslie Roberts's cho-reography for his Television Girls (and Leslie plays himself), but to realising that the film is pulling against its weight. At a rehearsal, Judy sings 'All through the Year', with Rogers intercutting scenes that were brightest with her lover, another John Robinson (John Ainsworth). When the show's backer drops out, the wealthy Dimwitty ('Have some jewellery') steps in. The show's tenor is missing, but Secombe steps in for 'One Love, One Lifetime'. Dimwitty returns to the island of Muck, where the comedians join forces for 'He's Been Around for All the Lasses'. They may not always amuse, but the comedians are unflagging in their energy, and who could fail to respond to the simple pleasure of Bentine and Secombe's walking-stick party piece? They return to London, where the show is about to open. From the show within the film, Judy, for some reason persuaded to look like a principal boy, admits 'I'm the Girl the Forces Fight For' in an oddball pugilistic choreography reminiscent of a League of Health and Beauty display. All things considered, it's a reasonable achievement for a Fancey production, neatly done, generous in its comedy and musical content, and better than we had the right to expect from so unpromising a source.

A noirish 'B' picture mystery around a shooting at an airport, blackmail and contraband, Banner Pictures' *The Limping Man* was headed by Hollywood import Lloyd Bridges, with Alan Wheatley and Leslie Phillips as the investigating policemen in amusing and leisurely support. Ian Stuart Black and Reginald Long's adaptation of Anthony Verney's *Death on the Tideway* was produced at Merton Park by David Ginsberg, and directed by Cy Endfield, here credited as Charles Lautour. With little reason, space was found for two cabaret numbers performed by Helénè Castle, 'I Couldn't Care Less' by Endfield (as Hugh Raker) and Arthur Wilkinson, and David Croft and Cyril Orandel's 'Hey Presto!', with Castle as on-stage assistant to Reginald Beckwith's conjuror. Lionel Blair is allowed to dance on what appears to be a giant xylophone, but the film's most unexpected moment is its final few moments, when it collapses into itself with a resounding cheekiness.

'In the silent era, Frank Randle would have gone to Hollywood, and would have made an international success as a droll. His comedy, directed along slapstick lines, could have been international instead of local, if a capable writer and a good director had spared the time.'[25]

Could it have been so? In fact, Randle clung to John E. Blakeley's Mancunian Film Corporation throughout his career and supported the company financially; without Blakeley's continued production of Randle's chaotic comedies, Britain's most anarchic, destructive, impossibly difficult comedian would long before have vanished from the screen, no longer delighting that perhaps mythical audience 'the industrial masses', that existed in the minds of *Kinematograph Weekly*'s writers.

Produced and directed by Blakeley, *It's a Grand Life* promises in its opening credits 'A musical comedy burlesque'. What part of 'musical comedy burlesque' did Blakeley not understand? The description was hardly appropriate when the only musical sequence was provided in the last few minutes. They are worth waiting for: it's time for Winifred Atwell, one of the sunniest personalities of the period, to tickle the ivories.

Randle's last film had been Mancunian's 1949 *School for Randle*. Four years on, Randle had very much aged, looking considerably older than his fifty-two years, but lacking none of his earlier vitality and losing none of his fondness for pratfalls. H. F. Maltby's screenplay effectually transported Randle back to the army atmosphere of his hugely popular 'Somewhere' films: *Somewhere in England, Somewhere in Camp, Somewhere on Leave,* and *Somewhere in Politics.* Randle was credited as co-writer (it would have been unfair for Maltby to shoulder all the blame). We soon suspect that Maltby's script is offered up for sacrifice whenever Private Randle stumbles into the frame.

Would we want it any other way? Randle's unique skills explode on screen because he throws the lighted match into the box of fireworks. It is because of him that the film doesn't get hopelessly bogged down in whatever Mr Maltby has contrived to enliven a vague storyline about the arrival of glamorous Corporal Paula Clements (Dors) of the Women's Royal Army Corps at an army camp. Her mild romance with Private Philip Green (John Blythe) is beyond insipid (but all romantic scenes in Mancunian are), and there is very little reason for Dors turning up at the studio. As it happens, matters of the heart will never stir us so long as Randle is rampaging alongside, hilariously filling in forms about new recruits, demolishing a tea trolley, falling through open doors, wrestling, or discussing the matter of 'thwarts'. Mayhem is king, and we are thankful.

At last, after Winifred has fled to another appointment, Randle collapses on some stairs, happily smiling and laughing direct to camera at the film's close. Perhaps it was just after this that he made his public apology to the company (see below). It's just as likely that he knew this was the last time he'd make a film and did the gentlemanly thing. As was sometimes his custom, he shows respect for this farewell scene by putting his teeth in.

For Blakeley to persuade Atwell into the Manchester studio to play her compositions 'Dixie Boogie' (no. 5 in the 1952 UK charts) and 'Britannia Rag' (written to mark the Queen's recent coronation) was a distinct coup. Randle seems to have been unwilling to give this splendid artist the space and respect owing to her. As she played piano 'Randle was to appear doing a silly little dance [but] in one of his tasteless pranks thought that doing it blacked-up complete with white gloves, minstrel-like, would be funny.'[26] Blakeley got wind of this, but arranged the filming so that Randle's prank went unfilmed. Randle professed himself delighted with his interpolation, but was furious when he saw the rushes. Atwell was understandably offended, informing Blakeley that 'Had I known there was going to be two coloured artistes I wouldn't have appeared.'

Dors, contracted to Mancunian for £1,000, was equally unhappy, recalling that 'the film was an utter shambles, for Randle was mad and usually drunk into the bargain. But, as he owned the film company, we had to put up with him shooting guns at the dressing room wall or dragging his girlfriends by their hair along the corridors.'[27] There was more disruption when Randle insisted on the sacking of the assistant director Bert Marrotta and refused to resume filming if he remained. Eventually, after filming was stopped for a few days, pressure from the other technicians persuaded Blakeley to reinstate Marrotta. 'Perhaps surprisingly, after the filming of the party scene, which appears at the end of the film, Randle asked John E. to keep the cameras rolling. John E. duly obliged to his request and in front of the camera Randle went up to Bert Marrotta and apologised for being an absolute bastard.'[28] In today's climate, Randle's behaviour would be roundly condemned. We do not have to ponder why major British studios refused to countenance him. Yet in that apology (filmed but, for obvious reasons, never making it to the screen) we discover something of Randle's complexities; his extremes of personality were assuredly responsible for at least some of his unarguable brilliance.

Gerry George tells us that 'It's generally accepted – and particularly where Frank Randle is concerned – that for each 'take', Blakeley just kept the camera running, while the toothless wizard pulled every subliminal, inspirational spark of genius, out of his bag of tricks [...] and the rest of the operation was concluded in the cutting room, with a goodly proportion of the day's shoot left on the floor. The usable footage, however, was nothing short of 'liquid gold' [...] and that showed-up, every time, at the box-office.'[29]

DECEMBER

Falling about with laughter came easily to Norman Wisdom's little chap, also called Norman in the vehicular comedy ***Trouble in Store*** that began a series that dominated the British cinematic landscape for many years to come. The Two Cities' film was produced by Maurice Cowan and directed by John Paddy Carstairs, with a screenplay by Cowan, Carstairs, and Ted Willis. A pattern was quickly established, a template to which its creators, content with the reaction of the public, stuck. A fit of hysterics, leaving Norman gasping for air, would erupt, usually after some extraordinarily complex sequence of disasters, to which his inoffensive character, 'the gump', was prone. The perpetual underdog, existing on the fringe of what others considered normal life, always willing, too often overlooked. Dog-like as he was, he was also a worm ready to turn, ultimately a solution to the problem, as faithful as an old but clumsy dog, the sort that knocks over the Crown Derby tea services or may even, as here, make a decent job of destroying a department store.

He is ever luckless in love, although film after film finds him hopelessly attracted to a girl who seems to be, if we can use the phrase from an earlier generation, 'above his station': a better-educated, socially confident, nicely turned-out girl. On this occasion, it's Sally (Lana Morris) from the record department of Gorringe's, where Norman works in the storeroom before being promoted to window dresser. Morris gets a look in by singing Mischa Spoliansky and David Arkell's 'I Want to Put on Record That I Love You, Love You, Love You' into a recording microphone, reprised by the already adoring Norman. It is then that we hear a change in Norman, almost as if his singing voice belongs to somebody else. It doesn't, but singing brings out a confidence, a poshness that intercedes when sentimentality or a longing for love arrives. When Formby broke into song, there had usually been a ukulele on hand, and a lyricist (sometimes he was his own) to provide sexually suggestive lyrics of which the average Briton would not have disapproved. This is not our Norman's way; indeed, one suspects he's too shy or innocent to come out with anything that might be misconstrued. It may also make his screen persona seem more real than Formby's, and *Trouble in Store* has the perfect number, written by Wisdom with June Tremayne, 'Don't Laugh at Me 'Cos I'm a Fool'. In this, a confession of the very attributes that make up Wisdom's on-screen character, Wisdom had his signature song. Morris's recording scene reminds us of the devastatingly cruel gramophone recording that Richard Attenborough's Pinkie makes for Carol Marsh in *Brighton Rock* (1947). Aside from this moment, Morris's contribution is negligible. Just as Beryl Formby made sure the spotlight never favoured anyone but her George, the producers of the Wisdom films made sure his on-screen girlfriends (not that they ever considered themselves as such) remained incidental.

However, *Trouble in Store* has the advantage of Margaret Rutherford as a busy shoplifter – no more than a prolonged 'turn', but a splendid addition to the general uproar. More importantly, it has Jerry Desmonde as the star's 'straight man'. Desmonde had already proved his skills as Wisdom's 'straight man' on stage, a role in which he'd excelled opposite the Scots comedian Dave Willis, and opposite Sid Field (a partnership that remains one of the best reasons to investigate the catastrophically sub-Hollywood 1946 *London Town*), and now proved invaluable to the Wisdom film comedies.

The film had not been released to the West End, but in Christmas week it achieved 25 per cent above the normal box-office expectation. Nevertheless, the critics had reservations. This was 'not a very good film. It is poorly written and shabbily made [but] its success is due entirely to Wisdom, a fine droll, with a screen character as strong, in its way, as [Harry] Langdon's'.[30] While the *MFB* thought it no more than a string of incidents and 'not as funny as it should be',[31] *Kinematograph Weekly* celebrated the fact that 'his clever and tireless performance not only establishes him as a great screen comic, but puts the extravaganza in the top box-office bracket'. In fact, this was 'Excellent, nay infallible, British box-office light fare'.[32] To describe Carstairs's product as extravaganza was an obvious exaggeration, but a template had been forged, a relationship with the British public had begun, a relationship comparable to that enjoyed by very few comics except Formby.

1954

The romantic scenes between Neagle and Flynn border on the grotesque

Lilacs in the Spring

The Gay Dog *Lilacs in the Spring*
Harmony Lane *One Good Turn*

JUNE

The year was half through before cinemagoers caught a glimpse of a British musical film. Some made do with Wilfred Pickles and Megs Jenkins repeating their husband-and-wife partnership in the Piccadilly Theatre stage production of 1952 in Coronet Films' warm-hearted **The Gay Dog**. Not surprisingly, Pickles (a superb but consistently under-rated actor) won *MFB*'s praise for 'an interesting character study of a hard-working miner, whilst retaining his customary mannerisms'.[1] The musical titbit was Joe (Mr Piano) Henderson's 'A Long Way to Go', sung by Petula Clark. Modest fare in a year lacking distinction, the best the British musical film could come up with was a patched-together half-hour musical revue, a supposedly lush theatrical romance based on the West End Anna Neagle vehicle *The Glorious Years*, and more Norman Wisdom.

OCTOBER

Small but neatly proportioned, **Harmony Lane** is a curiosity worth exploring. Presented by Daniel M. Angel, produced by Morris Talbot, and directed by Lewis Gilbert (holidaying as Byron Gill), this miniature revue was made in 3D at Gate Studios, Boreham Wood. Visually, it's a delight. The cartoonish design by Michael Stringer is tasteful and inventive, even beautiful when it presents its ballet segment, with the various 'turns' enacted in Harmony Lane's shops, linked by a prancing policeman (Jack Billings). The Television Toppers welcome us with Billings's neatly choreographed street dancing before lining up for their expected high-kicking routine, complete with performing dog. We see a snatch of The Skating Sayers before the Jack Billings Trio's spanking tap number invigorates the display; these dancers are at the top of their game. Another notable 'spesh' artist, Jack Kelly, dazzles with some complex juggling, although the most impressive feat of his stage act (throwing a lighted cigarette up from his heels and catching it in his mouth) is missing. Gilbert sensibly moves the various segments on before we grow weary of them.

The friendly local bobby turns to the 'Ballet Shoes' shop for the central sequence of the picture. A young woman (Svetlana Beriosova, soon to be prima ballerina of Sadler's Wells) is trying on the stock, helped by the shopkeeper (David Paltenghi). As he turns away to the window, she steps through a curtain. Gilbert's trick, simple but effective, is to immediately switch to Beriosova, now transformed into *Odette*, followed by the shopkeeper, now transformed into Prince Siegfried, ready for the six-minute White Swan Pas de Deux from *Swan Lake*. The sylvan landscape of moody trees, a setting that takes every opportunity to exploit the 3D effects, is unexpectedly exquisite.

From here on, the film's tone shifts less satisfactorily back to variety performers. In their only film appearance, the Beverley Sisters sing 'Side by Side', followed by what we must assume is top-of-the-bill Max Bygraves in a dismal sketch with Dora Bryan, culminating in his performing 'The Bygraves Boogie'. This eludes the charm that has gone before, but things pick up in the kilted Television Toppers' finale, built around a medley of Scottish melodies, before Constable Billings dances out of Harmony Lane. Another fascinating short presented as revue is the 1956 *Five Guineas a Week*.

DECEMBER

We may never know Errol Flynn's true feelings when he was contracted to make a series of films in Britain for director Herbert Wilcox, an arrangement that was to result only in **Lilacs in the Spring** and in the following year's *King's Rhapsody*. Both were redolent of Ivor Novello, who had died in 1951. Great swathes of lilac were thrown over Novello's hearse as it wound through the thousands of tearful mourners on its way to Golders Green crematorium.

Lilacs in the Spring was one of the handful of musical films of our period based on a theatre production. In this case it was intended to celebrate not only the coronation of the new young Queen Elizabeth, but the sheer brilliance of being British. This lumbering historical leviathan, *The Glorious Days*, played in London at the Palace Theatre from February to November 1953, involving Neagle in a multitude of costume changes in what was as much a pageant of British history as a musical entertainment. No time was wasted in turning it into a Wilcox film, its original script reformed for the occasion by Miles Malleson, who had been one of those responsible for the stage play. Its pedestrian nature permeated the proceedings, with a young heroine of the London Blitz, Carol Beaumont (Neagle), being regenerated not only as a young Queen Victoria (Neagle) scandalously learning how to dance the waltz (a polka would have been even more mutinous), but as orange-selling Nell Gwyn (Neagle, who had already played the title role in Wilcox's 1934 biopic), before turning up as Carol's daughter Lilian Grey. These impersonations had now and then caused

Lilacs in the Spring, Herbert Wilcox's 1954 film adaptation of
Anna Neagle's stage revue pageant *The Glorious Days*, was
intended to celebrate the coronation of the new Queen Elizabeth
in a spectacular *mélange* of minced history.

ripples of amusement among the more sophisticated audience members at *The Glorious Days*, although the faithful *Theatre World Annual* insisted that 'Neagle more than deserved the great personal triumph she scored in four exacting roles and it was impossible to believe that the enchanting dancer of the last act [it was a tango] was herself in musical comedy over twenty years ago.'[2] Indeed, there has been no British actress whose popularity with the domestic audience achieved such longevity, none who put herself to the wheel so determinedly as Neagle did, on stage for eight performances a week, playing so many characters in such a spectacular *mélange* of minced history.

Remembering *The Glorious Days*, the theatre critic Philip Hope-Wallace recorded that Neagle went at the musical numbers 'with a will. But the connecting links are feeble to the point of fatuity, and it was only our respect for the gallant spirit and wholesome personality of the leading lady that made us repress our yawns', and then there was her dancing, 'fleet but unsensational.'[3] The *MFB*'s opinion of Malleson and Wilcox's adaptation was more an admission that the film existed than a review, allowing that 'In energy and confidence [Neagle] is certainly not past her prime.' Forbearing to mention Flynn, it somewhat backhandedly conceded that 'Direction, dialogue, décor and other performances are of the standard we might expect.'[4] For one of Flynn's biographers the film was 'a mess – fascinating, but a mess [...] Neagle was over fifty, wasn't much of a dancer and telegraphed everything – you can tell she was a trouper.'[5]

A Novello-ish flavour pulses through the opening credits, which are shown as we hear his 'We'll Gather Lilacs', originally written as a duet for Muriel Barron and contralto Olive Gilbert in the 1945 stage musical *Perchance to Dream*, for which Novello also wrote the lyrics. The Germans are bombing London. At ENSA HQ's Drury Lane Theatre, Carol is going through some of her genteel dance manoeuvres to music. In the local pub, she buys a pint for a venerable Chelsea Pensioner ('Thank you kindly, miss!'). He reminds Carol of the history of Nell Gwyn. An air raid knocks Carol for six, leaving her shell-shocked. The story bursts into colour as we see sweet Nell prancing mischievously into view. She only has to offer him one of her juiciest oranges before King Charles (David Farrar) invites her to a flirtatious supper. A little army of Chelsea Pensioners appears as if in a vision, singing Odoardo Barri and Fred Weatherly's 1881 '[Boys of] The Old Brigade'.

Back in what passes for the real world, Carol is romanced by Charles King (we recognise him as King Charles) on a trip to Kew. She wears a lilac-coloured coat, and to her delight 'The lilacs are out!' Several cups of tea are consumed. Although the cups are patently empty, the merest teaspoon is grist to the mill of Neagle's armoury of nervous mannerisms, but soon we are whisked back to Queen Victoria's reign. For this occasion, Carol becomes Britain's very own Empress of India. At her daintiest, Neagle warbles 'Drink to Me Only' (it would have been a kindness to have had her dubbed) to Peter Graves's Prince Albert, before (much to Albert's disgust) insisting on a waltz. This develops into a ridiculous royal barney, an incident unknown to any of Her Majesty's biographers.

As Wilcox's imitation of contemporary life returns, Kathleen Harrison's barmaid recalls Carol's parents, and back we go again, to when Carol's mother Lilian Grey (yes, Neagle *again*) is a small part player in a 1914 show starring Beaumont. He and Lilian perform Leslie Stuart's 'Lily of Laguna', devised by the film's choreographers Philip and Betty Buchel. Lilian's finest moment comes with a glamorous Spanish dance in a London revue, *Hello Tango*, with Neagle framed by male dancers.

In his dugout in France, Beaumont breaks into the 1916 'Take Me Back to Dear Old Blighty' by the prolific song-writing duo A. J. Mills and Bennett Scott and Fred Godfrey, before returning to England, where Lilian is starring in an Andre Charlot revue, *By Jingo*. She and Beaumont are reunited, and (almost inevitably) it's off to supper at Romano's. Time flies. It's 1925 and Lilian is dancing on a giant piano to Noël Coward's 'Dance Little Lady' in a C. B. Cochran revue. The romantic scenes between Neagle and Flynn border on the grotesque. He leaves for Hollywood, where he finds success in talking pictures. At last returning to England, he meets Carol at the theatre where Lilian is starring: an excellent dance sequence of 'Lilacs' follows. A happy ending is expected, but Lilian dies in a plane crash en route to joining Beaumont in Hollywood.

Neagle had done this sort of thing before in the 1948 *Elizabeth of Ladymead*, when she had played (sometimes to unintended comical effect) four chatelaines of Ladymead: the 1854 Beth, the 1903 Elizabeth, the 1919 Betty (a flighty flapper with Ross Parker's 'I'll Make Up for Everything' to sing), and the 1946 Liz. *Lilacs in the Spring* is unmentioned in Wilcox's autobiography, but did not pass unnoticed by *Films and Filming*'s Dennis Millmore, who thought Neagle's routines 'Lilac Tango' and 'Dance, Little Lady',

> which, for Anna Neagle's contribution, might conceivably be called witty and, as far as the young men who support her are concerned, disgraceful. It is high time that an English film produced a chorus line that had some semblance of discipline and efficiency. That a dozen or so dancers cannot be put in front of a camera and raise their arms and legs in unison is quite deplorable. Thereafter the film rushes to a grand finale in Burma with everyone gaily gathering lilacs in the jungle and Anna Neagle happy with the man of her choice. As may also be gathered, practically no one has anything worth doing in the film except Anna Neagle and she does it for all she is worth, which, when all is said, is still a great deal.[6]

Two Cities' Norman Wisdom comedy **One Good Turn** had an unlikely provenance in Dorothy Whipple's 1944 novella *Every Good Deed*. When two more of her novels, *They Were Sisters* and *They Knew Mr Knight*, were made into British films in 1945, Whipple visited the studios at the time of a Herbert Wilcox film, and may well have looked in at Pinewood in 1954 to see how Norman was shaping up as he did his good deed. Much of the production team for the 1953 *Trouble in Store* remained in place: producer Maurice Cowan, director John Paddy Carstairs, and co-writers Cowan and Ted Willis, with Sid Colin and Talbot Rothwell contributing additional material. The runaway success of *Trouble in Store* had begun a series that kept his films in front of the public until the mid-1960s. His reputation as a theatrical performer was already established before he set foot in a British studio, but how would he fare in a medium that, post-Formby, had never promoted another comedian so vigorously? This, anyway, was a talent with much more dimension; everything about Wisdom was multi-faceted. His art, like that of the greatest clowns, is difficult to define. John Fisher attempts it: 'His act is a frenetic spiral of continually renewed disaster, anger, and isolation, pain, reconciliation, and laughter, between immaculate stooge and helpless waif.'[7]

The *Guardian* had its doubts, suggesting that 'If this likeable comedian is to be turned into a film star he will need to be completely supported by far more than haphazard direction, the ancient gags, the inadequate cast, and the generally slapdash devices which have gone to make *One Good Turn*' and adding that 'Chaplin would never have taken a job of film-making as casually as this.'[8]

The *MFB* agreed that those behind the camera were responsible for the handling, 'almost fatal to his individual gifts', of their star, complaining that 'The attempt to exploit the pathetic quality which once arose easily and naturally from his comedy here results in a mawkish, tasteless pathos, deliberately imposed from outside, and using such obvious devices as orphans.'[9] In sympathetic mood (its usual mood), *Kinematograph Weekly* agreed that

> Most of the critics patronised Norman Wisdom's latest, but I can assure you it's got away to a 'flyer' at the Odeon, Leicester Square. Obviously, Norman still has a lot to learn, but although he has not yet reached the Chaplin class, he is easily Britain's number one comedian, both on stage [he had spent a year in the West End in Frank Loesser's musical *Where's Charley?*] and screen.[10]

Whatever situation the opening scenes of any of his films placed him in, he was identified by his everyday uniform, the peaked cap at the cock-eyed angle, the twisted collar of his shirt, the disarrangement of his shirt collar, the waywardness of his tie, the shabby tightness of his suit. Now, as ever, there's a girl he's sweet on (this time Joan Rice, as thanklessly parted as any of the idols of his eye), with Shirley Abicair occasionally plucking her zither on the sidelines. The Greenwood Children's Home is the setting for protracted scenes of sentimentality, with its orphans insisting they won't go to bed until Norman sings to them. Such moments, manufactured as they are, exhibit aspects of Wisdom that offer relief from the obligatory knockabout routines (for this film without benefit of his excellent 'straight man' Jerry Desmonde). That song before bedtime is Norman Newell's 'Take a Step in the Right Direction', perhaps reminding us that Wisdom's own childhood was probably more miserable than the life of the little tots seen here. Wisdom had literally been thrown into the streets by his father.

Another scene that strikes home has a fairground booth where Norman gets into the boxing ring. We see at once that, whatever life has thrown at Wisdom, he has fought against it. Small of stature he may be, but he has a muscularity and gymnastic nimbleness that is the equal of Arthur Lucan. Even better, he is unencumbered by a Kitty McShane. As he pleads in Newell's 'Please Opportunity', he only needs the chance to prove himself. Unmemorable as the two songs are, we can see that they reveal another aspect of the singer. Song alters him, and will remain an important ingredient of the many pictures to follow.

1955

There were any number of young British composers who, given the opportunity, might have jumped at the chance to write the score

As Long as They're Happy

As Long As They're Happy   *King's Rhapsody*
You Lucky People!   *Gentlemen Marry Brunettes*
Value for Money   *An Alligator Named Daisy*
Man of the Moment   *All for Mary*
Oh … Rosalinda!!

MARCH

The mid-1950s selection of musical films painted several reasonably dismal pictures, of ambition overreached and misdirected (*Oh … Rosalinda!!*), a third attempt to make an Ivor Novello stage hit work on the screen with a famous Hollywood refugee and two leading ladies who couldn't sing, a Norman Wisdom vehicle whose individuality was subsumed into the industrial regularity of his comedies, a pedestrian comedy taken from a West End play and saved only by its cherished star, and three comedies with vague pretensions to the zany, the first to appear being Rank's *As Long As They're Happy*, 'a patchy but sometimes funny star vehicle' according to Halliwell,[1] 'a feeble farce' according to Shipman.[2]

Kinematograph Weekly, ever ready to cheer, found its tunes 'haunting and certain to join the hit parade', a hope doomed to disappointment.[3] The *MFB* thought Alan Melville's tepid screenplay, adapted from Vernon Sylvaine's songless play, 'a script deficient in humour' through 'a sprawling series of "big" scenes, few of which come off. The basic joke […] has lost much of its edge, and is scarcely in itself sufficient to carry a film of this length.'[4] For *Variety*, the story was 'told with full force in scenes which are reminiscent of the bobbysox demonstrations witnessed here in the past few years,'[5] although it is unlikely that it made much impression on American audiences with its parade of British character actors and artists plucked from stage revues: Dora Bryan, Joan Sims, Ronnie Stevens, and Vivienne Martin, and 'guest stars' Diana Dors, the professionally grumpy Gilbert Harding (a blatant sop to the British television audience), and, in the last frame, the arrival of no less than Rank's very own Norman Wisdom plugging his 'Don't Laugh at Me 'Cos I'm a Fool'.

The undemanding mildness of Alan Melville's original play *As Long As They're Happy* took little advantage of being turned into a musical film in 1955. Jack Buchanan displayed a stylishness that now seemed to belong to another age.

Filming began swiftly; the stage production of Melville's play had closed in May 1954. If it served any purpose, the film could be identified as a harbinger of the changing trends in British musical films, while keeping its mild but unmistakable middle-classness on the ground. Teenage singing idol Bobby Denver 'The Crying Crooner' (Jerry Wayne) is a prophecy of the Tommy Steele story in store, but neither Sylvaine nor Melville nor director J. Lee Thompson could conceivably be considered the best person to discuss a phenomenon that was waiting just over the horizon and was to have so radical an effect on British society. The best that Melville can do is to watch from the sidelines as youth asserts itself in a way that would have been unthinkable at the beginning of the decade; unfortunately, youth did not assert itself in those departments of the film industry that needed new ideas or quarrelsome philosophies. Despite its implicit insistence that *As Long As They're Happy* is all about young people, it is only about young people as seen through the eyes of an Old Guard sophisticate like Melville. He was to write a lyric about the younger generation, for his 1959 stage musical *Marigold*, when the heroine's aunts contemplate the sad state of 'Present Day Youth' as seen through the eyes of elderly Victorians living in Peebles:

> Each thinking only of things to be done
> And all very different from when we were young.
> Youth of today, youth of today
> Headstrong and flighty they go their own way
> All very lazy the few that we've met

Morally hazy we elders regret
Simply a crazy mixed-up foreign set
Obstinate, pert and uncouth
Preposterous present-day youth.

In just such a way does *As Long As They're Happy* pitch happily married couple John and Stella Bentley (Jack Buchanan and Brenda de Banzie) against their daughters Pat (Jean Carson), Gwen (Janette Scott), and Corinne (Susan Stephen) when Bobby moves into their home, although he surely could have afforded a smart London hotel.

It is a pleasure to see Jack Buchanan at the centre of it but in the last phase of his career. His many qualities essentially belonged to the 1930s, a decade that understood and welcomed his insouciance, his ability to not exactly sing a song but waft into and weave gently around it, so that when he reminded a lover 'You Forgot Your Gloves', there was never a doubt of the deeper significance as a message from the heart. Melancholy triumphed. The fact that his film career had lasted until the mid-1950s is proof of his place in the public's affection, even as he blusters through scene after scene, notching up an alarming number of double-takes, until he revives the memory of style long gone by, lurching and nonchalantly loping across the studio floor in 'I Don't Know Whether to Laugh or Cry'. It's better than the film deserves.

As the supposedly sexy young pop singer Bobby Denver who sets the Bentley girls' hearts fluttering, American Jerry Wayne is surely miscast. Or is he? *Kinematograph Weekly* told its readers that he had sung at a local dance hall, 'and by the look on the young women's faces I cannot imagine one of them missing the film'. Even more off-beam, it told its followers that 'all the seven [?] tunes are haunting and certain to join the hit parade'.[6]

If the film meant to take a soft swipe at the famously lachrymose American crooner Johnnie Ray, it might have found an actor who had some of Ray's sex appeal. When the American stage musical *Bye Bye Birdie* reached London in 1961, its producers had the good sense to cast a young pop singer Marty Wilde as Conrad Birdie, vaguely based on America's own Elvis Presley.[7] *As Long As They're Happy*'s producer Raymond Stross helped to cut his film off at the knees in casting Wayne.

The songs have little to commend them. Bobby is mobbed by fans when he arrives in England, and begins serenading the public including the unmistakably Edwardian little old lady in the crowd (Edie Martin) with Sam Coslow's 'You Started Something', and the all-female household of John Bentley (Buchanan) at Acacia Avenue in Wimbledon with his smooching rendition of 'Liza's Eyes' and 'I Don't Know Whether to Laugh or Cry'. Deserving of better, Carson sings Coslow's 'Quiet Little Rendezvous', 'Merry-Go-Round', and 'My Crazy Little Heart', for which she is joined by a neat routine by Irving Davies and Paddy Stone, whose several contributions to the British musical film deserve to be better remembered. On stage, Bobby's 'Be My Guest' sends his audience into hysterical acclamation. Inspired by Johnnie Ray's tearfulness, Bobby's ability to cry at will, evidenced in his singing Churchill Kohlman's 'Cry', is at the heart of his success. It is disappointingly revealed to be induced by onions. The rest of Coslow's numbers hardly stick around long enough to take root, at a time when there were any number of young British composers who, given the opportunity, might have jumped at the chance to write the score. As it is, the cast have to make do with mundane Tin Pan Alley product, as when Buchanan does what he can with Coslow's 'If Your Heart Aches'. Coslow is also responsible for the ghastly 'Hokey Pokey Polka' headed by Diana Dors. At this low point we cannot but be reminded of hapless Sid Field and Kay Kendall in *London Town*, made to perform the lamentable 'The 'Ampstead Way'. There is one minor number by Hubert Gregg, 'I Hate the Morning', sung by Buchanan, and Norman Wisdom hangs on the film's coat-tails with a mercifully brief rendition of his signature anthem 'Don't Laugh at Me' written by himself and June Tremayne. Noticeably absent is a title song, when the film's title seems to be a gift; it's an odd omission. The takeaway song is Paddy Roberts and Jack Woodman's 'In Love for the Very First Time', briskly performed by Jean Carson, but it's limply choreographed around a run-down garage. Miss Carson deserved better than to be palmed off with this.

JUNE

Even the most enthusiastic admirer of director Maurice Elvey's attempts to entertain the nation would be excused for thinking **You Lucky People!** an inferior effort. The title (originally *Get Fell In*) would have been widely recognised as the catchphrase of cheeky Tommy Trinder, whose substantial film career had consolidated through the 1940s with some of the most enjoyable British musical films of that decade: *Laugh It Off* and *Sailors Three* (both 1940) and Ealing's dazzling *Champagne Charlie* and *Fiddlers Three* (both 1944). Six years later, Adelphi Films' producer David Dent offered the comedian a way back to the screen after Trinder had spent long periods abroad. Trinder, used to the resourceful finances of Ealing, was now reliant on Dent's modest company run on more frugal lines. Uncredited Fiona Clyne remembered that she was paid £12 for one day's filming, but had to bring her own costumes to the Beaconsfield studios.

The film was to have been made in colour, but Adelphi's use of the new French process Ciné Panoramique, now named Camerascope and not to be confused with the more expensive Cinemascope, was so costly (funds had already been stretched by signing their star) that the project became black and white. Used for such a modest affair as *You Lucky People!*, perhaps Camerascope was a case of stretching things a little too far, although Adelphi also used it for *Fun at St Fanny's* (1956).

Based on Sidney Nelson and Maurice Harrison's BBC Home Service 1953 radio play *Fifteen Days*, the Antony Verley screenplay was bolstered with additional dialogue by Peter Aldersley and, sensibly, Trinder. The results were dismal, with a lacklustre cast obliged to wade through material that would have disgraced a shabby provincial panto. When Trinder tells Dora Bryan's doe-eyed Sergeant Hortense Tipp, 'I think I'm a misogynist', she replies, 'Oh, you can get treatment for that nowadays.' The humour seldom rises even to this level; the lines are delivered without finesse, even Trinder under par as he goes through a string of gags with Mr Elvey's stupefied extras standing around.

Again, a decade after the war was over, here was a British film centred on the comic aspects of British army life. It was by no means the last gasp of the genre. Two years later, Independent Television began *The Army Game*, a comedy series about life in barracks that flourished until 1961. *You Lucky People!* followed the adventure of Tommy Smart (Trinder), now a successful and wealthy businessman called back by the government to attend a compulsory refresher course imposed on men who had enrolled during the war as 'Z Men' (Class Z reservists). Ultimately, the film does none of its inhabitants any favours. The slapstick scenes, notably in the army canteen when Trinder and Private Sally Briggs concoct an unsavoury stew for the constantly barking Sergeant-Major Thickpenny (Rufus Cruickshank), mark a nadir in the proceedings with performances and antics that would never have got by in a Mancunian film.

For some reason, there is a glimpse of Max Bygraves singing a snatch of something called 'Opportunity' on a television screen, and Rolf Harris in a nondescript cameo draws a cartoon of Thickpenny. In time, Harris famously painted the Queen of England, who subsequently returned it to him. Some decent musical numbers might have brightened things up, but instead we have two totally unmemorable songs credited to Eric Moss: Trinder's 'Who Puts Stripes on the Humbug?' and his duet with Sally (Mary Parker) 'Top Secret'.

The industry's press whooped with delight at the film, with *Today's Cinema* reporting it as 'expertly handled by the doyen of English directors',[8] and the picture did good business. To Dent and Adelphi's surprise, in the absence of any other major film, the official premiere of *You Lucky People!* became the centrepiece of the year's Cinema Exhibitors' Association conference in a wet and windy Llandudno, although Trinder was now in summer season at Great Yarmouth's Windmill Theatre. Like George Formby before him, he had established a strong link with that venue and the holidaymakers in what was to some the Blackpool of East Anglia. For many years, travellers through the Acle Marshes en route to Yarmouth passed a derelict cowshed that had been cleft in two. A huge poster on either side of the crack read, 'I've split my sides laughing at Tommy Trinder.'

AUGUST

Sergei Nolbandov's production *Value for Money*, a Vista Vision and Technicolor comedy made at Pinewood, had a decent script by R. F. Delderfield and William Fairchild, based on a novel by Derrick Boothroyd. It owed much to Alex Vetchinsky's wonderfully glum grimy up-North décor. We get the message in the opening shots as the town's band (played by the Hanwell Silver Band) march through the rain-sodden streets of Barfield led by their miserable conductor (Charles Victor). Barfield, we are informed, 'is no beauty. Its pride is its "rag and shoddy" wool trades. It firmly believes that where there's muck there's money. It has plenty of both.'

We meet Chayley Broadbent (the 'son' of J. H. Broadbent and Son, Rag Merchants, played by John Gregson) on the day of his penny-pinching father's funeral. Father and son have the reputation of being 'too mean to part with the steam off their porridge'. Chayley's father has stipulated in his will that his coffin handles will be brass, and Chayley barters with the undertaker to get a reduction on the price of the wreath. In fact, he has been left a fortune. On a works outing to London's West End, he is taken on stage at the Prince of Wales Theatre by glamorous Ruthine West (Diana Dors). Her interest is spurred when she discovers Chayley's wealth. Good sense ultimately prevails when he returns to his homely, sensible sweetheart Ethel (Susan Stephen). John Gregson and Diana Dors worked well as the star-crossed lovers, beyond them a splendid supporting cast: Frank Pettingell as pompous Mayor Higgins, Hal Osmond, Joan Hickson, and Ernest Thesiger's silent elderly gentleman at the opening of a kiddie's playground. Throughout, there are deftly witty touches by director Ken Annakin, but not enough to please the *MFB*, for which the two stars fought 'a losing battle with the script'.[9]

Malcolm Arnold's fine score is supplemented by the musical sequence at the Prince of Wales's revue, 'tamely executed' according to the *MFB*.[10] The two numbers are by composer John Pritchett and lyricists Peter Myers and Ronnie Cass, all three from the world of London intimate revue, then enjoying its heyday. Neither item is of much note, and 'Dolly Polka' of almost no significance, although sung by one of Myers and Cass's favourite revue artistes, Ronnie Stevens. 'Toys for Boys' is another typically workmanlike number from the Myers–Cass songbook, but it's worth seeking out, the song and dance routine framed by Vetchinsky's modernistic décor. For this brief time, the world of London revues takes over in a routine brilliantly danced by Paddy Stone and Irving Davies, accompanied by female dancers including Eleanor Fazan (herself the director of some of the Myers–Cass shows), Amanda Barrie, Pamela Davis, Frances Pidgeon, Mavis Traill, and Sheila O'Neill.

SEPTEMBER

Rank's executive producer Earl St John had invested heavily in Norman Wisdom's potential as a major film performer. The evidence was on screen for the third of the unfolding Wisdom comedies, **Man of the Moment**, sporting higher production values than its predecessors and those that followed it. Produced by Hugh Stewart and based on a story by Maurice Cowan, the screenplay by Vernon Sylvaine and director John Paddy Carstairs had our Norman as a humble Foreign Office clerk who finds himself responsible for the remote volcanic island of Tawaki. The various problems are resolved when Tawaki obligingly sinks into the sea, by which time he has been united with Penny (Lana Morris). The chaotic sequences follow fast one on another, not least Norman's entanglement with a television studio when he interrupts the soufflé-making of the BBC's first television chef Philip Harben, announcer MacDonald Hobley, awkward grouchy Grandma (Nancy Roberts) from the BBC's soap opera *The Grove Family*, an apache act, an acrobatic troupe, and a ballet. The songs are lightweight and unmemorable, with the title song performed by the Beverley Sisters and three numbers for the star: Jack Fishman's 'Yodelee Yodelay', Arthur Groves and Peter Carroll's 'Dream for Sale' (in which Morris duets), and Norman's own composition 'Beware'.

Noting an improvement in story and script, for the *MFB* the film was:

'still overladen with an overbearing superfluity of unrestrained, frantic incident, which gives the comedian no chance at all to display his qualities in any sort of repose [...] Between the consequent exhaustion and embarrassment, it is easy to overlook the moments of real comedy; but there are enough to show that, given opportunity and discipline, Wisdom might still be a good film clown.'[11]

Noting that the film had 'negligible export appeal' and its musical numbers 'are neatly staged and warmly delivered', *Variety* agreed that 'Instead of giving the star a chance to show his ability as a talented artist, the producers are content to let him indulge in crude, broad slapstick [...] and as an extra gimmick there's a wild chase through television studios'.[12] Australia applauded a picture that showed Wisdom as 'seriously capable of challenging American comedians like Abbot, Costello, Dean Martin and Jerry Lewis on their own territory'.[13]

Two years later, reviewing Wisdom's *Just My Luck* (a film it thought might be his best so far), the *Observer* offered kindly advice: 'I do wish that some humane person would take the little man aside, and persuade him that he's far nicer and much more of a personality when he's not struggling to be funny.'[14]

NOVEMBER

Johann Strauss's *Die Fledermaus* premiered in Vienna in 1874 before accumulating its international reputation as what Richard Traubner has described as '*the* Viennese Golden Age operetta *in excelsis*'.[15] Michael Powell and Eric Pressburger's reinterpretation for the screen, carried out (essentially) with Hein Heckroth, has an undeniable stamp of brilliance, obvious if not consistent. In Powell and Pressburger's hands as writers, producers, and directors, the work is transposed to modern-day (i.e. 1955) Vienna, still enduring the post-war occupation shared by the British, French, American, and Russian forces. There is nothing inappropriate in such a rethinking. After all, one of the reasons for the initial sensation of Strauss's operetta was its up-to-dateness. The strikingly original opening tableaux of **Oh ... Rosalinda!!** are among the most effective, preparing us for a work clearly leaning to political satire. At one moment we even see a film within the film, as if its creators are preparing us to accept something somewhere between reality and fantasy. Coming from those responsible for *The Red Shoes*, *A Canterbury Tale*, and *The Life and Times of Colonel Blimp*, this is no surprise.

This is a film thoroughly contained within itself, keeping itself to itself, without adventuring, as it were, on location. In the circumstances, we accept the fire engine (one of the most enchanting visual delights). Courtesy of Heckroth's fantastic taste, that brave little contraption bears little resemblance to the real world, and has obviously raced to the rescue all the way from Toytown. Here, and time and again but, again, not consistently, the occasion is enhanced by Heckroth's use and exploitation and meld of colour and, in this respect at least, The Archers' film shimmers with extraordinary effect.

A stellar cast has been assembled, not all of whom do their own singing (for which we may be grateful). As the seductive Rosalinda, Ludmilla Tchérina has her songs dubbed by Sári Barabas, Mel Ferrer's virile Yankee Captain Alfred Westerman is sung by Alexander Young, Dennis Price's very British Major Frank is sung by a Sadler's Wells favourite of the time, Denis Dowling, and Anton Walbrook's sinuous Dr Falke by Walter Berry. Mismatches between the character's speaking and singing voices are liable to bring us to attention (Price's singing seems especially unlikely), and some poor lip-synching does not help matters. More happily, Michael Redgrave, a surprisingly spry Colonel Eisenstein even when cavorting in his underwear, and Anneliese Rothenberger as a delightful Adele sing their own vocals.

The film is a feast for the eye and, often, for the ear, but despite the wealth of its components, our emotions are not engaged. It is a crowded canvas with little of substance, frequently accompanied by Alfred Rodrigues's rhubarbing choreography (a real disappointment), which is contained between Walbrook's opening and closing speeches. As we have been enticed so effectively into the story by so eminent and brilliant an actor, it seems a shame that nothing strikingly substantial or touching is within, and tedium sets in. At the original stage performance's dress rehearsal in1874, the original Rosalinda, Maria Geistinger, disapproved of one scene because 'It's so boring when no one says a word for so long.' In *Oh ... Rosalinda!!* there are patches where both music and dialogue stretch the patience.

Without Pressburger, Powell went on to direct two more musical film productions, both designed by Heckroth. Neither is British. *Oh ... Rosalinda!!*'s lyricist Dennis Arundell provided the English script for the ballet film *The Sorcerer's Apprentice*, made in Germany in 1955. Its original thirty-minute duration was cut to thirteen minutes. Powell and Heckroth's final collaboration in Austria was their splendidly glum 1963 filming of Béla Bartók's *Herzog Blaubarts Burg* (*Bluebeard's Castle*). As Ian Christie has written, this 'stands as a final proof of The Archers' and Powell's claim that the essential unity of art can best be realised in cinema.'[16]

For *The Times*, *Oh ... Rosalinda!!* 'might have been impressive, amusing and enjoyable if only it had not been so brashly self-confident in its approach'. Furthermore, 'Powell and Pressburger are given to the belief that you cannot have too much of a good thing and that enough is nothing like as good as a feast.'[17] Hoping that its producers might move on to making a film based on the work of 'a British composer', *Films and Filming* saw 'none of the vitality of the Hollywood musical; but it does have gaiety, so rare in present day cinema.'[18] There was little to commend according to the *MFB*'s criticism of the 'elephantine treatment. The plot loses itself in hopeless convolutions; the presentation of songs and comedy alike is wearingly heavy; the design is a scrapbook of a sort of Teutonic House-and-Garden contemporary.'[19] The *Sketch* told its readers, 'the whole thing is prankish, stylised and a little vulgar.'[20] As observed by Ian Christie in 1985, the film 'now looks like another isolated prototype for a British cinema or ironic parody and stylistic *bricolage*. It combines some of Heckroth's most outrageous invention in studio décor with a determinedly *realist* approach to the operetta form.'[21]

In the *Illustrated London News*, Alan Dent saw little to celebrate in 'a frisky and savourless and tawdrily decorated version [...] One would ask, at this time of day, whether the sparkling music need be quite so poorly played and recorded. There is no excuse for such feeble reproduction in these days.'[22] David Robinson concluded that Powell and Pressburger 'even in their out-and-out failures like *Oh ... Rosalinda!!* have more invention and magic than most other films of their day.'[23]

In November 1954, looking forward to the filming of ***King's Rhapsody***, Anna Neagle told *Picture Post*'s Robert Muller

> I'll play the Phyllis Dare part – it will have to be built up of course – and it's quite a new departure. I have always liked playing parts which cover the years. We [she and Herbert Wilcox] like Pleasant People. Pleasant People

and Pleasant Things. Something that is not outside the realm of possibility, but that sends people out of the cinema with a kind of glow in their hearts.[24]

Muller wanted to know 'how Miss Neagle reacted to some of the vitriolic criticisms that some of her film and stage appearances have provoked. 'I never read the critics,' she replied. 'Herbert doesn't like me to be distressed. The critics are not like they were in the old days.'[25]

Determined to send cinemagoers home 'with a kind of glow in their hearts', Anna Neagle teamed with Errol Flynn for *King's Rhapsody* (1955), a fog of pomp and too much circumstance that weighed down Ivor Novello's last major operetta. The *Monthly Film Bulletin* regretted that 'the nonsense is magnified grotesquely'.

By now, Wilcox had probably abandoned his plan to follow up with Novello's *Perchance to Dream* as reported in *The Times* in July 1953. The splendour of *King's Rhapsody* was to be enhanced by location shooting in Yugoslavia, where 'the combined ballets of [the country] will be used in the production, which is to be made with the help of the Yugoslavian film industry and will be able to call on the services of 10,000 extras.'[26]

Originally, the film version of the last musical play written and composed by Ivor Novello was to have been made by Associated British and directed by Brian Desmond Hurst, who had been responsible for their 1937 *Glamorous Night*. Along the way, it was whispered that no less than Ronald Colman, Tyrone Power, and Douglas Fairbanks were eager to take on the role of Nikki, an apparently dissolute prince of Laurentia (a principality not on any map). Nikki is emotionally entangled with not only a 'snow princess' of a politically-arranged wife, but an ageing mistress. Novello had played, or perhaps more accurately glided inimitably through, the role on stage when the show opened at the Palace Theatre in 1949. It marked the apex of his career as writer, composer, and actor. There was no doubt that the piece worked, as the *Daily Telegraph* reluctantly admitted:

> The whole affair, though slightly preposterous, is astonishingly efficient: romantic story, neat dialogue, easy music, attractive settings, busy dancing – rather too busy at times – are all there, directed with skill by Murray Mac-Donald and all testifying alike to Mr Novello's unrivalled supply of trumps.[27]

This review, alas, is for the stage version; by 1955 the critics had changed their tune. In October 1954 it was announced that Herbert Wilcox had agreed to pay Errol Flynn £2,500,000 for between five and six films over the next three years, beginning with *King's Rhapsody*. The dust had quickly settled on the Ivor Novello phenomenon after Novello's death in 1951, almost as if his entire glamorous world of theatre had left the stage and turned out the light. Novello, ever a wise theatrical, had been conscious of changing tastes and was determined that *King's Rhapsody* would be his last, in many ways most resplendent, throw of the dice – essentially, his farewell to Ruritania. There would be one more stage musical, the 1951 *Gay's the Word*, a vehicle in lighter vein for Cicely Courtneidge, in which Novello even parodied the idea of Ruritania. In effect, Novello realised what Wilcox did not: the theatre and public were about to call time on Ruritanian extravaganzas. We may now see Wilcox's rash arrangement with Flynn as one of the several factors that would culminate in Wilcox's bankruptcy. It is no surprise that Flynn, *Lilacs in the Spring*, and *King's Rhapsody* go unmentioned in his autobiography.

The problems of adapting successful stage musicals to the screen had been abundantly illustrated in British cinema from 1929 onwards. The problems persisted. Wilcox seems to have misunderstood the very real difference between stage spectacle (on which Novello was an expert) and cinematic spectacle (which Wilcox looked at, as it were, from the wrong end of the telescope). For all its sudden bursts of ensembled splendour, not least in its final cathedral scene, the stage play is a pretty modest affair, an affair in the hands of a small number of characters armed with songs ringing with simplistic romanticism and occasionally rising to splashes of musical and scenic abandon. In all this, Novello never overreaches himself. We may disagree as to the amount of tosh he offers us, but the tosh is never vulgar, cheaply produced, tasteless, or over-garnished.

And so to Wilcox, making good on his promise by reuniting Neagle and Flynn after their partnership in *Lilacs in the Spring*, a box-office success that decidedly marked the end of Wilcox's and Neagle's glory days. There is not a distinguished or memorable line in *King's Rhapsody*, not a shred of wit in the screenplay of Pamela Bower, a regular writer for the Wilcox stable. Her subsequent screenplays for *The Heart of a Man* and *The Lady Is a Square* suggest that she had learned nothing from the feeble narrative of *King's Rhapsody*, which she had committed in collaboration with Novello's lyricist Christopher Hassall and A. P. Herbert. One can only think that these notable literary figures treated 'pictures' with disdain; they must have realised that Novello would have been dissatisfied with the result.

Without any signal of human emotion, Wilcox lays every excess at the picture's feet: hordes of extras lifting their fists in unison at signs of rebellion; no end of flaming torches held aloft (these are possibly obligatory in Novello; they are in the 1937 film of Novello's *Glamorous Night* too); trunks full of Anthony Holland's ridiculously inappropriate costumes for the leading ladies; a Niagara Falls flush of Robert Farnon's background music swishing meaninglessly around throughout; oodles of obsequious bowing and scraping at royal levees; lingering shots of Spanish mountains that closely resemble elephant dung; too much of Mutz Greenbaum's muddy photography and the unreality of William C. Andrews's sets. The whole envelops us in a fog of pomp and much too much circumstance. As the legend imprinted on the screen pompously informs us, we are about to visit 'a country of strange contrasts – the tenderness of romance, the venom of intrigue – and here, beneath these bastions of rock, we lay our story'.

There is, of course, something vaguely resembling acting. Top-billed Neagle will not disappoint her admirers, always arriving and leaving the screen with dignity and sometimes breaking into her strangely budgerigar vocalisations. Her memory of her love for Nikki (for some unfathomable reason rechristened here as Rikki) is remembered in 'The Years Together', written for the film. For Miss Neagle, all emotion is conveyed by mannerism, a style of acting that owes much to the fact that only once in her career did she work with a director other than Wilcox.

Flynn's deal with Wilcox handed the role of Cristiane, played on stage by Vanessa Lee, to Flynn's wife Patrice Wymore. We know why she is referred to as the 'snow princess' because she first comes into view running up and down in an unconvincing Elstree landscape of the white stuff, looking for all the world like a refugee from one of the big ice shows that were then so popular. We fully understand that Miss Lee may not have been film material, but Wymore is a poor substitute, lumbered with some ridiculously coy moments and much twirling, not least in Jon Gregory's dream sequence ballet with masked male dancers.

Flynn has been much criticised for the remoteness of his performance, the nonchalance, the fact that he seems to be impersonating the public perception of the actor's life rather than Rikki's. Certainly, he behaves in several scenes as if he has just been forcibly dragged out of bed into the film studio after a night on the plebeian tiles. Some have detected in his performance a want of majesty. From a personal perspective (the author once played 'Nikki' on stage and came in for exactly that criticism) this may be an unjust judgement. The role needs to be played as if it is 'the morning after the night before' if its closing scenes are to have any emotional bite. Only then at final curtain does Nikki show a much-needed maturity, warmth, sense of duty to his people. He grows up. He matures five minutes before final curtain. Flynn manages to do this (to some extent), only to be let down by Wilcox in the final shots. Having parted from Marta, he returns to Laurentia for his son's coronation, watching it discreetly from behind a pillar. When the cathedral empties, he walks to the altar. Wilcox tracks him walking away from the camera. Would the impact of the moment have been more effective if Wilcox had kept a close-up of his face as he made this meaningful journey? All that Wilcox achieves is to remove us even more from the emotional heart of the story, and to prevent Flynn from having to convey emotion. Nevertheless, clever actors can act with their backs. He stands before the altar. By now, the camera itself is almost hiding behind the pillar and does not encroach on his thoughts. Cristiane enters (at least we suppose it is Cristiane; the camera is so far away that we can only surmise) to stand beside him. Robbed of Novello's brilliant stage ending to the drama, with Cristiane's off-stage snatch of 'Someday My Heart Will Awake' as Nikki takes up the rose she has left for him while the curtain falls to a quietened orchestra, Wilcox leaves Flynn and Wymore looking as if they are waiting for a number 20 bus.

The *MFB* regretted that on screen 'the nonsense is magnified grotesquely' and that Wymore

> has the lifeless sparkle of a ventriloquist's dummy, while Errol Flynn has none of the required royal grace. Anna Neagle, on the other hand, suits per-fectly the role of Marta [...] Her own sturdy assurance carries her through some moments of considerable difficulty, presented by the stilted script, some singularly graceless costumes and one grotesque love-scene between herself (in the style of a coy, sensible British virgin) and Flynn (ageing Yankee wolf).[28]

The *Evening Standard* reported that 'The décor may be Ruritanian, but the emotions were pure West Kensington.'[29] The *Financial Times* summed up the experience as 'a blizzard of candy-floss whipped up by a wind machine', describing Neagle as 'the most daring lady in Eastbourne' and her leading man as 'a wastrel footballer bringing shame on his father's meat-packing firm.'[30] More charitably, *The Times* admitted that 'There is one abominable dream sequence, but, in general, the film provides some gorgeous scenes and moments of spectacle and is a generous, uninhibited, un-self-conscious splurge of, as it should be, nonsense.'[31]

The ultimate sadness for any Novello groupie is that no space was found to include the great Olive Gilbert, the sturdiest of Welsh contraltos, who interrupted the flow of the stage production with her deep-plumbed rendition of two of the best numbers, 'Fly Home, Little Dove' and the jocular 'Take Your Girl'. She is much missed in an irredeemable film that does disservice to Novello's reputation. I am reliably informed that in Novello's flat after returning from the theatre, Miss Gilbert regularly retired to the kitchen to prepare his cheese-on-toast supper.

After the success of Howard Hawks's Twentieth Century-Fox's *Gentlemen Prefer Blondes* (1953), based on the 1949 stage musical with its Jule Styne–Leo Robin songs that included Marilyn Monroe informing us that 'Diamonds Are a Girl's Best Friend', Hollywood looked to Anita Loos's follow-up novel **Gentlemen Marry Brunettes**. Contrarily, director Richard Sale and his screenplay collaborator Mary Loos borrowed the title but changed the plot. Jane Russell (Monroe's co-star in *Gentlemen Prefer Blondes*) was now Bonnie Jones, co-starring with Jeanne Crain as Connie Jones – sisters determined to make it in showbusiness. Lavishly staged flashbacks demonstrate the adventures of their 1930s progenitors, Mimi and Mitzi Jones, putting the roar into the 1920s.

Although the Russ–Field production released by United Artists was classified as American, not one foot of it was shot in the States, with *Kinematograph Weekly* referring to it as a British production.[32] Russell and Crain rehearsed Jack Coles's choreography at Chelsea Guards Barracks, and sequences were filmed at Shepperton and Boreham Wood, as well as location work in Paris and Monte Carlo. One of the most spectacular screen musicals of the 1950s, it has an attractive cast (including Alan Young, Scott Brady, and veteran Rudy Vallée as himself) who play the material for all it is worth, with various set pieces, not least a splendid over-the-top fashion parade, breaking through.

Herbert Spencer and Earle Hagen's title song is the only original number in a score that favours well-tried favourites. Also heard are Herbert Stothart, Harry Ruby, and Bert Kalmar's 'I Wanna Be Loved by You'; Rodgers and Hart's 'Have You Met Miss Jones?', 'My Funny Valentine', and 'I've Got Five Dollars'; Bobby Troup's 'Daddy'; Sidney Clare and Lew Pollack's 'Miss Annabelle Lee'; Walter Donaldson's 'You're Driving Me Crazy' and Fats Waller, Harry Brooks, and Andy Razaf's 'Ain't Misbehavin', this sung by Young dressed as a gorilla in a tree.

Unamused, the *MFB* decided that 'Brash, strident and in general scarcely remarkable for its good taste, this is a musical which attempts sophistication in dialogue and settings and achieves only a jaded and spurious brand of smartness.' It was 'Altogether, a disconcerting and inexpert production.'[33] The *New York Times* saw 'an aimless, uninspired charade' and 'witless adventure'; 'it is simple to understand why gentlemen prefer blondes'. As for the two stars, 'one wonders how they got involved in this witless adventure.'[34] It seems a harsh judgement on a film that so obviously does its best to keep us, if not enthralled, entertained.

Perhaps the various elements refused to knit together, but there was a certain quaintness about the 1955 *An Alligator Named Daisy*.

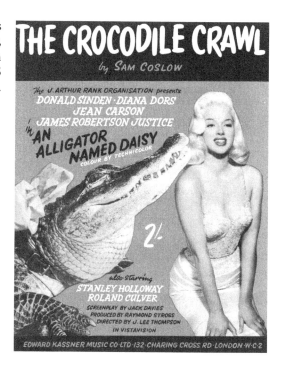

DECEMBER

Beyond its casting of an army of character actors and its fleeting guest artistes familiar to television audiences, Rank's *An Alligator Named Daisy*, adapted from Charles Terrot's novel with screenplay by Jack Davies and produced at Pinewood for Rank by Raymond Stross Productions, was directed by J. Lee Thompson. Donald Sinden was Peter Weston, the owner of the friendly reptile in question. Sinden, whose one stage musical role in the 1960 *Joie de Vivre* conclusively proved he could not sing, is not required to do so. The quaintness is accentuated, the light touch missed, and there should be more and better of

Jean Carson, for too long trapped in the long-running West End musical *Love from Judy*. It is no wonder Miss Carson upped and took herself to America, which did its best to cherish her. She has the only number that has had any afterlife, Paddy Roberts and Jack Woodman's 'I'm In Love for the Very First Time', roughly choreographed around a dirty garage. Sam Coslow provided the workmanlike other numbers, Carson's 'Midnight Madness', 'Your First Love Was Your Last' sung by Ronnie Stevens, and Ken Mackintosh and His Band performing 'The Crocodile Crawl'.

The Times complained that 'three quarters way through [it] surrenders to the kind of knock-about farce which went down well in the days of the Keystone cops'.[35] For *Films and Filming* it was 'a charming idea, but the story does not do justice to the theme'.[36] 'It remains a mystery to me', wrote C. A. Lejeune, 'why they chose to make a film about an alligator when they have got Miss Carson.'[37] The *MFB* didn't hold back, reporting that 'Little wit or comic invention, and aimless direction produces flat performances from the principals and gives small scope to the remarkable collection of small-part talent.' What was more, 'the staging of Jean Carson's dance sequences are deplorably unimaginative'.[38] *Variety* found it 'a somewhat disorganised merriment that disintegrates into uninspired farce'.[39]

Harold Brooke and Kay Bannerman's farce **All for Mary** was a mild West End stage success in 1954, largely thanks to Kathleen Harrison's performance as Nannie Cartwright. Rank's opening-up of the play ('contrived, stilted and pedestrian' according to the *Stage*[40]) involved a rigorous reworking of the original plot by director Paul Soskin and Peter Blackmore, with additional dialogue by that master of light confection Alan Melville. The humour depended heavily on the nursery atmosphere and (for those seeking subtext) on the threatened regression to childhood when mature males fall into the hands of state-registered nurses. Scenes of the Alps in Eastmancolor fleshed out the story of Nannie's looking after two grown men quarantined with measles as if they were her little charges. You can almost hear the theatre curtain coming down as Nannie makes her first entrance bearing gifts: a teddy bear and a model yacht. David Tomlinson and Nigel Patrick work hard to enliven the unlikely proceedings, Tomlinson having been retained from the stage production but now playing the role of 'Humpy'.

Robert Farnon's title song with its Norman Newell lyric is sung by the Stargazers. Jill Day, displaying no enthusiasm about acting, is a little out of place, at one point announcing with not a shred of doubt, 'There's a fancy dress party tonight and I'm going as an ostrich.' She seems little more at home when singing Milton Delugg and Bob Hilliard's cabaret act number 'Far Away from Everybody'. We watch on because of the always welcome Harrison, wondering what might have happened had director Wendy Toye insisted her star should sing.

1956

At St Fanny's, the boys could expect a sound education, answering life's important questions. What, after all, is an herbaceous border? A lodger who only eats vegetables.

Fun at St Fanny's

Fun at St Fanny's	*A Touch of the Sun*
Charley Moon	*On the Twelfth Day*
It's Great to Be Young	*Stars in Your Eyes*
Ramsbottom Rides Again	*Up in the World*
Invitation to the Dance	*Five Guineas a Week*
It's a Wonderful World	

JANUARY

By the mid-1950s the veteran director Maurice Elvey was in the final phase of a career that had prospered since 1913 with his first feature, Motograph Film Company's silent *Maria Marten*. He not only directed but wrote it and appeared as Captain Matthews. Before the advent of sound, he had 123 films to his credit; between 1930 and his death in 1967, he added another sixty-three, among which are several significant British films (many of them musical) that served as vehicles for leading performers of their day: Gracie Fields in *Sally in Our Alley* (1930), *This Week of Grace* (1933), and *Love, Life and Laughter* (1934); Ivor Novello in the brilliant *I Lived with You* (1933); *Soldiers of the King* (1933) for Cicely Courtneidge, and *Under Your Hat* (1940) for Courtneidge and Jack Hulbert; *Road House* (1934) for Violet Loraine and Gordon Harker; and *Princess Charming* (1934) for Evelyn Laye. His last pictures from the mid-1950s include three tightly budgeted entertainments, including Tommy Trinder in the army-life comedy *You Lucky People* (1955) and in 1956 **Fun at St Fanny's** and *Stars in Your Eyes*, two films that seem to accentuate the very particular tastes of a director (and deviser) still, at the age of eighty, displaying a greedy appetite for innocent enjoyment. Courtesy of Elvey, a visit to St Fanny's will answer many questions that may confound us. What are the inhabitants of Malta called? The boys at St Fanny's have the answer: Maltesers.

By 1956, the British fondness for shows built around young boys at public schools and their not infrequently ill-educated and intoxicated teachers was nothing short of excessive. Will Hay had exploited the formula through the 1930s, appearing as Dr Alec Smart (think *vice versa*) in the 1935 *Boys Will Be Boys* and Dr Twist in *Good Morning, Boys*. During World War II, Hay was tutoring German pupils in *The Goose Steps Out* (1942), notably instructing them in how to give the 'V' sign. In November 1957, the highly popular 'weekly school report' *Whack-O!* premiered on British television, starring the artful, corporal-punishment-enthusiast headmastership of 'Professor' Jimmy Edwards as the headmaster of Chiselbury public school. A radio series followed in 1961.

Also by 1956, the cream-cake-devouring 'fat owl' of Greyfriars, Billy Bunter, was known throughout the land via a BBC Television series that ran from 1952 to 1961. Bunter's shrieks of 'Yaroo!' echoed from the pages of school stories by Frank Richards (alias Charles Hamilton) in the boys' magazine *The Magnet* These unlikely schoolchildren were eventually joined by 'Cardew the Cad of the School'. Cardew had been part of British culture since 1949 when his adventures, inspired by one of Richard's 'St Jim's' stories, were cartooned by Reg Partlett in the comic *Radio Fun*. Widely enjoyed as these school-based diver-

sions were, not one of them had transmuted into a musical entertainment until *Fun at St Fanny's*, the school where Cardew the Cad (Cardew Robinson) remained at the unlikely age of twenty-six. Even more unlikely, Robinson himself was thirty-eight.

It is, of course, Elvey who is ultimately responsible for the fun at St Fanny's, although some share must be taken by David Dent, who produced for Advance Films and Grand Alliance. Bolstered by Peter Noble and Denis Waldock's story and adaptation, and additional dialogue by Fred Emney, the screenplay by Anthony Verney is merely a device on which to impose a seemingly inexhaustible parade of very old gags. It is as well that they seem not to have lost their efficacy, for which we must principally thank the star of Elvey's enterprise, Fred Emney. Indeed, it is Mr Emney's willingness to display his ample proportions (especially

Among the delights of Adelphi's carefree frolic *Fun at St Fanny's* (1956) were Fred Emney tickling the ivories and dusting the keyboard and modelling some startling beach-wear, pleasant American import Johnny Brandon, and Francis Langford's Singing Scholars.

in some eye-catching swimwear) that provides one of the many reasons for watching. He also appears to striking effect as a scoutmaster and his own sister. As she explains, 'The only difference between us is that my moustache is a little thicker.' If only one reason is needed to visit St Fanny's for fun, Mr Emney owns it. His brief recital at the piano is a comic gem that may forever affect how you look at popular pianists. There is also the strenuous twisting routine he enjoys with St Fanny's French mistress before tossing her about above his head. He excels, too, in a protracted attempt to spell 'pernicious' and 'incoherent'. Mr Emney may seem one of the most grumpy of comic actors; he is certainly one of the funniest, with a style to which he has exclusive rights. He is comedy gold, and the most is made of him here.

We can only regret the *MFB*'s inability to enjoy such tomfoolery, its critic reporting only that 'The talents of excellent music-hall performers [...] are atrophied by the wretched story and puerile dialogue of this depressing farce.'[1] The *Times* agreed, finding 'farce of the crudest order'.[2] The film was launched as one half of a double-bill with Adelphi's comedy mystery *Miss Tulip Stays the Night*, in which the greatest mystery was why Cicely Courtneidge and Jack Hulbert agreed to take inferior billing to Diana Dors.

In fact, *Fun at St Fanny's* is chock-a-block with well-observed cameos: Miriam Karlin as the hard-bitten private eye sent to the school to investigate the Cad's situation; Gabrielle Brune's amiable school matron; Peter Butterworth on television as a camp potter at his wheel (reminding us of this 'filling-in' film when BBC Television had run out of programmes); Stanley Unwin as a gallery guide describing modern sculptures. It is appropriate that the Henry Moore school of sculptures (involving gaping holes) should be described in Unwin's invented nonsense language of Unwinese. Indeed, this is typical of Elvey's sly approach to his comedy.

We must also thank Elvey for St Fanny's musical outbursts, including the brief romancing of Vera Day by Cardew in 'I'd Love to Learn All About You' (Cardew its lyricist, Norrie Paramor its composer). The opening credits introduce St Fanny's school anthem, 'The ABC Song', in expectation of the ultimate school concert with its embarrassment of riches. Chief among these is Welsh promoter Francis Langford's Singing Scholars making their only known film appearance. In 1952 the group was already thriving in the variety tour *Lads and Laughter*: 'The Greatest Parade of Youth Ever Presented by Francis Langford and the Welsh Miners' Boy Choir: 15 Voices of Wales in a Teen-Age Sensation', plus guest artiste Violet Evans, the '15-year-old Wonder Girl Soprano', supported by such as Jimmy Foote (Phenomenal Boy Whistler) and Pamela's Royal Wolf Hounds.[3]

Prominent in Langford's company was 'the Welsh Recording Boy Soprano Graham Jones'. It may be that this is the boy who (as 'Jones Minor, The Boy With The Wonder Voice') sings the solo part in the hymn-like 'There But For the Grace of God Go I'. The scholars also throw themselves into Bob Merrill's 1954 hit 'Mambo Italiano' and provide a backing for Johnny Brandon performing his own soft-shoe number (credited to Ed Franks) 'Anyone Can Be a Millionaire'. Through it all, Robinson is an amiable, highly likeable presence, a preposterously tall, angular bean-pole with protruding teeth. In the closing scene, he gets to play a gormless Hamlet in a potty version of Shakespeare's tragedy, with Gerald Campion as Ophelia, in which the rhyming couplets are worthy of a Planché pantomime.

A year after Langford's scholars became film stars, his organisation was still going strong, advertising for 'boy sopranos as soloists and choristers. Two-year engagement, also talented boys, 14–18, all types of voices. Young pianist under 20, boy for wardrobe. Chance for bright beginners.'[4] At St Fanny's, the boys could expect a sound education, answering life's important questions. What, after all, is an herbaceous border?

A lodger who only eats vegetables.

MARCH

The opening phrases of Francis Chagrin's background score momentarily make us think we are about to see a work of importance. As produced at Shepperton by Aubrey Baring and Colin Leslie, and written by Leslie Bricusse but 'adapted' by John Cresswell from a novel by Reginald Arkell, the film quickly disabuses us. Can this really be just another claptrap warming-up of the ancient theme of rags to riches? This one is different: it's almost a case of rags to riches to rags.

What is it about *Charley Moon*, sixty-six years after its debut, that remains so dispiriting? Is it the murky Eastmancolor that casts a pall over everything? Is it all to do with the casting: Dennis Price at his stiffest and most predictable as hammy old pro Harold Armytage, forever going on about his press notices in provincial rag-newspapers; Florence Desmond in the seriously underwritten role of difficult ageing leading lady (Desmond's acceptance of the part smacks of desperation); Shirley Eaton's vacant glamour; Patricia Driscoll (perhaps re-membered for turning the pages of BBC Children's Television's *Picture Book*, and Richard Greene's Maid Marion in ITV's *The Adventures of Robin Hood*) with nothing to do as the star's childhood sweetheart? What of the dance routines arranged by Vida Hope and George Erskine-Jones? Hope was best known for directing Sandy Wilson's stage musical *The Boy Friend*. Her skills had nothing at all to do with choreography; she was all about period theatre, having been nursed in that abiding sanctuary of pastiche, the Players' Theatre.

The songs of Leslie Bricusse and his lyricist Robin Beaumont do little more than fill gaps. The one exception is their fondly bucolic 'Out of Town', ridicu-lously staged (Hope's fault, perhaps) with ancient, toothless crones leaning over rustic gates while scantily dressed village maidens frolic. It's a sad indication that although Bricusse and Beaumont had written a decent number, nobody concerned with the production knew what to do with it. The other songs come unbidden and go unmourned: a funnyman routine for Bygraves and Price with

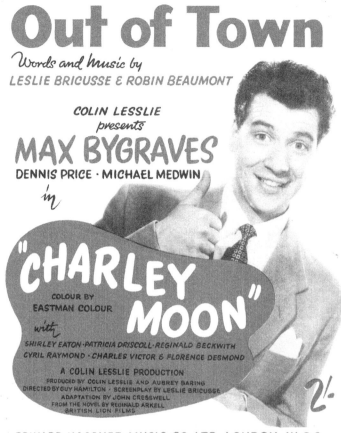

The British public cheered up when Max Bygraves came into view, and there was a vogue for Leslie Bricusse's bucolic hymn 'Out of Town', but *Charley Moon* (1956) failed to reach the sunny uplands.

'Fingers Crossed' (the star surrounded by delighted kiddies), 'It Isn't That One' (the star winning over a theatre audience against the odds), and a sort of 'rags to riches' anthem, *à la* Al Jolson, for the star to boost himself as 'The Fabulous Golden Boy', clearly intended as a parable of his celebrity: 'This is the story of a young man's rise to fame'. The level of invention is low, the lack of originality obvious, wit out of sight. There is no need for the remnant of a duet between the star and his frosty-faced leading lady in 'I'm Head Over Heels in Love'. As if acknowledging its unimportance, it peters out.

Bygraves was ill-served by a script that was 'untidy and contains few snappy lines'[5] and players who were shackled to it. Alan Dent thought that the film

> shows us that he may one day bring his good looks and his cheeky Cockney charm to full fruition on the British screen. His aim, at the moment, would seem to be to create an effortless performance rather than an innately funny one. But the effect of real effortlessness is only to be achieved by making a prodigious effort and having the art to conceal it.[6]

The *MFB* was not in word-mincing mood.

> This faltering attempt at a British musical chiefly makes one regret the lost efficiency and certainty, the unaffected freshness of British musicals of the early thirties, like *Evergreen*. The script is slack and wandering; the back-stage music-hall atmosphere is embarrassingly phoney; the characters are mainly threadbare types [...] The great misfortune of the whole thing is that Max Bygraves is most sympathetic and really talented, and that the story, fairly done, might have had genuine charm.[7]

Overall, this film has nothing to offer the senses, with its blatantly sub-standard attempts at Hollywood gloss collapsing within a country mile of the real thing. Ten years after the end of the war, it seemed unthinkable that a British studio could turn out so careless a product when America had shown the way.

MAY

The first sight of Angel Hill Grammar School's impressive façade will probably strike fear into the heart of many grammar school pupils of the late 1950s; for one horrible moment, I thought it was the façade of the City of Norwich Grammar School: no girls except for one mysteriously female secretary, a tuck shop, the ever-threatening possibility of being called to the headmaster's study, detention for misbehaviour, and playing one of the little maids from school in one of the annual Gilbert and Sullivan operas. For good or ill, Marble Arch's Angel Hill Grammar in *It's Great to Be Young* has lots of girls as well as boys (it's co-educational). Many of them are much too old to be there; they are really potential RADA fodder, a fact that robs the film of much of its integrity. The freshness of having Ted Willis's dialogue spoken by children who were young enough to get away with it may have prevented us from noticing that Mr Willis has written a script of astounding dullness. Furthermore, as Andy Medhurst detects:

> In the light of the rock-and-roll revolution breaking out all around it, *It's Great to be Young* is irritatingly coy, indelibly conformist, irretrievably English. As the whiter-than-white kids go into their neutered jitterbug and sing, with a stunning lack of conviction, 'Rhythm Is Our Business', you wonder if the British will ever be able to make a film which dealt adequately with the raw, erotic, seismic ecstasy of the new music.[8]

Ted Willis's screenplay for *It's Great to Be Young* (1956) gives us an insight into the adolescents of the mid-1950s. Unfortunately, it is through the prism of Mr Willis's understanding. Any sort of reality existed elsewhere.

Willis's blindfolded influence does nothing to convince us that these children will thrive as teenagers, does his capable cast no justice, and never develops any of the characters (the other schoolteachers are ciphers, with such as Mary Merrall given nothing to do), none of it (even more damningly) making us laugh. His story is simply told: the new headmaster at Angel Hill, dry old stick Mr Frome (Cecil Parker), disapproves of music in general ('Scraping a violin will not win scholarships!') and jazz in particular, setting himself at odds with the enthusiastic and much-loved music teacher Dingle (John Mills), whose conducting might as well be an ancient Aztec rite. With the school orchestra's future in doubt, the children rebel. Dingle quits, getting by with playing honky-tonk in a local pub (but it's probably Winifred Atwell). Chaos ensues before settlement and agreement is reached, Dingle and orchestra restored, and Frome tearful at being so loved. Romance blossoms between Nicky (Jeremy Spenser) and Paulette (Dorothy Bromiley), tremulously expressed in Ray Martin and Paddy Roberts's 'You Are My First Love', with Bromiley dubbed by Edna Savage. The song is first heard in a prologue involving two junior sweethearts as they ramble through the countryside before checking into school; on this occasion, the unseen singer is Ruby Murray.

Musically, it's a fascinating *mélange* of different styles; classical; bursts of 'My Old Man' and 'I've Got Sixpence' as Dingle (or Atwell) plays piano in the pub; Ray Martin's stirring 'Marching Strings' performed by The Coronets; John Addison's 'Scherzo' played by the London Schools Symphony Orchestra; unseen Humphrey Lyttleton and His Band's 'Jam Session'; and an extraordinary about-turn into the one big production number, quaintly choreographed by Diana Billings, 'Rhythm Is Our Business'. It is one of the oddest but most enjoyable sequences in a film that above all is a triumph of dubbing. Returning to it almost seventy years later, we may wonder what audience it was intended to please, but please them it did, turning out a box-office success, with no one more surprised than its creators. *Films and Filming* noted

> its indecisive approach. At one moment it tends to farce of *The Happiest Days of Your Life* variety. At others there are traces of Searlish [a reference to artist Ronald Searle, famed for his drawings of St Trinian's School] satire. Also there are songs and dance numbers which provide yet another flavour. However, in spite of skilful dubbing these contain insufficient musical talent to sustain them.[9]

Comparing its theme with that of Ealing's *Hue and Cry* (1947), the *MFB* thought it a 'simple, boisterous schoolboy romp', regretting that 'the sugary, American-style songs strike an alien note in such emphatically British surroundings'.[10] Accepting the schoolchildren as 'teenage rebels', Roger Mellor realises that

> they are all terribly British and middle class, just the kind of youths that were rapidly going out of fashion in 1956, finding pleasure in light classics (the enthusiasm for the school orchestra reflects the prominence of the National Youth Orchestra of Great Britain in the 1950s) and wholesome traditional jazz music [...] These kids are far removed from the juvenile delinquents found in newspaper headlines or American films – *It's Great to Be Young* is no *Blackboard Jungle*.[11]

Produced by Victor Skutezky and directed with gusto by Frankel, *It's Great to Be Young* (its very title questionable) has a soundness and general air of decency and enthusiasm which retain much of the period potency, although in the midst of such cooperative schooling there may be some who would long for nothing more than to find a disruptive newly arrived pupil (probably expelled from Greyfriars School). Yaroo!

Only the most urgent apologist for John Baxter could claim that ***Ramsbottom Rides Again*** belongs among his best work. Stripped bare of the qualities that imbue his considerable contribution to British cinema, it is not readily recommendable. No other British director maintained a hand on the tiller so determinedly throughout their career, and he never let up on films that conveyed, no matter how naively, messages about social cohesiveness. With no pretension and, as often as not, not much budget, film after film (often with Baxter writing as well as directing) evinced his homely philosophy. The modesty of their presentation has hampered an appreciation of these essentially Christian morality tales. There are few in British cinema who achieved so much in straitened circumstances, all films with Baxter's name all the way through them. We may argue over their worth as art; we surely cannot question their sincerity. A random listing of some of his best works reminds us that Baxter spent a career treading the same path, making pictures for a reason: *Doss House* (1933) and *Say It with Flowers* (1934), *The Common Touch* and *Love on the Dole* (both 1941), J. B. Priestley's *Let the People Sing* (1942) and *Judgment Deferred* (1952), even the bargain-basement *Old Mother Riley in Society* (1940), the only one of the Arthur Lucan comedies to be imbued with Baxterisms.

Ramsbottom's ride was received with limited enthusiasm, as a film 'as English as the music-hall' and 'ideal escapist fare for the industrialites and family', made of the stuff that *Kinematograph Weekly* was fond of recommending to working-class cinemagoers, or the 'masses'. Sophisticated patrons were unlikely to make for the local kinema for a picture 'as North Country as black puddings and trotters, and much more hilarious'.[12] 'To the uninitiated', confided the *MFB*, 'it will probably appear only as a shapeless hotch-potch of weak slapstick, doubtful music-hall humour [lavatories and chamber-pots are involved], old gags and unsuccessfully aimed satire'.[13]

Throughout his long career, there must have been many occasions when Baxter opened the *MFB* with foreboding; it seldom regarded him as significant. Now, he was director, producer (in concert with Jack Hylton Film Productions), and co-writer with Basil Thomas for an adaptation from Harold G. Roberts's play. Some of the blame fell on Geoffrey Orme's additional dialogue and on comedy sequences worked up by the film's star Arthur Askey, very possibly the last man standing from that oddest of art forms, British concert party, with his comedy helpmate Glenn Melvyn. In the opening scenes we might expect a sort of satire about television, if only because publican Bill Ramsbottom (Askey) is losing business because his customers are too busy watching the gogglebox to buy alcohol.

Sadly, nothing so bracing as satire emerges; that would come later with Askey and Baxter's next collaboration, *Make Mine a Million*. Instead, Bill inherits his grandfather's property in backwoods Loveless, a run-down gun-toting settlement in Canada, constantly threatened by villainous Black Jake (Sidney James in the film's best performance), and decides to emigrate with his family. The boat journey from England finds the script and Bill's family all at sea in more senses than one, including wife Florrie (Betty Marsden struggling to maintain a t'up-North accent, and daughter Joan played by Shani Wallis). Also involved are Sabrina, the mascot 'discovered' by Askey, and the star's daughter Anthea Askey as a milk-and-water version of Calamity Jane.

Forty-two minutes in, burnished cowboy Elmer (Frankie Vaughan) rides into town to woo Joan with Michael Carr and Bert Wallace's 'This Is the Night'. *Kinematograph Weekly* told its readers that 'Tuneful songs round off the rooting-tooting lark', but Ross Parker's 'Ride, Ride Again' sung by Vaughan over the main title is the only other. Baxter was so happy to feature a genuine home-made heart-throb that he fills the screen with Vaughan's face. There is otherwise no reason for Vaughan's involvement. The wearisome plot ends with a shoot-out and with Askey given the gift of a pretty Indian squaw. His response is his familiar catchphrase: 'I thank you'.

JULY

Invitation to the Dance. The title could not have made it clearer: the film was about dance, and even more about Gene Kelly, whose commitment to it was unquestionable, as its deviser, director, and star. There was surely no one better placed to win the hearts and minds of the cinema audience than the man who had played so major a role in the Hollywood musical.

No holds barred, David Vaughan noted 'an almost unmitigated failure', detecting 'a conscious striving after art, that results inevitably (in a mass en-tertainment medium) in the production of *kitsch*'. Ultimately, 'It would need a dancer-mime of the most profound tragi-comic powers to carry off this role, and Kelly has made a grave mistake if he has allowed himself to be persuaded that he is an artist of this calibre'.[14] Despite 'the weaknesses in the choreogra-phy', Peter Brinson forecast that 'it is obvious that popular all-dancing films will influence the future of classical ballet on the stage', but it is doubtful if this happened.[15] The *MFB* noted that the film had 'undergone numerous vicissi-tudes since it was begun in England over four years ago, and it seems likely that not all Kelly's original conception has remained intact', suggesting that 'One cannot but feel that its director's main strength lies in the creation of lyrical, genuinely American dance forms which owe less allegiance to European "artistic traditions".[16] More sympathetically, Leslie Halliwell acknowledged a film 'which closed its star's great Hollywood period and virtually ended the heyday of the Hollywood musical. The simple fact emerged that European ballet styles were not Kelly's forte; yet there was much to enjoy in *Circus, Ring Around the Rosy* and *The Magic Lamp*.'[17]

This in itself demonstrates one of the problems with MGM's London-based *Invitation to the Dance*, produced by Arthur Freed. Originally intended to comprise four separate dance sequences, its British release comprised two: *Circus* (music by Jacques Ibert) and *Ring Around the Rosy* (the original score by Malcolm Arnold was replaced by a new score by André Previn). A third sequence and much the most entertaining, *The Magic Lamp*, was made in

America and is thus beyond the reach of this critique. There seemed little doubt that Kelly's ambitious project had suffered a prolonged and difficult gestation: filming had begun in London four years earlier, in August 1952.

Dance and mime are two distinct art forms; mime is one of the most consistently tiresome. Being exposed to it for any length of time cannot be encouraged. Where, in Mr Kelly's essays, did dance end and mime begin? More fundamentally, where did dance turn from what the British cinemagoer might consider conventional ballet (plenty of this, and lashings of mime to put up with, in *Circus*) to more modern, non-classical, popular dance, the sort of movement to music that British musical films were never shy of including in their efforts to beguile the public? Perhaps one of *Invitation to the Dance*'s problems was that it tried to mix these elements so blatantly. There is a sea of difference between the styles of *Circus* and *Ring Around the Rosy*, and of course a complete change of emphasis in the non-British *The Magic Lamp*.

Notwithstanding Kelly's brilliant performances in such as *Singin' in the Rain*, where his resolutely masculine, muscular style flourishes, when it comes to dance he was no leaping Nureyev, and when it comes to mime he was no Marcel Marceau. The white-faced clown of *Circus* presents a blankness that simply doesn't translate from the screen – Kelly seems unable to transmit from behind the make-up. Perhaps Kelly simply had too much going on to get the elements to work alongside each other. *Circus* hasn't the advantage of a strong or interesting story, lacking directorial decisiveness and constantly hampered by the hordes of extras (non-dancing extras, too) who stand about watching the principals. They may not dance, but they bray and make themselves heard throughout. Kelly's Pierrot is joined by Claire Sombert as Equestrienne and Igore Youskevitch as the High-Wire Walker.

There is a little more reason to see the second sequence, *Ring Around the Rosy*, and there is fine dancing from Kelly, Irving Davies, and Tommy Rall and their expertly drilled associates, but the general air, accentuated by Rolf Gerard's sets and costumes, is of many dance sequences from movies of long ago. Malcolm Arnold's commissioned score was discarded and replaced by Previn's, but the lack of narrative, of the use of words, of the human voice, does for it; there is little to demand the viewer's emotional involvement. Sadly, there is little to dance about in a film that was clearly beyond the comfort zone of *Kinematograph Weekly*, which recommended that 'The overall should captivate other than the cap and muffler brigade.'[18]

AUGUST

It's a Wonderful World, announced George Minter's Technicolor and Spectascope entry, perhaps unaware of a vastly superior MGM 1939 movie of the same name with benefit of James Stewart and Claudette Colbert, written by Ben Hecht and Herman J. Mankiewicz. Val Guest's 1956 version, enacted by

Terence Morgan and George Cole as flat-sharing wannabe songwriters, comes nowhere near the quality of its predecessor. Stanley Lupino and Roddy Hughes had played just such characters in the delightful *Cheer Up!*, with much happier results. It does, however, feature Prince Leleiohoku's 'Hawaiian War Chant' performed by Ted Heath and his band, little as the compensation is. Now the *Guardian* suggested that Heath should have been retained 'and let the rest of the cast go home.'[19]

Was the British musical film of the mid-1950s so utterly bereft of a few decent ideas that it served up such a tired, flabby piece as entertainment, inflicting further damage by casting two highly unsuitable contenders as the flat-mates? On one level, this is just another film about character misunderstandings and show-business success (unlikely as success seems in these circumstances) strung together with outdated gags.

It was sent forth from Shepperton under the pretence of being an up-to-the-minute picture with pop music, but the *Guardian*'s decision that with it 'British films reach a new low, in fact almost bedrock' was damning.[20] *Films and Filming*'s observation that it was 'lacking verbal subtlety' is somewhat surprising (was the reviewer expecting subtlety, verbal or otherwise?), but it referred to it as 'Emphatically entertainment for the younger generation of dance-band enthusiasts, for whom it is largely a deafening documentary.'[21] The extraordinary assertion that this is a film for the young demonstrates the studio's inability to cater for that 'younger generation' about to be denied films that genuinely reflected the vibrancy of new music breaking into British culture.

Does Guest really expect us to believe that in 1956 teenagers (and young teenagers too, if the shots we get of the audiences are to be trusted) went into a screaming frenzy at the very idea of seeing nice middle-aged Mr Heath or, come to that, the agreeable Dennis Lotis as he reiterates his fascination with the opposite sex in 'Girls, Girls, Girls' (music by Mr and Mrs Moira Heath), in which he includes 'The minky kind with men on her mind'? And what teenager would be in the least interested in the inane plot about Ray Thompson (Morgan) and Ken Millar (Cole) doing their own ironing and trying to break into the music business? Across the way, the glamorous and very French Georgie (Mylène Demongeot, credited here as Mylene Nicole) practises her scales and gets to sing with Heath. The band's appearances are the film's only saving grace, but Mr Heath's acting is a dead weight.

Musically, beyond the band there is little to report, although Lotis is usually around the fringes, ready to sing 'A Few Kisses Ago' (by Robert Farnon and Guest) and 'Roseanne' (by the Heaths), while Morgan and Nicole duet in the Heaths' 'When You Came Along'. There are attempts to satirise the sort of songs that the film regards as outdated, in such feeble cod numbers as 'When the Moon Shines Down' (tried out by Morgan, James Hayter, and Reginald Beckwith) and 'The Girl I Love Best Is My Mother'. Things reach rock-bottom in a dream sequence with Morgan, Cole, Nicole, and Hayter stumbling through vague choreographic movements as they limp through a mist that is not thick enough to disguise their obvious embarrassment. It proves, as so much else in British musical films does, that performers will do anything for money.

Another strand, which might even pass as the plot, is the juvenile effort by our two heroes to pass off 'D'You Ken John Peel?' (when played backwards) as the work of a modern composer, Rimsikoff. The work is eventually played at the Albert Hall, where it is greeted as a masterpiece. The sounds it makes are probably at least as interesting as those that precede it. It gives Guest ample opportunities for side-swipes at 'modern' music, although Jon Pertwee's frantic conducting of the premiere is unfunny. By then, subtlety, in all its forms, is out of the window. Others will decide if we can believe *Kinematograph Weekly*'s assurance that 'the new numbers are ear-tickling' and that 'As for the songs, all are destined to be whistled by errand-boys.'[22] In a truly wonderful world, that might still be true, but errand-boys are extinct.

SEPTEMBER

A supreme clown, Frankie Howerd never established a consistent film career in the manner of George Formby or Norman Wisdom. The outrageous information that he conveyed to an audience worked brilliantly on stage; on screen, the effectiveness is blunted, and the lack of a live response negates his effectiveness. He is more sedentary than Wisdom, and could hardly be expected to attain that comic's extravagant use of pathos. Unlike either Wisdom or Formby, Howerd was no singer, as proved by his strained efforts to put over his numbers in the disastrous stage musical *Mister Venus* – a major contribution to his career's decline at the end of the 1950s. His career survived several cinematic disappointments, not least *The Cool Mikado* (1963), but ***A Touch of the Sun*** survives as one of his more successful assignments.

One of Howerd's biographers considered the Raymond Stross production 'Probably the least effective and, indeed, least-seen of Frankie's 1950s vehicles [but] it's still worth catching for the bucketloads of typical Frankie moments and even more so for the less characteristic bits of pathos' in a script by Alfred Shaughnessy that was 'charming'.[23] Shaughnessy's story of William Darling, a hall porter at the smart Royal Connaught Hotel, finds Howerd surrounded by a giddy assortment of characters, all beautifully cast.

Dismissed by the *MFB* as a 'woefully unfunny and badly acted hotel romp',[24] it was no more appreciated by another Howerd biographer, who saw Howerd 'act embarrassingly badly opposite a supposed "love interest" – Dorothy Bromiley – who acted even worse, exuding all the warmth and unforced sincerity of a woman languishing in an ancient commercial for powdered gravy'.[25]

It's a harsh verdict on a film that constantly strives to amuse, offering a wealth of opportunities to a cast including Gordon Harker as elderly lift-attendant Sid, especially splendid when putting on his posh cockney voice ('Will you partake of a glass of waine?'), and Colin Gordon, blown in by a gale as a frenetic photographer. The pace picks up when three northern businessmen (Alfie Bass, Willoughby Goddard, and ever-welcome Reginald Beckwith) arrive to consider investing in the hotel, sending its staff into a deceptive frenzy. Howerd relishes impersonating a duchess ('A glass of champagne? I never touch it, except at launchings').

At least, *A Touch of the Sun* provides Irish singer Ruby Murray with her only (and minor) film role as hotel staff member Ruby; her recording of 'Softly, Softly' in 1955 – a year in which she had five songs in the Top Twenty British hit parade – exemplifies the gentleness of her performances. A French song by Pierre Dudan, it was anglicized by lyricists Robin Hugh Scutt (as 'Mark Paul') and Paddy Roberts. There is nothing notable about the two cabaret numbers Murray performs in the final moments of *A Touch of the Sun* ('Me? Sing in public?'), 'In Love' and 'O'Malley's Tango', both by Norrie Paramor and Jack Fishman, and her few lines of dialogue are timidly conveyed, despite encouragement from director Gordon Parry: 'I'm amazed at her naturalness. I really believe that she has a big future in British films if she is properly handled.'[26] No offers came.

NOVEMBER

Devised and directed by director-dancer Wendy Toye, ***On the Twelfth Day*** is among her best work; it is certainly her most distinctive. George K. Arthur's production is 'scripted' by James Matthews and Val Valentine, with additional material by David Deutsch, a visually exquisite dance piece built around the rhyme of 'The Twelve Days of Christmas', with a complexity and wealth of invention unequalled in British dance films (it beats Gene Kelly's more pretentious *Invitation to the Dance* hands down). The music is by Doreen Carwithen, a composer whose potential was forfeited to her marriage to another composer, William Alwyn. Carwithen's task was made more difficult because the choreography had already been worked out. She watched as the piece was danced on set to the improvised accompaniment of a pianist.

After research at the British Museum, Carwithen began the laborious task of matching her music to the film, visiting the studio at Beaconsfield, where cows were being painted in Technicolor and with noughts and crosses. Carwithen's score expertly defines each of the verses. As for the sequence of 'Twelve drummers drumming':

> On arrival for recording this I discovered George K. Arthur who produced the film took it quite literally and ordered twelve timp players. The London Symphony Orchestra obliged. It was a huge noise and really not necessary as I can score to make a big noise with the normal orchestra. However, this was what he wanted so I obliged and wrote for twelve drummers, much to their amusement.[27]

The score was finished at 5.00 a.m. on the day of the recording; when Carwithen told Muir Mathieson, he replied, 'I told you that you would most likely have to do this. Now do you believe me?' The film enjoyed considerable success, was given a Royal Command Performance, and gave its composer the largest Performing Rights Society cheque she ever received. Carwithen also provided scores for two other films directed by Toye: *The Stranger Left No Card* (1953) and *Three Cases of Murder* (1955).

Kinematograph Weekly's Frank Hazell told his readers that

> In the last few weeks I've come to the conclusion that the BBC's *Picture Parade* should either have drastic revision or be scuttled without trace [...] The first extract – from *Stars in Your Eyes* (British Lion) – was a not funny comedy sequence of a type frequently seen on TV but usually done rather better. If anyone thought this was going to bring people to the cinema they must have totally different ideas on exploitation from my own.[28]

A few weeks earlier, the trade paper had written encouragingly about this 'Cheery, disarmingly inconsequential show business musical', 'a good star and title frolic for the nine pennies and family', that was (as the *Kinematograph Weekly* had so often decided) 'Just the thing for the tired working man and woman and their nippers'.[29]

Such a verdict may have served in 1956, but this is a picture that deserves as much reassessment as any of its period. We can overlook its attempt to sneak into the consciousness of 1956 youths by its trumpeting publicity call 'Rock'n'roll with Laughter!' It has not the least hint of rock'n'roll, but then almost all the so-called rock'n'roll British musical films of the 1950s had nothing to do with it either. Our best hope is that some may have been seduced by this most beguiling, modest picture to discover variety and music hall, albeit as its life blood seeped from it.

Produced by David Dent, devised and directed by Maurice Elvey, Adelphi Films' **Stars in Your Eyes** was scripted by Talbot Rothwell from an original story by Francis Miller, with additional dialogue (and possibly co-direction) by Hubert Gregg. That tired working man (was he a different beast from that other much-maligned male, the tired businessman?) and their various 'nippers' would probably have found little originality or excitement in this celebratory vaudeville. Attendances were poor; financial failure beckoned. The *MFB* didn't seem bothered, merely recording 'a few passable songs and dances' (really? The dances are nowhere to be seen) in a film that was 'insufficiently inventive to raise the material out of its depressingly familiar rut. Nat Jackley contributes some very broad humour and the other players work hard, notably Hubert Gregg, who, apart from writing the two best songs [but which two?], is occasionally amusing as the TV producer'.[30] In fact, Elvey's

Adelphi's 1956 *Stars in Your Eyes*, a valentine to the declining world of music-hall and concert party, was imbued with fondness for such lost art forms. There are effective performances from all, notably Pat Kirkwood, Dorothy Squires, and Bonar Colleano.

final paean to music-hall shimmers with a genuine fondness for the vanishing art, strongly supported by this most interesting cast.

In 1956, the old halls were closing. Some stood for a while yet, empty, awaiting demolishment. These local havens of music-hall would be lost for ever. After struggling on by presenting underfed variety bills, strip shows, films, and repertory companies playing to empty houses, Norwich Hippodrome closed its doors in 1960, awaiting its 1964 demolition and its replacement with a car park. The plague covered the country. Closures in the 1950s included the Bristol Empire; Bedford, Camden Town; Croydon Hippodrome; East Ham Palace; Ealing Hippodrome; Ilford Hippodrome; New Cross Empire; Poplar Queens; Wolverhampton Hippodrome; Chiswick Empire; Kingston upon Thames Empire and Croydon Palace.

Where were the old artists supposed to work? There is a telling moment in *Stars in Your Eyes* when Elvey shows us some banner headlines; is it merely accidental that we can just see on the right-hand side of the frame on the front page of the *Stage* a heading: 'Any Offers?'? We can just see the top of a head, too. It is the head of Jessie Matthews. The *Stage* explained that 'because she has no play, film, radio or television offers in Britain', she was off to South Africa. She explained, 'I just couldn't face more Morecambes and Prestons now, with those stage down-draughts you get in mid-winter.' If this was the fate of Britain's top musical star of the thirties, what hope for the variety artistes, whose knowledge of Morecambe and Preston and all the other worn-out dates throughout Britain was so depressingly extensive? Those stage down-droughts blew through the country.

Husband-and-wife team Jimmy Knowles (Nat Jackley) and Sally Bishop (Pat Kirkwood) are in Oldham, playing to near-empty houses in their touring variety show. Business is bad and the outlook grim, but Jimmy, aware that the theatres are dying, resists the idea of trying to get into television. To them, after all, television has been an enemy. Now he auditions for producer Crawley Walters (Hubert Gregg) but isn't successful until Walters, urgently needing acts to fill a last-minute gap in the television schedule, takes on Jimmy and Sally's stage show. There is nothing original here, the dire effect of television on so many aspects of British life having been exhibited in British films from the 1930 *Elstree Calling*, where they were trying to *invent* television, to such 1950s pictures as Alan Melville's *Simon and Laura* (1955), where a married couple become Britain's first reality stars, and to the Arthur Askey–John Baxter comedies *Ramsbottom Rides Again* and *Make Mine a Million*.

As in all showbusiness-based films, success for those who have struggled is guaranteed, and originality is not expected, but Elvey is particularly fortunate to have a company and writers who bring a surprising naturalness to the situations. Running alongside the fortunes of Jimmy and Sally, we have the relationship between famous cabaret star Ann Hart (Dorothy Squires in her only film role, singing her own composition 'With All My Heart', and Colleano as alcoholic songwriter David Laws, and Edwin Astley, Albert Elms, Hazel

Astley and Malcolm Harvey's 'Without You'). Squires and Colleano (especially effective) also perform Astley's melancholic 'I Saw the Look in Your Eyes'. Their scenes add another layer of conviction to a film that does much on many levels; we can see that Squires might well have gone on to other roles, with Colleano wholly convincing in the most dramatic scenes played against Astley's impressively filmic orchestrations.

For Kirkwood, *Stars in Your Eyes* stands alone as her best film. Her on-stage reputation as a pantomime principal boy is unassailable, but her film career had not prospered. The teaming of Kirkwood and Jackley (along with Colleano's presence) is the film's greatest asset; the honesty shines through. Gregg's three songs for his newlywed wife are tailor-made. Forever remembered for his World War II hit 'I'm Going to Get Lit Up When the Lights Go On in London', he now came up with the equally stylistic 'If I Could Take My Pick I'd Pick Piccadilly' with Kirkwood as a tattered paper-boy in Piccadilly Circus. It's a song redolent of much that had gone before. It has echoes of the pre-Professor Higgins's Eliza Doolittle. Hadn't we already seen Mary Clare binding violets into posies in the gloriously sentimental *Say It with Flowers* (1934); Betty selling flowers below Eros in *Squibs*; the great Violet Loraine selling flowers in *Britannia of Billingsgate* (1933); and Tessie O'Shea shifting daffodils in front of Eros in *London Town* (1946) before going into a St Vitus-choreographed frenzy?

Nowhere else on film does the camera catch Kirkwood's superbly glamorous talent as in Gregg's entrancing title song. This is the musical high point of the picture, magically and vividly captured in superb cinematography. There is recognition of Kirkwood's expertise in male impersonation in Gregg's witty pastiche 'The Man That Wakes the Man That Blows Reveille', and Kirkwood revives the music-hall atmosphere with C. W. Murphy and Will Letters's old chorus-pleaser made famous by Florrie Forde, 'Has Anybody Here Seen Kelly?' complete with Directoire stick. In March 1956 she played Vesta Tilley in Gregg's musical biography of the music-hall star on BBC Television's *The Great Little Tilley*.

Then, Nat Jackley, that 'animated, rubber-necked genius',[31] brilliantly real in the off-stage scenes, really brilliant on stage in routines the like of which we will never see again, in the company of little Jimmy Clitheroe (as 'My Son' to Jackley's elderly mother). The sketch of itself is pretty feeble; it is also unmissable, a rare example of the sort of unabashed sentimentality that imbued so much mother-son material on the halls (we only have to recall 'It's My Mother's Birthday Today'). At the time of settling on Jackley's petticoated knee, Clitheroe was thirty-five years old and no singer, as we can clearly see. When he finishes his solo in Don Pelosi and Leo Towers's 'My Boy', he lifts up his eyes, clearly knowing he has made a fist of it by singing out of tune, and probably thinking that Mr Elvey is about to say 'Cut!' Thankfully, he didn't. It's a moment that adds another moment of charm to an already beguiling sequence.

As for the brilliant Jackley, he's far from done. A holiday camp chalet scene displays many of his skills, but the guardsman sketch removes any doubt about his eminence as a superb comic actor, magnificently and hilariously supported by the largely unremembered Sammy Curtis, Dennis Murray, and Sonnie Willis, making their only appearance on film. In vocal and bodily contortions Jackley's style here is hugely reminiscent of Sid Field; compare Jackley's demeanour with Fields's in the photographer's sketch of *London Town*. Throughout, Jackley's physical comedy collides with the surreal via techniques now long extinct. S. D. Onions's photography in Camerascope and Eastmancolor is remarkably vibrant. On the periphery of the story is a fascinating collection of British character actors, including Gabrielle Brune, Joan Sims, Freddie Frinton, Jack Jackson performing his own 'A Man and His Music', Meier Tzelniker, and Vera Day.

The professional difficulties that had plagued their *Stars in Your Eyes* characters, with the threat of live theatre surrendering (with all that this implied) to television, came back to haunt Gregg and Kirkwood when they starred in the British musical *Chrysanthemum*. What at first seemed an assured success foundered when the BBC televised an extract, against the advice of impresario Peter Saunders, who warned that 'A TV excerpt makes a straight play, but ruins a musical'.[32] The week after transmission, the box office dropped by £1,700.00. Gregg blamed television for killing the show: 'We had gone on television and as good as told ten million people not to come'.[33] Future attempts to revive the Kirkwood–Gregg partnership proved troublesome.

Rocking around the clock meant little to the British public before 1956. Two years earlier, Bill Haley and His Comets had recorded the song, subsequently used in Hollywood's 1955 *Blackboard Jungle*, and in March 1956 the first American film to be built around the rock'n'roll phenomenon *Rock Around the Clock* marked a weather change in popular music, a change deeply felt in Britain, whose shores it reached in late 1956. The effects could not be exaggerated: in panic mode, the *Melody Maker* warned Britain that 'the current craze for Rock-and-Roll material is one of the most terrifying things to have happened to popular music'.[34] More fundamentally, it was one of the most worrying things to happen to British cinemas at a time when attendances were sharply declining. The *Aberdeen Evening Express* reported that the police used truncheons and hoses to stop young cinemagoers from rioting, breaking shop windows, destroying road signs and tearing down the corporation's Christmas decorations. At the Victory, Rochdale, the management brought in vigilantes to keep order during the film.[35]

Without viewing the film, the watch committee of Belfast banned it, while Londonderry's corporation sat through it at a special midnight preview and declared it 'completely harmless'.[36] The *West London Observer* headlined its disapproving opinion with 'The New Jazz Is Just Cannibalistic Tribalism'.

Rock'n'roll was mentioned in the same sentence as 'voodoo'.[37] In Halifax, teenagers told reporters 'that the music "sends" them, that it was "the living end", and that they got a terrific kick out of it. These, apparently, were the reasons for nothing more than downright hooliganism.'[38]

When the film was shown at Dagenham's Gaumont, 'girls spat in police-men's faces as two youths were marched off to the station'.[39] Indeed, *Rock Around the Clock* seems to have been directly responsible for a mass breach of the peace in Britain's cinemas and streets. There was more outrage when two youths were up before Derby magistrates after seeing the picture. One, eighteen-year-old labourer Patrick Morley, wore a drape coat with velvet collar and cuffs, an outfit that, according to the prosecuting Police Superintendent Redfern, 'would make King Edward VII turn in his grave'. Morley's friend, seventeen-year-old fishmonger Dennis Clarke, had ended up dancing on top of a telephone kiosk. Suggesting that the police should have referred these miscreants to a mental welfare team, Redfern urged the court to deliver 'sharp punishment'. Transportation to Australia no longer being an option, the boys were each fined £2.

The Bishop of Woolwich wanted the film banned from British cinemas, but the unrest and destructiveness that picture-houses were now faced with did not always accompany a showing of *Rock Around the Clock*. Norwich's unassuming little Theatre de Luxe had problems enough of its own without this new threat. Hoping to cling onto its dwindling clientele by introducing 3D in 1953, and then offering Norwich a constant diet of Westerns (so persistent that the de Luxe became known locally as 'The Ranch House'), it finally ran out of time in February 1957. At the last showing of *Outpost to Morocco*, a work of crushing boredom starring George Raft, the young audience (among them, no doubt, those drape-coated, velveted, and sleekly brilliantined Teddy Boys and their girls) destroyed the place, smashing 236 seats, ripping down the screen, and unravelling fire hoses. Wise heads nodded over the reports of such destructive events up and down the country. Some will have wondered if these stirrings in the subsoil of British culture were of any serious significance. Some may have realised that, against the background of a confluence of changing mores, sociological worms were beginning to turn.

Norman Wisdom was on good form for ***Up in the World***, produced for Rank by Hugh Stewart. The screenplay by Jack Davies, Henry E. Blyth, and Peter Blackmore had its star as an accident-prone window-cleaner threatened by a band of crooks. The drama is indistinct, but John Paddy Carstairs's appre-ciation of Wisdom's skills ensures an unflagging pace. As girlfriend Jeanne, Maureen Swanson, in place merely because Norman croons his title song at her, is given no opportunities. The usual indignities visited on casts of a Wisdom film include Jerry Desmonde being submerged in a water-butt and Ambrosine Phillpotts falling flat on her face in a football field. A precocious boy accompanies Norman to a splashy nightclub where the chorines sing Philip Green and Marcel Stellman's 'Talent'. Unlike Formby, whose dialogue usually segued naturally into song, Wisdom's vocal gear-change has a curious effect on his 'little chap' persona; he is never quite the same person when an orchestra strikes up.

As well as devastating a conjuror's act, Wisdom copes with being sentenced to twenty-five years' hard labour, and almost destroys a country house. On the sidelines, Michael Ward has some delightful moments when (a touch of the Ernest Thesigers) embroidering, or exercising his chest-expander. We should not overlook the lingering look of disbelief on the face of Colin Gordon. Credit is given to the hamster that plays a crucial role, but knowing the tricks that film-makers play on us, can we be sure it's always the same one?

The whiff of intimate revue, an art and craft that persisted in British theatre into the 1960s, arrived on screen with Archway's delightful ***Five Guineas a Week***, 'a new British quota film in Eastmancolor [and Cosmoscope]' produced by Jacques de Lane Lea, directed by Lea and Donald Monat, and written by Monat and Donald Cotton with music by Basil Tait and Brian Burke. Archway's press book described the 33-minute entertainment as 'an unusual, musical featurette set in a gay contemporary mood [...] the first production of its kind to be made in this country'. Its closest relation in post-war British musical films is probably *Harmony Lane* (1954), notably in the cartoonish designs by John and Catherine Flatman. There is no attempt to work the individual numbers into any sort of narrative.

The writers had provided material for the stage revue *Light Fantastic*, first seen at Hammersmith in 1954 and subsequently for a brief West End run the following year, but only two of the items were retained for *Five Guineas*: 'Picnic', a satire on the 'Teddy Bears Picnic', and the light period charm of 'Everyone Has Got to Have a Dream'. *The Times* had more or less dismissed *Light Fantastic* as 'unoriginal and harmless'.[40] As much could be said of *Five Guineas*, its wares lacking distinction, with no hint of breaking new ground at a time when another intimate revue, John Cranko's inventive *Cranks*, was breaking the rules. *Five Guineas* happened because, one night at the Fortune Theatre, Lea went round to see Monat after the show. As it happened, Lea had been planning a truncated film version of *Cranks* until Cranko's appointment to the Stuttgart Ballet scuppered the project. Monat persuaded Lea that a film could be made from his team of composers and lyricists (there is no dialogue), loosely interwoven with the idea of a young woman (Georgia Brown) trying to find reasonably priced accommodation in London.

The film was shot in five days at the Elephant and Castle swimming baths, the soundtrack having been pre-recorded. None of the cast of *Light Fantastic* made it into the film, but Lea's young cast is a display case of burgeoning British musical talent of the mid-1950s, headed by Brown crooning 'Without

Love', Sally Bazeley introducing the picture with her carolling of 'I Get Up in the Morning Early', and dancer Sheila O'Neill, all of whom had significant careers, with a young Teddy Green (destined to be a strong supporting player in stage and musical films) and a small ensemble of West End dancers, imaginatively and moodily choreographed by Malcolm Clare. The air of despondency apparent in 'Rehearsal Room', 'Without Love', and 'Don't Tempt Me' lends a profundity to the work's perception of London life in the mid-1950s. One of the highlights is the Teddy Boys' 'Picnic' performed by Green, Glenn Wilcox, and Ken Smith, and Nevil Whiting has his 'Lute Song', as well as duetting with Bazeley in the finale. Visually, the film is a joy, a minor gem that deserves to be seen and appreciated, with its main players, young and hopeful of their futures, brought together in its last moments among the paraphernalia of a mid-1950s coffee bar.

1957

It was not known how long the craze for coffee would last, or how quickly the craze would grow

The Tommy Steele Story

The Good Companions   *After the Ball*
Let's Be Happy   *These Dangerous Years*
The Tommy Steele Story   *Davy*
Rock You Sinners

Seen in the context of the mid-, approaching late, 1950s, the British musical film presents what can only be described as a bland response to the confluence of social change when the tectonic plates of domestic life were skidding beneath the nation's feet. Change seemed to be everywhere, in a country that, remarkably, had only recently disposed of its ration books (meat was the last commodity to be restricted, in 1954), but the country's severe housing problems, exacerbated by the slum properties that proliferated throughout the country during the Depression of the 1930s, and the war-shattered buildings that scarred London and other cities, persisted as a grim reminder of what the country had been through.

The social whirl so favoured and promulgated through to the end of the decade and beyond by Herbert Wilcox and Anna Neagle was so entrenched in the British cinemagoer's expectation of what films were that nothing seemed to threaten its continuance, even though Mr and Mrs Wilcox did their bit in recognising that the landscape beyond the studio floor had altered. Their trick was to preserve the status quo by acknowledging, as if out of the corners of their eyes, shades of a perplexing modernity that they had no hope of representing. They spoke, as it were, for the Opposition, so desperately off-piste that they seemed to suggest that the star of their *These Dangerous Years* might even be a teenager.

Teenagers, of course, had much to answer for, having been invented (and in America, too) only in the mid-1940s before becoming an identifiable, viable reality in 1950s Britain. Their relevance to economic prosperity was recognised, apparent from an awakened interest in teen fashions in a society that for decades had forced British men to wear distressingly unattractive apparel. Trousers out, jeans in. The sales of sheet music (unrivalled since the age of the parlour song) declined as sales of gramophone records sold to teenagers soared. Throughout the country, the listening booth was a direct call to the teenage market, a place of refuge, sanctuary.

In the mid-1950s Willmotts of Norwich was the first port of call for bicycles, model railways, perambulators, refrigerators, Hoovers, gramophone records, and the gramophones to play them on. It also had listening booths – *sit-down* listening booths – one of the more civilised inventions of the twentieth century, providing an almost monastic experience. Entering the listening booth and closing its door on the world (and at Willmotts the booths seemed to be soundproof) was the nearest some of us got to a religious experience. As a teenager, one only had to ask the shop assistant in order to listen to a particular record (even a *long-playing* record). Halfway through your visit, the request to 'listen to the other side' was readily granted.

Perhaps Prime Minister Harold Macmillan had the listening booth in mind when he assured an audience in Bedford in July 1957 that 'most of our people have never had it so good', but the remark cut through at a time of considerable unease, not least in politics. The Suez Canal crisis of late 1956 had jolted Britain's international reputation and led to the resignation of Prime Minister Anthony Eden in January 1957, accentuating the accelerating decline in Britain's importance in the world. A relaxation of certain constrictions played its part in the newly emerging atmosphere. Conscription into the armed services, introduced at the beginning of the war in 1939, was wound down by 1957. The last man standing was officially discharged in 1963, by which time the state's interference in an individual's life had been considerably curtailed.

The 1954 conviction of Peter Wildeblood for homosexual activities resulted in a prison term of eighteen months, during which he wasted no time in writing his personal account of what being gay meant. His *Against the Law*, published in 1955, encouraged a new discussion about the laws relating to queer behaviour in Britain. We can see a clear line between the Wolfenden Report of 1957, with its recommendation that sexual activity between consenting men should be legalised, and Wildeblood's calm explanation.

The abolition of capital punishment marked another milestone in the advance of civilising the country's attitudes. There had been widespread disgust at the execution of 29-year-old Ruth Ellis in 1955. She was the last woman to be hanged in Britain, but executions persisted until 1964 and were officially abolished in 1969. It was appropriate that the public executioner Albert Pierrepoint should write in later years that 'executions solve nothing and are only an antiquated relic of a primitive desire for revenge'.[1]

Theatre, too, was expected to respond to a new dawning. John Osborne's legendary *Look Back in Anger* (1956) has, perhaps glibly, been identified as largely responsible for the New Wave of British theatre that rolled into London, at once rendering so much work by previously respected playwrights of lesser importance: think Terence Rattigan, Wynyard Browne, or the intellectually cool works of N. C. Hunter. It was generally accepted that *Look Back in Anger* had wreaked havoc in British drama, but it was a trick that Osborne

J. B. Priestley's warm-hearted love song to concert party *The Good Companions* had been successfully filmed in 1933 with Jessie Matthews and John Gielgud. Many appreciated the 1957 opportunity for Technicolor, but some of the original charm was in short supply.

had difficulty in repeating. Nevertheless, a door had been opened. The kitchen sink had crashed into the drawing-room of West End light comedies, causing considerable damage.

By the mid-1950s, television had increased its grip on the public pulse. It was beginning to be realised that it was a medium that could react without delay to changes of taste. No sooner had those rioting Teddy Boys and their girls been taken off to court after *Rock Around the Clock* than ITV put out *Cool for Cats* in late 1956, a series that ran until 1961. The BBC followed up with *6.5 Special* (1958) and *Juke Box Jury* (1959–67), in which a panel of a burgeoning breed of 'television personalities' decided whether a new pop recording was going to be a Hit or a Miss.

The jukebox was one of the most enthusiastically sought-after pleasures of life when luxury goods began to be imported from America, with the *Financial Times* proclaiming it as a 'Defining Moment: The American Jukebox arrives to corrupt British teenagers.'[2] The most natural habitat for the jukebox was the coffee bars that had begun to spring up around 1952 when espresso machines reached Britain. It was not known how long the craze for coffee would last, or how quickly the craze would grow. There was something intrinsically home-made about those coffee bars, 'not designed to last for more than a few years.'[3]

The brassy presence of both the jukebox and the Gaggia coffee-making machine could be traced back to the iconic gleaming grilles of American cars. Something very un-British had grown up in league with the new-trending coffee bars, an emboldened development from those mysterious 'Milk Bars' that had apparently been so popular in the 1930s. By the end of 1957, it was estimated that the US had imported 8,000 jukeboxes into Britain. The Lord Mayor of Birmingham spoke of an 'aimless juvenile café society'. He did not consider it proper that young people should 'spend hour after hour listening to records, buying cups of tea and coffee and bottles of pop.'[4]

MARCH

J. B. Priestley's *The Good Companions* enjoyed long life. His 1929 novel quickly found itself transformed into a semi-musical adaptation in the West End in 1931, the music by Richard Addinsell, its stars Adele Dixon and John Gielgud. Two years later, Gielgud and Jessie Matthews headlined a British film version, its songs by composer George Posford and lyricist Douglas Furber. The 1957 remake of the 1933 picture, Cinemascoped and Technicolored, was followed by a 1974 London stage musical with a score by André Previn and Johnny Mercer. A major television adaptation by Alan Plater for Yorkshire Television made between 1980 and 1981 once again proved the work's vivacity, with its new score by David Fanshawe. It is highly recommended.

'A Gay Glad Film', trumpeted the trailer for Associated British Picture Corporation's new version of **The Good Companions** ('That's what people ought to be'), Priestley's meandering tale of a nomadic concert party, 'The Dinky Doos', struggling from tatty theatre to seaside pier in search of an audience. T. J. Morrison's screenplay updated the action to the present day, bolstered with additional dialogue by J. L. Hodson and John Whiting. Whiting's recent work had included such distinguished plays as *A Penny for a Song* and the 1953 *Marching Song*; goodness knows what he was doing contributing dialogue to a musical film. Produced at Elstree by H. G. Inglis and directed by J. Lee Thompson, this revival of The Dinky Doos' adventure was carefully mounted, with high production values and solid leading players: Celia Johnson as nice middle-aged Miss Trant, leaving her comfortable family home to seek new life after the death of her father; Eric Portman as blunt northerner Jess Oakroyd, walking out on his unhappy marriage and job to take to the open road; John Fraser as Inigo Jollifant, a talented and valiant young schoolteacher freeing himself from the horrors of working in a dismal private school. In the footsteps of Dixon and Matthews, the troupe's ambitious starlet Susie Dean was now played by Janette Scott. For *Films and Filming*'s critic 'P.G.B', the role revealed her as 'a star of international significance'; the critic went as far as comparing her to Judy Garland. A strange comparison, especially since Scott's singing was done, in the manner of *Singin' in the Rain*, by off-screen popular singer Jill Day.

Reaction to this resurgence of The Dinky Doos was discouraging. As Roger Mellor states, 'This film had the misfortune to open just as rock'n'roll was taking off as music for teenagers'.[5] The *Guardian* thought it 'preserves only a sketchy outline of that rich piece of English picaresque to support another embarrassing English imitation of the snap and gloss of the American musical: one can hardly imagine a more unlikely match'.[6] The American press concurred, noting 'a pedestrian musical. Much of the characterization and writing quality of the original is lost in the conventional screenplay. An old-fashioned story line, without surprise twists, is not aided by the moderate quality of the score'.[7] For the *MFB*, it was 'superficially modernised with a few "pop" songs (including a painful title number), intermittent attempts at an American style, and several references to television. The result is as incongruous as might be expected. Characterisation is consistently two dimensional, and the dialogue is dogged but flat'.[8] In noting the 'vast cast', *Films and Filming*[9] congratulated the production for 'the fact that the story maintains shape and does not sink into a series of cameos'. Philip Oakes suggested that the director had 'put his players in a no-man's land' by 'bringing the action up to date'.[10]

Really? More than sixty years on, we may look more kindly on it. The accusation that the story itself was somehow out of place in the mid-1950s seems odd when such modest little stage entertainments as this were still popping up all over the country, if not thriving. Indeed, they existed well into the 1960s. I was sitting there myself, in the stalls, waiting for Roberta Pett to come on stage at the end of Cromer Pier dressed in leafy green and singing 'I think that I shall never see a po-em lovely as a tree' while the chorus girls waved behind her in costumes that spoke of England's woods. Tired comics with ancient gag-books were still wandering up and down the country flanked with curious instrumentalists (once, even, a shooting act with a fearsome gun-toting, whip-lashing female described in the theatre programme as 'an actual descendant of Wild Bill Hicock'). In this sense, neither the story, setting, or content of *The Good Companions* was out of gear.

Nothing from the score has had any afterlife, but it is serviceable and might have been worse. The honours are shared between two pairs of writers. Composer Alberto Rossi and lyricists Paddy Roberts and Geoffrey Parsons wrote the title song, 'Where There's You There's Me' (Paddy Stone, dubbed by Michael Holliday, dancing with a chair) and two torch-songs for Susie, 'If Only' and 'This Kind of Love'. John Salew, as the old-timer performer of stirring drawing-room ballads, shows his stuff with Billy Reid's 'I Believe', a number that would have worked just as well in the 1933 original. One of the main faults of the new score is that it contains few of the type of songs that such a company as The Dinky Doos would have performed. There would have been a deal of fun in creating some for us here, as in the original film. Nevertheless, Rachel Roberts is briefly seen doing her stage act, insisting that 'The Gentleman Is a Heel' (writers unknown). The second pair of writers, credited with both music and lyrics, are Paddy Roberts and Geoffrey Parsons, with two of the most effective numbers, 'Today Has Been a Lovely Day' and the film's all-stops-pulled-out finale 'Round the World'. The always apposite arrangements of Laurie Johnson, supervised by veteran Louis Levy, do their best with the material at hand.

MAY

'I don't think people in the States will be able to tell the difference between this and the average Hollywood musical', said *Let's Be Happy*'s director Henry Levin, adding that 'Ours is primarily a story with music interwoven.'[11] Shooting for the Technicolor Cinemascope Associated British Picture Corporation film had started on the bonnie bonnie banks o' Loch Lomond in July 1956. Few cinemagoers were aware that Diana Morgan's screenplay was in effect a remake of the 1941 *Jeannie*, via Aimée Stuart's play of the same name. The 1940s Jeannie had been non-dancing Barbara Mullen, awaiting legendary fame as Dr Finlay's housekeeper in a BBC Television series. Now stellar Hollywood performer Vera-Ellen took over, flanked by American singer Tony Martin as Stanley Smith, the romancing 'Man from Idaho', and ramrod-backed Robert Flemyng as Lord James MacNairn.

For David Shipman, 'Vera-Ellen was one of the screen's best dancers, and, after a poor start, an attractive performer in musicals. Her career, however, never really got into first gear.'[12] By the time she signed for overseas duty her best work was probably behind her, including her partnering with Gene Kelly for the 'Slaughter on Tenth Avenue' ballet in *Words and Music* (1948), MGM's 1949 *On the Town*, and dancing with Astaire in *Three Little Words* (1950) and *White Christmas* (1954). She had already chanced the British studios with the 1951 *Happy Go Lovely* with less than brilliant results; the new returning suggested that her American career was waning. *Let's Be Happy* turned out to be her last film, 'even worse than her previous British musical. It must have made her regret that her decision to retire hadn't been made some months earlier.'[13]

Early scenes of rustic simplicity give way to dollops of supposed sophistication as Jeannie, making ends meet on her own in rural America, imperfectly created in a corner of Elstree, inherits her grandfather's modest fortune and decides to travel. A backyard celebration ensues with the local kids vaguely choreographed as they jump about with her to 'I'm Going to Scotland'. En route to Edinburgh, she meets pipe-smoking charmer-crooner Stanley. They re-meet fleetingly in Paris, and then in a train's dining car where he urges her to 'Hold On to Love'. Jeannie dances around her swish hotel room in a curiously unsensational routine. Stanley is entertaining partying Scots to an American dance sensation, 'The Golfer's Glide', a dance reminiscent of the equally ridiculous 'The 'Ampstead Way' of *London Town*. By now, Jeannie is appearing in outrageously inappropriate costumes, especially absurd when she goes to the ballet looking like a half-pulled Christmas cracker. As she watches the ballet from the stalls, she seems to imagine herself as the prima ballerina.

At last, we get a glimpse of Edinburgh and the country when almost penniless Lord James shows her his paupered estate and romances her. At a wedding celebration, Jeannie joins in at the 'Piper's Wedding'. Lord James ('Call me Jimmy') proposes; she accepts. A disappointed Stanley sits at the hotel piano, reflecting that 'One Is Such a Lonely Number', a song title that gives an inkling of the profundity of Nicholas Brodszky's music and Paul Francis Webster's lyrics. When Jimmy learns that Jeannie has spent her fortune, he confesses that he only wanted her for her money, robbing his lordship of our sympathies (we have been led to believe he's a good 'un) and rendering Flemyng's stiff upper lip (and, beyond his kilt, decidedly non-Scots manner) thankless. Alone, Jeannie returns to Scotland unaccompanied, ready to pick up her old country-hick life, but the man from Idaho pops up outside her window contentedly assuring her 'Let's Be Happy' as the local kids begin jumping about with joy all over again.

The *MFB* dashed producer Marcel Hellman and director Levin's hope that the picture would stand comparison with Hollywood. Instead, 'an unpretentious little Cinderella story has been blown up into an elaborate musical, losing most of its charm on the way' via 'production numbers which are for the most part vulgar in conception and undistinguished in execution', suggesting that 'success still eludes the Anglo-American musical'.[14]

We must exempt the star's dancing, dazzling as it fleetingly is, although Vera-Ellen comes over as a rather anonymous presence. But then, Morgan's dialogue gives her nothing to strive for. As for the choreography, questions remain. Pauline Grant is credited with 'Jeannie's Pyjama Ballet' and the 'Card Ballet' (the latter unquestionably the best thing in the picture). George Carden has the dubious privilege of choreographing the dreadful 'Golfer's Glide', with Alfred Rodrigues responsible for 'other dance numbers'. However, Olga Lehmann is credited with having 'devised and designed the Card Ballet'. It is to her that the plaudits seem due. With its echoes of *Alice in Wonderland*, the film momentarily gets somewhere close to what Levin was hoping for when the various disciplines of dance, choreography, lighting, cinematography, design, and music coordinate to create something that might be considered artistry. And why was the story set in Scotland? For all the use it makes of its location, the film might as well have been made in Timbuctoo.

JUNE

As spring turned to summer, 'The long, laborious, noisy life of a much-loved and admired jazz-exponent who is still in his adolescence and obviously sees no point in growing out of it'[15] marked a sea-change in the progress of the British musical film. It defined a new sort of musical entertainment designed to appeal to a younger cinema audience. Its character is probably best expressed in the first four features produced by British studios: *The Tommy Steele Story* and *Rock You Sinners* (both 1957), followed in 1958 by *The Golden Disc* and *6.5 Special*. Significantly, in the early phase it was often minor British film companies that enthusiastically explored projects that might appeal to the younger generation, basically films involving pop singers of the day. It was a trend begun by Steele that lasted until the mid-1960s, along the way encompassing the Cliff Richard and Beatles films, and other showcases for such as Billy Fury, Freddie and the Dreamers, John Leyton, Mike Sarne, Gerry Marsden and the Pacemakers, and the Dave Clark Five:

1957	*The Tommy Steele Story*
	Rock You Sinners
1958	*The Golden Disc*
	Six-Five Special
	The Duke Wore Jeans
1959	*Tommy the Toreador*
1960	*Climb Up the Wall*
1961	*The Young Ones*
1962	*Play It Cool*
1963	*Summer Holiday*
	Just for Fun
	It's All Happening
	What a Crazy World
	Live It Up

> *It's All Over Town*
> 1964   *A Hard Day's Night*
> *Wonderful Life*
> *Just for You*
> *Every Day's a Holiday*
> *Ferry Cross the Mersey*
> 1965   *I've Gotta Horse*
> *Be My Guest*
> *Catch Us If You Can*
> *Help!*
> *Cuckoo Patrol*

The shift of emphasis is succinctly described by Andy Medhurst's recognition that

> Tommy Steele was Britain's first pop star, in the [Elvis] Presley sense of the term, and *The Tommy Steele Story*, released with ferocious speed only eight months after his first hit record, was appropriately the first British pop film. To some extent, then, it had *carte blanche* to map out the new terrain, but what it was most concerned with was seeking to negotiate a space between its specific topic of British pop and two established film genres, the rags-to-riches biopic and the Hollywood musical.[16]

Even if the major British film studios were enthusiastic about rock'n'roll and the teenage market, their elephantine reactions to social change prevented any immediate response to the new music, and the possibility of their contributing to the current craze was lost because the rock'n'roll phenomenon in British musical films had no sooner arrived than it departed. By the time Steele was back on screen a few months later with *The Duke Wore Jeans*, the rock'n'roll film had already morphed into something much less exhilarating, and the trend would not be reversed.

The Tommy Steele Story was made by Nat Cohen and Stuart Levy's Insignia Films, producer Herbert Smith, and director Gerard Bryant, with a screenplay by Norman Hudis, interrupted occasionally by an attractive calypso narration written and performed by Russell Henderson. The ideal accompaniment to the film was the 'genuine Tommy Steele Rhythm Knitwear by Montford'; each garment sold came with a signed photograph of Tommy, adding that final touch of enjoyment to what Insignia's publicity insisted was 'Grand entertainment for the whole family – Mum and Dad as well as the Hep-Kids'.

The story was simply told of the rise to fame of a humble lad from Bermondsey achieving celebrity. On this occasion, the marvel was that Steele was playing himself in his own biopic made at the very beginning of his career. He was catapulted into national prominence, having no sooner begun than he's in cabaret at the Café de Paris, a sure indication that a bridge has been crossed between rock'n'roll and theatrical sophistication. He tells his story. Taking a knock at judo, he lands in hospital, where he encounters his first guitar (cue one of the oddest moments in the film, when we see that one of his fellow patients is engrossed in a Henry Green novel, equivalent to Sid James being caught in a 'Carry On' film reading Ivy Compton-Burnett). Before long, patients of all ages from all over the hospital are being wheeled into his ward to hear him sing of 'Butterfingers'. It perks them up wonderfully. Restored to health, Tommy wants to see the world, but instead decides to join the Merchant Navy, taking his guitar with him. 'You've got gold in those hands, that voice,' they tell him.

Fame and fortune beckon. The navy decides he isn't for them, but in the outside world he finds a café that needs something to pep it up. Tommy soon has the customers bopping to 'Two Eyes'. His parents (acted by Charles Lamb and Hilda Fenemore) disapprove: 'Tommy Steele,' exclaims Fenemore, a perennial charwoman of British comedy, 'you're not playing your guitar in a café in Soho if I know anything about it!' Much is made of such homely attitudes, but he packs the café out, is noticed by an agent, and records 'Elevator Rock'. Underlining the importance of the industry that he has invigorated, his records are seen being pressed. At home, mum is darning socks and content in the knowledge that 'You're one of them, and you understand them.' She could not be more thrilled when she hears he's going to be in variety. His respectability is confirmed. This is the film at its most prescient, for when Steele returned to the screen with *The Duke Wore Jeans*, he had already been remoulded as an all-round entertainer, and it is in this sphere that his career has thrived.

The writer-cum-social commentator Colin MacInnes saw Steele's on-screen debut as of great social significance: 'a picture which I believe to be enormously revealing of contemporary English folk-ways, was, so far as I could check, entirely ignored by serious film critics'.[17] Perhaps the film's trailer summed it up by insisting this was a film about 'The boy who never knew where he was going until he knew just what he wanted to do', eventually encouraged by his socially conformist mother: 'You can give the young people the sort of music they want.' Finally, it seems as if those 'young people' have a reason for being, a voice of their own, and furthermore a power that belongs to them. This is perhaps the heart of Steele's story, and the heart of *The Tommy Steele Story*, at least in 1957. More recently, David Parkinson has described 'an unremarkable meteoric-rise story, not made any easier to swallow by Steele's swaggering performance'.[18] The *MFB*, by no means a journal that let its hair down when films intended for teenagers turned up for its approval, thought Steele 'a completely real person with an ability to project his reality with wholly unaffected ease', and even seemed to enjoy 'quite good rock'n'roll numbers'.[19]

MacInnes's enthusiasm for Steele is almost off the scale:

> He is Pan, he is Puck, he is every nice young girl's boy, every kid's favourite elder brother, every mother's cherished adolescent son [...] Even in the film

which, by any serious standards, is a dreadfully bad one, his charm, verve and abundant *joie de vivre* continually rescue scenes of otherwise total banality.[20]

Sight and Sound decided that 'Whatever the reason (it may be an ingenious publicity line to identify Tommy a closely as possible with his unsophisticated teen-age admirers) it seems healthy and optimistic enough.'[21] The film's dash of skiffle is exemplified by Nancy Whiskey's classic underplaying of Paul James and Fred Williams's 'Freight Train', backed by Chas McDevitt's Skiffle Group, while Humphrey Lyttleton's Band and Chris O'Brien's Caribbeans provide some relief from the film's obvious star. Reading MacInnes's assessment of the Steele phenomenon, we wonder if MacInnes was president of Steele's Fan Club. Extolling Steele's talent, MacInnes even invokes the memory of the legendary music-hall singer Marie Lloyd, of whom Steele 'seems to me to be, in so many striking ways, the popular reincarnation'. In this, Mr MacInnes is barking up a very wrong tree.

Many young performers who followed in Steele's rock'n'roll footsteps learned that fame, once grasped, could easily slip away. Steele's younger brother Colin Hicks's bid to establish himself as a rock'n'roll artiste failed to replicate Tommy's success. Fourteen-year-old Laurie London got to the top of the American hit parade with the spiritual 'He's Got the Whole World in His Hands', and Terry Dene was in the wings to become the new rock'n'roll sensation via *The Golden Disc*. Meanwhile, MacInnes could enjoy the feast of numbers included in *The Tommy Steele Story*, mostly written (in various combinations) by Steele, Lionel Bart, and Mike Pratt: 'Take Me Back Baby', 'Butterfingers', 'I Like', 'A Handful of Songs', 'Water Water', 'You Gotta Go', 'Cannibal Pot', 'Will It Be You?', 'Time to Kill', 'Two Eyes', 'Build Up', 'Elevator Rock', and 'Doomsday Rock'. Humphrey Lyttleton contributed the 'Bermondsey Bounce', and Bernard Hunter sang Roger Paul's 'It's Fun Finding Out about London'. Russ Henderson's singing of Tommy Eytle's 'Fifteen Cents Sweetheart Calypso' is a welcome intrusion, but for some the highlight may be Whiskey's classic rendition of the traditional 'Freight Train' with its new lyrics by Paul James and Fred Williams, supported by the Chas McDevitt Skiffle Group.

If *The Tommy Steele Story* suggested there would be much more of his rock and rolling to come, Britain's next musical film cast its net wider, dredging a fascinating collection of singers and musicians whose often made-overnight careers disappeared with just as much speed. If it wasn't for the wonderfully enjoyable **Rock You Sinners**, we would know much less of Dickie Bennett (introduced as 'that dynamic singing personality'); of Joan Small (previously known, but unseen, as the dubbed singing voice for Vera-Ellen's British films); of brilliant singing drummer Don Sollash and His Rockin' Horses; of little Curly Pat Barry (presumably let off school for the day); of Rory Blackwell and His Blackjacks

(Blackwell has been credited with creating the very first British rock'n'roll band, and giving Terry Dene his first break); of the great Tony Crombie (he had 'a vigour that could lift the spirits of almost any kind of band'[22]) accompanied by His Rockets; of the perfectly-at-home-bringing-calypso-to-Britain George Browne; and, far from least, Art Baxter and His Rockin' Sinners.

Jeffrey Kruger and B. C. Fancey's Small Films company hired Beatrice Scott (not surprisingly, her name doesn't crop up again in British films, but she was Mrs Fancey) to write the ridiculous screenplay, and Denis Kavanagh to oversee the cast as it negotiates its way around the cheap cardboard sets worthy of an Ed Wood film. The lackadaisical plot has nice young Johnny (cravat-wearing Philip Gilbert) trying to get together a television series featuring rock'n'roll turns, encouraged by his girlfriend Carol played by Adrienne Fancey, here credited as Adrienne Scott. Along for the ride are live-wire Pete (Colin Croft) and his partner Jackie (Jackie Collins), but this is a film belonging to the guests and, as mentioned, Art Baxter.

In September 1956 young Art was earning £10 a week as a road-worker in Stevenage, but everything changed a few weeks later when he found himself fronting his own band, The Rockin' Sinners, and earning £200 a week. Over-excitedly, he was sometimes referred to as 'Britain's answer to Bill Haley'. He certainly had the quiff and had put a few pounds on, too, and was signed up to appear in *Rock You Sinners* and on the BBC's *Six-Five Special* (his name was in the *Radio Times*, but the BBC pulled him before the show). At the end of May 1957, Baxter told the *Sunday Mirror* he'd bought himself a car and his parents a television set, but both had now been returned as he was penniless. 'I was a big star', he explained, 'but I never had any money. All the royalties from my records and fee from the film went to reduce the £300 debt I owed my agent [...] for the uniforms of the band, their shoes, shirts and ties'. Now, even before the film was released, he was reduced to standing in the dole queue at Canterbury Employment Exchange, having been fired by Kruger for turning up late for a theatre appearance. Mr Kruger rather unhelpfully explained that 'I knew he was difficult when we signed him up'. In 240 days Baxter had gone there and back from obscurity. 'Rock'n'roll is dead in Britain', he told the paper. 'And as far as the teenagers and public who clamoured for me are concerned, I am dead, too'.[23]

In fact, Baxter and His Rocking Sinners live on in *Rock You Sinners*, performing the title song he co-composed with P. Phillips, Jimmie Deuchar's 'Art's Theme', and Don Sollash's 'Dixieland Rock'. Sollash also contributes his 'Rock'n'Roll Calypso' performed by George 'Calypso' Browne, and joins His Rockin' Horses in singing his own 'Rockin' the Blues'. Rory Blackwell fronts The Blackjacks in his own composition 'Rockin' with Rory' and Deuchar's 'Intro to the Rock'. Curly Pat Barry puts over Jimmie Currie's 'Stop It – I Like It'. Tony Crombie and His Rockets appear with Crombie and Currie's 'Let's You and I Rock' and Gerry Eily and Alex Lee's 'Brighton Rock'. Dickie Bennett brings style and class to his three numbers, 'How Many Times?' by Diane and Don

Johnston, 'Cry upon My Shoulder' by Charles Aznavour, Geoffrey Parsons, and John Turner, and Elvis Presley's 'Heartbreak Hotel' by Mae Boren Axton and Tommy Durden. Joan Small breaks through the all-male line-up with Johnny Franks and Larry Boyn's 'You Can't Say I Love You'.

Baxter's physical connections with rock'n'roll remain undeniable, and it's to Kruger's, the Fanceys, and Kavanagh's credit that the film succeeds in conveying the vital excitement of the new music and its infiltration of dance halls, with the four actors worked into dance sequences performed by unpaid members of the public. Despite its absurdities (a prize example is Croft's big moment performing the excruciating and uncredited 'You've Got to Get the Message Now', which sounds very much like a third-rate revue number), this is a film too often overlooked and regularly scoffed at. As Roger Mellor describes, it

> captured the birth pangs of British rock in dance halls at a time when it was still outside the mainstream. Energetic dancers strut their stuff as tenor saxes honk to a rim shot off-beat. The 16mm location filming here is guerrilla film-making, *cinéma vérité* style, capturing the moment. In 1957, this was cutting edge stuff.[24]

In June 1957 *Rock You Sinners* was booked for an indefinite run at the London Pavilion. It is doubtful that many of its patrons bothered to take notice of the reviews, even if *Kinematograph Weekly* sounded as if it was getting into the swing by recognising that the film 'gives out with a solid beat' and that 'Unpretentious as it is, the film clearly proves that the Americans have no monopoly of rock'n'roll fare.'[25] Noting the 'negligible' plot, *MFB* suggested that the musical acts 'however lively, can hardly satisfy the more exacting initiates of the style'.[26] More generously, Chibnall concedes that the film 'captures (albeit crudely) the first enthusiastic scrabbling of young people for a music that was genuinely their own.'[27]

Rock You Sinners remains redolent of the year Art Baxter became a star, and here he stays, in the midst of a fascinating collection of material that now and again seems almost to have come from an Age (such as Bronze or Ice) vaguely recognised but estranged from us.

JULY

For wall-to-wall dullness, you could do no better than ***After the Ball***, a biopic of the Edwardian male impersonator Vesta Tilley. Her sway in Victorian and Edwardian music-hall is the stuff of legend, and as a performer she was said to have had a face 'like a city in illumination'. She is probably best remembered today, when the art of music-hall is dead and its qualities misunderstood, for her artistic contributions to the Great War, notably in her rallying cry of 1914, 'The Army of Today's All Right' by Fred W. Leigh and Kenneth Lyle, and their rumbustiously cheery 'Jolly Good Luck to the Girl Who Loves a Soldier'. There was some justification in her being known as 'England's Greatest Recruiting Sergeant'. Forty years on, her role in sending thousands of young men into battle might have suggested a strong line of interest to decent writers, but not here. Tilley's other characterisations included the wayward juvenile found in E. W. Rogers's 'Following in Father's Footsteps', but all the songs here are un-imaginatively staged, in unconvincing settings and without the essential period style. It is little wonder that Pat (Patricia) Kirkwood expressed no fondness for this depressing production.

The theatrical historian Ernest Short pointed to the problems involved in recreating Tilley's art in his 1946 *Fifty Years of Vaudeville*:

> Is there any chance of doing justice to the career of this trim little packet of mingled charm, good-nature, and impudence? Perhaps she was at her glorious best at the time of the Boer War, when no male impersonator could approach her dapper soldiers and sailors. Here was a girl who really did wear the clothes of a man with grace. No corsets, no high-heeled shoes, for Vesta Tilley. Previously most girls had played boy parts in tights, and a feminine dinner-jacket. An eyeglass, an opera hat, and a walking-stick completed the disguise, but it deceived no one.[28]

Finding it 'less hysterical than the majority of its kind', *The Times* found that *After the Ball* made it 'impossible to believe that this Vesta Tilley [Patricia Kirkwood] and her act would have impressed a village hall let alone conquered London and New York', while the absurdly inflated audience reactions created for the film were so over-enthusiastic that 'the thinness of the material becomes, by contrast, the more obvious and pathetic'.[29] This was endorsed by *Films and Filming*'s review of a 'phlegmatic survey' in which Tilley's audience, 'a diverting assortment of extras, react with conscientious gusto. Yet none of it ever strikes a spark, let alone a Vesta.'[30]

For Kirkwood, *After the Ball* was another disappointing film outing, co-starring with Laurence Harvey at his most sleek and charmless. They are mismatched. One wonders why Kirkwood insisted on playing another trouser role (although she and her husband Hubert Gregg had wanted to put her into a biopic of another music-hall great, Marie Lloyd, for which she would have been just as unsuitable) after having done two 'trouser' numbers the year before in the much more entertaining *Stars in Your Eyes*. Now, having to cope with so many more such numbers exposed her lack of natural swagger. The un-relentless focus on Kirkwood's impersonation would have made it difficult for any performer, further hampered by Compton Bennett's pedestrian direction, dreary settings, and a general visual muddiness.

Romulus Films' biography was loosely based on Tilley's autobiographi-cal *Recollections of Vesta Tilley*, written under her own name Lady de Frece (marrying into the aristocracy was something of a habit for female performers in music-hall). If the film's script is to believed, hers was a life of great success and little incident. The limping screenplay by Gregg and Peter Blackmore and the lacklustre production by Peter Rogers were in urgent need of assistance. In desperation, the authors seized on the fact that Tilley had once been sent to hospital suffering from a rhubarb allergy, presented here as the one enlivening moment. When it came to shooting this dramatic highlight, Kirkwood confessed that 'it was difficult to keep our faces straight, let alone concerned and serious'. She and Gregg 'were both glad when the film was finished.'[31]

A less unhappy *MFB* reported that Kirkwood 'performs Vesta Tilley's songs well and wears male costume with rare success', but it's distinctly faint praise.[32] Nevertheless, emboldened by the recent production of *The Tommy Steele Story* and especially *After the Ball*, Peter Rogers announced, 'We now know that nothing is impossible at Beaconsfield. This singularly difficult subject made heavy demands upon the studio's facilities and resources.'[33]

The mid-1950s marked a desperate acceleration of Herbert Wilcox's and Anna Neagle's attempts to respond to shifts of public taste. Aware that rock'n'roll had taken a grip, and that the British film's new-found realisation that the young people of Britain could not be ignored by those hoping for commercial success, they changed direction, wanting films that not only would appeal to the young and the apparent interest in youth's modern ways, but would maintain their popularity. The early 1950s had seen Wilcox morphing his star into what might be thought of as a 'serious' actress. Much was made of her dramatic impersonation of a war heroine in Wilcox's 1950 *Odette*, and the following year Neagle played Florence Nightingale in *The Lady with a Lamp*. In 1954 there was a return to romance with *Lilacs in the Spring* with Errol Flynn flown in to partner Neagle in a lumpy adaptation of her recent stage hit *The Glorious Days*. The following year they were paired again for Wilcox's film of Novello's last musical spectacular, *King's Rhapsody*. It effectively proved that the days of Novellian romance, no matter how memorable his songs, were, if not over, peacefully drawing to their close.

Neagle's successful screen partnership with Michael Wilding had ended only when Wilding effectively walked away from them (never, it had to be said, regaining the distinction the Wilcox films had given him). Wilcox now pinned his hopes on partnering Neagle with Errol Flynn, but plans to reunite them in further projects were dashed when Flynn reneged on his contract. Fighting on, the Wilcoxes returned with the 1956 *My Teenage Daughter* (played by 22-year-old Sylvia Syms) with Neagle as an upper-middle-class mother mystified by the doings of modern British youth, but the fustiness that had permeated Wilcox's work for years was a spectre at the feast. Now the intention to make films that bore some resemblance to, indeed *reflected*, modern life set the Wilcoxes on the path that would see them to the end of the decade with the 1959 *The Heart of a Man, sans* Wilding and Flynn but *avec* Frankie Vaughan. The first of the Wilcox–Vaughan–Neagle projects was ***These Dangerous Years***, in which Neagle did not appear but was credited as producer.

The trailer promised 'the new screen sensation' in 'a story of today, told with the force and ferocity of today', presumably realised in Jack Trevor Story's insipid screenplay. We may be deluded by the opening legend on screen (Wilcox was fond of such portentous announcements) that invites us to enter 'an unsupervised world where boy is king'. In this case, it's the Dingle boys, incipient disturbancers of the truth but basically decent, underprivileged lads, led by Dave Wyman (Vaughan). The opening moments suggest we might be in for some gritty realism. This, after all, is the Cast Iron Shore, that 'desolate backwater of Liverpool's prosperous river-front', with troublesome teenagers scarpering from the coppers against a bleak industrial background and going home to goodness knows what domestic abuse.

An officer, no doubt expressing the views of many of his elders, tells the Dingle lads that the army will sort them out. At the local palais, Dinah (Carol Lesley) seems likely to win the singing competition with 'Isn't This a Lovely Evening?' Wilcox seems undisturbed that she is identified variously as Diane or Dinah or Diana, but she sends the clapometer (overseen by Eric Morley, the man behind the then hugely popular 'Miss World' contest) into the stratosphere. Urged to better her score, Dave tears the roof off the palais with his gyrating title song's lyric that attempts to explain why these years are so dangerous:

Take a look, a look at your parents
If you do, you must agree
That they're displaying all the symptoms
Of old age delinquency.
They don't know what it means to rock
They go to bed at ten o'clock
It figures that they're gonna knock
These dangerous years.
What do they know?
They never heard a voice inside that cried out
'Go, go, go, go man, go!'

It's hardly Lorenz Hart, but Dave wins the prize. No sooner has his inevitable romance with Diane/Dinah/Diana begun than he gets his calling-up papers for National Service. He's barely into uniform before he's getting into scraps and smashing up the barracks. Oh, those Dingle boys, eh? Fortunately, there's an on-site Canadian padre (George Baker in what is possibly the most embarrassing role of his career) who brings with him the sort of celestial serenity with which Conrad Veidt was imbued in *The Passing of the Third Floor Back* (1935). Along with Diane/Dinah/Diana, this man of God will be Dave's saviour.

The one laugh-aloud moment comes when Dave is sent for his army regulation haircut in the hut labelled 'Camp Hairdresser'. We may safely assume that Wilcox meant this notice as defining the location of the camp's barber. This line must surely have raised eyebrows at any public viewing. To roar with laughter or to sit straight-faced as barber Reginald Beckwith delivers the one funny line in the whole shebang, that is the question. For which Mr Beckwith should have won an award. There is, however, a problem. That haircut *can never have happened*: throughout the film, Vaughan's thick helmet of hair remains firmly in place. It's just another sloppy thing about a film that makes us wonder if anyone was bothered. The demand to 'Get your hair cut!' was surely never more urgently required.

Never mind: Dave is made up to Lance-Corporal. Another officer (John Le Mesurier) looks on his soldiers sympathetically. After all, they are 'grocers, butchers, clerks. They're passing through the dangerous years between leaving school and call-up.' Indeed. No previous Wilcox film has ever seemed so concerned with the fate of the common man. Perhaps the officer hasn't noticed that Dave looks years older than any of the other new recruits, although he can rock'n'roll with unmatched frenzy. At a concert for the boys, Ralph Reader, as well known for his exuberant promotion of the Boy Scout movement as for his contribution to light entertainment, introduces the third of the numbers written by composer Bert Waller and lyricists Richard Mullen and Peter Moreton, 'I Want a Cold, Cold Shower'. A less appetising lyric cannot be imagined. The appearance of a male soldier dressed as Diana Dors only adds to the awfulness. From thereabouts, the film degenerates into a predictable charade that sees Dave wrongly accused, reviled, hunted before the padre and Diane/Dinah/Diana, save him.

Kinematograph Weekly came to Story's defence, noting the 'compelling teenage angle' while admitting that 'The film's alchemy may not be subtle.' Subtlety had never been part of Wilcox's armoury. Nevertheless, 'The picture borrows the best ideas, gags and situations from time-honoured mixed-up kid melodrama and evergreen square-bashing comedy and vigorously shakes them against authentic backgrounds.'[34] Less enthusiastically, the *MFB* regretted the 'flat script' that 'invokes every old joke about Army life; and the outcome of the mawkish drama is always obvious. Frankie Vaughan, a popular singing star, makes a vigorous if not particularly likeable screen debut' backed by a 'dull supporting cast.'[35]

Wilcox subsequently recalled

> How I had to knock against a brick wall to sell Anna Neagle at the beginning of her career. It was the same with Michael Wilding. And, more recently, I was looked at aghast when I started to sell Frankie Vaughan. 'But he's a pop-singer' (tones tinged slightly with contempt). 'Yes', Anna and I said.[36]

DECEMBER

Some context is needed if we are to understand Ealing's **Davy**, produced by Michael Balcon and Basil Dearden and directed by Michael Relph, to the full: we need to consider it alongside other domestic product of its period. From

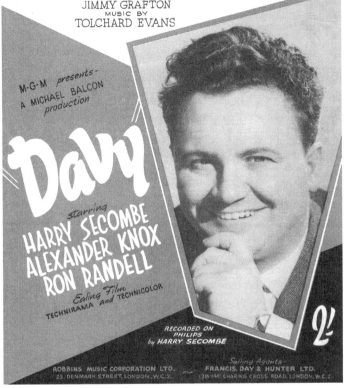

What to do with the conflicting talents of Harry Secombe?
Ealing's 1957 *Davy* tried to resolve the predicament, but its
components struggled to coalesce.

1956 on, the industry's obsession with the decline of music-hall and variety
is clearly discernible, through *Charley Moon* (Max Bygraves and, unconvincingly, Dennis Price as a no-hope double-act) and the admirable *Stars in Your
Eyes* with its gallant music-hall turns making one last stand before succumbing
to the inevitability of television and ending up as a walk-on in *Dixon of Dock
Green*, through *The Good Companions* as heated up for a second serving, in its
way a lament for the final bow of concert party, on its last legs by the mid-1950s.

Emerging at the end of 1957, *Davy* may be the summation of films about
British music-hall. Its lack of airs and graces catches something of that lost
art's earthiness, just when the domestic audience is about to be bombarded

with product allegedly directed at a newer, 'with it' younger clientele. The old-troupers of *Stars in Your Eyes* are threatened by the advent of television, whereas the Mad Morgans are threatened by the possible break-up of their act. As their frequently sozzled patriarch Uncle Pat insists, 'It's a family act, and a family act is the closest kind of partnership there is. You don't desert a family act. It's just not the thing to do.'

This, rather than the slow death of music-hall, is the central dilemma of a film that is always well-intentioned and occasionally moving, focused on Davy (Harry Secombe), the essential cog in the hermetically sealed familial relationship that binds the Mad Morgans together. Settling down to watch the film, we already know that its star has a two-sided appeal to his admirers. As a zany Goonish comedian, he is well represented in a protracted slapstick stage routine. The problem is that Davy and Secombe can also sing, here performing Jimmy Grafton and Tolchard Evans's 'My World Is Your World' (somewhat prescient of Secombe's hit number 'If I Ruled the World' in the 1963 stage musical *Pickwick*). It's not enough for Davy; he wants to sing seriously, and he auditions for and is accepted by the Royal Opera, Covent Garden. Realising that the family act will die without him, he returns to the miserable, dank dressing-room at Collins Music Hall. As an ending, this is hardly satisfactory; we are left unsure whether his decision is (a) happy or (b) unhappy. It is possibly (c) unwise, but the sudden joyful reunion with the rest of the Mad Morgans at the end of the film is somehow unconvincing.

We should not, however, under-rate the importance of that dressing-room, where a great deal of the action takes place. The picture's opening shot is of Collins Music Hall on Islington Green. This theatre, grandly converted from a public house, was created by Irish artiste Sam Collins in 1863. At the time of filming, it was still very much a working hall, the only London theatre that could, like the Windmill, boast that it had never closed. By now, the management had adopted another feature of the Windmill, female nudes. One of the most prominent in 1957 was Manchester's Blondie Haigh. The days when famous entertainers appeared on its bills were gone, but business continued (only four shillings for a stalls seat) with the likes of contortionist Eliza Rae and male impersonator Billie Roche on the bill. Its reputation as one of the last bastions of genuine music-hall was proved when in 1957 Laurence Olivier visited in advance of playing Archie Rice in John Osborne's play *The Entertainer*.

The authenticity of the Mad Morgans' subterranean dressing-room that we see on screen cannot be doubted. Secombe recalled that many of the scenes were filmed there, with water running down its walls. He wondered why so dark and drear a background was being exposed in Technicolor and widened in Techni-rama. There is no hint of those absurdly extravagant dressing-rooms we see in so many other British musical films. The Mad Morgans' environment may be unattractive and patently atrocious, but looks very much like the real thing.

We can compare the scenes that take place there with similar scenes in *The Entertainer*, where Archie's famous music-hall father Billy Rice is a leftover from an age when music-hall reigned supreme. The comparisons between *Davy*'s Uncle Pat (beautifully played by George Relph) and John Osborne's Billy Rice are unmistakable. It is no coincidence that Relph had created the role of Billy in the original stage production of *The Entertainer*. The similarities and differences between the two works may help us appreciate both. Osborne wraps on-stage musical numbers into the fabric of his play; for *Davy*, screen-writer William Rose doesn't, and only when he gets to that Covent Garden audition does Secombe sing again, performing Puccini's 'Nessun dorma', on the stage where another auditioner, Joanna Reeves (Adele Leigh), has just delivered Mozart's 'Voi che sapete' to maestro Sir Giles Manning (excellent Alexander Knox). The number is not necessary to the film, and is one of several sequences that merely slows the action. In compensation, we get a glimpse of the Covent Garden canteen, behind whose counter serve Liz Fraser, Joan Sims, and Gladys Henson.

The Entertainer sustains our interest in the dynamics of the Rice family, not only via its on-stage songs, but attempts in *Davy* to interest us in the fate of the Mad Morgans is somewhat half-hearted. At one point it seems that Uncle Pat is having a complete breakdown, but the scene lacks development, having no dramatic comparison with Brenda de Banzie's emotional collapse in *The Entertainer*. The film never quite helps us know the Mad Morgans as people, so that when Davy turns his back on a possible operatic career we care less than we should. Instead, you can almost feel the film fizzle out. Ultimate-ly, we must be grateful that *Davy* was made when it was. In September 1958, a fire begun in a wood-merchant's behind Collins Music Hall destroyed all but the theatre's façade. In the last throes of British music-hall, *Davy* at least lets us peep into a theatrical world that already seemed to be in perpetual mourning. It marks a passing.

1958

a rare glimpse of British Rail catering in the late fifties

6.5 Special

The Golden Disc
6.5 Special
The Duke Wore Jeans
Wonderful Things
A Cry from the Streets

The Sheriff of Fractured Jaw
tom thumb
Hello London
Life Is a Circus

FEBRUARY

By any standards, Butcher's tribute to the coffee bar culture of the late 1950s is a dismal piece of work that somehow made it to the screen despite battling its crushing budget constraints. Nevertheless, *The Golden Disc* has much to offer, and for those susceptible to its naïve charms, it remains vastly entertaining. It is a wonderful example of what we may call demi-choreography, rather than

Sometimes dismissed as being of little importance, Butcher's quietly seminal *The Golden Disc* (1958) was an affectionate memento of burgeoning rock'n'roll and coffee bars in the late 1950s.

dancing as we know it. Naturally, hand-jiving plays its part, being especially handy as it doesn't take up much studio space, a distinct advantage in a film in which characters are forever coming through suspiciously curtained areas that no doubt hide a multitude of production sins (it was produced at Walton studios by W. G. Chalmers). Director Don Sharp and Don Nicholl provide a screenplay based on a story by Gee Nicholl.

Dennis Lotis, a considerable catch for Butcher's Film Services, obligingly starts the film off by singing Philip Green and Ray Mack's attractive 'I'm Gonna Wrap You Up' to a theatre full of screaming teenagers. One Lotis enthusiast has 'Denis' (wrongly spelled) writ large across her top. Some time later, we see her again, with 'Terry' writ large on her top, a clear indication that allegiances in the pop world can swiftly shift, and that Mr Lotis may not be exempt from the effect.

These, after all, are changing times, in a cinematic era where the British public have already been offered *The Tommy Steele Story* and *Rock You Sinners*. Now young Terry Dene continues drawing what passes in Butcher's Films for a crowd with Green and Mack's restful 'Charm' and Len Paverman's jaunty 'Candy Floss'. Later, we move to the recording studios, where Phil Seaman's Jazz Group perform his 'Lower Deck' complete with manic drummer, and Murray Campbell performs Green's sub-Eric Coates 'Balmoral Melody'. It falls to Sheila Buxton to have the most interesting number of all, Green and Mack's 'The In-Between Age'. It probably deserves a better film, its lyric a wry, sympathetic comment on the generation it attempts to represent:

> They say we're adolescent
> Too young to fall in love
> We haven't reached the grown-up stage
> Why do they have to tell us
> This is an in-between age?
> They say our minds are open
> They read us like a book
> But wait until we turn the second page
> A growing-pains age

Similarly reflective, Michael Robbins and Richard Dix's 'The Golden Age' has the teenage onlookers thoughtfully swaying in quirky demi-choreography as Dene softly insists:

> Don't let their golden age slip through your fingers
> Don't let the golden age pass us by
> These are the golden years that offer everything
> So let the love they bring never die!

It is Aunt Sarah (Linda Gray), the owner of a dim little teashop, who is persuaded to become 'with it' by Joan and Harry Blair (Mary Steele and quiffed Canadian actor Lee Patterson familiar to B movies), although Sarah sees nothing wrong with her café:

Aunt Sarah:	The coffee's good, too, if I do say it myself.
Joan:	But it's not espresso.
Aunt Sarah:	Espresso? That's coffee? Oh, two boys came in the other night and asked if we had espressos. I thought they wanted newspapers!
Joan:	Oh, you've got a lot to learn, Aunt Sarah. This place could be a gold-mine!

They recommend a thorough overhaul of Auntie's premises, with 'plain walls and mad line drawings' against which the geometrical intricacies of hand-jiving will stand out, although Sarah is still confused ('Can we have a jackbox?'). Business booms, the Gaggia gushes and steams, the transparent cups and saucers tilt and satisfy, the jukebox is throbbing, the teenagers enraptured and presumably full to the gunnels of espresso coffee. In short, Aunt Sarah is with it where she had previously been without. Failure threatens one night with the jukebox on the blink. Saving the day, young Terry Dene, guitar always on standby, lures the teenagers back in by performing Len Paverman's 'C'min and Be Loved'. For *Kinematograph Weekly*, Dene was 'a close rival to Tommy Steele', in a 'triumphant debut'.[1] The coffee bar thrives, and there is no holding Aunt Sarah, Harry, and Joan, who set up their very own label Charm Records.

One of *The Golden Disc*'s most appealing attributes is its apparent innocence, set in a milieu where tyro vocalist Joan wears elbow-length evening gloves to complement her summer frock, and a yet-to-be-convinced-as-to-the-relevance-of-Terry-Dene enthusiast asks for a record of Pat Boone. As Roger Mellor has noted, Steele 'looks and sounds as if she has just stepped out of a 1950's television commercial for Omo or Daz, and probably has'.[2] Her performance of Green and Norman Newell's 'Before We Said Goodnight' suggests she isn't en route to stardom.

We even have the beautifully enunciating disc jockey David Jacobs. We sense that having him spending a couple of hours in the film studio was considered by a film of this type to be no less than a cinematic coup, when one of the film's real achievements is having the surely legendary Nancy Whiskey belt out Paverman's 'Johnny O!' backed by Sonny Stewart and His Skiffle Kings, reminding us that Sharp and Nicholl's film is paying homage to skiffle as much as to what some might define as rock'n'roll. It's skiffle that grabs our attention when the Les Hobeaux Skiffle Group zip through Tommie Connor's fantastic 'Dynamo', or when Sonny Stewart and His Skiffle Kings go into Stewart's 'Let Me Lie'.

Dene, remembered as one of the five-minute wonders of the British musical film, had been heralded in some quarters as the British Elvis. Indeed, he followed in Presley's well-exploited footsteps by joining the British army, but his tenure was brief; by January 1959 he was in military hospital suffering from 'emotional strain'. Newspaper reports charted the dégringolade of 'a somewhat nervous and restless young man' who was 'more or less pitch-forked into a life of great publicity which had never come his way before.'[3] He had worked variously as a messenger, film extra, timber hunker, crate maker, plumber's mate, and packer. To some, his unexpected propulsion to fame and fortune augured the rise of a new type of celebrity.

The Golden Disc holds a special place in the history of the British musical film. The *MFB* complained that 'the performances which the film wraps in its somewhat vapid plot are all genteel and disappointingly inhibited.'[4] *Variety* agreed that 'The pic [*sic*] would have been more acceptable had the screenplay by Don Nicholl and Don Sharp not been completely devoid of wit and suspense, and also had Sharp's direction not been so plodding.'[5]

MARCH

It's a shock to discover that the rock'n'roll locomotive that was the **6.5 *Special*** was not only a steam engine but a corridor train. An inappropriate vehicle, perhaps, for the BBC Television series begun in 1957 as a 'hip', up-to-the-minute musical showcase for the newly visible generation of British teenagers, an homage to the now forgotten art of hand-jiving. In fact, Anglo-Amalgamated's film version, written by Norman Hudis, produced at the Alliance Studios in Twickenham by Herbert Smith and directed by Alfred Shaughnessy, is a very odd affair, seemingly unaware of the earth-shaking effect of Elvis Presley. On this evidence, it is no wonder the television series (highly popular on Saturday nights) lasted only until the end of 1958, by which time the original cornerstones of the enterprise – producer and presenter Jo Douglas, disc jockey Pete Murray, and ex-boxer Freddie Mills, all present in the film – had fled the scene.

Tom Sloan, Assistant Head of BBC Television Light Entertainment, explained. Mills 'finally developed into a clown. Like all clowns he needs material and we need changes. Hence our decision not to renew his contract.' Douglas 'made up her own mind to leave' apparently because she wanted to spend more time with her family and 'wants to have her Saturday evenings free' (hardly a ringing endorsement of the programme). As for Murray, 'his agent made certain demands and there was nothing we could do.' Despite this bloodbath, all three are on show for Anglo-Amalgamated's film, strange beast that it is. By 1958, Sloan was anyway expressing doubts, suggesting that 'Rock'n'roll and skiffle appear to be declining. There is a definite swing back to ballads.'[6] Subsequently, this apparent swing in public taste away from what teenagers wanted (or what the BBC decided to offer them) had Max Bygraves brought into the mix. Cheekily, he even finished one of the shows with a waltz. Could it be that the broadcasters had taken their finger off the pulse of the nation?

Hudis's plot uses the slenderest of devices, around wholesome Anne (Diane Todd) dreaming of becoming a performer although admitting, 'I'm strictly a bathroom soprano.' Thus, the picture begins with her 'You Are My Favourite Dream' written by Shaughnessy, a sweetly innocent offering that would not have been out of time in the 1930s, and could hardly be thought appealing to the film's intended audience of 1958. As Anne later explains, 'It's a Wonderful Thing to Be Loved' (by Gerald Marks and Milton Pascal).

Undeterred, in search of an audition, Anne catches the train (it leaves at 6.5) for London. Luckily, Jim Dale, who happens to be passing in the corridor, is on hand not only to explain that this is a 'pro' train carrying a galaxy of pop singers, but to start the ball rolling by fetching his guitar. He entertains the girls with Charlie Phillips and Odis 'Pop' Echols's 'Sugartime' and Louis Mann, Myron Bradshaw, and Howie Kay's 'The Train Kept a-Rolling'.

The compartments are busy on the 6.5 special, its theme music by Julian More and Johnny Johnston. In another compartment, the endlessly harmonising Ken-Tones are trying a new arrangement of Clay Boland and Moe Jaffe's 'The Gypsy in My Soul'. Petula Clark pops out into the corridor to ask Anne to listen to a new number someone has sent her: it's Wandra Merrell's 'Baby Lover'. Other female vocalists are Joan Regan with Billy Reid's plangent ballad 'I'll Close My Eyes' and Cleo Laine with John Dankworth in his 'What Am I Going to Tell Them Tonight', but this is predominantly a male outing during which Don Lang and His Frantic Five perform their 'Boy Meets Girl', Bruce Hamilton performs his own composition 'I Had a Dream', Desmond Lane entertains with Joseph D. Newman's 'The Midgets', and John Barry gets to promote his 'sound' with his 'You've Gotta Way' and Mel Tormé's 'Ev'ry Which Way'.

Other passengers include comic duo Mike and Bernie Winters (popular in the television series) and – much more welcome – velvet-voiced Victor Soverall and Trinidadian Jimmy Lloyd as cooks in the train's kitchen (a rare glimpse of British Rail catering in the late fifties). Soverall sings Peter Kreuder, Harry Link, John Turner, and Geoffrey Parsons' 'Say Goodbye Now', and Lloyd sings Bobby Sharp and Jerry Teifer's 'Ever Since I Met Lucy'. The long train journey is further enlivened by middle-of-the-roaders Dickie Valentine and the Popular King Brothers, Valentine singing Clive Allen and Bobby Joy's 'The King of Dixieland' and Aldo Piga, Maurizio De Angelis, and Jack Elliott's 'Come to My Arms', and the King Brothers singing an arrangement of the traditional 'Hand Me Down My Walking Cane' and Geoff Love and Johnny King's title song. Love also wrote 'Ice Blue', featuring a dance duo by Paddy Stone and Leigh Madison.

One of the most enjoyable sequences is reserved for Jackie Dennis's 'La Dee Dah' by Bob Crewe and Frank Slay, but for many the outstanding contributor will be Lonnie Donegan with Woody Guthrie's 'The Grand Coolie Dam' and an arrangement of the traditional 'Jack O'Diamonds'.

The oldest theatrical survivor on view is the great Finlay Currie, hidden behind his theatrical newspaper. He is here to lecture Anne on the inadvisability of a youngster going onto the stage. It's a curious scene; Hudis seems to be issuing a stern warning against considering showbusiness as a career (sensible enough when you consider the future of some of the film's performers), as if teenagers' heads may have been turned by the prospects of instant fame and riches. Russ Hamilton's first disc sold a million copies. In later years he recalled, 'I was going round the world singing my head off, and I was swindled out of a fortune.'[7] Edinburgh's Jackie Dennis's anthem 'La Dee Dah' took him into the Top Ten at the age of fifteen. Described as 'Fame in a Kilt' (he explained 'I would'ne be without it'), he may have been Scotland's first pop star, although he disagreed ('I always maintain it was Lonnie Donegan').[8] It is Donegan, undeniably the 'King of Skiffle', who closes the film. As the *MFB* reported, 'The singers of long experience shine like beacons amongst some alarming "overnight" rock'n'roll successes.'[9] And Donegan shines the brightest.

When we sit through the film today, the mystery remains: why did 1950s British teenagers scream whenever Dickie Valentine (and others of his ilk) came into view? Why do so patently middle-of-the-road performers invoke such frenzied response? We can appreciate it as an archival document of its period, telling us as much about the BBC as about the popular music atmosphere of the time. If all else fails, there is the parade of patterned frocks for the girls and the generous selection of period men's knitwear. The *Daily Mirror* informed its readers that they would need number 2 and number 4 needles if they wanted to 'Get in the mood with the 6.5 Sweater': 'Jo and Pete had theirs in green and beige.'[10] Somehow, the dangerous undercurrents of rock'n'roll are given no space in this tamest of memorials, with nothing so modern and innovative that it would not have done equally well for the BBC's radio series *Housewives' Choice*.

Having already starred in his own biopic *The Tommy Steele Story* for which he was paid £3,000, the 'tousle-haired hero from Bermondsey, who all in a year jumped from the Merchant Navy to film star and £2,000 a week'[11] followed on with *The Duke Wore Jeans*, produced for Nat Cohen and Stuart Levy by Peter Rogers and directed by Gerald Thomas; their star's contract was for £20,00 plus a share of the profits. How to build on the success of owning his very own biopic? *The Times* thought the follow-up 'a puerile affair', wondering:

> If this talent was to be fostered, both in the interests of his producers in particular and of the British film industry in general, one would have imagined that much care would have been given to the choice of story for his second picture, and that this young player would have been granted the benefit of more subtle direction and a strong supporting cast.[12]

In its way, this semi-Ruritanian fantasy showed the way forward for Steele's career, veering from an acknowledgement as Britain's most promising rock'n'roll performer to a wholesome musical Everyman. He plays Tony Whitecliffe, heir to an upper-class family (not much of one; his mother puts milk in her cup before pouring the tea) who want him to marry Princess Maria of faraway Ritilla, a seriously strapped-for-cash principality apparently dependent on under-financed set designers with bad taste. Happily, a spitting image of Tony in the shape of chirpy cockney sprig Tommy Hudson, arrives on Tony's doorstep. He looks uncannily like Tony (were cinemagoers confused?), who arranges for this assembly-line cockney sparrow to take his place, travel to Ritilla, and meet the princess. Once he is in Ritilla, his artless charm quickly wins over the populace, and talk of a political take-over rebellion does not get in the way of his falling for Her Royal Highness, whose bedroom lacks aesthetic charm.

As in *The Tommy Steele Story*, the songs are by the still-up-and-coming Lionel Bart and Mike Pratt: Tommy's breezy opening number 'It's All Happening'; Tommy and Tony duetting with themselves and somehow getting through Pauline Grant's utilitarian choreography in the stagey 'What Do You Do?'; 'Our Family Tree', in which Tommy attempts to explain his genealogy to foreigners understandably mystified by their first experience of hearing the sort of songs written for British films (Steele said the song was 'a bastard to sing, but I relished it'); 'Happy Guitar' with Tommy at large in a musical instrument factory; Tommy entertaining at a Royal staff do in 'Let Your Hair Down Everybody'; 'Princess', his duet with Maria (the only chance for June Laverick to join in); 'Photograph My Baby' at a press reception for their engagement; and 'Thanks a Lot, I've Had a Ball' when a Pearly King and Queen are flown in to prove that Tommy's blood is blue as blue. Throwing decorum to the wind, the company leaves us with a spirited rendition of that most rasping of East End choruses 'Knees Up Mother Brown'. There have, frankly, been far too many songs.

A kindly review in the *MFB* welcomed Steele's new vehicle, although 'the august supporting cast too often betray a sense that they are "slumming" – with rather embarrassing results'.[13] *Variety* encouraged the star, who 'emerges as a likeable personality with acting potential';[14] Mark Cunliffe saw a 'dim comedy with numerous woeful songs'.[15] As David Parkinson has written:

> Where movies are concerned, a single Tommy Steele is usually one too many, but two are more than flesh and blood can bear [...] The 'trading places' plot is one of the venerable old chestnuts of drama and the jerry-built sets and fifth-rate pop songs that adorn this tosh considerably scuff the sheen. Gerald Thomas [director] and Peter Rogers [producer] made cheapskate part of the *Carry On* [films] appeal, but here it simply seems tatty.[16]

Credulity is soon put to bed, not least in Ritilla, where the royal palace and its spindly trappings bear no comparison to Buckingham. The divide between the classes and cultures is ridiculously accented. Tony's mother's lapse of breeding (milk last!) is not the only social solecism that cinemagoers are obliged to witness in an unremittingly witless compendium. Many can only have squirmed at hearing Princess Maria, her brain obviously turned by Tommy's Harry Champion-like banter, confront her Prime Minister: 'What's on your mind, mate? I'm going to be his trouble and strife.'

Its obvious shortcomings overlooked, *The Duke Wore Jeans* helped to con-solidate Steele's special place in British cinema as he managed his transition from Britain's Elvis (which he never was) to the nirvana awarded to those sometimes referred to as 'all-round' entertainers. There is no denying the quantity of bright musical moments, with Bart and Pratt providing a score that points the way to the sort of anonymously vigorous stuff that Peter Myers and Ronnie Cass would churn out for the Cliff Richard series of musical films begun with the 1961 *The Young Ones*.

JUNE

Why do so many Herbert Wilcox pictures have such terrible opening shots behind the title credits, whether distant shots of London (Mayfair, natural-ly) traffic, the hideous mountainous scenery of the imaginary principality in which the ponderous *King's Rhapsody* is set, presumably intended as pictur-esque but in fact resembling nothing so much as elephant dung, or the aerial shots of the Rock of Gibraltar, guaranteed not to set a tourist's heart beating, for the Wilcoxes' **Wonderful Things**. Somehow, there's never a doubt, from the opening titles onwards, that we are in for a *big* film within which a very much smaller one lurks. Producer Anna Neagle had also produced Frankie Vaughan's *These Dangerous Years*, assuring the public that 'I'd like to have him in a dramatic story *without* singing. He can do it, but is the audience ready for Frankie without a song? After all, Sinatra has done it.' She was convinced that 'He'll be one of the really big stars of the future, I think. Really big box-office.'[17]

What was more, *Wonderful Things* promised a Wilcoxian up-to-dateness as the film's fierce promotion made it almost impossible to avoid. In British cinemas, it was booked for simultaneous release in sixty-five 'key locations' on August Bank Holiday Monday. Inexplicably, the Wilcoxes seemed de-termined to reach a younger audience, despite the generally conservative and antediluvian attitudes of their product. Not a bit of it, declared *Kine-matograph Weekly*: 'Herbert Wilcox Is No Square.' This was the man 'who has handled high society in Mayfair [...] and is bringing the same shrewdness to bear in the teenage markets'.[18] One lucky couple won a competition in *Woman's Mirror* to spend a weekend at the Metropole, Brighton, including dinner with Frankie, who was also sent on a foreign promotional tour to coincide with the film's continental release.

Jack Trevor Story's screenplay concerns two conning fishermen brothers, elder Carmello (Vaughan) and younger Mario (Jeremy Spenser), both enamoured of Pepita (Jackie Lane). In search of prosperity so that he may marry her, Carmello relocates to London, working his passage as a waiter and a wrestler on a fairground ('Remember, boys, no gouching or biting!'). No oppor-tunity to emphasise Carmello's (or Vaughan's) undoubted manliness is over-looked, incorporating lingering moments of his romanticising. Balancing this youthful virility (although Vaughan seems a little too mature and his presence on screen strangely solid) we have one of the staple Wilcox old codgers, Wilfrid

Hyde-White, completely out of place in a film apparently aimed at that 'teen' audience. There is little help from a supporting cast that includes Jean Dawnay's socialite butterfly characterisation as Anne, or from ex-model Barbara Goalen making what Wilcox coyly credits as a 'courtesy appearance', in which talent plays no part. The best, uncluttered, freshest show comes from Spenser. In other hands, he might have shown promise as an incipient British James Dean, but it is only too obvious that, although prominently billed, he is little more than the inevitable add-on to the star. The one element in this dullest of love stories that might have grabbed the interest of the young is given no chances.

The music doesn't help much, either. For some reason, the songs are by the American Harold Rome, composer of several musicals, among them *Gone with the Wind* and *Fanny*; it was memorably claimed that his *Fanny* was 'the biggest on Broadway'. His music was widely known to be serviceable rather than exciting, and is true to form here. 'Little Fishes' goes some way to creating a salty atmosphere and sense of communal living among the sea-going fraternity, but the main focus is on Vaughan's singing of the title song to the fairground crowds. Inexplicably, he suddenly loses his Gibraltarian accent – just as well, as Wilcox lets him put it over as if he were on stage at the London Palladium. If we were in any doubt, Carmello's solo is rapturously received by the onlookers ('A wonderful song, wonderfully sung!').

The melodramatic love triangle is worked out to everyone's satisfaction except, possibly, that of the cinemagoer. All this despite Wilcox's publicity machine insisting that Vaughan is 'perhaps our greatest star yet' and lining him up alongside 'Valentino, Al Jolson, Chaplain and Danny Kaye', at the same time as persuading local fishmongers the length and breadth of the country to promote the picture by using the caption: 'You can cook Wonderful Things to eat from fresh fish'. This level of invention is at least on a level with the film's script. The *MFB* politely dismissed the whole affair as a 'quaint production', 'unsophisticated and ingenuous'.[19] Whether Wilcox enjoyed watching such stuff is unknown.

AUGUST

Max Bygraves's follow-up to the 1956 *Charley Moon* was the social drama *A Cry from the Streets*, written by Vernon Harris from Elizabeth Coxhead's novel *The Friend in Need*. Produced by Ian Dalrymple for Film Traders and directed by Lewis Gilbert, this 'definitely down-to-earth'[20] film had Barbara Murray as a perfectly made-up, meticulously coiffured, impeccably dressed, cool and collected, and RADA-trained social worker, Ann, with a caseload of abandoned children. Murray was no more authentic an example of that hard-worked and under-appreciated species than Celia Johnson's perfectly made-up (etc.) social worker in Ealing's well-meant (and likeable) *I Believe in You* (1952), a film that sought to introduce British post-war audiences to the concept of social work.

Ann's way with hopelessly inept mothers is of the no-nonsense variety; she tells a drunken mother, 'an habitual slut' (Eleanor Summerfield), to 'Stop drinking, Gloria, and get yourself a job.'

Beginning against a background of almost brutalist post-war new building, the film promises to be a hard-hitting treatment of contemporary social issues, but perhaps winds up as what Leslie Halliwell classifies as a 'mildly pleasing but unconvincing semi-documentary, with children competing with the star at scene-stealing'.[21] They are well represented here, explaining why Gilbert won a silver medal, for directing a film with children, at Moscow's first film festival. After *Charley Moon*, Bygraves was used to working with children; some of his best moments, in both films, are spent among them. Now, he has his own composition 'You Got to Have Rain', perhaps a little intruding on the seriousness of Gilbert's philanthropic theme.

There is excellent supporting work in a cast that includes Mona Washbourne as a children's home matron of the old school, Kathleen Harrison on top form as an inadequate mother, and most notably Sean Barrett as a teenager emotionally at sea. Throughout, Gilbert manages the various relationship vignettes with sensitivity. Alan Dent imagined that

> they will be deemed crude or merely sentimental by the more casual kind of filmgoer. They seem to me to be utterly true to a sort of life which is in reality crude and sentimental as well as harsh in its values even if [Bygraves] does not really 'belong' to [the film]. But this amiable and widely popular young comedian has a way of saturating any kind of show with his own personality.[22]

The background score is by Larry Adler, with harmonica, an instrument rarely appreciated by the British public.

NOVEMBER

In a year dominated by films vaguely intended to please younger elements of British society, *The Sheriff of Fractured Jaw* brought unexpected relief in its spirited adventure of the Wild West, a location almost unknown to the British musical film but more likely to be found in Hollywood's product: think *Seven Brides for Seven Brothers* and *Calamity Jane*. Although not of the same quality, Daniel M. Angel's romantic comedy is at least an attempt to do something different for the domestic market. Howard Dimsdale's screenplay, from a story by Jacob Hay, seems untroubled by its central conviction that guns are a good thing, especially in the wilder parts of the USA. Jonathan Tibbs, gentlemanly and sophisticated, the heir to a British gunsmith company, sees the unexplored potential for gun sales beyond the grouse-shooting clients of his St James Piccadilly shop. He has heard, too, of 'some frightful female there called Jessie James. She's shooting at everyone.' Arriving in the hillbilly

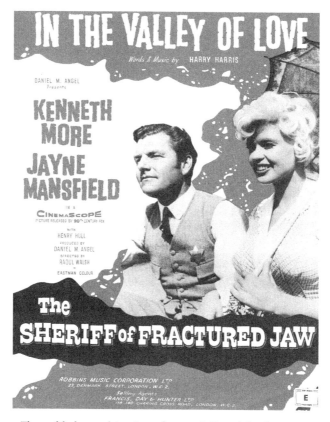

The unlikely combination of staunch British leading man
Kenneth More and Jayne Mansfield did not altogether
overshadow the British attempt at making a Wild West
musical film in the 1958 *The Sheriff of Fractured Jaw.*

backwoods outpost of Fractured Jaw (courtesy of the turf war between the
gun-slinging gangs that rule the place, its cemetery is always busy), Tibbs
soon finds himself appointed the town's sheriff, no sooner done than the
local undertaker is measuring him for his soon to be expected coffin. Unused
to the rude ways of the locals, Tibbs nevertheless charms Kate, the overtly
glamorous owner of the local inn (Jayne Mansfield).

In such unlikely surroundings, Kenneth More's gentlemanly presence
carries the day in a light characterisation completely at ease with the material,
and it is More who sustains the interest. Fortunately, he is not called upon
to sing, as he would be in the 1964 West End musical *Our Man Crichton.*
He had already played J. M. Barrie's butler Crichton in the non-musical *The
Admirable Crichton* (1957), but the musical version proved he was no singer.

In *Fractured Jaw*, the songs by Harry Harris belong to Kate: two numbers with her girls' chorus worked into her cabaret act ('If the San Francisco Hills Could Only Talk' and 'Strolling Down the Lane with Bill'), and (most memorably) the appealing 'In The Valley of Love' (rather in the style of 'The Black Hills of Dakota'), sung to More.

In the background, Robert Farnon's score kicks up an orchestral dust-storm of rumbustious enthusiasm with frequent bursts of 'Rule Britannia' that remind us of the hero's stubborn Britishness. Mansfield's Kate is nicely drawn, but her songs are dubbed by Connie Francis. The choreography (basically Kate's on-stage routines) is by George Carden.

Films and Filming suggested that 'Like most situation comedies, it goes on too long. [It does, for 103 minutes, by which time the central idea is exhausted] A twenty-minute cut would prevent the basic joke going a little stale.'[23] For the *Observer*, 'It's simple-minded, simple-hearted, and the exaggerated display of ferocity conceals the minimum of violence',[24] while the *MFB* found Raoul Walsh's direction 'surprisingly pedestrian', his two stars giving 'oddly mistimed and limited performances'.[25] *The Times* described 'a truly bizarre historical aberration'.[26]

DECEMBER

The quality of MGM's fairy tale ***tom thumb*** insists on its inclusion as the only patently musical film for children in these pages. Working from the deft screenplay by Ladislas Fodor based on the Brothers Grimm story, producer and director George Pal, with an army of puppeteers and special effects specialists, has created a wonderland of colour and charm that is genuinely magical, simple enough for children to enjoy, and clever enough for adult attention. Russ Tamblyn, remembered for his Gideon in *Seven Brides for Seven Brothers* of 1954, is the captivating miniature hero, adopted by the poor but kind and childless Jonathan (Bernard Miles) and Anna (Jessie Matthews). There is romantic enchantment between friendly and lovable Woody (Alan Young) and the apparently ethereal Queen of the Forest (June Thorburn). The sustained comedy sequences with Terry-Thomas and Peter Sellers are brilliantly effective, but everything here suggests perfection and an impeccable cast list that has the benefit of Ian Wallace's happy Cobbler and Peter Butterworth (incomparable if you need protracted exasperation) as a frustrated bandmaster.

Technically, this is a superb piece where everything combines to ensure success: Pal's assured direction, the utterly seductive Pal's Puppetoons, the artwork of Elliot Scott, the vivid photography of Georges Perinal, the photographic effects by Tom Howard, and the commendable score by Douglas Gamley and Ken Jones, with Peggy Lee's theme 'Tom Thumb's Tune'. Matthews had last appeared on screen in the little-seen short *Life Is Nothing Without Music* in 1947. One of her proposed numbers, 'Take a Little Time to Smile', was dropped, but Fred Spielman and Janice Torre's sentimental 'After All These Years' was retained, although Matthews's singing is dubbed by Norma Zimmer. Spielman and Torre's 'Talented Shoes', introduced by the Cobbler and taken up as one of the film's most zestful set pieces, is cleverly choreographed by Alex Romero and irresistibly danced through by the superb Tamblyn. Pal's Puppe-toons have their finest moment in 'The Yawning Song' with music by Spielman and lyric by Kermit Goell, sung by Stan Freberg. Woody serenades the Queen of the Forest with Peggy Lee's 'Are You a Dream?' The film's admirable achieve-ment was appreciated by *Variety*'s comparing it to a Disney classic, and *Time*'s unarguable opinion that it was 'unusually fresh and appealing'.[27]

Kinran Pictures' **Hello London** was concocted by producer George Fowler and co-authors Herb Sargent, Ken Englund, and Guy Elmes, with a generous and sprightly if unmemorable score by Philip Green and Michael Carr. It is disguised as a travelogue around London undertaken by the Norwegian ice-skating star Sonja Henie and companions Eunice Gayson and Michael Wilding (all playing, unlikely as it appears on screen, Themselves), with Ronny Graham as Himself or Henie's manager.

Here is a vanity project by Henie, who planned the film as the first of many she would release wherever she rested her caravan around the globe, in effect what we might now understand as a promotional 'video' intended to boost attendance at her live ice extravaganzas. We must be thankful that the idea was realised with such enthusiasm, resulting in director Sidney Smith's hotch-potch of scenes set on London buses (a cramped location for some ridiculous choreography), in under-populated night-spots, at a gentlemen's outfitter in Savile Row (one of its sales assistants is Welsh tenor Trefor Jones, who two decades earlier had sung Ivor Novello melodies with Mary Ellis in *Glamorous Night*), at Battersea's funfair, and in protracted extracts from Ms Henie's ice show of the moment. Presumably, these routines are offered as the main course, but they are so uninventively filmed, and exposed in such cavernous spaces (you can almost feel cinemagoers wishing they'd brought a cardigan), that they fail to warm the spirits. The luxury of Eastmancolor and the expansiveness of Cinemascope do nothing to melt the glacial atmosphere.

The permanently fixed smiles of delight on the faces of Wilding, with none of the charisma that sustained him through his long years as Anna Neagle's on-screen lover, and Gayson, and the dialogue they are obliged to reiterate, remind us that actors must eat and will at times do just about anything for the money. Dennis Price is among the supporting players in the same situation; he sings. The script encourages the audience's low expectations, as when a nightclub host introduces 'The man you've all been waiting to see – Roy Castle!' There is a gruesome seduction scene between Graham and Gayson, and a Julie Andrews-type moment when Henie sings, cutely but weakly, to a gathering of children.

Unencumbered by any of the surrounding nonsense, Joan Regan pops in to remind us that she was one of the finest singers of her type with 'When You Know Someone Loves You'. We are also relieved to see Dora Bryan in one of her 'barmaid'-type roles. An artist who rarely got the opportunity in films to show her skills learned in the now lost art of revue, she knows exactly how to put over her number. Another distinguished guest is Stanley Holloway in one of those thumbs-in-the-braces cockney numbers that have persisted throughout time, at least in British musical films, with its reassuring lyric bereft of original thought, sung by Holloway as he is surrounded by genuine Pearly Kings bussed in for the occasion but chronically under-rehearsed.

> All me China's shouting out 'Wot Cher, me old cock sparrer'
> They're simple blokes that's never bin to Eton or to 'Arrer,
> But all me life they'll stick to me, me missus and me barrer,
> Down Petticoat Lane on Sunday morning

Tellingly, *Hello London* came out the year that London's Harringay Arena, one of the principal venues for spectacular ice shows, closed. High season for ice shows, often with huge casts far outstripping the numbers of skaters employed by Henie, had faded by the end of the 1950s. At Harringay, monumentally staffed iced productions of American operettas flourished in the early years of that decade, including in 1951 *Rose Marie*, with 'Canada's Queen of the Ice' Barbara Ann Scott in the title role, while at the Empress Hall the revue-like *London Melody* was followed by Claude Langdon's third ice pantomime *Puss in Boots*. Henie's travelling shows required industrial organisation, with their own portable ice-making equipment; her credits even listed 'the Sonja Henie 1953 Orchestra'. Her pre-eminence as a skater (at the Empress Hall in 1953 she was announced as 'the incomparable queen of the ice') was emphasised by the programme's boast that she 'has rightfully been called the world's best dressed actress', whose speciality the 'Hula-on-Skates' was 'evolved from many hours of practice, with the greatest Hawaiian dancers'.

The Philip Green and Michael Carr score yields 'The Way to Make It Hip' for Roy Castle; 'Do It for Me' performed by Castle, Henie, Wilding, and Gayson; 'On Top of a Bus' for Henie, Wilding, and company; 'My Four British Tailors' performed by Ronny Graham, Dennis Price, and Trefor Jones; 'Petticoat Lane' for Stanley Holloway; 'That Deadly Species the Male' for Dora Bryan; 'Fly Alight Fancy and Free' with its Jack Fishman lyric for Henie and children; 'The Truth of the Matter' for Price, Gayson, and Wilding; and Joan Regan in 'When You Know Someone Loves You'. Henie and company presented the finale, 'The Magic of You'.

A last cinematic hurrah for the Crazy Gang, Vale Films' ***Life Is a Circus*** was produced by E. M. Smedley-Aston and scripted by Val Guest. In their first film since the 1940 *Gasbags*, the Gang had lost none of their verve or aptitude for quick-fire repartee or physical vitality at a time when they might be regarded as

venerable, pensionable leftovers from an earlier generation. A unique phenom-
enon, the Gang comprised three sets of double-acts: Jimmy Nervo and Teddy
Knox, Charlie Naughton and Jimmy Gold, and (most famously) Bud Flanagan
and Chesney Allen in a partnership that seemed to connect the working class
(Flanagan) with the better-educated upper (Allen). To these might be added
'Monsewer' Eddie Gray and the Gang's regular understudy (of all six of them)
Peter Glaze.

The popularity of Flanagan and Allen owed much to their songs, which
were delivered in a manner quite unlike anything else in popular music of their
time; together, they made a remarkable sound that emphasised the emotional
tug of the numbers they sang. They and the rest of the troupe were masters
of brilliant wordplay, broad comedy, delicious (and often sexual) irreverence,
and absurdity. They had been brought together in 1931 by the impresario Val
Parnell, and were pre-eminent in the London Palladium's history between 1935
and 1939. After the war, their run of variety-cum-revue shows at the Victoria
Palace made more theatrical history. In May 1962, part of the last night of
their final Victoria Palace revue *Young in Heart* was transmitted live on ITV,
preceded by an affectionate poetic tribute by John Betjeman. This indeed was
the end of an era of comic history. Charlie Chaplin sent a tribute, as did Bob
Hope and Sophie Tucker.

Watching that television broadcast confirms what we might already have
known: filming only constricted the Crazy Gang. Their comedy thrived on
their personal relationships (one felt certain that there was never much division
between how they behaved off stage and on). Their comedy was sparked by togetherness, vibrant, reacting to the moment and the affection their audiences
felt for every one of them. That most percipient of theatrical historians John
Fisher recognised qualities in Flanagan and Allen that distinguished them
from most other double-acts.

> It differed curiously from the others, namely in the complete absence of any
> deep antagonism between the two partners. Any disagreements they shared
> were fleeting, superficial, a pretext for single gags and nothing deeper.
> Whereas in the other acts a rivalry informs the whole atmosphere, the es-
> sential ethos of Bud and Ches was one of pure and simple comradeship.[28]

That ethos, exhibited by the bringing together across the social divide
pervading British society, that sense of comradeship, of each helping another,
made them ideal subjects for the films of director John Baxter.

Life Is a Circus does not show the Gang at its best. We may blame ageing. A
slim storyline has Joe Winter's run-down travelling circus struggling to survive
against opposition from Rickenbeck's Circus, but fighting back with some assistance from a genie summoned by an Aladdin's lamp, an idea already used
in the Gang's 1938 Gainsborough film *Alf's Button Afloat*. On that occasion,
the genie was Alastair Sim. Now it is Lionel Jeffries, who, according to *Kinematograph Weekly*, 'easily steals the honours as they are'.[29] *MFB*'s faint praise

that the Gang 'disarm criticism by their innocent and undisciplined enthusiasm'[30] extended to a recognition of Michael Holliday, singing pleasantly but moving self-consciously, and Shirley Eaton, who were added to the mix as the picture's young-blood romantics.

Composer Philip Green and Guest wrote the title number and the lovers' duet 'For You, for You', both utilitarian but reprised and not much encouraged by Denys Palmer's cut-price choreography, but Holliday and Eaton make little impression against the Human Cannonball and the brilliantly filmed high-wire sequence amid the circus extracts that enliven the picture.

There is, too, a scene that pulls us back. Bud is alone somewhere under some arches when he hears a voice he recognises. It's Ches. It's the film's most touching moment, beautifully judged, as Bud and Ches inevitably go into their most famous number, written by Bud in Derby during the Great Depression of the 1920s. It's a song that tells of homelessness, of deprived, disappointed lives, and in their delivery, of comradeship, faithful friends, our struggles against adversity and belief in one another.

> Pavement is my pillow, no matter where we stay
> Underneath the arches, we dream our dreams away.

The song done, the old friends part, Ches walking out of the film as quietly as he arrived.

1959

It may be that the cinema was never going to be the right place for
Mankowitz's affectionate inspection of the underbelly of show-biz

Expresso Bongo

The Lady Is a Square	*Sweet Beat*
Make Mine a Million	*Tommy the Toreador*
Idol on Parade	*Desert Mice*
Serious Charge	*Follow a Star*
The Heart of a Man	*Expresso Bongo*

FEBRUARY

Writing of the new Anna Neagle film, *The Times* considered that 'The productions of Mr Herbert Wilcox are generally designed with considerable shrewdness to make the best of a variety of different worlds. Here [he] metaphorically
speaking, marries Miss Anna Neagle to Mr Frankie Vaughan, thus ensuring
the approval of the middle-brows [...] and of the shriekers and swooners.'[1]
Philosophical matters had never really come within the compass of Herbert
Wilcox's films; the lack of them probably encouraged their often enormous
success at the box office, but there might be a suspicion of imponderable quan-
daries lurking within his productions, each to be dealt with as superficially
as possible. His 'serious' films made with Neagle, with her impersonations of
Nell Gwyn, Florence Nightingale, Amy Johnson, Queen Victoria (twice; having
made one film about her, Wilcox enjoyed it so much that he made another),
Edith Cavell, and Odette, suggested that the frothiness of their other work had
been put aside for the duration. Throughout a long and distinguished career,
Neagle's professionalism and sheer hard work were unquestionable, and the
British cinemagoer had kept her prominently at the coal face for thirty years.

As the 1950s drew to a close, the Wilcoxes needed to place themselves ad-
vantageously at the beginning of a new decade, fifteen years after the end of a
war that had in no way damaged their progress. Looking over their shoulders,
they must have realised the difficulties that awaited them. David Shipman has
succinctly described the final phase of Neagle's work in pictures after *Lilacs in
the Spring* and *King's Rhapsody*. Wilcox

then put her into an 'up-to-date' story, *My Teenage Daughter*, cruelly referred to as 'My Stone-Age Mother', and – in another attempt to re-interest the public – loaned her to ABPC to play a hospital matron in *No Time for Tears*. But it was: *The Man Who Wouldn't Talk* played just a week in a small West End cinema and didn't make the circuits; and many cinemas showing her last film *The Lady is a Square*, omitted her name. It was a harsh verdict on someone who had coined a lot of money for the same houses.[2]

Neagle's on-screen relationship with Michael Wilding had seen the Wilcoxes through five 'London' social comedies. When Wilding fled the scene, Errol Flynn was signed up (a deal lucrative to Flynn but financially disastrous for Wilcox) as Neagle's new partner. When Flynn, too, slipped away, reneging on his long-term contract, there was the need to find her a new 'regular' leading man, singer Frankie Vaughan. It was an unlucky choice. Reporting on one of his stage performances in 1959, *The Times* saw that 'His aim is to act as an erotic stimulant, and his swarthy good looks and big voice are single-mindedly addressed to that end.'[3]

Vaughan was the wrong man for the job: his heavy frame didn't suit the screen, and in no way could what he did on it be described as acting. Just as wrong was the new project, ***The Lady Is a Square***, a lumpen error of judgement saddled with a suet dumpling of a screenplay by Harold Purcell, Pamela Bower, and, inevitably, Nicholas Phipps. Derek Conrad suggested that 'if [Vaughan] goes on appearing in pictures like this he'll finish his cinema career before it has properly got under way'. The film showed 'Anna and Herbert trying desperately to "get with it" […] And just how far does it get them? At a rough guess, I should say 1949.'[4]

The *MFB* remained unconvinced by this 'attempt to reconcile "pop" addicts and serious music lovers. Wilcox's direction suffers through straining too hard to contain both the gloss of "high life" and the more suburban course dictated by the screenplay […] Unfortunately, this latest variation in the Wilcox–Neagle dream world lacks two essentials – glamour and excitement.'[5] Patently non-intellectual in the way it manages to keep 'classical' music pigeon-holed upon a pedestal, its feeble premise crashes at the last-minute *volte face* when Vaughan sings Handel's *Largo*: it's past ridiculous. If it achieves anything, *The Lady Is a Square* does its best to persuade us that there is really no difference between pop and classical; Wilcox's trick is to make each as dreary as the other.

Elements of an upstairs-downstairs comedy showing the extreme witlessness of high society play out as Frances Baring (Neagle) floats across the screen in a series of highly impractical outfits, with no one around brave enough to suggest she might be overdressed; no hope of even a Marks and Spencer nightie. But Frances loves classical music and is the teeniest bit snobbish about it. She is condescendingly amused to learn that her new footman Johnny (Vaughan) knows about Mahler and Tchaikovsky, although he insists on singing the vacuous 'Honey Bunny Baby' (one of Vaughan's own compositions, credited to 'Frank Able', so he has no one else to blame). No wonder Frances complains of 'croaking crooners' as beloved of her teenage daughter Joanna (an especially vapid Janette Scott), who is forever making doe-eyes at Johnny. As someone remarks, 'That boy's great. He's another Frankie Vaughan!' This 'Hitchcockian' trick of mentioning the very stars the audience is watching on screen is a recurring embarrassment in the Wilcox–Neagle canon, at a stroke undermining any sense of what in the circumstances passes as 'reality'.

Never mind: Johnny has songs to sing, performing Dick Glasser and Ann Hall's 'That's My Doll' ('A pair of arms that are just my size / And she's got those twinkling eyes') at the Talk of the Town, and intimately serenades Joanna with Ray Noble's 'Love Is the Sweetest Thing'. 'What does it feel like, being a star?' demands Joanna. We may prefer to look away at the ensuing billing and cooing. Having struggled throughout with gloves (putting them on and taking them off an essential part of Neagle's art) and used up every mannerism in her exhaustive catalogue, she loses her sophisticated assurance when she makes a hash of replacing a telephone on the receiver. Wilcox did not think it worth shouting 'Cut'. In this, we may team Neagle with Tod Slaughter's ham-fisted struggle to replace the instrument in his 1952 pot-boiler *King of the Underworld*.

A long-overdue finale to this pop-versus-classical thesis comes with a concert given by the National Youth Orchestra. Wilcox simply points the camera at it and lets it get on with what it does. To everyone's consternation, Johnny strides out to sing Handel's *Largo*. This is best imagined. Inevitably, Frances succumbs to the native lure of pop music, marking her farewell appearance before the British cinemagoer with something that looks a little like 'the Twist'. As Conrad remarks, 'Miss Neagle cutting a rug at the end of this tedious picture is *quite* forgettable.'[6]

In fact, *The Lady Is a Square* (with its title song by Johnny Franz and Raymond Dutch) was something of an omen for the Wilcoxes in the way it presaged their fate. The plot steers Frances into troubled financial waters. Suddenly, the telephone bill goes unpaid, and creditors demand payment: 'We are temporarily embarrassed'. She and Joanna have been living on an overdraft: 'It's the only thing that makes living possible', Frances tells her. Joanna agrees: 'I don't think I'd like to go bankrupt'.

On the silver screen, such trifling matters are mere blips easily overcome before the final moment, but in the real world the Wilcoxes faced a turbulent future. In the early sixties Wilcox was bankrupted (his biography describes the parlous state of their finances), and their home was lost. Neagle set up a dance school, but it was wound up. With Wilcox dangerously ill, she enjoyed a successful theatrical renaissance in the British musical *Charlie Girl*. Her modesty, graciousness, and willingness to work hard continued to be appreciated by a great number of the British public. Her final engagement was as Fairy Godmother at the London Palladium in 1985, doing two shows a day for three months. Exhausted, when the show closed she went into a nursing home, dying in 1986. Wilcox had predeceased her in 1977.

Neatly turned out and consistently genial, ***Make Mine a Million*** is a happy mating of concert-party survivor Arthur Askey and favourite cinematic con-man Sidney James, directed by Lance Comfort. The trade's *Daily Cinema* welcomed 'a happy comedy, full of laughs and with a long parade of popular TV personalities ensuring easy selling and warm reception with mass audiences.'[7] Askey played Arthur Ashton, the make-up man at National Television (understood as the BBC) persuaded by Sid Gibson (James) to slip a 'live' television advertisement for a 'wonder detergent' called Bonko into a broadcast. Had this been the inspiration for an Ealing picture, it would have ranked as satire; it is never that here, although Peter Blackmore's screenplay, based on a story by Jack Francis with additional material from Talbot Rothwell and (of course) Askey, comes close, as when the outraged controller of National realises the damage done to its reputation for 'perfect entertainment, unmarred by unsavoury interruption': 'It will take at least three poetry readings and a visit to Glyndebourne to pick it up again.'

Designer Denis Wreford's giant dimensions for National's boardroom not only emphasise the broadcasting station's unassailable dominance, but effectively diminishes the already diminutive Askey. His performance here is one of his most pleasing, coping with the occasionally riotous (as in a launderette when the addition of Bonko to the wash gets a little out of hand) but convincing us that the character is real. The success is achieved without resource to a scintillating script, but as Brian McFarlane has written in his monograph on Comfort, 'This is not dialogue meant to be read coldly on the page but heard delivered by those who know how.'[8] There are notable walk-ons (and quick walk-offs) by some distinguished visitors: Evelyn Laye, Tommy Trinder, Dickie Henderson, Askey's daughter Anthea, and the alarmingly constructed Sabrina, whose waist would be the envy of the most figure-conscious wasp, but none of them do much more than cross the screen.

The musical sequences are sparing but quite effective, skilfully exploiting the television studio context, with close-ups of Dennis Lotis singing 'Valentina' taking us immediately into the picture. Pleased as we are to see them, the featured duettists might have been a little more prominent – we want to hear more of Stanley Black's pleasing romancer 'I'll Remember This Night of Love' sung by Patricia Bredin and Leonard Weir. Bredin's career in British films was brief, although in 1959 she was more prominent in the ENSA-inspired *Desert Mice.* In 1957 she was the first British entry for the Eurovision Song Context, coming seventh. Weir's career seems to have been short-lived, although in 1958 he played Freddy Eynsford-Hill in the original London production of *My Fair Lady.*

Gillian Lynne, supported by 'The National Ballet', leads in extracts from *Swan Lake*, beautifully lit and not surprisingly interrupted by Askey in tights. More formally, the regimented Television Toppers kick through their routine, and the automaton Penge Formation Dancers are a troupe beyond parody. The musical spectacle of five grand pianos being hammered by five pianists adds to the unexpected sumptuousness of the set pieces as well as the sheer foolishness of the enterprise, reminding us of similar excesses in *London Town* and John Baxter's Hazel Ascot vehicle *Talking Feet*, with its Kafka-nightmare-like pyramid of the Minipiano Ensemble of child pianists.

During filming at Shepperton, this sequence must have reminded Baxter, producing for Jack Hylton Film Productions, of his earlier successes. It was in part appropriate that *Make Mine a Million* marked Baxter's farewell to the film industry, for he too was moving on to the last phase of his career, in television. It seems clear that his fascination with music-hall and variety, and the use of popular music within a predominantly straight 'social' context, has its corollary in some of Comfort's work; it assumes significant importance in his *Band of Thieves* (1962), *Live It Up* (1963), and *Be My Guest* (1965). The essential difference is that Baxter had what we may understand as an obsession with such material; Comfort merely bows to the inevitability of its inclusion in films that might otherwise struggle even harder to attract a 1950s audience already saturated with 'pop'.

In truth, Baxter's mantle could not be shuffled onto a descendant's shoulders: how could it, why should it, when society, cinema, commerce, taste had moved on? Baxter's contribution to British musical films had been one of the most remarkable, and least remarked, in its history. Never the trumpeter of his own incalculable achievements, in retirement he wrote that

> if I were to sum up my life's work in show business, it has been to provide 'family entertainment'. Certainly laughter has been an important ingredient, but problems have been faced and opinions ventilated ... When it comes to a laugh or a tear, no monetary value can be put on them, nor can money necessarily buy them. That is why films produced with little money can achieve a special purpose; and while my films have not been measured in terms of millions of dollars they have been successful in some degree, through the pleasure and encouragement they have given to ordinary men and women.[9]

Baxter died in 1975, barely obituarised. He was given a retrospective at the British Film Institute in 1989.

MARCH

Riding the wave ridden by British pop singers since *Rock You Sinners*, Anthony Newley, for long a favoured boy actor in British films, was the ***Idol on Parade*** in Warwick Films' Cinemascope army comedy filmed at Shepperton, produced by Irving Allen and Albert R. Broccoli, and directed by John Gilling. Here was a film that was 'a muddle of half-developed storylines and characters',[10] in which, as the *MFB* wrote, the star 'works hard against trite material, and apart from isolated bright moments the film is simply a waste of good comedy talent'.[11]

John Antrobus's screenplay (his first) has none of the skilfulness or surrealist tones of his subsequent work, which included his 'New Wave' play *The Bed Sitting Room* (1963) written with Spike Milligan. The shadow of Elvis Presley having joined the US army in March 1958 hangs over what vaguely resembles a plot. Presley's conscription was also the inspiration for the 1960 American musical *Bye Bye Birdie*,[12] and with happier, wittier results. Wit is in short supply in Antrobus's creation, which is perhaps not always treated with the respect it deserved, despite strenuous promotion by the film's stars as the picture wound its way around British cinemas. When making a personal appearance at a cinema in West London, the performers had ice creams (still in their tubs) thrown at them.

Nevertheless, it seemed that in 1959 the British cinemagoer was still fascinated by life in barracks, especially when pop singers were conscripted to them. Antrobus had form as one of the scriptwriters for Granada TV's comedy series *The Army Game* produced from 1957 to 1961 (National Service in Britain ended in 1960). In the cinema, a patently absurd depiction of army life as experienced by budding pop star Jeep Jackson (Newley) was an odd melting-pot of poorly assembled components. A musical rather than dramatic performer, Newley showed more than a dash of cockiness in his persona. Neither top-billed Hollywood veteran William Bendix as a sergeant major, nor Lionel Jeffries in one of his on-the-verge-of-a-nervous breakdown St-Vitus-affected characterisations, was shown to advantage, with Anne Aubrey making the mildest of impacts.

Throughout, Newley was poised precariously between romantic lead, pop singer, and rock'n'roll performer, without any of the raw edge of the true rock'n'roll delineators. He was already, perhaps in chrysalis form, the all-round-entertainer, out to please. There is only one moment in *Idol on Parade* at which we get even the faintest whiff of anything approaching rock'n'roll, when we glimpse Larry Martyn flitting across the screen in a leather jacket. Musically, the rest is pretty bogus, boogie-woogie in place of the red meat and (for those who know the real thing when they hear it) very probably not very good boogie-woogie either. Anyway, how can we believe any of the musical moments when the echo chamber takes them completely out of context of what has gone before? The crudity of the device does nothing to promote credulity.

Not having read the novel by William Camp on which the script is based, I cannot vouch for its qualities, only assuming that the premise of a pop singer being able to pursue his career by leaping over the wall of the barracks to attend gigs was more deftly handled in print than on screen. Luckily, the musical numbers found considerable commercial success, and according to his biographer, 'Overnight, Anthony Newley the actor and "serious" comedian, was a pop star. He was a sensation.'[13] Newley and Joe Henderson contributed 'Sat'day Night Rock-a-Boogie' and 'Idol Rock-a-Boogie', while Jerry Lordan and Len Paverman contributed the title song and 'Waited So Long'.

APRIL

'If you are still shocked by vicars fancying choirboys, I suppose this film will have some impact', suggested *Films and Filming*'s review of **Serious Charge**,[14] probably remembered more for Cliff Richard's screen debut than as a socio-logically significant contribution to British cinema. Philip King's songless play had reached the West End in 1955, with Patrick McGoohan as the young vicar accused of sexually assaulting one of the boys from his youth club, a hotbed of ping-pong, spontaneous jiving, and character-building boxing. Acknowledging its good intentions, *Plays and Players* nevertheless regretted that 'Our theatre appears to be incapable of approaching serious contemporary subjects in an adult manner.'[15] It has largely been forgotten that King, best known for writing farces such as the brilliant *See How They Run*, was at the vanguard of 'gay' British drama, daring to venture where few had gone. In 1963, *How Are You, Johnnie?*, another of his dramas dealing with homosexual issues, had a short run at the Vaudeville Theatre with Ian McShane and Derek Fowlds.

An Alma Films presentation, *Serious Charge* was adapted from King's original play by producer Mickey Delamar and Guy Elmes, and directed by Terence Young. Their concern must have been that the introduction of the 'teenage' scenes with their three musical numbers by Lionel Bart might undermine the work's essential, and for its day quite daring, drama. Howard Phillips (Anthony Quayle) is a highly regarded unmarried vicar living with his mother (Irene Browne). He is much admired by Hester Peters (Sarah Churchill), the spinster daughter of Phillips's predecessor and commando of the parish magazine, but he seems disinterested in her. He runs a youth club for the local teenagers, including Curley Thompson (Cliff Richard) and his elder lawless brother Larry (Andrew Ray). When one of the local girls gets pregnant by Larry and dies, Phillips confronts him. Alone with Phillips at the vicarage, Larry sees an opportunity to get back at Phillips by pretending the vicar has 'tried to interfere with me'. Hester arrives to find the room in disarray, Larry shirtless and crying; she is the only witness to what has happened. The village reacts with contempt and poison-pen letters; as one character remarks, 'You trying to tell me we've got one of *them* down at the vicarage?'

All is resolved when Mrs Phillips persuades Hester to expose the truth of what happened. At last, we know that Phillips will stay, possibly united with Hester, and his good work will continue, his reputation unsullied. The interpolated sequences in the youth club and espresso bar are no more or less absurd than any other such scenes in other British musical films of the period, but they quickly pass, and the three Lionel Bart numbers given to Richard – 'Livin' Doll', 'No Turning Back', and 'Mad about You' – do not detract from the central, 'serious' story. The *MFB* approved: 'The story in outline seems melodramatic and contrived, but an imag-inative script, sensitive and crisp direction, and the authoritative performance of Anthony Quayle make this an absorbing film [while] the personal conflicts that occupy the foreground are authentic and well observed.'[16]

Films and Filming 'loathed' the picture, describing the performances as 'adequate, if undistinguished'.[17] In this I think the critic is misguided. Watching Quayle and Browne is taking a masterclass in acting (not necessarily film acting; Browne is the epitome of mature leading West End ladies circa 1950s), but the picture is full of skilful character vignettes: Judith Furse's jolly probation officer, only just managing to tuck herself into her little Austin 7; Wilfred Pickles as a sympathetic JP; Jean Cadell as an elderly matron; Wilfrid Brambell as a nervous verger; Jess Conrad's knife-drawing teenager; and a fleeting appearance by Olive Sloane. Throughout, Young handles the obviously stagey sections with tact and assurance.

JUNE

The second Herbert Wilcox-directed picture of the year, after Anna Neagle's final film appearance in *The Lady Is a Square*, was Everest's ***The Heart of a Man***, produced by Neagle. It continued the Wilcoxes' association with Frankie Vaughan, in whom they put their trust as a leading man whose popularity would carry them into the 1960s. The Vaughan–Wilcox–Neagle portfolio had

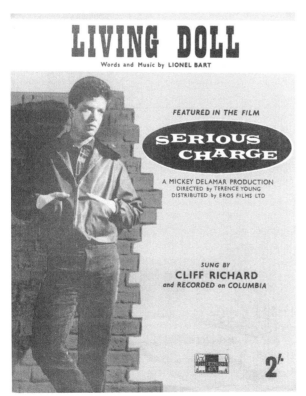

Adapted from Philip King's stage play, *Serious Charge* (1959) involved gay sexual issues. A mostly forgotten pioneer of such drama, King went on to write another West End play with a homosexual theme, *How Are You, Johnnie?* (1963).

already survived *These Dangerous Years* (1957) and *Wonderful Things* (1958). Vaughan had played a substantial role in the Wilcox's fortunes, but Wilcox's autobiography, with fulsome recollections of Michael Wilding, fails to mention Vaughan. Meanwhile, the *Guardian* wrote of 'Frankie Vaughan's peculiar attractions',[18] which, courtesy of the work he did for Wilcox, seemed curiously inappropriate for the purpose.

We catch the whiff of a stolid Wilcox production from the legend that follows the opening titles: 'WESTMINSTER. The Houses of Parliament where 630 wise men and women formulate the laws of the land ... but ... Where There's a Law – There's a Flaw!' Wilcox has always seemed most at home in the metropolis, where once again we find some of the spacious, almost baronial, houses we recognise from his other films.

Swarthy out-of-work ex-sailor Frankie Martin (Vaughan in a polo-neck sweater) meets old codger Bud (Peter Sinclair). Bud is down on his luck but turns out to be Frankie's saviour. Frankie is taken on as a bouncer for gambling den mastermind Tony Carlisle (Tony Britton cast against type). Frankie's method of dealing with troublemakers is to throw them in the Thames, between which episodes he is smooching Carlisle's songbird girlfriend Julie (Anne Heywood) via some deathless prose from the hapless screenplay.

Julie: Sex – the difference between motherhood and mink

Frankie: You know all the answers, don't you?

Julie: You know all the questions

Back at her apartment, Julie, doing something unconvincing with spaghetti in a saucepan, is again dressed in most unsuitable apparel, especially worrying as she is using a tomato-based recipe. The spaghetti has some effect, because she and Frankie go into a dream-sequence choreographic entanglement that might have been in *Spring in Park Lane* but on this occasion has been arranged (to little effect) by Neil and Pat Delrina. Lots of dry ice attempts to disguise the inadequacies of their footwork. Julie becomes a dance hostess. Frankie gets a break on television singing a nonsensical, supposedly rock'n'roll, number, and gets to record 'Walking Tall', accompanied (unintentionally and hilariously) by a backing group playing paper and comb. When played on the jukebox in screamingly modern cafés, it sends the kids crazy. Disc jockey Ken Walton introduces Frankie singing 'Sometime, Somewhere' as teenagers look on, apparently hypnotised. Throughout, Anthony Newley flits in and out as the frankly irritating Johnny Ten Per Cent.

Things are expected to take an emotional turn when Frankie and Julie visit Bud in Charing Cross Hospital, where the ward sister is such a dead ringer for Anna Neagle that we suspect that this actress (Christine Pollon) may have been Neagle's stand-in. Once more, Miss Heywood's costume is wide of the mark: she is wrapped in a pelmet, crowned by a hat that might have been constructed by a vengeful three-year-old peeling onions and wondering what to do with the segments. Unrestrained mawkishness takes over at last, with Bud feeling chippier and sitting up in bed, surrounded by a gaggle of nurses (at least it shows how well-staffed the National Health Service was at the end of the 1950s) and dabbing his eyes as he watches Frankie on television.

Neither producer or director found favour with the *MFB*. As for Neagle,

> she remains content to cling to the outworn conventions; moreover she has chosen a script [by Jack Trevor Story and Pamela Bower, based on a story by Rex North] whose witlessness and banality make it almost a parody of the worst British comedies of the Thirties [...] it is hard to believe that the director is the veteran Herbert Wilcox. He has, in the past, shown a keen awareness of popular taste, but this time he may find that he has overestimated the tolerance of his audience.[19]

Kinematograph Weekly struck an unusually unencouraging, even sardonic note, complaining that 'The script, flecked by whimsy, lacks originality, but at least the "corn bin" is full to the brim [...] Thanks to [the cast's] persistence and energy the majority will willingly take it. They always have!'[20] When all else palled, cinemagoers might be amused by the extravagant costumes designed by Eileen Idare, whose hugely impractical creations had been featured in a 1922 Pathé short. Each scene reveals that once again Miss Heywood has been changed into yet another absurdly inappropriate confection by Idare. Attending a boxing match enveloped in chiffon with a whole bunch of flowers for a corsage does seem a little wide of the mark.

The musical numbers are efficient but lack distinction, although Vaughan had a recording success with Peggy Cochrane and Paddy Roberts's title song. Lionel Bart and Mike Pratt provide 'Walking Tall', while Bart and Vaughan contribute 'Sometime, Somewhere'. Also heard are Boyd Bennett and John F. Young Junior's 'My Boy Flat Top' and Leslie Bricusse and Robin Beaumont's 'Love Is' sung by Heywood. Vaughan returned to British studios in 1964 for *It's All Over Town*.

NOVEMBER

'I never wanted to go through with this fantastic nonsense in the first place, but I did.' Apt as it would have been, this is not the comment made by the leading lady Julie Amber about Flamingo Films' **Sweet Beat**, which the *MFB* labelled 'A mild and artless warning to the stage-struck [in which] direction and performance are very uneven.'[21] It was a little late to promote it as 'The First British Rock'n'Roll Film', not least because it had little to do with that too often misrepresented art form. These supposedly torrid sequences were filmed at British holiday camps at Clacton and Cliftonville, where Bonnie Martin (Julie Amber) is hoping to further her career as a singer.

At least *Sweet Beat*, produced by Jeffrey S. Kruger and directed after a fashion by Ronnie Albert, had a purpose: to promote some of the recording artists signed up with the American labels Ember and Herald Records. Ron Ahrans's screenplay, based on a storyline by Sheldon Stark, suggested it might be a warning to the curious: it follows the meteoric ascent to stardom of Bonnie, beginning with her appearance in a 'beauty and talent' competition at Butlin's holiday camp at Clacton. Paraded before ogling British holidaymakers (not paid extras, but the genuine article before the British discovered sunnier destinations), the swim-suited girls are identified each by their number. Bonnie complains ('I feel like a joint of meat in a butcher's shop window'), but she is already on the way to pop-singing fame, despite what we suspect is minimal talent. Older men take an interest in promoting her career. She is wined and dined at the West End's Stork Room by Al Burnett (he owns it). Mr Burnett plays himself, badly. She is whisked off to meet disc jockey Keith Fordyce live on Radio Luxembourg. Here, as in other scenes, the sound technicians twiddling the knobs make us think that everyone involved in the recording of pop music has long been in receipt of the old-age pension. Her number 'Recently' is by Tommie Connor.

She attracts unwelcome attention from leering record promoter Dave Laffert (Irv Bauer), who effectively abducts her to the USA and away from faithful but dull Bill (Sheldon Lawrence). Once in America, Bonnie realises that Laffert's interest is not musical. He is no gentleman ('You dumb broad!'). Ahrans's dialogue is a ludicrous compilation of polite exchanges laced with prissy gentility. Bonnie (soon to be a genuine innocent abroad) insists about the beauty competition, 'Those other girls will probably be much better than I.' She congratulates fellow performer Tina Miller (played by Herald Records' artiste Leoni Page): 'May I too compliment you on your song?'

In 1962, *Sweet Beat* underwent an alarming personality change when it was released in America. Retitled *The Amorous Sex*, it promised more than it could deliver: 'When a man lusts for a woman … there is nothing he won't do to get her! See beautiful girls with practically nothing on parade unashamed before men.' Transatlantic patrons must have gaped at the dreary goings-on in Clacton and Cliftonville, although an element of striptease seems to have been added. Through it all, the film retained its air of seediness, its participants looking just as bored as they had been in Britain. The awfulness of *Sweet Beat* can barely be concealed, but must be balanced against its impressive cache of musical items, begun when Bonnie sings Peter Warren, Adrienne Birkhard, and Kruger's 'Thanks' in front of the holiday camp audience for the combined 'beauty and talent' contest. Already established chanteuse Tina Miller (Leonie Page) contributes Buddy Kaye and Leon Carr's 'Just for the Asking'.

Disc jockey Keith Fordyce hosts Bonnie on his Radio Luxembourg record show, playing her recording of Winfield Scott's 'How Do You Mend a Broken Heart?', and we hear a snatch of Lee Allen's 'Boppin' at the Hop', co-written with A. Tyler. Another of Herald's signed-up vocalists, Cindy Mann, sings George Scheck's 'Luva Luva Love', eclipsed by 'Tonite Tonite' written by Myles and performed by The Mello-Kings (a 1957 hit for Herald Records). Another standout is Fred Parris backed by The Satins in their 'In the Still of the Night'. Whatever *Sweet Beat*'s faults, it contains some brilliant examples of Doo-Wop music. Also included are Lou Stallman and Joe Shapiro's 'It's New to Me' and Tony Crombie's 'Sweet Beat'. And we hear Tina in Billy Myles's composition 'Careless Caresses'. Outstandingly, Myles sings his signature ballad 'The Joker'; for this alone, *Sweet Beat* is worth sitting through.

Cheap and not particularly cheerful, its extras decked out in a job lot of theatrical costumiers' Spanish outfits that may have recently been used in a bargain-basement production of *Carmen*, **Tommy the Toreador** (who could doubt that this meant Tommy Steele?) continued the downward trajectory of the Bermondsey wunderkind's career in British films, following the spectacularly successful autobiographical *The Tommy Steele Story* of 1957 and *The Duke Wore Jeans* of 1958.

The producer for Nat Cohen and Stuart Levy's Fanfare film was George H. Brown, responsible for cobbling together the dismal story and screenplay with the assistance of Patrick Kirwan. In case of need, Nicholas Phipps (whose prominence as a writer for British films must remain a mystery), Talbot Rothwell, and Sid Colin came up with additional dialogue. Taking advice from the *MFB*, we must agree that 'the confused and preposterous plot can be overlooked'.[22] A fence-sitting *Times* declared that 'Mr Steele is a symbol, a banner to rally fanatical adherents, and approval, or its reverse, is largely a matter of age – the cleavage between the generations is nowhere more apparent than in their contrasting ideas of what constitutes entertainment and what does not'.[23] On this occasion, John Paddy Carstairs's direction is slapdash and Malcolm Clare's occasional choreography fairly desperate, the now-and-again talented supporting players puppets conveying what Carstairs and his writers consider to be human emotions. The clicking of castanets cannot convince us of the film's Spanish-ness.

More might have been expected from the songs by Steele (behind his pseudonym of Jimmy Bennett), Lionel Bart (about to see the success of his stage musical *Oliver!*), and Mike Pratt, although 'Little White Bull' wormed its way into the public consciousness. The rest, 'Take a Ride', 'That's Fiesta', 'Singing Time', the title song, 'Where's the Birdie?' (the only number that Steele shares with Sid James and an under-par Bernard Cribbins), and 'Amanda' sung to a miscast Janet Munro, are barely fit for service.

DECEMBER

It seems inevitable that the British musical film would concern itself with ENSA (the Entertainments National Service Association, more or less fondly better known as 'Every Night Something Awful'), but fourteen years after the end of war it was a late arrival. The Artna–Welbeck–Sydney Box production by Basil Dearden was directed by Michael Relph, who had directed another theatrical saga, *Davy*, two years earlier. The potential to poke fun at a much-maligned but fondly regarded wartime institution intended to keep the troops entertained was obvious, but unfulfilled by David Climie's disappointing screenplay.

The prospect of an entertainment around ENSA should have been a gift to any talented writer, and Climie had long experience of writing sketches and lyrics for London revues. His inability to enliven **Desert Mice** is surprising, especially when he was writing for an experienced cast capable of making it work. Much of it was impeccably drawn: Irene Handl's Miss Patch, redolent of all-female trios playing in the palmed courts of Eastbourne's hotels, tickling the ivories even as bombs descend, and charming when, accompanying herself on piano, she revives a dour Victorian parlour ballad, Charles Harris's 'Break the News to Mother'; Dora Bryan's Gay, played in Bryan's grandest slightly common style; Sidney James's wonderfully perky Bert Bennett, holding the troupe together through thick and rather a lot of thin; delightful Reginald Beckwith (a specialist in slightly gay characterisations) as illusionist Fred, with his assistant Edie (Liz Fraser); duetting Dick Bentley and Joan Bentham, lifting spirits with Hugh Charles and Ross Parker's 'There'll Always Be an England'; Patricia Bredin, hoping to make it as a female Percy Edwards but finding her feet as the pleasant performer of Climie and Stanley Myers's 'Christmas Star'; and Philip Green and Tommie Cooper's 'Till the Right Time Comes'. In their way, these strolling players are second cousins to the gallant 'Good Companions' as seen in two earlier British musical films.

Indeed, *Desert Mice* shares something with the 1933 Jessie Matthews and John Gielgud version of *The Good Companions*, incorporating some of the material the artistes perform as part of their act into the film, but – one of Relph and Climie's poor decisions – these are never expanded into full numbers, so we never get the full flavour of the film, only the sentimental and not very satisfactory songs given to Bredin. How we might have warmed to fuller versions of Bryan and James's 'Give Me a Pair of Pig's Trotters', but pastiche continues with fragments of 'cod' numbers that we might have enjoyed more if they had been given more space, as when contortionist Margery Manners twists herself out of shape while attempting Philip Green and Tommie Connor's Victorian-styled ballad 'There's a Little White Cottage'. Elsewhere, there is Dora Bryan's outburst of 'I'll Peek-a-Boo Sergeant Major' and 'Together Again', and Joan Bentham's 'Home Is Where the Heart Is' by Green and Climie, also responsible for the company's 'Sing Goodbye to Dear

Old England', with servicemen chipping in with Fred Godfrey, Jimmy Hughes, and Frank Lake's 'Bless 'em All'. Climie uses Hans Leip and Norbert Schultze's German classic 'Lili Marlene' (made famous in its English lyric by Tommie Connor) to spin out a running joke that runs out of steam long before the finishing post. Otherwise, the parodic snatches of song promise more than they deliver, with none of the delight such examples provide in the 1933 *The Good Companions* or the superbly parodic concert-party stylishness of David Fanshawe's natty score for the 1980 Yorkshire Television adaptation.

Alfred Marks's twitchy Entertainments Office Posket, with his detestation of ENSA ('Why is there always a piano accordion?'), is the film's rock, aghast at the prospect of these unworldly characters let loose to entertain servicemen in a war-torn Middle East. What possible experience of soldiering can they have? Gavin (Dick Bentley) explains that he spent two years in *The Chocolate Soldier*, but is warned that things 'are likely to get pretty sticky here, you know'. 'Things were pretty sticky in *The Chocolate Soldier*,' he replies.

An unimpressed *MFB* complained that a 'boorish script and amateurish handling combine to make a quite undistinguished farce out of some promising ideas',[24] but *Kinematograph Weekly*'s review found it 'refreshingly free of malice or grit' although 'embellished with lavatory humour' (presumably the mirage of ladies' lavatories that appears in the desert).[25] Ultimately, *Desert Mice* is a disappointing tribute to the organisation and the army of hopeful entertainers who did their best to brighten the lives of the armed forces. It seems unable to see beyond the conventional view of what ENSA was: a well-worn theatrical joke; in short, it's unworthy of its subject. Fred may own up that 'We're not the best in the world, and we know it' – although some of the biggest names in British entertainment willingly worked abroad under the ENSA banner – but they did their best and put themselves in the face of danger.

A publicity campaign playing on the title verged on the absurd. The staff of the Astoria on the Old Kent Road placed an advertisement in the local press that resulted in 'several hundred pet mice' being brought to the cinema; once 'the problems of the female staff had been solved [presumably providing chairs for them to stand on] a dozen of the all-whites were placed in a cage in the centre of display on the film in the main foyer'.[26]

Over-long, intermittently entertaining, and now and again amusing, Rank's **Follow a Star** owed not a little to a Gene Kelly–Debbie Reynolds Hollywood classic, with its plot of a no-hoper wannabe crooner (our Norman) being revealed as the voice of scheming declining star Vernon Carew (Wisdom's invaluable straight man, without whom). The screenplay by Jack Davies, Henry Blyth, and Norman Wisdom left the *MFB* cold: 'The potential that Norman Wisdom once indubitably possessed is quite obscured by this film – with its silly, tawdry script and the inept direction of Robert Asher'.[27] Taking over from John Paddy Carstairs, Asher, who had worked on *One Good Turn* (1954) and

Man of the Moment (1955), would remain in place for the next five Wisdoms. The change of direction was not much noticed, with little new ground broken, but Hugh Stewart's production was bolstered by a decent supporting cast and some effective musical numbers to speed its 104-minute stay.

Laundry worker Norman Truscott (Wisdom) is thrilled to meet ageing puffed-up singer Vernon Carew (Jerry Desmonde), who gives him two tickets to see his act. Norman takes his girlfriend Judy (a luckless engagement for June Laverick) and is enthralled when Carew sings Philip Green and Sonny Miller's 'Give Me', but chaos and a custard-pie battle threaten to destroy the theatre. Norman proceeds to perform Carew's number to acclaim, and the failing star is booed off stage. Aware that the shades of night are drawing in on his career, Carew plots to steal Norman's voice. Thus Rank has stolen the central plot of *Singin' in the Rain* and contrives for Norman to move in with him. Still, Norman can only sing when Judy is close by. She plays piano for his performance of the title song; the switches from knockabout comedy to sickly sentimentality are grindingly managed, underlining the fact that disabled Judy is in a wheelchair. Examined by a psychiatrist (Richard Wattis), Norman regresses into childhood, but is restored to adulthood for the protracted production number in a gentleman's club, 'You Deserve a Medal for That'. It's an unusually complex musical sequence for a Wisdom comedy, and doesn't sit well. The best scenes occur whenever Hattie Jacques turns up as elocution and voice coach Dymphana Dobson. Along the way, we hear 'I Want to Go to Heaven for the Weekend', 'I'll Sing You a Song', and 'I Love You', with some here-and-there choreography by Eleanor Fazan. It serves Carew right that he should be shamed on stage at the London Palladium, leaving Norman to bask in success. Despite its blatant warming-up of its well-used gloopy storyline, the film did excellent business.

The opportunity to turn the spotlight on British film's relationship with London stage musicals of the late 1950s comes with **Expresso Bongo**, produced and directed at Shepperton by Val Guest, its screenplay by Wolf Mankowitz, who had co-authored the original stage version of 1958 with Julian More, and its music by David Heneker and Monty Norman. After a collection of British stage musicals in the mid-1950s that exuded charm and bucolic contentment but resisted satirical content, there was a brief glut of shows with a freshening, social bite between 1958 and 1962, although the steam had effectively gone out of the new genre as early as spring 1960. These were *Expresso Bongo* (April 1958), *Fings Ain't Wot They Used t'Be* (February 1959), *The Crooked Mile* (September 1959), *Make Me an Offer* (October 1959), *The Lily White Boys* (January 1960), and *Johnny the Priest* (April 1960). Beyond the West End, Theatre Workshop contributed *What a Crazy World* as late as 1962, by which time the 'verismo' British musical caravan had moved on into decidedly uncharted territory. Of these, the best-known was *Fings*, with a title song by Lionel Bart that was widely heard (and sometimes compared with Rodgers and Hart's 'Mountain Greenery'). *The Crooked Mile* and *The Lily White Boys* enjoyed some critical success, but could not be classified as popular or commercial winners. The quite modest *Make Me an Offer* had much to offer. It should be noted that the songless 1954 film version, adapted from Mankowitz's novel, preceded the musical adaptation.

On stage, *Expresso Bongo* was the first real blast of what we might call the 'verismo' British musical, slices of life intercut with songs. In a way, the show took on the air (and airs) of a British 'B' movie, and the Soho nightclub milieu had its antecedents in such pieces as *Pal Joey* and Nöel Coward's 'Soho' musical *Ace of Clubs*. The generally contemplative romantic numbers, hardly recommending love as a recipe for happiness, also sound as if they are out of some black and white British 'B' picture of the forties or fifties.

A year later, the impact of the screen version of *Expresso Bongo* was less seismic. *The Times* detected whiffs of Gilbertian wit, as in Gilbert and Sullivan's send-up of artistic pretensions *Patience*, but for the *Guardian* it was 'too long for its matter and, by comparison with its American prototypes, it is, even at its best, slightly amateurish.'[28] Hollywood's version of Rodgers and Hart's *Pal Joey* had covered some of the same ground with rather more wit and acerbity. David Parkinson acclaimed the new film as 'One of the best musicals ever produced in this country [...] Harvey is perfectly cast as the talent agent hoping to get rich quick [...] Val Guest captures the fads and fashions of the late 1950s, but it's Wolf Mankowitz's crackling script that gives the film its authenticity.'[29]

Yes and no. It may be that the cinema was never going to be the right place for Mankowitz's affectionate inspection of the underbelly of show-biz. There is no denying that 'backstage' stories have been the staple of the musical film since the cameras first rolled. *Expresso Bongo* is a creditable example, and the ground has been more smothered than covered, but does *Expresso Bongo* add anything distinctive to that list? What relationship did it have to the stage show? Presumably, Mankowitz's collaborators on the original musical approved of the many, one might say crucial, adjustments made for the film? But why did Mankowitz sanction them?

A stark comparison might be with the Hollywood Rodgers and Hammerstein adaptations: think *Oklahoma!, Carousel, South Pacific*. There would of course be differences between the stage and film score, but essentially the original stage score remained in place for R and H. The idea of other composers and lyricists being brought in to bolster what was already there (certainly for R and H) unthinkable. The makers of the filmed *Expresso Bongo* took a different view; this was a British stage musical and therefore not of a quality to be transferred, as it were verbatim, to the screen. The validity of its having been chosen for cinematic treatment was inevitably undermined.

Those not associated with the stage production were brought in to provide new numbers: Robert Farnon (also its musical director), Val Guest, Norrie Paramor, Bunny Lewis, and Paddy Roberts. Their contributions cannot be described as substantial or adding anything of value. Only four numbers from the theatre score are retained, and (apart from 'The Shrine on the Second Floor') they are considerably truncated. The four remaining bolster the tone of Mankowitz and More's original downbeat perception and have qualities not shared by the film's new interpolations.

The team of Mankowitz, More, Heneker, and Norman had known what it was about. It was Mankowitz's intention to create a new 'school' of British musicals, a plan that met with mixed success. The school had few pupils, and any political bite threading through *Expresso Bongo* was dissipated in the team's subsequent works. This, after all, is a story that emerges under the shadow of Prime Minister Harold Macmillan's claim made during an iconic speech at Bedford Town's football ground in July 1957 that 'most of our people have never had it so good'. It's a view corroborated by Johnny in one of Mankowitz and More's most pertinent lyrics, retained, if in shorter form, on screen:

I never had it so good since the day I was born
Corn is growing!
Where there used to be barren soil
What a lark – I've struck oil!
I never had it so good, never made such a kill till this moment
Now I know I'm the lucky type,
Got the plum, picked it ripe!

Missing from Guest's film is Johnny's final hymn to disillusionment, 'The Gravy Train', a step too far for a British musical film. Fortunately, it is archived in Paul Scofield's performance on the original cast recording. It's all you need to hear to convince you that Scofield's performance shoots Harvey's out of the water.

What of Bongo Herbert himself, James Kenney on stage, and Cliff Richard on screen? There is no contest, even though we have only the evidence of Kenney singing his numbers in the cast recording. Richard conducts himself well throughout, with smooth vocals, but the central point of the piece is sacrificed. What is the point of Mankowitz showing us scenes of Bongo's shabby, dysfunctional parental home (at least it's a chance for wheezing Wilfrid Lawson to steal his brief scene) when he sings 'The Shrine on the Second Floor' with no hint of parody? This is hardly surprising: Richard could hardly be expected to *parody* the sort of pop singer that Mankowitz and More had created. Because he plays and sings everything straight, the absurdity of the number is rendered meaningless. But then, the opportunity to hire Richard for his film was something Guest could hardly be expected to resist. With Kenney in place as Bongo, the film might have shown its teeth; instead, we have puppy-fat niceness and milk teeth. *Sight and Sound* acknowledged 'a gentle, likeable performer, but it seems astonishing that anyone should confuse that authentic air of well-fed abstraction with virginal innocence and professional naïveté'.[30] Instead of sad tawdriness, Richard's involvement marks a destructive diversion from the play's spirit. So it is that Kenney was robbed of this role, despite the fact that he had form as a 'teenage' hoodlum, having played the lead in the 1953 *Cosh Boy* and, in 1958, *Son of a Stranger*, in which he was another no-gooder who attacks elderly ladies.

And so to *Expresso Bongo*'s star, Laurence Harvey. Harvey was riding a wave of popularity following the previous year's box-office hit *Room at the Top*, of which there are echoes in Johnny's intimate scenes with Maisie. His participation in *Expresso Bongo* may be very fine; it may not. He gallops through the film with unremitting confidence but little nuance. If only we could see how Scofield played the part. According to his associates and those who saw his performance, Scofield was superb, as might be expected of so distinguished an actor. Opinions of Harvey's account will vary, but watching him go through the motions is a tiring experience. The skill would have been in making Johnny likeable, but Harvey has no reserves to take the character to interesting places. So it is that Harvey and Richard take the film down roads originally unintended for travel.

Four numbers are retained, sometimes truncated, from the original stage production, with music by David Heneker and Monty Norman and lyrics by Julian More and Wolf Mankowitz. These are 'Nausea' sung by Meir Tzelniker, 'The Shrine on the Second Floor', the Harvey–Tzelniker duet 'Nothing Is for Nothing', and Harvey's 'I've Never Had It So Good'. For Richard and The Shadows, Norrie Paramor wrote 'Bongo Blues' and with Bunny Lewis wrote 'A Voice in the Wilderness' and 'Love'. Farnon collaborated with various lyricists to make up the rest of the score, teaming with Guest for 'You Can Look at the Goods but Don't Touch' performed by Sylvia Syms and Girls and Syms's 'Worry Go Lucky Me', and with Paddy Roberts for 'You Can't Fool You'.

1960

When, at curtain call, Archie sings 'Hide Your Face, Mum' to the disinterested huddle in the stalls, it is as if the last trumpet has been blasted on a whole regiment of light entertainment

The Entertainer

Jazz Boat
Let's Get Married
Girls of the Latin Quarter
Climb Up the Wall

In the Nick
The Entertainer
Too Hot to Handle
Beat Girl

FEBRUARY

Anthony Newley's gregarious career mined deeply into the British musical film industry in a year that offered no other major opportunities to young male artists beyond Tommy Steele in *Light Up the Sky* (barely qualifying as musical) and Adam Faith in *Beat Girl*, while Newley had three bites of the cherry: *Jazz Boat*, its sequel *In the Nick*, and *Let's Get Married*. For some, Warwick Films' *Jazz Boat* had its own identity issues, the *MFB* labelling it a 'lively' and 'muddle-headed' affair in which 'The general farce and fantasy mix uneasily with the spirited caricaturing of David Lodge and Al Mulock (playing The Dancer) in the gang', leaving Newley 'a most ineffectual hero' in 'a juvenile crime story barely strong enough for a B-feature'.[1] Newley's biographer recognised the dichotomy, deciding that 'its explicit and random scenes of violence made it reminiscent of Brando's *The Wild One*, but in the midst of this were songs staged by Lionel Blair, turning the whole into a lesser *West Side Story*'.[2] Equally confused, *Kinematograph Weekly* found it 'a bit short on emotional appeal and suspense'.[3]

Its beginnings were in a story by Rex Rienits, worked into a screenplay by John Antrobus and director Ken Hughes. Their hero, electrician Bert Harris (Newley), persuades a gang of leather-jacketed thugs that he is a cat burglar, so persuasively that he is brought in to take part in a jewel robbery. The screenplay skitters between moments of considerable violence, lingering shots of Newley smooching The Doll played by Anne Aubrey with sultry intensity, quirky humour, riotously choreographed sequences, punch-ups, and musical numbers by Joe Henderson that just about do service: a title song, the instrumental and dance number 'I Wanna Jive Tonight' played by Ted Heath and His Music in clubland, 'Take It Easy' (its lyric by Henderson and Hughes) as the gang moves through a street market causing chaos, and Newley's especially mournful lament 'Someone to Love' as he wanders alone by the dockside. For no discernible reason Jean Philippe is found in a nightclub singing 'Oui, Oui, Oui' (music by Hubert Giraud, lyric by Pierre Cour).

Jazz Boat has the advantage of sharp characterisations from the company, not least Spider's band of thieves, the ever-threatening Dancer (Al Mulock) and Holy Mike (David Lodge) with his biblical small talk. As the more innocent Jinx, Bernie Winters (*sans* Mike) suggests what a decent actor he might have become if Fate had dealt a different hand. He also gets one of the nicest lines: 'If we get a fair trial, they'll hang us.' At the centre of the web, James Booth's Spider is by turn seductive and immoral, leading to some final moments of violence against The Doll that lurch into flick-knife territory.

Justice is served by worn-down Detective Sergeant Thompson (Lionel Jeffries) as he follows the crooks on the jazz boat to Margate. There, Hughes takes every opportunity offered by that resort's pleasure beach of Dreamland, hurtling his players into a surreal world of halls of mirrors and fairground horror. The happy ending for Bert, his girlfriend Renee (Joyce Blair), and Jinx makes for a surprisingly soft landing after a film whose grittier moments recall some of the atmosphere of Carol Reed's *Brighton Rock* (1947).

Anthony Newley's many competent performances as a boy actor in British films (memorably as the Artful Dodger in David Lean's *Oliver Twist*) contrasted with his adult contributions to the industry, which included (thankfully beyond the timespan of this book) *Mister Quilp* (1975); Newley's performance as the dwarfish wife-pincher faded into nothingness in comparison with that of Hay Petrie in Thomas Bentley's 1934 version of *The Old Curiosity Shop*. Newley's biographer sees **Let's Get Married** as 'a dog's dinner of a screenplay [by Ken Taylor, from the novel *Confessions*], one moment a "kitchen sink" drama [produced by John R. Sloan for Viceroy Films], the next a love-in for Newley. It didn't know what it was, where it was going or what it was trying to say.'[4] The *Spectator* thought that 'An inepter British comedy it would be hard to find, with Anthony Newley, potentially one of our brighter young comedians, lost in a story, script and direction [Peter Graham Scott] so abysmally awful that nothing need be said about them.'[5] The film served as a means of promoting one of Newley's best-known numbers, Lionel Bart's insouciant 'Do You Mind?' As well as Bart's title song, there was 'Confessions' sung by Anne Aubrey.

MARCH

E. J. Fancey formed his own production company in 1954, with his son Malcolm as co-director. E. J.'s wife, B. C. Fancey (also credited as Beatrice Scott), produced the rock and rolling but mostly twisting *Rock You Sinners* in 1957; in films, her daughter Adrienne doubled as Adrienne Scott. The Fanceys were strong on family. Their **Girls of the Latin Quarter** was a title intended to summon up visions of scantily clad females. Between 1949 and 1952 'Latin Quarter' revues were a constant attraction at the London Casino, while tatty touring shows persisted in offering such frequently disappointing titillation well into the 1960s. In May 1958 the *Latin Quarter Strip Show*, with its 'Six Latin Quarter Lovelies', stopped off for a week at Aston Hippodrome (Old Age Pensioners a shilling). Sadly, this was also the year in which Phyllis Dixey, once the refined queen of British striptease, planned to commit suicide at Beachy Head, but was saved by a spiritualist and persuaded to return to the stage, her glory dimmed, in a cut-price tour of *The Phyllis Dixey Show* (she got £75 a week).

The Fanceys' Latin Quarter exploited striptease in the only way available to the British musical film of 1960: cheaply and modestly, vaguely suggesting sexual stimulation. Not without reason, *Kinematograph Weekly* recommended the film's 'eager contributions by *Folies Bergère*-like dancers' to 'the tired businessman and most certainly the troops'.[6] 'Almost everything about this film is shoddy', reported the *MFB*. 'Even the editing, lighting, colour and sound quality cannot maintain acceptable standards', and it was 'primitively directed' by Alfred Travers, previously director of *Meet the Navy* (1946) and the 1947 *Dual Alibi*, the only feature film to star Dixey.[7]

Surprisingly, the timid screenplay was by the (subsequently) celebrated team of Brad Ashton and Dick Vosburgh, based on an idea by Travers, concerning Clive (Bernard Hunter) putting on a show to gain a fortune. This charade of reality involved the bubbling organist Cherry Wainer (seen in the same year's *Climb Up the Wall*), singer Sonya Cordeau, and 'Britain's first rock and roller' Cuddly Dudley, frequently booked for television's *Oh Boy!* and often deputising for Cliff Richard. Mimi Pearce, who had starred in the *Folies de Londres* stage revue of 1956, was principal dancer. Whether Mimi fulfilled the tantalising promise from Fancey's publicity department – 'Striptease in London's Soho' – is open to question.

MAY

Produced by Olive Negus-Fancey for Border Film Productions, and directed and co-written by Jack Jackson and director Michael Winner (his first feature), **Climb Up the Wall** was a feeble attempt at a rock'n'roll picture, with its 'turns' forced into a scenario 'so chaotic and inconsequential in construction and presentation that it is almost surrealist'.[8] The connecting antics of Jackson and his son Michael as they lurch through the proceedings, introducing meaningless snippets of old movies (from Frances Day to Peter Sellers), represent infantile fun. The first guest to appear, wandering about Kensington Gardens, possibly in search of a personality, is Mike Preston singing 'Try Again'. For some reason, we see bits of old Westerns, and shots of pianist Charlie Kunz, Antonio and his stamping Spanish dancers, and toothsome 1930s comic actor Claude Dampier, and George Browne performs 'Frankie and Johnny'. In a nightclub, belly dancer Rahnee Motie lies on a bed of nails.

We then see proof of the fascination that pianist Russ Conway inspired in women. They begin screaming at the very mention of his name. Mr Conway smiles as much as he plays. In 1959, he was the composer (as Trevor H. Stanford) of a disastrous West End musical, *Mister Venus*, starring Frankie Howerd and Judy (Judith) Bruce. During rehearsals, Miss Bruce recommended him to not only play the piano but also communicate a gleaming pleasure with his audience. As we see here, he took Miss Bruce's advice, but nothing can disguise his self-consciousness. The fun continues with Glen Mason in a strangely under-equipped kitchen asking, 'What's Cooking, Baby?' Not much, apparently.

In the bar, pleasant Craig Douglas, alarmingly clothed, wants to be a star (this seems to be the only qualifying reason for his being in the picture) but has to make do with being a dishwasher. He sings 'My Miss Inbetween' and 'Of Love'. Only as the film drags itself to its grateful conclusion does energy burst out with the engulfing enthusiasm of Cherry Wainer's keyboard-playing and manic drumming. She almost jumps out of the screen in her efforts to gain our approval. For some reason, the talented Canadian Libby Morris does nothing but stand shivering by the Albert Memorial, although Winner must have been aware of her skills as a quirky chanteuse whose repertoire included a love song to a vulture. It might have livened things up.

JULY

A follow-up to its *Jazz Boat*, Warwick Films' ***In the Nick*** resumed the misadventures of Spider (James Booth) and his gang, again written and directed by Ken Hughes, based on a story by Frank Norman, then noted for supplying the book for Lionel Bart's stage musical *Fings Ain't Wot They Used t'Be*. The *MFB* had mixed feelings, finding it 'conventionally weak and structurally uneven, yet it gets closer to contemporary feeling than numerous more ambitious comedies'.[9]

The milieu of a friendly prison sympathetic to the needs of its crooked guests would have been familiar to those acquainted with Flanagan and Allen's *Here Comes the Sun* (1945), and there was a similar setting for Acker Bilk's amusing *Band of Thieves* (1962). Anthony Newley returned in the new guise of kindly prison psychiatrist Dr Newcombe, with Lionel Bart's title song and 'Must Be'. In more thoughtful hands, the film might have contributed something valuable to the seemingly unsolvable problem of in-prison rehabili-tation, but the publicity machine promised a tale of 'living it up … behind bars' choreographed by Lionel Blair. James Booth repeated his authoritative Spider, and Anne Aubrey transmogrified into The Doll, a striptease artist.

As a film about a comedian with barely a laugh in it and almost guaranteed to send you home feeling more depressed than when you went in, John Osborne's *The Entertainer* was not the first and not the last, although as an adaptation from his stage play it might have made room for more comedy, but neither Osborne nor brought-in screenplay co-author Nigel Kneale was known for comedy. Producer Harry Saltzman and director Tony Richardson presided over a film that successfully opened up Osborne's claustrophobic drama, moving a little uneasily between the cramped, unstable confines of the Rice family's home life and the stage life of its patriarch, washed-up, fast-fading, leftover music-hall comic Archie Rice.

Unlike his elderly, once theatrically revered father Billy (Roger Livesey), himself a leftover *lion comique* of an Edwardian age, Archie epitomises the fag-end of music-hall-cum-variety. Osborne uses Archie as a mouthpiece of 1950s disillusion and despair, living out the last weeks of his career just as he has spent it, drinking, womanising, scratching at existence in tawdry revues in cavernous and grossly uninhabited theatres in whose wings lurk a man from the Inland Revenue. But where to begin an understanding of this in several ways unsatisfactory parable? Perhaps by overcoming any discussion of the younger characters: Frank Rice (Alan Bates), Mick Rice (Albert Finney), Jean Rice (Joan Plowright), and Jean's boyfriend Graham (Daniel Massey). These characters seem almost irrelevant to what is happening, representing a new generation but mere appendages to the tragedy unfolding before them. It is a film that fixes our attention on the oldies: Archie, his pathetic alcoholic wife Phoebe (Brenda de Banzie), game Billy, and gritty cameos from Thora Hird as the mother of Archie's new lover Tina (Shirley Ann Field), and – briefly but effectively – from experienced hands Gwen Nelson and Hope Jackman.

The opening-out of the stage play allows us to move around Archie's lodgings (surely his chaotic lifestyle would never have resulted in his owning a house of his own) and be, as it were, in the wings of his latest show. This fluidity is used to advantage without ever sacrificing the centrifugal force of the stage play. On the other hand, it throws up potential problems. In the theatre, the audience watching the performance doubles as the audience watching Archie and his supporting artistes (represented here by Miriam Karlin as a brassy chanteuse going through her stuff with gathering desper-ation), having paid to sit through it. Thus, by participating in a piece of 'live' theatre, the theatre audience becomes very much more of the play as it is acted out. The audience had the potential to affect the performance as it reacted to Archie's exhausted patter, put over with techniques that remind us of greater comedians and probably reached back to the great Regency clown Joseph Grimaldi. In the film, all this is distanced, although we are in no doubt that we are trapped in that milieu familiar to tatty tours of nude revues that travelled up and down the country as the Hippodromes and Palaces, drained of vitality, prepared to shut their doors and awaited the demolition men. Untouched by the recent intervention of rock'n'roll, Archie's world crouches on its beam ends as oblivion beckons.

Osborne's tragedy (how else to describe it?) unfolds against the impression of a country that, like Archie, is hanging on by its fingernails, most recently knocked out of its post-war complacency by the Egyptian president's nationali-sation of the Suez Canal. In National Service, Mick is taken prisoner and killed. Archie's animal howl of agony is one of the play's most searing moments, but it is less effective on film, where it somehow lacks impact. Nevertheless, Olivier moves his stage performance to film with ease. His characterisation is equalled by Brenda de Banzie's deeply moving Phoebe; the scene in which she discovers Billy eating the celebratory cake that she has bought for Mick's expected home-coming is a devastating *tour de force* from an actress whose work (including her brilliant Maggie in *Hobson's Choice*) deserves to be better remembered. It can be no accident that Richardson insisted on her being retained from the stage production.

Hovering as it does between straight play and musical play, *The Entertainer* has survived as one of Osborne's most revived works. It was in 1956 that his *Look Back in Anger* broke bonds with the Shaftesbury Avenue social dramas so familiar to the theatrical management of H. M. Tennent, jumping a barrier that crossed beyond such playwrights as Noël Coward, Terence Rattigan, Wynyard Browne, and N. C. Hunter and seemingly promising a new school of British dramatists. 'However you look at it', wrote Michael Billington, 'as social document or Strindbergian study in self-torment – [*The Entertainer*] remains a great play.'[10]

In his preface to the play's published script, Osborne explains that 'The music-hall is dying, and with it a significant part of England [...] something that belonged to everybody', and it is to the lost art of music-hall that composer John Addison's pastiche score turns. It is pitch-perfect, not least in Archie's principal numbers, the haunting 'Why Should I Care?' and 'Thank God We're Normal', the latter having been especially effective when the play premiered in 1957, the year of the Wolfenden Report. By the time of the film, the song's potency is a little less obvious, but still telling. Together, Osborne's lyrics and Addison's second-hand tunes support, underpin, express the work's essential sense of hopelessness, in sympathy with young Graham's belief that 'Everything about this country's dead.' Death stalks through the piece: the death in the wings of old trouper Billy as he makes a last attempt to repeat past triumphs; the death of music-hall itself; the death of world peace; the death of Mick; the death of Phoebe's hopes; and ultimately the professional and emotional death of Archie, who has already confessed to being dead behind the eyes.

In 1959, Osborne fulfilled a desire that had surely been gnawing at his creative ambitions for years: at last, he wrote a work that can justly be classified as a truly British musical play, *The World of Paul Slickey*. Its spectacular critical and commercial West End failure did much to damage his reputation. Its music was by the little-remembered Christopher Whelen. As can happen in the teeth of instant rejection, that world of Mr Slickey has never been revived, or justly reassessed. It resides undisturbed in the catalogue of Osborne's work, vaguely recalled as a muddled, spiteful, coruscating, disorganised, badly written splatter-gunning assassination of British society, and has rarely (except on occasion by your author) been considered worthy of a moment's concern. In the public's mind, the nearest Osborne ever got to writing a musical was his book and lyrics for *The Entertainer*. Consider what it would be without its songs, and be grateful for them.

Osborne's conviction that music-hall was 'something that belonged to everybody' is evidenced in the film's skilful use of authentic music-hall material. It's there in Nelson's public house singalong of 'Don't Let 'em Scrap the British Navy' (music by Melville Gideon, lyric by R. P. Weston and Bert Lee), accentuating a celebration of a bygone day. It's there when the younger generation (Bates and Plowright) sing a snatch of Charles Collins and Harry Castling's 'When There Isn't a Girl About'. It's there when Livesey and friend (George Doonan) break into Harry Gifford, Alf Lawrance, Tom Mellor, and Huntley Trevor's delightfully communicative 'Kitty the Telephone Girl'. It's there when Karlin robotically puts over C. W. Murphy and Dan Lipton's 'Put Me amongst the Girls' at Blackpool's Winter Garden. Most poignantly, it's there when de Banzie and Plowright join in George Ware's evergreen 'The Boy in the Gallery'. Elsewhere, Addison never fails to point the theatricality. When, at curtain call, Archie sings 'Hide Your Face, Mum' to the disinterested huddle in the stalls, it is as if the last trumpet has been blasted on a whole regiment of light entertainment.

OCTOBER

'Bad enough, ripe enough, to be thoroughly enjoyed' might have been taken as a commendation of Associated British and Wigmore's ***Too Hot to Handle***, but *Films and Filming* amplified its displeasure: the film was

> Bad to the point of becoming outrageously so, it pushes its unlovely ripeness at you with such persistence, with such effrontery, that it leaves you with a kind of stunned admiration for its grandiose banality. [It is] fairground cinema, strictly lunatic stuff, bearing little more connection to life than, say, *Juke Box Jury* or *Double Your Money*.[11]

The Times sniffed in unison, seeing a 'dubious' film purporting to expose scandals 'while fully and generously illustrating them', and 'every now and again the film takes time off to present a "cabaret" number and show the girls undressing. The colour throughout is garish, but then so is the film.'[12] *Kinematograph Weekly* saw how 'the bizarre trimmings cunningly insulate its steamy plot', noting that its star 'sings adequately, meets all acting demands and makes the most of her fabulous upholstery'.[13] *The MFB* recognised 'the kind of immoral film which exploits the vices it pretends to condemn', offering 'a titillating glimpse of nudity and brutality' alongside 'some atrocious acting'. In fact, 'Apart from some lavishly staged cabaret numbers, only two things relieve the tedium.'[14] Halliwell dismisses a 'rotten, hilarious British gangster film set in a totally unreal underworld and very uncomfortably cast'.[15]

These are harsh verdicts on a film that, after all, was only doing its job, to depict the remarkably seedy, calmly sordid, world of Soho's gangster-run strip joints, apparently up-market but decidedly questionable. David Shipman dismisses it as a Soho thriller 'of the sort beloved by British B Picture-makers',[16] but despite at one point threatening to involve even the Archbishop of Canterbury, *Too Hot to Handle*, with its elderly men leering at young women in various states of undress, seems as relevant in our time as it did (to some) sixty-odd years ago. It pretends to be only what Herbert Kretzmer's screenplay, worked up from a story by Harry Lee, intends. As Novak (a crooked manager of the Pink Flamingo Club, played by Christopher Lee) says, here is 'Sexy, sordid Soho, England's greatest shame. Send for the missionaries before it's too late.'

There is no doubting the potency of its star, Jayne Mansfield. By now, with her American popularity waning, she had been farmed out to Britain, and in 1958 she co-starred with Kenneth More in *The Sheriff of Fractured Jaw*. By the time of *Too Hot to Handle* the slope was more slippery. It is possible that her 'fabulous upholstery' – that extraordinary structure that the cinema audience confronted – made it difficult to arrive at an accurate assessment of her dramatic capabilities, but despite the unavoidable diversion that her appearance starts up, she makes her sad cabaret-singing heroine Midnight Franklin flesh and blood. Where, anyway, is that 'atrocious acting' noticed by the *MFB*? The film is strongly cast across the board: Leo Genn excellent as the ruthless, unfeeling Johnny Solo, Carl Boehm as Robert Jouvel, and the girls of The Pink Flamingo including Barbara Winsor, Toni Palmer, and Judy (later Judith) Bruce.

Eric Spear's score is apposite and well-employed, including a background melody with a yearning sweetness that is completely at odds with much of the unpleasantness happening on screen. The in-house cabaret numbers (Spear's title song for Mansfield and the boys, and 'You Were Made for Me' with Kretzmer's lyrics) are neatly done, while David Lee's 'Monsoon' and Bill McGuffie's 'Midnight' orchestrate on-stage routines.

A notable development in the portrayal of the rock'n'roll and beat generation, *Beat Girl* (1960) had an interesting, somewhat elliptical, screenplay by Dail Ambler (otherwise the real-life Betty Mabel Lilian Williams).

In March 1959 **Beat Girl**, produced for Renown by George Willoughby and directed by Edmond T Gréville, was the first of Dail Ambler's screenplays to reach the British Board of Film Classification. It was coolly received. The reader reported 'the degredation of this story; the author may pose as a realist or a reformer but this seems to me to be machine-made dirt – the worst script I have read in years'. Was the reader aware that Ambler was the pseudonym of Betty Mabel Lilian Williams, better known as Danny Spade by those who lapped up her many thrillers in the manner of Mickey Spillane? Few recognised the author of *Beat Girl* as the blonde (whether natural or bottled we do not know, but the blondeness is somehow in harmony with Spade's fiction) author of such virile American-styled yarns as *The Dame Plays Rough* (1950) and *Honey, You Slay Me* (1953).

Miss Williams was about to change the tone. As the new decade dawns, Williams turns her back on the wholesomeness of Cliff Richard and Tommy Steele, turning the screw and turning up the heat on British youth. In some way, *Too Hot to Handle* prises open the door on permissiveness in the British musical film. Lending his very particular and confidently topical sound to the film is John Barry, whose musical contribution underpins the carefully assembled X-certificated social drama.

One of *Kinematograph Weekly*'s main observations was that Gillian Hills (playing the Beat Girl Jennifer Linden) was the closest British films had ever got to Brigitte Bardot, in what was an 'outstanding British "gimmick" offering [in which] the dialogue crackles, and Walter Lassally's photography is first-class. No mistake: *Beat Girl* will send 'em to the box-office.'[17] The *MFB* agreed that Lassally 'occasionally gives the general farrago, with its confusing time continuity, a distinction it hardly deserves'.[18] For the *Illustrated London News* it was 'a staggering film (almost harrowingly directed)',[19] while *The Times* argued, 'It would be possible to get very angry indeed about *Beat Girl* and the tendency it stands for, but it is actually no worse and no better than others of its kind.'[20] Stephen Glynn has succinctly defined the film's *raison d'être*, stating that 'for all its stylisation and excess [it] provides the full cinematic treatment of the "beatnik" scene in the Soho/Chelsea district in the late 1950s–early sixties and, by focusing on teenagers from upper-middle-class backgrounds, it reveals the ubiquitous nature of youth problems'.[21]

Now, the older generation is represented by Jennifer's father Paul Linden (David Farrar), a wealthy architect obsessed with his plans and forever toying with his impressive model for a perfect city ('I call it City 2000'). These plans do not seem to have been commissioned and will almost certainly never be realised, although we suspect they would have resulted in something along the lines of J. B. Priestley's blissful but unseen settlement in Ealing's *They Came to a City* (1944).

Paul returns home with his glamorous new French wife Nichole (Noelle Adams) to a cool reception from teenage Jennifer. Farrar's presence seems to belong to a previous decade: he is a staunch, unyielding and slightly eerie figure that one might have seen in a mild 1950s West End drawing-room comedy by Hugh and Margaret Williams, a man who wears a dressing gown when fully dressed. Introducing Jennifer to Nichole, he asks his daughter if she admires his taste. The cuddly old pussycat of a housekeeper (Margot Bryant, eventually immortalised as Minnie Caldwell in television's *Coronation Street*) is all smiles to meet her new mistress, although one suspects that their mutual sweetness will be short-lived. But at once there is a sort of sexual frisson between Jennifer and her new stepmother, the stirrings of a disturbing relationship. But it's that imaginary city that excites Linden: 'Grime, filth, poverty, noise, hustle and bustle. These things'll be unknown, an almost silent place.' Jennifer meanwhile has her opinion about the marriage, insisting that 'Love is the gimmick that makes sex acceptable', one of Miss Williams's snappiest lines and one that deserves to be in collections of quotations.

At night, Jennifer creeps out, becomes the Beat Girl (she has twenty cardigans), and meets Dave (Adam Faith) at a nightclub, where he sings John Barry and Trevor Peacock's 'Do What You Told Me', for which the echo chamber has been switched on. Dave remembers his poverty-stricken past, playing on the bomb sites, playing chicken on railway lines. This younger generation has stuck with the relaxed language we heard in *Rock You Sinners* and its like: 'Try me, daddy-o!', 'Oh, fade out!' It's a language unknown to Paul Linden. 'This language!' he expostulates. 'These words! Whatever does it mean?' 'It means us,' Jennifer explains, 'something that's ours. We didn't get it from our parents. We can express ourselves and they don't know what we're talking about. It makes us different. It's all we've got. Live now before the world explodes!' Dave sings Barry and Peacock's 'Made You', admonishing heavy-drinking pal Tony (Peter McEnery) 'If you wanna fight, go and do it in the Army. That's the place for squares!' What's more, 'Drink's for squares, man!'

Jennifer learns about striptease ('Do I hear aright?' asks Linden), visiting the seedy nightclub run by creepy Kenny (excellent Christopher Lee). Elderly men (among whom may lurk Monsieur Gréville) follow the girls' gyrations with interest. There is an especially graphic striptease routine performed with a scarf by Pascaline. Jennifer is taken on by Kenny for '£25 quid a week'. Jennifer's friend Dodo (Shirley Ann Field) sings Barry and Hyam Maccoby's 'It's Legal', promising that

> I won't be wicked again
> I'll never be bad no more
> Just think of the things that we can do
> Without even breaking the law.

While her father's away, Jennifer invites her gang back to the house for a late-night party. Plaid Shirt (Oliver Reed) and others urge her to strip. The noise awakes the sleeping Nichole, who also had a career (unknown to Linden) in striptease, validating the film's publicity campaign: 'My mother was a stripper … I want to be a stripper too!' *Beat Girl* marked a notable development in the portrayal of the rock'n'roll and beat generation, misunderstood and never to be accepted by Linden, and heightened when Jennifer becomes embroiled at the strip club, where murder resolves the situation.

1961

Disappointingly, it lacked originality, but had much to commend it

The Young Ones

Rag Doll   *The Johnny Leyton Touch*
The Young Ones

MARCH

With remarkable tenacity, the Mancunian Film Corporation survived up to the mid-sixties, having at last turned its back on the 'low' comedy pictures of Frank Randle, Norman Evans, Sandy Powell, and associates. The line was effectively drawn at the start of the decade with **Rag Doll**, enticingly retitled *Young, Willing and Eager* for the American market. This and Mancunian's next production *The Painted Smile* were directed by Lance Comfort: two slightly drawn, downbeat, melancholy social dramas that exhibited Comfort's conscious concession to the era of pop music, followed by his *Band of Thieves* (1962) and *Live It Up* (1963) and reaching a sort of apogee with *Be My Guest* (1965).

Brian McFarlane has recognised that 'In all of these unremarkable, but not unenjoyable, programme fillers, which represent the most strained circum-stances in which Comfort as a director for the cinema would work, there are recurring incidental pleasures.'[1] There is a good supply of them in *Rag Doll* with its typical Comfort protagonist, young crook Joe Shane (Jess Conrad), 'who, for reasons of naivety or other sorts of disadvantage, is made vulnerable to criminal intentions.'[2]

The picture may be remarkable only for the obvious care that Comfort bestows on it. Produced by Tom Blakeley at Walton-on-Thames, it has a screenplay by Brock Williams and Derry Quinn, from Williams's original story. Not without justification, the *MFB* thought that 'it wastes no time on things like conviction and characterisation, but achieves nothing compensa-tory either.'[3] Inhabiting seedy transport cafés on the North Circular, London's alluring illuminations, and subterranean nightclubs of dubious intent, it is a morality tale of unhappy seventeen-year-old Carol (Christina Gregg), who runs away from home. She is courted by successful businessman Mort Wilson (Kenneth Griffith) but irresistibly attracted to wannabe pop singer Joe, despite Mort informing her that 'A pop-singer is only a cowboy once removed.' The simplistic developments are expertly portrayed by a cast with the benefit of Hermione Baddeley as an ageing tart with a heart of gold, and Patrick Magee briefly seen but brilliant as Carol's sozzled dad.

As its nominal star, Conrad is effective enough. Martin Slavin's deft jazz-orientated score underwrites the action, with Conrad and the Mike Sammes Singers in the suitably mournful 'Why Am I Living?' with its lyric by Abbe Gail. A title song written for Conrad was subsequently unused.

DECEMBER

From its opening moments, with Teddy Green clambering back to terra firma via London scaffolding, **The Young Ones** bursts with exuberance and confidence. There is at last the possibility that the British musical film may be turning a corner. The *MFB*, always reticent in approval, praised 'a tremendous impression of overall pace and drive' in 'a rare and robust shot at a British musical'.[4] Disappointingly, it lacked originality, but had much to commend it. Concocted by producer Kenneth Harper, director Sidney J. Furie, and writers Peter Myers and Ronald (Ronnie) Cass, the film took its principal idea from the 1939 Judy Garland and Mickey Rooney *Babes in Arms* and a great number of similar plots: a bunch of kids putting on a show against the odds. In various forms, this had been almost endlessly regurgitated in the ensuing twenty-two years. The trick of *The Young Ones* was to bring a reinvigorating freshness to what was unmistakably a vehicle for Cliff Richard. In *Expresso Bongo* he had been 'an attractively surly presence, but here he is merely precise of diction and beaming of smile'.[5] Now, *Variety* thought him 'inexperienced as an actor, but he has a pleasant charm'.[6] Beyond *Expresso Bongo*, Richard had not registered as an actor, and he never became the actor-performer that his contemporary Tommy Steele was. In 1963, Steele found himself engulfed in yet another musical film about putting on a show against the odds, *It's All Happening*, a much less adroitly managed affair than *The Young Ones*, lacking the cohesiveness of Richard's major film debut and lumbered with Leigh Vance's screenplay. At least superficially *The Young Ones* seemed newly minted and looked expensive, and it moved briskly across the screen avoiding *longueurs*.

In a film that emphasised the energy of youth, it is surprising that Harper and Furie enjoined Myers and Cass to write the screenplay and much of the score. Previously, Myers had worked only intermittently in films, contributing some material to *Value for Money* (1955), *Storm over Jamaica* (1958), and Norman Wisdom's *Follow a Star* (1959), while Cass had composed the 'Winter Garden Waltz' for *The Entertainer* (1960).

Their association with Richard revitalised their careers. Through the 1950s they had written a string of satirical revues that had long runs in the West End, but critics and audiences had turned their backs on their last major effort *The Lord Chamberlain Regrets* (1961), one of the final flings of that specialised genre. Ironically, it would be another revue, the four-hander *Beyond the Fringe*, whose enormous success effectively rang the knell on the sort of revues that had proliferated in London. It comes as no surprise that the musical numbers Myers and Cass wrote for the three quintessential Richard films are redolent of the snappy but unmemorable material they had written for these entertainments. They bore little likeness to the sort of material expected by young cinemagoers. There was little need of them in *The Young Ones*, packed as it was with liveliness and more fashionable items by The Shadows. It was more likely that the Myers–Cass numbers evaporated by the time the audience was out on the street. There had been nothing memorable about Cass's score for the 1957 British musical *Harmony Close*, but they brought an energy to *The Young Ones* that at the time seemed like a breath of fresh air.

The young ones in question are Nicholas Black (Richard) and his gang of somewhat mature teenagers, among them Toni (sophisticated Carole Gray), long, athletic Chris (Teddy Green), toff-like Ernest (Richard O'Sullivan), and sidekick Jimmy (Melvyn Hayes). Their favourite place, where they can be young together, is Nicholas's youth club. Its future is threatened when his father, property magnate Hamilton Black (Robert Morley), buys the land for redevelopment. Undeterred, the gang take over a broken fleapit of a theatre to put on their show, illegally jamming BBC transmissions to publicise their campaign. Whatever we see as its faults, we happily concur with Nathan Rabin's assessment that ultimately 'the film's vibrancy, sense of humour, and catchy songs render such quibbles irrelevant: *The Young Ones*' unabashed, zestful high spirits are infectious'.[7]

The components are excellent. We need only list Furie's assured direction, with *Films and Filming* admiring the skill with which he concealed the film's limitations, American choreographer Herbert Ross's vital staging of the musical numbers, and Douglas Slocombe's impeccable cinematography. As Andy Medhurst has written, the Richard musicals knew what they were about, embellishing their star with 'lots of wide-screen colour, well-behaved heterosexual romance, sunshine and teeth'.[8]

A highlight is the extended medley of musical entertainment's history, brilliantly done. Myers and Cass would pull much the same trick in the last of their screenplays for Richard, *Wonderful Life* (1964). As in all the three films, the generation gap between the old and young yawns widely. Richard's admirable, thoroughly decent and hugely popular backing group The Shadows hover self-consciously at the edges of the picture, as if they were nothing to do with some of its best numbers.

The Myers–Cass songs are the ensemble 'Friday Night', 'Nothing's Impossible' performed by Richard and Carole Gray (her singing dubbed by Grazina Frame); 'All for One' and a protracted dance routine for Richard and ensemble, the rather insipid love song 'No One for Me But Nicky' performed by Gray, and the central set piece 'What Do You Know, We've Got a Show', as well as the vividly choreographed 'Just Dance'. Sid Tepper and Roy C. Bennett wrote the title song and Richard's 'When the Girl in Your Arms'. The Shadows' Bruce Welch and Hank B. Marvin wrote 'Got a Funny Feeling'; Welch, Marvin, and Peter Gormley collaborated for 'We Say Yeah'. Sung by Richard and Patti Brook, 'Lessons in Love' is by Shirley Wolf and Sy Soloway. The Shadows play Norrie Paramor's 'Peace Pipe' and 'The Savage', while Cliff Adams's melancholy 'Lonely Man Theme', written for the television commercial of Strand cigarettes (with its depressing tag line 'You're never alone with a Strand'), makes a surprising appearance.

The maverick pop record producer Joe Meek was the driving force behind Viscount Films's modest ten-minute short *The Johnny Leyton Touch*, directed by Norman Harrison. Under the musical supervision of Charles Blackwell, following the orchestral introduction of Margarita Lecuona's 'Taboo', Leyton sings two ballads that border on the melodramatic, Geoffrey Goddard's 'Wild Wind' and 'Son, This Is She', overlooked by adoring angora-sweatered girl singers. The opportunity is taken to introduce a hopeful contender for a new pop idol, Iain Gregory, singing 'Can't You Hear the Beat of a Broken Heart?' by Robert Duke (alias Joe Meek). Gregory was subsequently seen in the 1964 *Gonks Go Beat*. Harrison's direction is distinctly light-touch, but succeeds in conveying Leyton's cool naturalness.

1962

Bogarde may have been embarrassed by the words he uses, but he obviously knew that in those moments he was in the presence of cinematic greatness

I Could Go On Singing

Play It Cool	*Some People*
The Painted Smile	*Band of Thieves*
It's Trad, Dad!	*I Could Go On Singing*
The Road to Hong Kong	

MARCH

Director Michael Winner had already made a contribution to the pop films of the decade with his 1960 *Climb Up the Wall.* His exploitation of the genre continued with Independent Artists' **Play It Cool**, produced by Julian Wintle and Leslie Parkyn at Pinewood. Written by Jack Henry, the plot is vaguely constructed around pop singer Billy Universe (Billy Fury) and his musicians, who are flying to Brussels. At a 1962 airport (unrecognisably homely) Fury is fascinated by three air hostesses: 'I wouldn't mind crashing with those three!' This is a fair example of the uninspired dialogue that cobbles together a sequence of not uninteresting performers. Critical plaudits were in short supply, with *Films and Filming* pronouncing, 'It's Bad, Dad [...] amateurish and tatty [...] As Billy Fury can't act, he sensibly acts natural instead, while his musical-saw accent is left unblunted – a

Despite the sometimes-dispiriting surroundings, Michael Winner's cut-price *Play It Cool* (1962) featured Billy Fury, Danny Williams, and Bobby Vee among its notable artistes.

good touch.'[1] In this at least *MFB* agreed, explaining that Fury 'who, while apparently suffering from an Elvis Presley complex, can't quite shake off an Old Kent Road perkiness which is rather endearing'.[2] Over half a century on, this quality still comes through, despite the sometimes dispiriting surroundings.

In the airport lounge, Billy entertains expectant travellers by singing Norrie Paramor and Richard B. Rowe's 'Once upon a Dream'. There's no stopping him in his efforts to keep everyone's mind off the perils of air travel. If we are to believe *Play It Cool*, getting airborne was a distinctly quaint experience in 1962. Before take-off he's moving up and down the aisle relaxing the passengers with song. All appear delighted. On dry land, everyone is doing 'the Twist', which seemed to be enjoying a bumper year; even Margaret Rutherford as Miss Marple was having a go in MGM's *Murder at the Gallop*. Along the way, it's good to see Shane Fenton and Jimmy Crawford, and the always unpretentious Helen Shapiro in natty knitwear in two Paramor–Newell numbers. Mike and Bernie Winters provide a thermometer reading of British film comedy in the early sixties. They had already sneaked into the 1957 *6.5 Special* and make a late appearance here. Fury's items are central to the film's relevance, but Winner pulls out all the production stops for Danny Williams singing 'Who Can Say?' in a nightclub setting. Winner even provides a line-up of violinists (reminiscent of John Baxter's human pyramid of child pianists in his 1937 *Talking Feet*) for the guest appearance of American Bobby Vee performing 'At a Time Like This'. Between them, Fury and his fellow artistes provide the compelling reason to 'play it cool'.

Fury sings 'Play It Cool' (Paramor), 'You're Swell' (Rowe), 'Once upon a Dream' (Paramor and Rowe), 'Let's Paint the Town' (Paramor and Rowe), and 'Twist Kid' (Paramor and Larry Parnes). Paramor and Norman Newell wrote Shapiro's 'Cry My Heart Out' and 'But I Don't Care', Vee's 'At a Time Like This', Williams's 'Who Can Say?', and Jimmy Crawford's 'Take It Easy'. Paramor and Bob Barratt wrote Shane Fenton's 'It's Gonna Take Magic', and Fenton (alias Alvin Stardust) performed 'Why Little Girl?' co-composed by Fenton (as Bernard Jewry) and Ron Fraser.

APRIL

Director Lance Comfort's second pop-affected picture of the decade was Mancunian's *The Painted Smile*, a neatly produced 'B' feature, redolent of the Edgar Wallace series, each made in three weeks at Merton Park studios. Written by Pip and Jane Baker from an original story by Brock Williams (who had been the original source of Comfort's 1961 *Rag Doll*), it is notable for offering Liz Fraser a dramatic role as doomed nightclub hostess Jo, opposite Kenneth Griffith as nightclub owner Kleinie. Again, 'As in his major films [Comfort's] sympathies are for life's victims, even when their weakness helps to expose them to danger.'[3] As in *Rag Doll*, the score is by Martin Slavin, who wrote the title song with its Abbe Gail lyric. We also hear 'Another You', music by Norrie Paramor, lyric by Bunny Lewis and Michael Carr, sung by Craig Douglas.

Director Richard Lester is probably most often associated with being responsible for the critical and popular success of The Beatles breaking into films with *A Hard Day's Night*, but this was two years away. He is less well remembered for one of the most deft and inventive of pop musical films of the decade, Amicus's entertaining *It's Trad, Dad!*, aka *Ring-a-Ding Rhythm!* The posters promised 'The Kings of Dixieland Jazz together with the world's top recording stars', delivered in a co-mixture of New Orleans-infused Dixieland jazz from Kenny Ball, rhythm and blues in the hands of Gary 'US' Bonds, a dash of unpretentious lighter fare from the British contingent of John Leyton, Helen Shapiro, and Craig Douglas, and the legendary rock'n'roller Gene Vincent.

This was 'Dick' Lester's debut feature following two 1959 shorts, *The Running Jumping and Standing Still Film* and *The Sound of Jazz*. Now, Lester was recognised as the man who 'here revives the tradition of W. C. Fields, Eddie [Edward] Cline and *Hellzapoppin* by satirising his script, his actors and any number of cinema conventions between the feverish jazz tunes which make up the bulk of the picture'. Furthermore, the film had qualities 'which have succeeded in turning a basically threadbare, trashy plot-line into a genuinely comic occasion'.[4] *Films and Filming* regretted that 'musically, it's a little monotonous of course (and not a little deafening either). But visually, it's a spruce affair'.[5] For Donnelly, *It's Trad, Dad!* is 'remarkably energetic and technically adventurous [...] probably the most varied compendium of versions of the performance mode available'.[6] George Perry understood 'a routine assemblage of musical turns [it most certainly is not that] connecting with a current fad in the world of pop', a verdict that seems at least to be uncharitable.[7]

'Trashy' as producer Milton Subotsky's deceptively slight screenplay may be, it provides a perfect framework for Lester to work with as Helen and Craig (neither of them great actors) try to organise a jazz festival, pinning their hopes on the cooperation of some famous British disc jockeys who, in true pop-film tradition, make cameo appearances: suave David Jacobs, Alan Freeman, and Pete Murray. At the Town Hall, Felix Felton's splenetic Mayor thoroughly disapproves of the modern craze for enjoyment, 'a matter of grave importance to the governing of our fair community. The teenagers of this new town are disrupting its peace, its serenity, its calm and graceful dignity with the wild, the furious, the frantic music which they play constantly.' It is, in fact, 'Creeping jazzism!'

Subotsky and Lester reveal a Pandora's box of delights. First to escape is 'Tavern in the Town' from Terry Lightfoot and His New Orleans Jazz Band; they return for James Ryder Randall's 'My Maryland'. In the same mode, Kenny Ball and His Jazzmen have the traditional 'Nineteen Nineteen March', followed later by W. C. Handy's 'Beale Street Blues'. A close-upped Gene Vincent delivers Subotsky and Norrie Paramor's 'Space Ship to Mars', giving way to the neatly choreographed and well-turned-out Brook Brothers (Geoff and Ricky) performing their own 'Double Trouble'. Musical eccentricity is represented by the stiffly serious Temperance Seven, firstly in Jack Palmer and Spencer Williams's

'Everybody Loves My Baby' and then in Paul McDowell and Clifford Bevan's pleasantly lugubrious 'Dream Away Romance'.

After Subotsky's 'Bellissima', Bob Wallis and His Storyville Jazzmen move on to a spirited rendition of Wallis's own composition 'Aunt Flo'. An obvious highlight is Doc Pomus and Mort Shuman's fabulous 'Seven Day Weekend', stormingly done by Gary U. S. Bonds. Pomus and Shuman also contribute 'What Am I to Do?', semi-whispered by the gentle trio of The Paris Sisters (Priscilla, Albeth Carole, and Sherrell), and the vital 'You Never Talked About Me' sung by Del Shannon. The Dukes of Dixieland drop in to perform 'By and By', preceding one of the most effectively atmospheric sequences with Burt Bacharach and Hal David's superb 'Another Tear Falls' in a cigarette-smoke fog inhabited by a masterful Gene McDaniels.

The downbeat beauty of McDaniels's performance is countered by the happy appearance of Chubby Checker and dancers for Kal Mann and Dave Appell's 'Lose Your Inhibition Twist'. Checker, after all, was at the vanguard of the dance craze that swept the world. He had first danced it on American television's *Dick Clark Show*. In some form, the Twist had been around for years and might be attributed to the rhythm-and-blues exponent Hank Ballard, who introduced it in 1958, but it was Checker who realised its potential and helped the dance to its phenomenal popularity. Despite involving pelvic thrusting, manoeuvring of the hips, bending of the knees, balancing on the balls of the feet, and grinding of the heels, the Twist was unquestionably less hazardous than the Can-Can, and – perhaps its only recommendation to an older generation who still lamented the degrading effect of rock'n'roll on the young people around them – involved no touching of your partner.

Even after the wealth of talent that Lester and Subotsky had already welcomed in, the enjoyment carries on. It was inevitable that Acker Bilk, one of the most popular of the mature generation of performers, should feature, as he does in three items that have some historical relevance: Albert Ketèlbey and Mack David's 'In a Persian Market', Clarence Williams and A. J. Piron's 'High Society', and Subotsky's version of 'Frankie and Johnny'. On the lighter side, John Leyton (was there ever a British pop singer with so timidly appealing characteristics?) breaks through with Geoff Goddard's 'Lonely City'. Craig Douglas negotiates Paramor and Bunny Lewis's attractive 'Rainbows' ('There'll be rainbows in your tears'), and Helen Shapiro sings their 'Let's Talk about Love' and Clive Westlake's melancholic 'Sometime Yesterday' before she and Douglas duet with the Paramor–Lewis 'Ring-a-Ding', backed by Sounds Incorporated.

Finally, the film folds back to its jazz-oriented beginnings, with Chris Barber's Jazz Band playing his own 'Yellow Dog Blues' and his arrangement of the traditional 'Down by the Riverside' before James Milton Black and Katharine E. Purvis's 'When the Saints Go Marching In' sung by Ottilie Patterson.

The most amusing of the year's British musical features was Melnor Films' *The Road to Hong Kong*, a collaboration of producer Melvin Frank and director Norman Panama, sharing credit for the nimble screenplay. Halliwell explained its provenance: 'A curious, slightly dismal-looking attempt to continue the series in a British studio and on a low budget. A few good gags, but it's all very tired [...] and the space fiction plot makes it seem more so.'[8] Hollywood had begun the Crosby–Hope–Lamour musical comedies in 1940 with *The Road to Singapore*, subsequently setting off on the roads to Zanzibar (1941), Morocco (1942), Utopia (1946), and Rio (1947). It had now been a decade since the last of the series, *Road to Bali* (1952). It seemed inevitable that Hong Kong would be the series's final destination. Adding to the sense of occasion, Frank Sinatra, Dean Martin, and David Niven drop in, but there is excellent support from Peter Sellers as an Indian doctor, Joan Collins as the girl whom Hope has no hope of getting, Robert Morley as a Bond-type villain, and the gloriously punctilious Felix Aylmer as a Grand Lama with a penchant for drop-earrings.

The script needed only to accommodate the well-worn gags, with the occasional reference to the here and now, as in the mention of the unexpurgated version of D. H. Lawrence's *Lady Chatterley's Lover*, but there are inspired moments, one involving a great number of bananas before Crosby, Hope, and Collins are propelled into outer space. More might have been expected from the songs of Jimmy Van Heusen and Sammy Cahn: the opening number 'Team Work' and title song, both sung by Crosby and Hope, and Crosby's romantic duet with Collins, 'Let's Be Sensible'. Dorothy Lamour sings Van Heusen's 'Personality' with its Johnny Burke lyric, and Van Heusen and Sammy Cahn's 'Warmer Than a Whisper'. The musical numbers are staged by Jack Baker and Sheila Meyers.

For *Films and Filming*, 'The easy-going confidence of it all is admirable. A film by Jacques Tati is more important, and Jerry Lewis at his best is more brilliant [...] but this free-wheeling humour is serviceable and durable, and after all this time as road-worthy as ever.'[9] Less enthusiastically, the *MFB* thought it 'genial if, like its leading players, a bit weary'.[10]

JULY

The place of the teenager in British society at the beginning of the 1960s is at the heart of Vic Films' *Some People*, made in Bristol, produced by James Archibald, and written by John Eldridge, with much ad-libbing encouraged by Eldridge and director Clive Donner. Not all cinemagoers would have realised that the film was made to promote the work of the Duke of Edinburgh Award scheme as it followed a group of youngsters trying to make sense of adolescence: Johnnie (Ray Brooks), Bill (David Andrews), and Bert (David Hemmings). Under the aegis of kindly organist and schoolmaster Smith (Kenneth More) the film's striving to qualify as something like 'New Wave' collided with the suspicion that it was a dressed-up sermon on morality. There is no doubting the integrity of the enterprise; it was the final work of Eldridge, who died the same year, a last assignment that was 'among his finest and still ranks as one of the most nuanced portraits of youth to be produced in this country', 'at its best when it simply hangs out with them: a single-take stroll around a shopping centre that sounds entirely ad-libbed; a quiet chat down the pub between father and son'.[11]

Ron Grainer and Johnny Worth wrote the attractive title song (with calliope accompaniment) that pronounced the film's argument, apparently sung by Angela Douglas but dubbed by Valerie Mountain, a singer with the Bristol group The Eagles, who also perform Grainer and Worth's 'Yes You Did', 'Too Late', and Grainer's 'Bristol Express' and 'Johnny's Tune'.

> Some people think that kids today have gone astray
> But they should know 'cos they're all mixed up too
> Some people think that kids are bad, well that's too bad
> 'Cos they don't know the kids the way I do.

Alan Dent was unsure of the film's effectiveness.

> Though feeling quite certain that this film is meant quite sincerely in spite of its general inconclusiveness, and feeling hardly less sure that most of my colleagues are right to make elaborate allowance for it, I cannot be brought to believe that among the classes it is meant to reform it will evoke anything but jeers and guffaws of utter incredulity.[12]

Others were more forgiving of the film's disguised sermonising, as was Gordon Gow, who described 'essentially a director's film' in which 'The approach is welcome, and the technique remarkable.' For Gow, 'interest seldom, if ever, wanes',[13] but the *MFB* was not persuaded: 'Relying mainly on superficialities for its effect, the film finally outcasts the one thoroughly rootless delinquent who should have been its main concern.'[14]

AUGUST

'Trad's not a lark, it's a full-time occupation,' explains the governor of the prison where Acker Bilk and His Paramount Jazz Band are cosily incarcerated, although it is obviously not so full-time as he has imagined. It is not only crime, but a passion for traditional jazz that has brought the men together as **Band of Thieves**, making it a pleasure to be detained by Her Majesty. The Guv (jazz-loving Geoffrey Sumner), encouraged by 'The Duchess' (a sparkling Maudie Edwards in one of her most successful film roles), is desolate when the boys come to the end of their jail sentences and go their separate ways. Old lags such as Getaway (Arthur Mullard) make the best of it all. How long has he been 'inside', asks the Duchess. 'I don't remember the exact date', replies Getaway, 'but it was the day they started shooting *Cleopatra*.' 'Oh, you poor thing,' she sympathises. 'Oh well, never mind. You'll both be released one day.'

There are several good lines in Lyn Fairhurst's nimble screenplay based on a story by Harold Shampan, and decent direction by Peter Bezencenet, but Filmvales's *Band of Thieves* owes much to its cinematographer Nicolas Roeg and producer Lance Comfort, notably in the musical sequences when inventive camerawork and settings frame the amiable Mr Bilk. As the *MFB* reported, 'Bilk – both musically and personally – is a welcome addition to the screen ranks [...] the film knows its place and its public and isn't afraid of either. The plot is as zestfully slapdash as the production and the acting.'[15]

The prison scenes have the brightest dialogue and the best performances (Sumner and Edwards), but interest slides when the Honourable Derek Delaney (Jimmy Thompson) reunites Acker and his boys after their release and sends the 'Band of Thieves' on a tour of other prisons, effectively as a cover for the string of lucrative burglaries Delaney has organised. Delaney's romancing of Anne (Jennifer Jayne) is tediously spun out, while the musicians of the Paramount Jazz Band suffer the sort of personality anonymity suffered by The Shadows, The Pacemakers, and The Dreamers, those eternally swaying back-row attendants of the star turn. Sensibly, this film's star is kept mostly on the sidelines when anything resembling dramaturgy is attempted, coming into focus when the music starts up. It is then, in some multi-imaging of Bilk that Comfort's influence is evident; one of Comfort's abilities was to make the best of an obviously limited budget by tasteful use of pared-back décor.

The value of *Band of Thieves* lies in its documentation of Bilk's talent, his fatherly, benevolent persona. Musical items include 'Jazz at the Jails'; Colin Smith's 'Dudley D'; John Harris and Archie Leonard's 'Paradise Avenue', and 'Lovely' by Bilk, Norrie Paramor, and Kermit Goell, whose musical *Pocahontas* was to be a major West End flop the following year. We also hear Bilk insisting 'All I Want to Do Is Sing' (by Bilk, Paramor, and lyricist Peter Pavey), and the same author's 'Kissing' performed by 'guest singer' Carol Deane.

The thieves are captured, and the Honourable Derek is nabbed by Anne, now in police uniform. Acker and his boys return to prison to carry on happily as before, to be seen again on film in *It's Trad, Dad* and the 1964 *It's All Over Town*.

DECEMBER

And so to the probably incomparable Judy Garland in her final musical film, Barbican's production of **I Could Go On Singing**, based on an American television play, *The Lonely Stage*, built around Hollywood veteran Mary Astor. Scripted by Robert Dozier, *The Lonely Stage* (the working title of what became

I Could Go On Singing) told the story of celebrated actress Harriet Brand making a nervous return to the profession that had brought her much unhappiness, a role with which Astor clearly identified. It did not take a great leap of imagination to consider this a framework for a film fit for Garland. Jack Klugman was the one actor in the television play to be retained in the film as the star's manager George.

On screen, Dozier is credited with the story, with American Mayo Simon writing his first screenplay, a major opportunity for a writer who just previously had handed in an episode of television's *Dr Kildare*. In the event, Simon suffered the indignity of neither Garland nor her co-star Dirk Bogarde relishing his dialogue, some of which they adapted to their own needs. We may not know if Bogarde's conversation with Garland in the hospital scene is Simon's work or Bogarde's revision, but it certainly smacks of Dr Kildare. Bogarde may have been embarrassed by the words he uses, but he obviously knew that in those moments he was in the presence of cinematic greatness. Nevertheless, were it not for Garland's incandescent performance as performer Jenny Bowman, Lawrence Turman and Stuart Millar's production, directed by Ronald Neame, would not be so fondly remembered, or held in such esteem.

Mayo's screenplay is simply told. Jenny has come back to London to star at the London Palladium. She decides to seek out the son Matt (Gregory Phillips) whom she had with Dr David Donne (Bogarde). Having walked out of their lives, she wants, *needs*, to bring the young boy back into her muddled, conflicted existence. At curtain call of this predicament, she must acknowledge that the claim of showbusiness cannot be repulsed. There can have been very few cinemagoers who failed to recognise the unhappy comparisons to Garland's life.

Variety's main complaint was that 'the production is constructed on a frail and fuzzy story foundation.'[16] *Films and Filming* thought it 'a subject crying out for boldness and imagination, but it gets gentility'. Without Garland, the film was 'unthinkable. With her, for all its faults and there are many, it has moments of infinite richness and variety. Her alchemy turns paste to diamonds, her unique talent moulds and colours the work in which it is a centrepiece.'[17] The *MFB* experienced 'an enjoyment that will not bear analysis', but 'Within the limits of the writing, this performance probably brings us as close as we are ever likely to get to understanding the temperament of a great entertainer.' All this despite it being 'a back-stage *East Lynne*, the writing maddeningly superficial, the direction impersonal, the cutting commonplace'.[18] Penelope Houston went on to note that 'The total purpose, object and achievement of the film is contained in Judy Garland's performance; and even performance, here, is a word to be used diffidently, since the essence of her quality – as actress, if not as singer – has always been her ability to seem not to be performing.'[19]

It is inevitable that the film takes flight in its musical items, only one of which seems foreign to its star: Gilbert and Sullivan's 'I Am the Monarch of the Sea' when Jenny goes to see Matt in his school's production of *H.M.S. Pinafore*. Garland's artistry imbues the songs with myriad qualities, encompassing the liquid fluidity of Kurt Weill and Maxwell Anderson's 'It Never Was You' from their 1938 Broadway musical *Knickerbocker Holiday*, and Arthur Schwartz and Howard Dietz's 'By Myself', a number originally performed by Jack Buchanan in the 1937 New York production of *Between the Devil*. Garland is at full strength for Cliff Friend's 'Hello Blackbird' and Harold Arlen and E. Y. (Yip) Harburg's storming title song. At every turn, the direct line of communication between Garland's soul and our own holds firm.

1963

Cuteness is avoided, and offers no concessions to the often sub-Brechtian wholeness of both dialogue and song

What a Crazy World

The Cool Mikado	*A Place to Go*
Summer Holiday	*What a Crazy World*
Just for Fun	*Live It Up*
It's All Happening	*Farewell Performance*
Take Me Over	*It's All Over Town*

JANUARY

In welcoming Frankie Howerd to Shepperton for the filming of **The Cool Mikado**, director Michael Winner told him, 'You must remember that I'm a genius.' We must bear this in mind when considering this by turn tasteless, unintelligible, deeply irritating, amateurish, luridly colourful, disorganised, sexist adaptation of Gilbert and Sullivan's *The Mikado*. In writing of Howerd's involvement, his biographers describe Winner's production as 'an insult to the intelligence of any self-respecting film fan'[1] and 'a movie bad enough to make the most ardent moviegoer contemplate staying at home'[2] We suspect that Maurice Browning, modestly fêted as the librettist of a little British musical of the fifties, *Twenty Minutes South*, regretted that Winner's ramshackle screenplay was credited as being 'based on an adaptation by Maurice Browning' of Gilbert and Sullivan's most celebrated opera, with further intervention by Lew Schwartz and Phyllis and Robert White. Mr Browning was surely not responsible for such exchanges as that between Judge Mikado and a female witness:

Witness: My husband Mr Smith, well, he's a beast. He insulted me and he treated me cruelly and, well, he just didn't care where he hit me.

Mikado: And where *did* he hit you?

Witness: He hit me once in a grocery store and once on the corner of Elm Street.

Mikado: Oh, you poor thing. A bruise on the corner of Elm Street can be pretty painful. Is there anything else you'd like to tell me, my dear? Your phone number, for instance.

We may yet be fascinated by so gory a spectacle involving some notable names, the most prominent being Howerd as Ko-Ko, Tommy Cooper as Pooh-Bah, and Stubby Kaye as Judge Mikado. These at least retain some dignity, with the patently non-singing Howerd steering his own comic path through the mire. The patience of saints is required for the all-too-frequent manifestations of Mike and Bernie Winters (their billing matter on the halls had once been 'Just Nuts') and the choreography and dancing of Lionel Blair and his all-female troupe, whose work is never helped by his joining in. The desultory nature of his work may be compared with the vitality of Gillian Lynne's brilliant choreographies of the same period.

Gilbert's wandering minstrel, now Hank Mikado, is played by the ex-Broadway Kevin Scott, male juvenile lead in the London productions of two American musicals, *Fanny* (1956) and *Flower Drum Song* (1960). Mild-mannered he may be, but his agreeable playing is welcome, as is that of his Yum-Yum, Jill Mai Meredith. Contributing to the general embarrassment are disc jockey Pete Murray smooching one of Winner's chosen beauties ('Why don't you slip into something cool?') and one of the kingpins of the British 'B' movie, Dermot Walsh, with absolutely nothing to do. Extras stand about, understandably bewildered as to why Mr Winner has summoned them.

Martin Slavin's arrangements of Sullivan's score work well, with the assistance of John Barry's distinctive sound. Much of Sullivan's music is jettisoned along with Gilbert's lyrics, but the male ensemble's 'Gentlemen of Japan', 'Three Little Maids from School', Hank's 'A Wandering Minstrel I', Yum-Yum's 'The Sun Whose Rays', Ko-Ko's entrance 'Behold the Lord High Executioner', Kaye's 'A More Humane Mikado', Ko-Ko, Hank, and Yum-Yum's trio 'Here's a How-De-Do!', Hank and Yum-Yum's kissing duet 'Were You Not to Ko-Ko Plighted', 'The Flowers That Bloom in the Spring', and the 'For He's Gone and Married Yum-Yum' finale, are retained.

Ivy Films' black and white opening for the follow-up to *The Young Ones* probably reminded cinemagoers of the weather outside. On screen, it's summer in a denuded British seaside resort, and the rain is pouring down on the town's brass band bravely playing tiddley-om-pom-pom to the last bedraggled paying customers before they hurry to the nearest promenade shelter. Peter Yates's brilliant introduction to **Summer Holiday** points out the pitfalls of staycation before the youthful players, with some familiar faces among Cliff Richard's gang, burst into colour.

London Transport mechanics Steve (Teddy Green), Edwin (Jeremy Bulloch), and Cyril (Melvyn Hayes) help Don (Richard) to convert an AEC Regent III RT red London double-decker bus into a mobile hotel that will take them to the south of France. En route, the boys pick up the female singing group 'Do Re Mi', comprising Sandy (Una Stubbs), Angie (Pamela Hart), and Mimsie (Jacqueline Daryl). They also take on Barbara (Lauri Peters), a rich American heiress passing herself off as a boy in the hope of evading her frightful mother Stella (Madge Ryan), although it is beyond belief that Don and company would not recognise a young woman when they see one. Once the disguise is penetrated, there is no impediment to the blossoming romance between Barbara and Don.

Characterisation is not one of the film's strong points, but why should it be? Richard's gang of inevitably ageing teenagers (Teddy Green being among the most irreplaceable) are no more complex than they had been two years earlier in *The Young Ones*, and whatever depths they inhabit remain unexplored. The girls suffer most from this deficiency of delineation. They are what is sometimes classified as 'bright and bubbly', but a vagueness surrounds them, and they are too dim to recognise another girl when they so obviously see one. They need all their energy to cope with the next burst of movement induced by Herbert Ross's choreography, still impressive but perhaps not hitting the high spots of his work in *The Young Ones*. The generation gap is once again, this time without benefit of Robert Morley, at the heart of whatever drama is available, but Ryan's role is written so broadly that she can do little more than play it in the same manner. There is a somewhat superfluous guest appearance by Ron Moody as a mime artist that reminds us of his recent success as Fagin in Lionel Bart's stage musical *Oliver!* and of his work in the Myers–Cass West End revues.

These kids are aeons away from the rebellious teenagers in British dramas such as *Cosh Boy* (1953) and *Serious Charge* (1959). The coffee bar dancers and the palais-dancing couples we see jiving in the lovable *The Golden Disc* and *Rock You Sinners* are nowhere to be seen, presumably because they would no longer appeal to the British cinemagoer. For *Films and Filming*, 'At heart these teenagers are as square as the Huggetts and wouldn't have minded having Her Glorious Majesty Anna Neagle coming along to chaperone.'[3]

Sidney J. Furie had been slated to direct but was detained on another project and replaced by Peter Yates making an impressive directorial debut. James Oliver has acknowledged that

> Cliff's films were assigned to newcomers [...] The fact that, post-Cliff, British producers saw rock movies as a training ground rather than a retirement home was crucial to establishing the distinctive tone of British rock movies: younger directors were keen to make their mark, were in tune with their times and consequently more adventurous.[4]

The determination of producer Kenneth Harper to imbue his film with what we may call social currency was commendable, and Yates's cooperation in repeating what was by now the Cliff Richard format yields satisfactory results. The *MFB* might suggest that the film 'continually slops into the second-rate through lack of inventiveness in narrative and dancing',[5] but it does little harm to the Richard franchise. The retention of Myers and Cass for screenplay and several of the songs (the unmemorable ones) basically locks the film into the pattern established in *The Young Ones*.

The Myers–Cass numbers are the bright opener 'Seven Days to a Holiday', 'Let Us Take You for a Ride', and 'Stranger in Town' sung by Richard, the Richard–Peters duet 'Swinging Affair', 'Really Waltzing' for Richard and ensemble, and 'All at Once'. It is attractive stuff, but undistinguished. Myers and Cass also wrote the 'Yugoslavian Wedding' sequence. The carefree title song is by The Shadows' Bruce Welch and Brian Bennett, with 'Dancing Shoes' by Richard and Hank B. Marvin; both are performed by Richard. Richard also co-authored 'Big News' with Mike Conlin, and sings Philip Springer and Buddy Kaye's touching 'The Next Time'. The Shadows' material includes their own compositions 'Les Girls', 'Round and Round', and 'Foot-Tapper', and Welch and Richard's enduring signature song 'Bachelor Boy' (added to the film in its post-production phase) is a standout hit.

FEBRUARY

By its very title, Amicus's ***Just for Fun*** suggests it need not be taken seriously. In fact, unsatisfactory and unresolved as it may be, this attempt at melding twenty-eight pop songs into a digestible product is not without interest, spreading its net to catch some of the current acts of the early sixties. Ultimately, it is for those twenty-eight numbers that we appreciate producer and screenplay writer Milton Subotsky and director Gordon Flemyng making the effort, if only to be dismissed by the *MFB*'s opinion that 'the numbers follow the TV variety show formula, and are unimaginatively presented in cramped settings' in a film 'strictly for incurable addicts'.[6]

But *Just for Fun* may not have been quite so inconsequential as we think. Its basic 'plot' considers the possibility that teenagers might create their own political party, with its ambition to rule the country with themselves in mind, even as it accentuates the difficult relationship between pop music and television, with the BBC turning its back on shows that feature the material teenagers crave. Great minds may not be at work here, but the points are made by a cast that, on the sidelines of the pop performers, includes John Wood, Irene Handl, Dick Emery, and the irreplaceable Reginald Beckwith.

As for those singers, *Films and Filming* was unimpressed. 'Most of them are sluggish and thick to the extreme, and the performances either grotesque, flabby, or so amateur as to evoke, of all things, pity [and] blown up for the cinema they become unbearable.' The younger performers 'were used to inject youthful vitality into the film, but you sense that it's all a matter of talking down, like a boring uncle at his niece's birthday party'.[7]

CAN YOU FORGIVE ME

Words and Music by KARL DENVER

Recorded by

 KARL DENVER

on *DECCA* Records

  And sung in the film

"JUST FOR FUN"

From the same team that made **ITS TRAD DAD!**

BOBBY VEE · MARK WYNTER

THE CRICKETS · FREDDY CANNON

JOHNNY TILLOTSON · KETTY LESTER

IT'S THE GREATEST POP MUSICAL SHOW ON EARTH!!

KARL DENVER TRIO	JOE BROWN & THE BRUVVERS	KENNY LYNCH
JET HARRIS	TONY MEEHAN	CLODA ROGERS	THE TORNADOES
THE SPRINGFIELDS	LYN CORNELL	THE SPOTNICKS	JIMMY POWELL
THE VERNON GIRLS	BRIAN POOLE & THE TREMELOES	LOUISE CORDET
THE BREAKAWAYS	SOUNDS INCORPORATED	AND INTRODUCING CHERRY ROLAND

| GUEST STARS | IRENE HANDL | HUGH LLOYD | DICK EMERY | MARIO FABRIZI |
| DISC JOCKEYS | DAVID JACOBS | ALAN FREEMAN | JIMMY SAVILE |

WRITTEN & PRODUCED BY MILTON SUBOTSKY · DIRECTED BY GORDON FLEMYNG · AN AMICUS PRODUCTION · A COLUMBIA PICTURE

A COLUMBIA PICTURE

HILL & RANGE SONGS (LONDON) LIMITED   **2/6**

Sole Selling Agents :

BELINDA (LONDON) LIMITED   17, SAVILE ROW   LONDON, W.1

The 1963 *Just for Fun* (and why not?) was a not altogether dismal attempt to introduce British teenagers to politics (as imagined by a British film studio). The entertaining compendium boasted twenty-eight 'pop' numbers.

At least the party has a surfeit of songs, kicked off by cheery Cherry Roland's title song, followed by Mark Wynter against a Gaggia in a café setting for Clive Westlake's 'Vote for Me', and Jet Harris and Tony Meehan's instrumental 'The Man from Nowhere'. They also play Meehan and Johnnie Rodgers's 'Hully Gully'. Clodagh (here billed as Cloda) Rodgers sings of her 'Sweet Sweet Boy'. Friendly Joe Brown offers Westlake and Subotsky's advice to 'Let Her Go' before American Ketty Lester, remembered for her 1962 recording of 'Love Letters', describes Smith and Maxwell's 'A Warm Summer Day'. Freddy Cannon is a welcome visitor, twisting and smiling his way through 'It's Been Nice' ('I've Gotta Get Up Early, Early in the Morning') and Doc Pomus and Mort Shuman's bouncy 'The Ups and Downs of Love' backed by Sounds Incorporated. These are some of the segments, filmed in America, that lend a truly transatlantic feel to the project. We are in classic pop company with Bobby Vee, his voice once described by Bob Dylan 'as musical as a silver bell', for Pomus and Shuman's 'All You Gotta Do Is Touch Me'. Kenny Lynch sings a number he co-wrote with Westlake, 'Crazy Crazes', and there is a fragment of Westlake and Subotsky's 'Everyone But You' performed by Birmingham's home-grown Jimmy Powell.

Former 'Vernon Girl' Lyn (sometimes Lynn) Cornell has Westlake's 'Kisses Can Lie', making way for Sounds Incorporated's instrumental version of Billy Preston's 'Go'. Alan Blakley, Brian Poole, and Mike Smith's 'Keep On Dancing' gets a lively rendition from Poole and his Tremeloes. 'Can You Forgive Me?' reminded cinemagoers of its author and performer Karl Denver, a Scots singer with many hit singles during the decade. Louise Cordet's 'Which Way the Wind Blows' and Joe Brown's performance of Westlake and Subotsky's 'What's the Name of This Game?' tirelessly continued the variety. Westlake is further represented by his 'Happy with You' sung by Mark Wynter. The Springfields bring a distinct quality of their own to Tom Springfield and Westlake's 'Little Boat'. Westlake's other contributions involve Kenny Lynch singing 'Monument' and the remaining few Vernon Girls in 'Just Another Girl'. There had once been seventy of them, but they were now whittled to three; the girls disbanded in 1965. Joe Meek's style is all over 'All the Stars in the Sky', an obvious cousin to his 'Telstar' as performed here by the Tornados. The Swedish group The Spotnicks appear as Martians for their treatment of 'My Bonnie Lies over the Ocean', and almost as silly an item is Pomus and Shuman's 'Judy Judy Judy' sung by American Johnny Tillotson.

The USA brings up the rear with The Crickets performing Sonny Curtis's 'My Little Girl' (a true highlight) and Jerry Allison, Glen D. Hardin, and Tom Leslie's 'Teardrops Fall Like Rain', before the great Bobby Vee ties up the show with Ben Weisman, Dorothy Wayne, and Marilyn Garrett's classic 'The Night Has a Thousand Eyes'. It is fitting that Wynter and Roland should bring the proceedings to a conclusion with Westlake's title song.

MARCH

Perhaps the purpose of *It's All Happening* was to make the just-around-the-corner *Summer Holiday* seem like a cinematic masterpiece. Vapid nonsense loosely constructed around vaguely connected elements, the new Tommy Steele vehicle's screenplay by Leigh Vance was condemned by *Variety* as 'lazy, old-fashioned and flabby.'[8] The parlous state of the British musical film needed to look no further for an exemplar. The film placed its star at some distance from his autobiographical film debut of 1957. Of this, Colin MacInnes had written: 'If Elvis is the teenage witchdoctor, Tommy Steele is Pan. His tunes, originally derived from "rock", but increasingly melodious and even, on occasions, tender, are an invitation to the forest, to the Haywain, to the misty reaches of the Thames from whence he comes.'[9] MacInnes goes on to recognise Steele's speaking voice as 'that of a descendant of a long line of Cockney singers – [Gus] Elen, Kate Carney, [Albert] Chevalier' before singling out Marie Lloyd, 'of whom Tommy Steele seems to me to be in so many striking ways, the popular reincarnation.'[10]

It's an astonishingly inaccurate suggestion from the author of *Sweet Saturday Night*, a splendid long essay by MacInnes that no one who wishes to understand the lost art of music-hall should ignore, for nothing suggests the least similarity between Mr Steele and Miss Lloyd. For example, she would never have consented to be connected with so sickly a sentiment as that which overcomes Tommy when he sings to the orphans ('The Dream Maker').

MacInnes well understood the easily overlooked profundities of the Victorian and Edwardian music-hall song, but if Steele is a true descendant of these largely forgotten stars, he is many times removed. Gus Elen, Kate Carney, and Albert Chevalier each in their way reflected the Britain in which they lived in their storytelling, rough-hewn in the case of the strangely angular, almost manic style of Elen, and determinedly strong and pugnacious in the case of Kate Carney, whose 1903 'Are We to Part Like This Bill?' by Harry Castling and Charles Collins remains one of the most moving laments of lost love, and overlaid with lashings of cloying sentimentality by Chevalier as he too sang his sad hymns of costermonger romancing. Chevalier wrote many of the numbers he sang, too, among them 'Alice – an East End Ecstasy', 'The Future Mrs 'Awkins', the exquisite 'Coster's Serenade', and the still remembered 'My Old Dutch', a mournful ditty occurring just as a long-married husband and wife part before entering the workhouse with its separate entrances for male and female.

Of course, storytelling was and remains at the heart of music-hall song, perhaps even its main reason. It reflected the audience's everyday lives back on them, a transmission that recognised shared experience. Thus the problems of housing and paying rent, never mind the sexual complications that might ensue, inhabit countless songs such as perky Vesta Victoria's 1897 'Our Lodger's Such a Nice Young Man' by Lawrence Barclay and Fred Murray, Dan Leno's delightfully innocent 'Young Men Taken In and Done For' written in 1888 by Harry King and George Le Brunn, the troublesome but superb Victoria Monks account of her enforced 'Movin' Day' ('It's moo-oo-oo-oo-oo-oo-oo-oovin' day'), and Marie Lloyd's 1919 singing of Charles Collins and Fred W. Leigh's indestructible 'Don't Dilly Dally', a description of the moonlight flits all too often performed by those unable to pay their landlord. Regretfully, Lloyd even used music-hall song as a recruiting call to young men via Collins and Leigh's 'Now You've Got Your Khaki On', with its artful chorus promising sexual fulfilment for men if they took the King's Shilling.

In contrast to the earthy numbers performed by Steele's supposed antecedents, *It's All Happening* rolls out a generalised smorgasbord of gloopy songs. Now, Steele is an unlikely record producer recording the latest pop sensation Johnny De Little. Unfortunately, Mr De Little proves to be anything *but* sensational, a performer whose career seems to have come to a shuddering halt shortly after. We see John Barry musically directing the recording of De Little's 'The Wind and the Rain', but it's as insipid a beginning to a film as you are likely to find. Neither producer Norman Williams or director Don Sharp (whose *The Golden Disc* is at least more entertaining) can disguise the shoddiness of what follows, the awful décor, the cramped sets, the lack of pace, the over-use of sentimentality, the crass depiction of the older woman. Sentiment leaks from the film's pores when Tommy does voluntary work at a children's orphanage. ('He's wonderful with them, isn't he?'). He himself, despite what *The Tommy Steele Story* would have us believe, has lost his parents and was brought up in just such an institution. When the orphanage is threatened with closure, Tommy (the excuse for so many musical film plots) plans a concert to raise funds.

Despite difficulties, performers are gathered together for the occasion, including an un-blacked troupe from George Mitchell's *Black and White Minstrel Show* of stage and television renown in a finale medley that seems to have forgotten that the film is supposed to be about Mr Steele. Also helping to save the children's futures are pianist Russ Conway hammering out 'Flamenco', Shane Fenton and the Fentones telling of 'Somebody Else, Not Me', Dick Kalyan singing 'Meeting You', and (most welcome of all) Danny Williams describing 'A Day Without You'. The other performers are almost without exception dreary, with undistinguished contributions from the workmanlike Marion Ryan, who gets a duet with Steele ('Maximum Plus'), as well as an unexciting solo ('That's Lovin' – That's Livin'), and dull work from Jean Harvey and Angela Douglas, although the Clyde Valley Stompers manage to liven things up for a while with 'Casbah'.

There is a generous original score by dependable Philip Green and lyricist Norman Newell, although nothing distinctive emerges. They trade on Steele's cockney barrow-boy charm with the ghastly 'Egg and Chips', which is blown up to epic proportions with dancers David Toguri and Sheila O'Neill in what seems like a country cousin of Steele's music-hall pastiche number 'Flash! Bang! Wallop!' from *Half a Sixpence*. Almost simultaneously with the release of *It's*

All Happening, Steele's career was boosted by his portrayal of Kipps in David Heneker and Beverley Cross's musical version of H. G. Wells's novel. A film version followed in 1967. By the time the company of George Mitchell's *Black and White Minstrel Show* show up (mercifully not in blackface), the affair has pretty well ground to a halt, but we are left with Dai Francis and chorus singing 'It's Summer', tenor John Boulter recalling 'Once Upon a Time in Venice', Tony Mercer 'Watching All the World Go By', and, a little feebly but most enjoyably, Carole Deene's story of 'The Boy on the Beach'.

MAY

The largely forgotten McLeod Productions' **Take Me Over**, produced by William McLeod, written by Dail Ambler (of *Beat Girl*) and directed by Robert Lynn, was a homespun affair that elevated some little-known British actors to temporary prominence, notably John Rutland (for years a leading performer at the Players' Theatre), as well as Mildred Mayne (the now-forgotten star of the 1957 West End musical *Zuleika*) and Totti Truman Taylor. It is more likely that the presence of the Temperance Seven – here playing 'The Twenties Group' – headed up by Paul McDowell, would have attracted customers; this year, the Seven notably appeared in a West End play, *The Bed-Sitting Room*, with Spike Milligan. McDowell co-authored the film's appealing title song with George Martin, but the project earned a thumbs-down from the *MFB*'s critic, who condemned it as 'totally unremarkable' and 'exceptionally weak'. [11]

JUNE

Excalibur's interesting **A Place to Go** earns its inclusion with two musical numbers by Charles Blackwell, written in collaboration with the film's male star, Mike Sarne. Based on Michael Fisher's novel *Bethnal Green*, producer Michael Relph's screenplay, with added dialogue by Clive Exton, paints a grim picture of East End working-class life in the early sixties as it follows the story of the Flint family's existence among the Peabody buildings and remains of the Blitz while all around them a new brutalist landscape is emerging from slum clearance and new council house provision. This is a place to escape from, but where, as young Ricky Flint (Sarne) asks himself, to escape to? He and his family are caught in a rhythm of life that centres around dodgy ways of getting by, punch-ups whose realism is one of the most effective features of the film, and sing-songs in rowdy pubs. It's no wonder that Ricky wants something better, as expressed in a lyric that might not have satisfied Ira Gershwin but hits the spot:

I'm goin' to get out and about
I'm goin' to get out and about
I'm savin' for a cruise
I'm givin' up me booze
I'm gonna get out and sing and shout
Cos I just wanna be free
I'm gonna get out and about and see the world.

Intelligently directed by Basil Dearden, *A Place to Go* deserves to be better appreciated not only as part of the 'New Wave' movement that spawned such as Shelagh Delaney's *A Taste of Honey* (1961), but as a very fine, almost intense, example of Dearden's commitment to cinema as social document, already evident in his cinematic reimagining of J. B. Priestley's *They Came to a City* (1944), *The Blue Lamp* (1950), Ealing's attempt to show the British public what social workers did, *I Believe in You* (1952), *Sapphire* (1959), and *Victim* (1961).

Rita Tushingham's elfin Catherine is infinitely touching as Ricky's on-off girlfriend, by no means overwhelming Sarne's performance or the strong support of Bernard Lee and Doris Hare as his valiant parents. The sudden explosions of manic joy that puncture the play, whether in the pub or when the Flints set their Christmas decorations alight, are brilliantly done, as is the unflinching violence of the punch-ups, outdoing anything that was to follow in *Eastenders*. Relph and Exton's screenplay propels the story forcefully, even if the slow slide from gritty working-class drama into more of a standard cops and robbers scenario seems a little forced. Ultimately, Ricky gets a slap over the knuckles from a kindly magistrate (the great Norman Shelley, inexplicably uncredited), pointing to a happy reunion between the young lovers. This cosy denouement comes as a relief after our wondering what Ricky can make of himself as he lies on his bed playing 'Greensleeves' on his mouth organ, or wondering how long it will be before his dad's busking escapology results in a stroke.

JULY

What a Crazy World stands out as the only British musical film to be made of a stage musical presented not in London's West End, but for a specified season of forty-eight performances at the Theatre Royal, Stratford East, in 1962; its transition to the screen should be celebrated. The show's genesis began with the title song, which is sometimes (understandably) compared to Lionel Bart's stage musical and title song *Fings Ain't Wot They Used t'Be*.

For Andy Medhurst the film 'remains fascinating, a neglected thread in that strand of white pop Englishness which later wove itself from the Kinks and The Small Faces through The Jam and Madness to The Smiths and Blur'. He argues that the film is 'in a tradition that has sought to avoid second-hand Americanisms in favour of a pop that addressed more pertinently English structures of feeling'.[12] For David Flint, the film's pop-singer-actors Joe Brown and Marty Wilde are 'mere puppets for the likes of Larry Parnes [prolifically the manager of pop singers of this period]. And frankly, by 1963, they already seemed old hat. It seems oddly apt that they should appear in a film where they pretend to be youthful delinquents but which feels essentially more like a Lionel Bart musical, complete with chirpy Cockney types' at a dramatic junction where 'Low rent kitchen sink drama meets throwaway rock'n'roll'.[13] For Graeme Clark, Alan Klein's musical was 'in the main a vehicle for celebrating a specific time and place and culture, and pretty sprightly as far as that went',[14] but David Parkinson does the film a disservice by describing 'an amiable but outdated musical [in which] the *longueurs* between the musical numbers, which the more generous might call the plot, are distinctly dodgy'.[15] Surely, we should accept the film as of its own time, in which it was *not* outdated. It could scarcely be otherwise.

The casting (with only Avis Bunnage, Larry Dann, David Nott, and Barry Bethel retained from Stratford East) could hardly be happier. Brown and Wilde both went on to achieve theatrical success: Brown when he co-starred with Anna Neagle in the British musical *Charlie Girl*, and Wilde as pop singer Conrad in the London production of Broadway's *Bye Bye Birdie*.

The minor roles provide much pleasure, not least Michael Ripper (a Hammer Film staple) in a variety of roles, stressing the theatricality of the piece and adding significantly to its atmosphere, and the briefest of appearances from one of the great actors from a bygone era, Wilfrid Lawson, worryingly breathless as a geriatric grandfather. We are reminded, not for the first time, that such actors no longer exist; this is a film steeped in the theatre of Joan Littlewood's era. Among the habitués of her productions (known as 'Littlewood's nuts') are Fanny Carby, Toni Palmer, and Avis Bunnage and Harry H. Corbett as Mr and Mrs Hitchens, with Michael Goodman as Alf's young brother Joey in a perfectly nuanced performance worthy of a Littlewood veteran. Together, in what is essentially an ensemble piece, the company instils the film with Stratford East virility. In this, *What a Crazy World* remains distinct in British musical films. Susan Maughan, a recording artist at the time riding the crest with 'Bobby's Girl', is not the strongest element as Alf's girlfriend Marilyn; she was subsequently briefly seen in *Pop Gear* (1965). Grazina Frame, whose pop musical film had begun with an uncredited moment in *6.5 Special* (1958), went on to the 1964 *Every Day's a Holiday*.

Klein had written a persuasive piece. Without exception, his songs work well, without any of the embarrassment in the ranks caused by the scores of such as *The Duke Wore Jeans*. Klein provides the real thing, a genuine transmission of working-class culture, or at least a feasible version of it. Cuteness is avoided, and offers no concessions to the often sub-Brechtian wholeness of both dialogue and song. Nothing stops for the song; the song belongs, even in the obvious set pieces technically divorced from the plot, as in those involving Freddie and the Dreamers. Songs heard in the stage production that are not heard in the film are 'Treat Them Hard' (sung by Herb), 'He's Not a Bad Boy Really' (Mary), 'Striped Purple Shirt' (Alf), 'Eggs, Beans and Chips' (Alf), 'There's Something Funny Somewhere Going On' (Alf), 'I Wanna Be a Beatnik Like Me Bruvver' (Jimmy), and 'Do Me a Favour' (Marilyn). Graeme Clark's vivid appreciation of Klein's film should make us sit up and take notice:

> But here's the odd thing: there's a kind of joy about the exuberance with which they all let rip (location filming in the exterior of an actual council block) at the end. This message of non-communication and dissatisfaction ought to be a downer, but the music seems to urge you to accept, or even celebrate, the contradictory nature of things – maybe it's even saying that all we need is a right good old moan at each other and then we'll all feel a whole lot better: primal therapy, East End style, as it were. That doesn't mean this musical is a social commentary without bite but it's not exactly urging affirmative action, either, just calling attention to the mess, the whole, er, crazy world.[16]

Klein's score moves the story on without introducing much memorable besides the title song performed by Brown. It was, nevertheless, not a negligible achievement. The songs and singers are 'A Layabout's Lament' (Wilde, Brown), 'My Two Brothers' (Frame, Brown, Michael Goodman), 'Oh What a Family!' (Wilde), 'Alfred Hitchens' (Susan Maughan), 'Wasn't It a Handsome Punch-Up?' (Brown, Wilde), 'Independence' (Larry Dann, Brian Cronin), 'This Is My First Romance' (Maughan), 'I Feel the Same Way Too' (Brown, Maughan), 'Just You Wait and See' (Brown), 'The Things We Never Had' (Harry H. Corbett, Avis Bunnage), and 'I Sure Know a Lot about Love' (Goodman). Freddie and The Dreamers appear for 'Sally Ann', 'Gonna Twist All Night', and 'Short Shorts' by Bill Crandall, Thomas Austin, Bob Gaudio, and Bill Dalton.

Brian McFarlane has suggested that while the pop performers of Three Kings Films' *Live It Up* may today

> seem extraordinarily wholesome, or even staid, they are instructive about what might have appealed to young people in the pre-Rolling Stones era. Even if they are not his personal cup of tea, Comfort doesn't patronise his guest singers, but gives them uncluttered access to the camera, putting the narrative on hold while they do their turns.[17]

In one of its snootiest reviews, the *MFB* conceded that 'The slight story has one good moment in which the boys briefly consider, and quickly reject, the possibility of calling their group "The Maggots"'; otherwise the film was 'a festival of electric guitars and echo chamber effects' in which Kenny Ball performed 'a perversion' from Mozart.[18] We have to ask why so unsympathetic a critic was put to the inconvenience of having not only to watch Comfort's film, but to give an opinion on it. Is it a better work than this glancing blow of a notice insists, or is it merely that time has enhanced the film in the rosy glow of reminiscence? May we agree with David Parkinson's opinion that Comfort was 'a decent director, but he was hardly cutting edge and he handles the drama as unimaginatively as he stages the songs'?[19] We at least owe it to Comfort to consider it more closely than the denizen of the British Film Institute did. Is the film worth the effort?

Made at Pinewood, it has a sound starting point with Lyn Fairhurst's solid screenplay, based on an idea by Harold Shampan, about the efforts of young GPO motorcycle messenger Dave Martin and his workmates Phil (John Pike) and Ricky (Steve Marriott) to become known as a pop group, 'The Smart Alecs'. Fairhurst is especially good in characterising the relationship between the boys, as well as with Ron (Heinz Burt) and Dave's girlfriend Jill (Jennifer Moss). The domestic scenes with Dave's parents (Ed Devereaux and Joan Newell) are convincingly natural, although pop music is foreign to them. Indeed, Mrs Martin has been in variety, singing 'Bluebells and Buttercups' with impresario Mike Ross (Peter Glaze). Mr Martin wants to see Dave in regular work; if he doesn't break into pop music within a month, he'll get Dave a job at the hotel where he works, insisting that 'He's got to get this music nonsense out of his head and settle down.' Nevertheless, Dave's father's attitude is less harsh than Harry H. Corbett's father to Joe Brown in *What a Crazy World*. Thus Fairhurst sets a context for the different music that is taking over from what has been acceptable. The boys reject being called 'The Maggots' but, a question audiences may themselves have asked of Fairhurst, 'Haven't you ever heard of the Beatles?' Mr Martin is more concerned about the health of his cacti, and doesn't like the look of his tomato plants.

It's difficult now to decide if the acts that Comfort presents were really what the younger cinemagoer wanted to see in 1963. The acts have a wholesomeness, even a cleanliness, and certainly a smartness (with the exception of Gene Vincent, whose very appearance might be a sort of affront to British sensibility): well-cut suits and ties, and recent visits to a barber. Throughout, Comfort adopts the method of letting each of the acts do its stuff, without unnecessary cutting-away or interruptions of dialogue; the plot obligingly draws into the sidings for these highlights, for these are what Comfort assumes the audience expects to see.

This, too, is the contract between Comfort and 'the paranoid, and finally homicidal record producer Joe Meek'[20] to promote not only his songs (uncredited as he is) but the groups that Meek was currently working with. We have Meek to thank for the echo-chamber effects that impressed the *MFB*. They are, in fact, essential to the film, not only as crucial components of Meek's music cooked up in his three-floor flat on Islington's Holloway Road (one of his most successful hits involved placing instrumentalists all over the premises, including the bathroom), but in marking the distinct separation of the musical sequences from the dramatic. This accentuated difference of spoken and musical elements is one of Comfort's main achievements; both elements – the musical items and especially the domestic scenes in the Martins' home – are successfully transmitted, reality (at which Fairhurst is so good) and the sense of unreality in the Meek numbers.

Andy Medhurst alerts us to a picture that is 'still unsure of its subcultural moorings', but explains that

> This collision of Meek, mod and Beatles (with some Shadows dance steps and Kenny Ball and his Jazzmen in post-Trad attendance) is then grafted on to yet another rags-to-riches plot, but the film has a shrewder grasp than most of its kind of that sheer sense of escape, of a youthful future, which pop offered to its devotees.[21]

Subsequently, *Live It Up* may be perceived as a memorial to some of those involved, and it is a rare sighting of such as Andy Cavell and Kim Roberts. Meek's extraordinary career came to its end in February 1967, when he shot his landlady and committed suicide. He was thirty-seven. Gene Vincent had been touring in Britain with the Outlaws, drinking heavily and using guns. He died at thirty-six. Jennifer Moss, so simply but effectively photographed on a rooftop for her delicate solo 'Please Let It Happen to Me', had success in *Coronation Street* before the bad times began. Alcoholism, five marriages (and domestic abuse), her children taken into care, and homelessness followed. She was dead at sixty-one. Peroxided Heinz Burt, originally one of The Tornados before being promoted by Meek as a soloist died at fifty-seven, worn down by the collapse of his career, two failed marriages, penury, and a prolonged battle with motor neurone disease. One way and another, we may with justification look back on *Live It Up* with sober reflection.

We also have the benefit of an interesting selection of numbers predominantly written and composed by the extraordinary Meek, not least the title song sung by Heinz, who also presents 'Don't You Understand' with the Smart Alecs. Kenny Ball and His Jazzmen play 'Rondo' and the traditional 'Hand Me Down My Walking Shoes'. 'Don't Take You From Me' is performed by Andy Cavell and The Saints, 'Keep Moving' by Sounds Incorporated, and 'Law and Disorder' by The Outlaws. Brylcreem-polished, Gene Vincent tackles 'Temptation Baby' as he gives some seriously heavy machinery a final rub-down. It's not an especially auspicious moment, but it's the film, and Comfort, at their most straightforward. Space is made for Meek's 'Loving Me This Way' sung by wasp-waisted Kim Roberts with a permanently faraway look, for Jennifer Moss to beg 'Please Let It Happen to Me', and for Patsy Ann Noble to perform Norrie Paramor and Bob Barratt's 'Accidents Will Happen'.

AUGUST

Considered to be a 'lost' film, *Farewell Performance* was produced for Sevenay Films by Jim O'Connolly and directed by Robert Tronson. The screenplay by Aileen Burke and Leone Stuart, with O'Connolly supplying additional dialogue, concerned the murder of pop singer Ray Baron (David Kernan). It reached a gruesome conclusion, but the musical content promised more interest. Joe Meek's name was stamped on the score, orchestrations, and musical direction, with Heinz Burt singing 'Dreams Do Come True' and The Tremeloes performing 'The Ice Cream Man'.

DECEMBER

The 'A' certificated short (at fifty-five minutes) *It's All Over Town* had the *MFB* pondering, 'Perhaps the psychologist might read a wealth of meaning in the extrovert antics of this superficial musical charade'.[22] Produced for Delmore Film Productions by Jacques de Lane Lea, it was written and directed by Stewart Farrar at Boreham Wood, with additional material by performers Lance Percival and William Rushton. Any hope that we are about to get an insider's look into West End shows of the time is soon crushed by the ensuing parade of items. It presents as a sort of studio-bound travelogue of central London, with star turn Frankie Vaughan more effective than in his 1950s films for Herbert Wilcox. Peter Proud's settings are imaginative and vibrant, and it's well photographed in Eastmancolor.

With no attempt at a plot, Percival and Rushton thread the musical numbers together in a variety of surrealist jests, although satire (at which both were adept) is not attempted. Everything is modestly done in a potpourri of pop and jazz that slightly predates 'swinging' London. Vaughan could never be officially linked to it, but his sexual flirtatiousness (much of it learned from the veteran male impersonator Hetty King) with its promise of hedonistic delight formed the basis of his appeal.

It wasn't until Carnaby Street turned iconic in 1966 that men's clothes underwent seismic change, but it's interesting to see that *It's All Over Town* makes sure everyone is nicely turned out. What anxious mother would not be pleased to see one of The Bachelors as a prospective son-in-law? Wholesomeness abounds, and despite the concern about what might happen to that girl on that bench in that moonlight, Vaughan is its godfather. There is, of course, no shortage of what we might see as sexism, or much doubt about Acker Bilk's virility, but he too seems safely stowed in pre-swinging London.

The visit to the Raymond Revuebar is one of the film's central features, featuring Ingrid Anthofer in a curious striptease in reverse, and the Paul Raymond 'Bunnies'. The sense of changing sexual attitudes is obvious, and this only a few months before the Windmill Theatre (as seen in the fascinating *Murder at the Windmill*) shut down. Why go to the Windmill to see static nudes when you could see them moving around? They seem distanced from the gentle manner of the singers, as witnessed in Clodagh Rodgers (credited as Cloda Rogers) and Alan Davison. We should be grateful, too, for Mitch Murray's Covent Garden 'Beetroot Song' with its splendid dash of music-hall nonsense:

My sister Jean's
Always eating beans,
My little brother leeks.
I just saw Ma lick
A piece of garlic
Everybody duck when she speaks.
I'll take you home to show to mater – come with me
It's corny but it's nice
When they throw rice.
Oh, lettuce get us to the church by half past two
And if you like beetroot I'll be true to you.

Naturally, Vaughan is well to the fore with Basil Tait (of *Five Guineas a Week*) and Dave Carey's title song and with Tait and Carey's 'Wouldn't You Like It?', Carey's 'Alley-Alley-O', Mitch Murray's 'Gonna Be a Good Boy Now', and his signature number 'Give Me the Moonlight' written by Lew Brown and Albert Von Tilzer in 1917. Carey also contributes 'Please Let It Happen to Me' sung by Alan Davison, and 'The Trouble with Men' sung by Jan (Hunt) and Kelly. The Springfields offer two of Tom Springfield's pieces, 'Maracabamba' and 'Down and Out'; The Bachelors appear for Don Pelosi and Leo Towers's 'The Stars Will Remember'; The Hollies turn up for Graham Nash and Allan Clarke's 'Now's the Time'; Cloda Rogers sings Michael Carr and Norman Newell's 'My Love Will Still Be There'; Acker Bilk performs his arrangement of the 'Volga Boatmen' with His Paramount Jazz Band and dancer April Olrich, as well as 'Sippin' Cider Beside 'er'. Wayne Gibson and The Dynamic Sounds are allotted Tony Hiller and Perry Ford's 'Come On, Let's Go', but Lance Percival gets the plum in the pudding that turns out to be a beetroot.

1964

If only the British musical film of so many past years had opened itself up to such joy as can be found here

The Rise and Fall of Nellie Brown

A Hard Day's Night	*Mods and Rockers*
Wonderful Life	*Every Day's a Holiday*
Just for You	*Ballad in Blue*
Swinging UK	*Ferry Cross the Mersey*
UK Swings Again	*The Rise and Fall of Nellie Brown*
Rhythm 'n' Greens	

JUNE

'For sheer youth and vitality this film knocks spots off Richard's *Wonderful Life*. It doesn't advance the technique of film-making, but it should be an object lesson to the film world in what makes for genuine personality.'[1] For *New Musical Express*,

> Scripted, slapstick and in thrall to Ealing comedies, **A Hard Day's Night** is nevertheless the closest we have to a true-to-life document of Beatlemania [...] whip-smart witticisms abound, stone cold Merseybeat classics arrive every ten minutes or so and the random plotlines [...] only tend towards the ludicrous rather than diving in mop-top-first.[2]

The *MFB* acclaimed it as 'streets ahead in imagination compared to other films about pop songs and singers'.[3] Geoffrey Nowell-Smith's tempered enthusiasm decided that the film,

> broken down into its individual components, is pretty poor and insipid stuff [...] About the only good single aspect of the film is the songs, which are musically and verbally among the best that the group has produced. It is utterly slapdash, but it is consistent with itself. It works as a whole. It is coherent and has a sense of direction to it and a point.[4]

On this occasion, director Richard Lester confronts his young stars with a considerable number of old codgers, fronted by Wilfrid Brambell, recently propelled to television stardom via the BBC's *Steptoe and Son*, as Grandfather.

Lester seems to delight in employing senior Equity members. These include the wonderful Edward (Eddie) Malin, the small-part player of many films perhaps best remembered as the steward who consoles a child during the sinking of the *Titanic* in Roy Baker's *A Night to Remember*, and as the silent Walter in the television comedy series *Nearest and Dearest*, with Hylda Baker forever solicitous as to his well-being ('Has he been?'). In sharp contrast to the apparently carefree attitudes of The Beatles, Alun Owen's inventive screenplay has roles for other traditionally stolid older British establishment types: Deryck Guyler, Michael Trubshawe, and Richard Vernon. The film brings together several of Lennon and McCartney's best numbers: 'A Hard Day's Night', 'I Should Have Known Better', 'I Wanna Be Your Man', 'Don't Bother Me', 'All My Loving', 'If I Fell', 'Can't Buy Me Love', 'And I Love Her', 'I'm Happy Just to Dance with You', 'Tell Me Why', and 'She Loves You'.

The always astute Roger Mellor acknowledges that *A Hard Day's Night* 'did not revolutionise the British film musical, but it is a key text of 1960s British cinema and culture, and its influence on television music video can be seen to this day. The film's French title (which translates as *Four Guys Caught in the Wind*) sums it up perfectly.'[5]

The minor miracle of **Wonderful Life** is that, following *The Young Ones* and *Summer Holiday*, it retained Peter Myers and Ronnie Cass as its creators, providing not only the screenplay but the lion's share of the score. *Films and Filming* thought it 'a sad little picture. It is so square. The musical numbers both sound and for the most part look like Hollywood of the "forties" [...] I would like to think British teenagers demand something with a bit more vitality.'[6] There was little enthusiasm from the *MFB*, which described 'a likeably bouncy, if not very good, film' in which the humour was 'depressingly unfunny', but conceded that Sidney Furie (who had directed *The Young Ones*) had been 'saddled with a more than usually imbecilic story.'[7] There was a distinct feeling that the Myers–Cass franchise was showing signs of exhaustion. Professional and expensive as the film looks, it trades in formula.

We should not be surprised. By now, Richard had moved far away from anything that might be recognised as rock'n'roll. Donnelly perceptively puts him among the 'wave of smooth pop stars [who] appeared in the early 1960s [...] more adult-friendly than the original rock'n'rollers had been.'[8] As before, Furie, Myers, and Cass depended on a story that emphasised the generation gap. Now, the old codger of *The Young Ones*, Robert Morley, and the female old codger of *Summer Holiday*, Madge Ryan, transmogrified into old codger Walter Slezak. In fact, Morley and Slezak end up in the same place at the end of their films: sharing a stage with our Cliff and doing a musical number to rapturous acclaim. Strangely, these unlikely climaxes are performed in front of highly unlikely audiences. We can only wonder, exactly who is this patently middle-of-the-road material of unremitting pleasantness being aimed at?

For the most part, it is well done, and successfully and consistently pro-mulgates Richard's clean-cut image, his permanently upturned features, the gleaming teeth, the carefully adjusted quiff, the semi-Americanised twang in the Peter Pan manner. This we have in abundance, but no Teddy Green. The other players are mostly poorly served. Our hero's gang (sadly lacking the presence of the ever-welcome Green) has little to do but follow where Richard leads. The now stale tomfoolery between Richard O'Sullivan's toffish Edward and Melvyn Hayes's scrawny Jerry is merely irritating. They join Richard in 'Home', a number that is dull, irrelevant, wholly predictable, and over-long. Hollywood would never have countenanced so badly danced a routine, for which Gillian Lynne can hardly be blamed; the fact that none of them can dance is all too obvious. Along the way, The Shadows (for whom the British public have always had a perfectly understandable fondness) remain pretty well, well, in the shadows.

Stranded on the Canary Islands, Johnnie (Cliff Richard) rescues pretty starlet Jenny Taylor (Susan Hampshire) from a runaway camel. In fact, she is filming a scene for a *Beau Geste*-like film directed by the temperamental Lloyd Davis (excellent Walter Slezak) and co-starring hopelessly weak leading man Douglas Leslie (an unusually funny Derek Bond). Johnnie and his crew decide to surreptitiously add musical numbers to Davis's dull picture. The romance between Johnnie and Jenny blossoms. When Davis discovers what is happening, he agrees to amalgamate his unsatisfactory rushes with Johnnie's footage. The result, of course, is a huge success, consolidating the love between Johnnie and Jenny, revealed as Davis's daughter.

The Myers–Cass numbers include the breezy 'A Girl in Every Port', 'A Little Imagination', the central extended set piece 'We Love a Movie' (the film's most successful sequence), 'All Kinds of People', and the finale's 'Youth and Experience'. Workmanlike but momentarily effective, these have all the characteristics of the sort of material Myers and Cass had turned out for their stage revues, bright numbers that sweep the thing along. Otherwise, Richard's numbers were crafted more skilfully by The Shadows. Brian Bennett and Bruce Welch's title song had an expansiveness and zest that Myers and Cass could only imitate. The numbers struck an immediate note of youthful enthusiasm and wonder, as did Bennett and Welch's duet for Richard and Hampshire, 'Do You Remember?', while Welch's 'A Matter of Moments' was performed by Richard and The Shadows and company. Among the most memorable items are Hank Marvin, Welch, and Richard's 'On the Beach' and the romantic 'In the Stars'.

Occasionally, and unusually, a little self-awareness creeps into the pro-ceedings, as when the impossibly difficult Davis explains, 'I am not making a New Wave avant-garde film.' As he confesses, 'Whenever did dialogue have anything to do with our picture?' Davis is perhaps the only character throughout the three Myers–Cass films who seems to know anything about a theatrical (rather than a cinematic) past. When Jenny complains that her yasmak gets in the way of her speaking her lines clearly, her father informs her that 'when Sybil Thorndike portrayed St Joan she spoke through a breastplate, a visor and an entire iron mask, and her voice boomed out'. Of course, Cass and (certainly) Myers had a profound knowledge of British theatre. It was knowledge that they exploited to the full in their stage pieces, which makes it all the more disappointing that their work here is so lacking in resonance and depth. The declining popularity of the Richard films was reflected in the sales of the long-playing soundtracks of the three productions, as measured by the number of weeks they featured in the LP charts: *The Young Ones* (42), *Summer Holiday* (36), and *Wonderful Life* (23). For the record, the decline continued in the sales of Richard's *Finders Keepers* (18 weeks in the LP charts) and the 1974 *Take Me High* (4).

The service that ***Just for You***, also known as *Disk-o-Tek Holiday*, was doing for posterity in compiling so rich an archival document of British pop in the mid-1960s was offered no sympathy by the growling *MFB*. Here was 'a vulgarly over-decorated musical fantasia [...] plotless, and altogether charmless'.[9] Strung together with a commentary by Sam Costa and producers Jacques de Lane Lea (*Five Guineas a Week*) and Ben Nisbet, *Just for You*'s fascinating programme of turns veers from the ridiculous to the almost sublime. It is also, as the *MFB* seemed not to appreciate, a credit not only to its director Douglas Hickox (he and Lea had conceived the film) but to production designer Peter Proud and the cinematography of Martin Curtis and Stan Pavey. The responsibility of linking the performers falls to Sam Costa, the godfather of British disc jockeys, older-looking than his fifty-four years and with a long career as singer, actor and pianist behind him; his popularity had increased through his ongoing association with the BBC from 1939 begun with radio's *ITMA* (*It's That Man Again*) and carried on by his programmes for Radio Luxembourg and his hosting of the BBC's *Housewives' Choice*. His currency continued through the sixties with *Juke Box Jury* and David Frost's *Frost on Sunday*. Now, his supine patronage acts almost as a benediction of the young people he introduces.

The programme consists of 'Tell Me When' (Geoff Stephens and Les Reed) sung by the West Midlands group The Applejacks. They enjoyed brief popularity but fell out with their recording company when they refused to record 'Chim Che Ree' from *Mary Poppins*. 'Mine All Mine' (Dave Carey) has Al Saxon playing and singing at a revolving piano. A Band of Angels arrive for 'Hide'n'Seek' (John Baker and Mike D'Abo). These Angels are smartly dressed, boatered, and suited ex-Harrovians, in a car showroom among glamorous girls.

'Mr Scrooge' (Tony Hiller and Shel Talmy) is performed by The Orchids, three Coventry schoolgirls named after Coventry's Orchid Ballroom, where their careers began when they won a prize of £1. The girls' preference was for jazz and soul, but they were encouraged to appear in school uniform and backed Johnny Great on vinyl recordings. They made little money from their brief fame: 'We just did as we were told.' They re-formed as The Exceptions in 1965.

The Bachelors, who had worked previously as The Harmonichords, sing 'The Fox' written by themselves (Conleth and Declan Cluskey, and John Stokes) as they play billiards to surprisingly filmic effect. Doug Sheldon, whose mild pop career segued into acting, is seen in an atmospheric nocturnal London setting for Dave Carey's 'Night Time', observing strolling lovers and meeting his girl. The attempt at narrative underlines the mood, with interesting use of shadow. Nolly Clapton and Mercy Hump's 'Teenage Valentino' is performed by Roy Sone, Caroline Lee, and Judy Jason. Sone had a reputation for taking over from household names in West End musicals, thanklessly understudying such stars as Tommy Steele, Joe Brown, and Anthony Newley.

'Leave Me Alone' is written and performed by Peter and Gordon (Peter Asher and Gordon Waller). Two boys with two guitars, it is a no-nonsense presentation in a garden patio setting, but one of the outstanding sequences. Their 1965 hit 'A World Without Love' was inspired by Buddy Holly and became a classic of the repertoire. 'You Were Meant for Me' (Mitch Murray) has Freddie and The Dreamers larking in their carefree manner. 'Sugar Dandy' (Derrick Harriott) welcomes bright Millie Small, one of the most refreshing pop performers of the period. Of minor importance, perhaps, but wearing a lollipop badge in recognition of her current hit 'My Boy Lollipop'. 'The Lo-co-Motion' (Gerry Goffin and Carole King) has Jackie and The Raindrops, three well-scrubbed young men in natty cardigans, four bowler-hatted male dancers, and one female dancer backing Jackie Lee, once a member of The Squadronaires and remembered for her 1968 recording 'White Horses'. Mitch Murray's 'I Wish You Everything' goes to Mark Wynter, one of the freshest-faced young pop performers of the period, who moved on to a busy career as actor. 'If I Had a Hammer' is sung by Johnny B. Great, real name Johnny Goodison, a Coventry singer, exuberantly celebrating Pete Seeger's song. Peter and Gordon return with their 'Soft As the Dawn' followed by a vibrant dance sequence, uncredited.

For 'Don't Make Me Blue' (David Foster) The Warriors arrive in a car and perform against a garden trellis. A white boy serenades his black girlfriend. Louise Cordet's 'I'm Just a Baby' had been a hit in 1962. Here, she sings Don Spencer and Mike Bradley's 'It's So Hard to Be Good'. The following year she was seen in *Just for Fun*, but by 1965 her recording career was over. Despite their frilled shirts, The Merseybeats were contemporaneous with The Beatles, and played Liverpool's Cavern Club. In 1964 they toured Germany and the USA, and they had their own show on Italian television. Tony Crane and Johnny Gustafson's 'Milkman' was one of The Merseybeats' 'B' side recordings in 1964, reaching no. 13 in the British charts. Michael Carr and Norman Newell's 'Low the Valley' is the second Bachelors' item, one of the best in the film, in which they describe powerful landscapes among statuary. Freddie and the Dreamers reiterate that the film is, as Mitch Murray's song insists, 'Just for You'.

JULY

One of the most prolific British film producers, Harold Baim (his untiring efforts are proved by the fact that there are, at the time of writing, seventy-three of his films listed as 'lost') happily made two attractive, uncomplicated compendiums of current pop artistes. The first, *Swinging UK*, is a 28-minute short directed by Frank Gilpin, a toiler at the industry's coal face whose career, largely consisting of unassuming documentaries, included Sooty on British television in the 1950s. Now, Gilpin has little need to do anything more than point the camera at the young performers who make up the company. In attendance are three popular disc jockeys of the day, Alan Freeman, Brian Matthew, and Kent Walton, who briefly commend the artistes, several of whom are little remembered today. Pinpointing a particular time of British pop music, Baim and Gilpin provide an archival service, reminding us of The Cockneys as they sing Mick Grace's 'After Tomorrow', and the Migil Five as they perform 'Have Some Fun Tonight' and Vaughn Horton's 'Mockin' Bird Hill'. The Four Pennies contribute Mike Wilsh, Fritz Fryer, and Lionel Morton's 'Juliet', as well as Roy Orbison and Joe Melson's 'Running Scared'. From the Merseybeats, we have Albert Hammond, Peter Lee Stirling, and Diane Warren's 'Don't Turn Around' and Jack Clement and M. Maddux's 'Fools Like Me'. Brian Poole and The Tremeloes perform Berry Gordy's 'Do You Love Me?', and, less well-known, The Whackers have Dewayne Blackwell's 'Love or Money'. The male line-up is joined by Millie Small performing Johnny Roberts and Morris Levy's hit 'My Boy Lollipop' and 'Oh Henry' written by Small and Johnny Edwards.

Harold Baim's **UK Swings Again**, a follow-up to his celebratory *Swinging UK*, reunited Brian Matthew, Alan Freeman, and Kent Walton as the ageing comperes at an unpretentious Eastmancolor parade of pop artists again directed by Frank Gilpin and filmed at the Kay Carlton Hill Film Studios. The Swinging Blue Jeans kick off with Ralph Ellis's 'Don't You Worry About Me', followed by Bryan Irwin's 'Blue, Blue, Blue Beat' performed by The Tornados with their pounding drummer. The Animals, with their impressively incisive soloist set among ladders, sing Bert Berns and Wes Farrell's 'Baby, Let Me Take You Home', and Brian Poole and The Tremeloes perform Edwin Greines and Violet Ann Petty's 'Someone, Someone'. The Hollies perform Mort Shuman and Clive Westlake's 'Here I Go Again', and The Swinging Blue Jeans return with Clint Ballard Junior's 'You're No Good'. The Hollies offer the undistinguished 'Baby That's All' written by Chester Mann (in fact by Allan Clarke, Graham Nash, and Tony Hicks). Matthew introduces the obviously self-conscious schoolboys who present as The Applejacks, self-consciously delivering Geoff Stephens and Les Reed's 'Tell Me When', but it's one of the best items on offer. The Applejacks change into natty knitwear for John Lennon and Paul McCartney's 'Like Dreamers Do' before Lulu and The Luvvers provide a vibrant finale in O'Kelly Isley, Ronald Isley, and Rudolph Isley's 'Shout'. The embarrassingly arch comments of the presenters are mercifully brief, making way for a smartly suited and booted collection of artistes. There is also evidence that British men's hairdressing is enduring a stylistic crisis.

SEPTEMBER

Throughout Britain in the 1960s, summer theatrical entertainments proved how potent was the attraction of pop performers. In the summer season of 1964 holidaymakers in Great Yarmouth were spoilt for choice. The Britannia Theatre's *Sunday Extra Special* one-nighters included Marty Wilde, Mark Wynter, Gene Vincent, The Gamblers, The Plebs, and The Applejacks. At the Royal Aquarium, *The Sunday Big Beat Show*'s star spot alternated between Brian Poole and The Tremeloes, and The Searchers, alongside lesser-known performers such as Johnny B. Great. Billy Fury topped the bill for fourteen weeks at the Royal Aquarium in *The Big Star Show of 1964*, with the Karl Denver Trio, Rolf Harris, Mike Yarwood, and The Gamblers in support. The main summer attraction at the ABC Theatre starred The Shadows in what presented as a more subtle musical entertainment: *Here, There and Everywhere: A Revusical Whirl of the World*. Fans of the 'other' Fab Four (Hank B. Marvin, Bruce Welch, Brian Bennett, and John Rostill) had to wait until the very end of the show for the boys to appear, having been entertained with her 'Little Bit of Ireland' by the softly sung Ruby Murray, Morton Fraser's Harmonica Gang, comedians Dailey and Wayne, and brilliant sour-faced ventriloquist Arthur Worsley. Authorship of this 'revusical' was unclaimed in the theatre programme, although Albert J. Knight was credited as deviser and director.

In fact, *Here, There and Everywhere* was to enjoy some sort of afterlife, when over ten days The Shadows made the 32-minute **Rhythm 'n' Greens**, produced by Terry Ashwood and written and directed by Christopher Miles. Made in and around Yarmouth, it's a delightfully refreshing skimming through British history, from protoplasm and cavemen through the Roman Empire, the Saxons, pillaging Hengist and Horsa, the discovery of cigarettes in the age of Francis Drake ('Armadas' are the thing to smoke), the daring of mixed bathing, and a finale with The Shadows showing a very neat set of pins as they twist on the beach among Great Yarmouth's windswept sand dunes. Originally to be titled *A Look at Rubbish*, the dialogue-free screenplay is narrated by Robert Morley, sensibly leaving the boys to cope only with the visual side of things. *Here, There and Everywhere*'s soubrette Joan Palethorpe was retained as one of the dancers, alongside the film's choreographer Audrey Bayley (assistant choreographer for the stage show). Cliff Richard makes an uncredited appearance as King Canute, singing 'La Mer', presumably in an attempt to turn the sea back to France. As a memento of The Shadows, it couldn't be bettered.

The overlooked curiosity of the dance film ***Mods and Rockers*** commands interest. Co-produced by the legendarily ruthless theatrical impresario Larry Parnes and director Kenneth Hume, in its form it invites comparison with Gene Kelly's *Invitation to the Dance*. In its way, *Mods and Rockers* comes over as the more meaningful, basically drawing the distinctions between the rivalries of those teenagers who defined themselves as members of one or the other unofficial social organisations, as interpreted by Peter Darrell's choreography for Western Ballet. Formed in 1957, twelve years later the company morphed into Scottish Ballet. Via Robert Amram's almost dialogue-free scenario, we can see how important it was for Western Ballet to break free of the classical tradition.

At a somewhat unusual vicar's tea-party (the vicar wears a leather jacket) Mods and Rockers come together but stay apart as a Mod girl and a Rocker boy link up against a background of music from John Lennon, George Harrison, and Paul McCartney and musical director Ian MacPherson, some of it played by rock group The Cheynes with Mick Fleetwood on drums. A substantial punch-up is broken up by the police, but not before we have witnessed movement to music as understood by the young people of Britain. Spaciously filmed at Twickenham, and beautified by Eastmancolor, *Mods and Rockers* earns our respect as a social document. It subsequently found its way into the 1965 American release of *Go-Go Big Beat*, incorporating both *Swinging UK* and *UK Swings Again*.

OCTOBER

Every Day's a Holiday is a truly patriotic film that doesn't want to go anywhere that's far away and unknown. It's not Cliff and his mates abandoning ship and luxuriating in the Technicolor splendour of a foreign summer holiday in the sun: it's a staycation, the closest the British 'pop' musical film gets to portraying enforced entertainment on an almost Orwellian scale. It's Butlin's luxury holiday camp at Clacton-on-Sea, opened by one of the legendary figures of the British hospitality business, Billy Butlin, in 1938. In some ways this was good timing. German misbehaviour soon ensured that foreign travel was inadvisable, that it was more sensible and more convenient and just as enjoyable to get closer to your fellow countrymen, in what at times reminded us of a Women's League of Health and Beauty get-together, with its swimming and beauty and talent competitions, perhaps even competitions to decide which of the stay-at-home holidaymakers had the knobbliest of knees. Nicolas Roeg's crystalline cinematography has captured many of the irresistible elements of this location, with its Gaiety Theatre, the Stage Coach Crazy Horse Bar, the Sunbathing Lawns, the Kiddies' Paddling Pool, the Sea Horse Lounge, the Boating Lake, the Viennese Ballroom (for the more sophisticated customer), the Regency Lounge Bar (with chandeliers), and the Rock and Twist Ballroom.

Whatever else it may be, it's an invaluable social document of the British at play and enjoying fine dining on a truly industrial scale.

Consistently entertaining, Fitzroy-Maycroft's *Every Day's a Holiday* benefits hugely from its location work at the Clacton Butlin's. There doesn't seem to be a single 'extra' in the crowds pouring out of the coaches rolling up to disgorge another consignment of Billy's guests in a film precariously positioned in the wake of the Myers–Cass Cliff Richard pictures and the various vehicles for popular groups at a time when it seemed almost inevitable that every Freddie and his Dreamers, every Dave Clark Five, would get their own musical film. Nothing about Maurice J. Wilson and Ronald J. Kahn's production, or James Hill's direction, is strikingly original; much is reminiscent. Indeed, Anthony Marriott, Jeri Matos, and Hill's screenplay has its very own three codgers accentuating the generation gap that rides through so many British pop films of the period. Gerry (John Leyton) dreams of becoming a pop star, despite the scorn of his ex-vaudeville star dad (superb codger Michael Ripper). Thus dad is following in the steps of other fathers distrustful of their children's ambitions, not least Harry H. Corbett's dad in *What a Crazy World*. Meanwhile, Christina (Grazina Frame) is being trained as an opera singer by an old codger professor (Ron Moody) at the insistence of her aunt (Hazel Hughes). Unlikely as it seems, the Honourable Timothy Gilpin (Mike Sarne) has slipped his moorings from the upper class to don Mr Butlin's uniform.

The *MFB* considered the film 'quite attractive and entertaining' and inexplicably 'at its best when unequivocally parodying the world of the colour supplements', singling out Leyton's 'engagingly melancholy personality' and describing Sarne as 'very funny. One is never sure whether it is the film sending up the upper-class Tim, or whether it is the pop lyrics that are being sent up by the cool Sarne.'[10] David Parkinson's thumbs-down found it 'often laughingly bad'[11] in contrast to the glowing review in *Films and Filming*, where David Rider argued that 'Where it differs from many of its predecessors is that all the well-known names give good value for money, the dancing (directed by Gillian Lynne) is intelligent and the songs are mostly above average. The film, in fact, carries no passengers.'[12] The parade of excellent character actors includes Hazel Hughes, an actress rather less used to such prominence, Ron Moody, and Michael Ripper. Nevertheless, Andy Medhurst saw:

> a film pulled apart by the strain of trying to reinvent itself during its actual period of production in an attempt to keep up with the volatile shifts in taste affiliation of the eventual target audiences. Its original conception, clearly, was to emulate the Cliff Richard musicals – lots of wide screen colour, well-behaved heterosexual romance, sunshine and teeth.[13]

No doubt, but *Every Day's a Holiday* is delightfully bright, with a constant flow of attractive and original numbers often accompanied by Gillian Lynne's energetic choreography, in which Sarne and Leyton, patently non-dancers, do their best. Lynne has skilfully monopolised a sort of loose-limb music with movement in which the presence of the less nimble is disguised. There is something so apparently spontaneous in the sunny title song performed as the company invade Clacton's beach. Much is made of Mr Butlin's attraction as in the thumping dance number 'The Fastest Gun in the West' filmed in the camp's Crazy Horse Saloon. The fact that it's completely extraneous is rescued by its being Leyton's dream sequence. He is at his melancholic best in the mournful 'All I Want Is You', sung as he wanders sadly through Mr Butlin's deserted fairground, and not much more hopeful when he duets with Grazina Frame in 'A Girl Needs a Boy'. Other numbers include the Baker Twins (Susan and Jennifer) bathing infants in the camp's nursery as they express their fondness for their little charges.

The abundance of song includes Clive Westlake and Kenny Lynch's 'Love Me Please' sung by Sarne, 'Crazy Horse Saloon' by Tony Osborne and Jackie Rae performed by Leyton and dancers, and the title song by Shuman and Westlake performed by Leyton, Sarne, Frame, and dancers. The Mojos perform their own composition 'Everything's Alright' and The Isley Brothers' 'Nobody But Me', and Sarne sings his 'Indubitably Me' co-written by Lynch. Leyton sings Westlake and Lynch's doleful ballad 'All I Want Is You', and in the holiday camp's crèche the Baker twins (Susan and Jennifer) serenade the tots with Shuman and J. Leslie McFarland's 'Romeo Jones'. Westlake and Lynch provide Frame with two of the film's most enjoyable numbers, 'A Boy Needs a Girl' and 'Second Time Shy'.

Freddie Garrity and the Dreamers contribute Tony Osborne and Jackie Rae's 'What's Cooking' and Garrity's own composition 'Don't Do That to Me'. A dash of old-fashioned variety arrives with Shuman and McFarland's 'Cor Blimey' performed by Ron Moody and Michael Ripper. An uncredited medley of songs has Leyton imagining himself in various musical guises as he looks at a mirror.

Despite its publicity material ('From the cellar clubs in London to the opening nights in Paris ... to the wild way-out world of the continental swingers'), admirers of Ray Charles are the most likely to seek out Alsa Films' ***Ballad in Blue*** produced by Herman Blaser, Alexander Salkind, and Miguel Salkind and filmed at Ardmore studios in Ireland. Paul Henreid directed Burton Wohl's screenplay, which is based on their story. Blind singer Charles, on tour in London with his orchestra and vocal group The Raelets, takes time to visit a school for blind children, where he meets emotionally isolated young David (Piers Bishop) and his widowed, over-protective mother Peggy (Mary Peach). As well as supporting David, Charles helps Peggy's boyfriend (Tom Bell) by employing him and facilitating his union with Peggy. Occasionally a remark strikes a vaguely original note, as when Steve remonstrates, 'You're always trying to get me discovered – as if I were some new Italian restaurant', but the melding of the real-life Charles into the fiction of his surroundings was not particularly well managed, the story lapsing into the star's musical moments.

Many of these were both written and performed by Charles: 'What'd I Say?', 'I Got a Woman', the traditional 'Careless Love', 'Talkin' 'bout You', and 'Hallelujah I Love Her So'. Other items performed by Charles include Don Gibson's 'Don't Tell Me Your Troubles', Charles and Rick Ward's 'Light Out of Darkness', Haven Gillespie and Beasley Smith's 'That Lucky Old Sun', Harlan Howard's 'Busted', Shirley Goodman and Leonard Lee's 'Let the Good Times Roll', Percy Mayfield's 'Hit the Road Jack', and Teddy Powell and Bobby Sharp's 'Unchain My Heart'. The *MFB* decided that 'In the face of the gimcrack script, Paul Henreid's anonymous direction can do little to disguise the banality of theme, characters and situation.'[14]

NOVEMBER

It's such an inspiring title: **Ferry Cross the Mersey**. There is a mythological ring to it, but measured against the film that hoped to do for Gerry and the Pacemakers what Richard Lester and his *A Hard Day's Night* had done for The Beatles, Gerry's apparently autobiographical effort cannot be called successful. A pity, because in its opening moments there's the feeling that we are rooted in the back streets and alleys and bomb-sites of 1960s Liverpool. For a while, it seems we are in for a relentless, even Orwellian, portrait of a deprived community. We can't help but wonder what future lies in store for the underprivileged children we are shown here. Territorially, we are in very different country from that inhabited by The Beatles. Sadly, the film almost immediately turns its back on such issues. What we are left with is the heart-warmingly fun-loving friendliness of our Gerry, not really convincing us that he's an art student or an actor but chasing about the place on a scooter in search of anything much of a plot and putting up with a lot of screaming.

'I don't know whether *Ferry Cross the Mersey* was filmed before, during or after [*A Hard Day's Night*] but stylistically it is almost exactly the same', claimed *Films and Filming*. 'Come to think of it, from nearly every angle, it's almost exactly the same.'[15] For Bill Harry, the film was 'one long cliché [...] With a decent plot, Gerry's personality, the film could have been an excellent vehicle to establish Gerry and the Pacemakers around the world and might have led to other film ventures for him', but it wasn't to be.[16] After seeing the film, one woman told the newspaper *Mersey Beat*, 'It's just like a look into hell.'[17] It was probably not particularly helpful that Suba Films' vehicle for the highly likeable Marsden was sent out with the American teen-fodder feature *For Those Who Think Young*, with its scantily clad younger generation doing their best to dance the Twist on a studio-staged beach dominated by a perfectly manicured James Darren. The double-billing of two such disparate efforts to show how vigorous young people were living their lives in the mid-1960s could hardly have represented two more polar opposites. Young James was an altogether more glamorous creature than brass-tacks Gerry, far from a beach and an over-enthusiastic tanning technician and filmed close to his Liverpool home because it was cheaper and more convenient than more adventurous location shooting.

The film seems to have been the inspiration of The Beatles' manager Brian Epstein, although proposing a similar sort of film to that group's *A Hard Day's Night* probably didn't seem especially inspiring. Tony Warren, whose achievements included the creation of television's soap opera *Coronation Street*, was

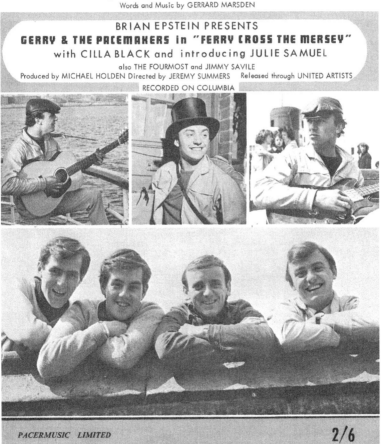

Likeable Gerry Marsden's adventure of *Ferry Cross the Mersey* (1964), very much in the wake of The Beatles, was filmed in Liverpool to save money on location shooting.

brought in to provide a script but was replaced by David Franden, whose screenplay based on Warren's original seemed home-spun. The style of production under Michael Holden lacked the immediacy and quick invention of what The Beatles had already done, and the score, mostly written with a few exceptions by Marsden, could not compare. Pleasant company as these young men are, they are non-actors shoehorned into a film that seems to mimic Richard Lester's homage to The Beatles, but hangs about, despite desperately speeded-up sequences *à la* Keystone Cops comedies, dotted with mostly unmemorable songs. Wilfrid Brambell's token old codger of *A Hard Day's Night* is replaced here by a whole gallery of the older and generally disapproving generation, among them Mona Washbourne, Deryck Guyler, and George A. Cooper. A sort of artificial reality creeps into Franden's script, with the Epstein-like pop group manager Hanson (T. P. McKenna) catapulting Gerry and the boys to greater success as they battle all that screaming.

According to the *New York Times*, Marsden's opening number, 'It's Gonna Be All Right', was 'well, all right, but most of the songs are standard copies of better beats'.[18] The critic advised that the group should 'Drop the conformity kick, boys. The world isn't ready for more Beatles'.[19]

Nevertheless, the evocative title song by Marsden and Les Chadwick establishes an atmosphere in which the star's natural personality might flourish, but most of the other numbers are by Marsden alone: 'Why Oh Why?' performed at Liverpool's Cavern Club, 'Fall in Love', 'This Thing Called Love', 'Think About Love', 'I'll Wait for You', 'Baby, You're So Good to Me', and 'She's the Only Girl for Me'. At Liverpool's Locarno Ballroom, Cilla Black sings Bobby Willis's 'Is It Love?' The pop world beyond Gerry and the Pacemakers is represented by four other groups: The Black Knights in Kenny Griffiths's 'I Gotta Woman'; Earl Royce and The Olympics in Royce's 'Shake a Tail Feather'; The Fourmost performing 'I Love You Too' at the Locarno, where Jimmy Savile is master of ceremonies; and The Blackwells performing their own composition 'Why Don't You Love Me?'

Rarely seen since its original release, the often-overlooked *Ferry Cross the Mersey* has been pushed into the hinterland of the decade's pop musicals. It may be consoling to know that the *MFB* decided that 'In the competition finale, this group sound, and look like conservative classicists by comparison with some of their uninhibitedly moronic rivals'.[20] Meanwhile, the mere presence of Savile as master of ceremonies at the Locarno Ballroom is enough to scupper the film's chances of ever being seen again.

DECEMBER

'I can hear bells! I can hear bells! Maybe nobody else can hear them, but I can hear bells!' They can be heard in a production 'specially written and composed for Anglia Television'. The continued existence of Anglia Television's superb

Christmas musical *The Rise and Fall of Nellie Brown*, transmitted live on ITV
as its 'Play of the Week' on 28 December, has a legitimate claim to inclusion
in these pages despite never having been released as a film. Its score is by the
Canadian composer Dolores Claman, with book and lyrics by Robert Gould;
both had regularly contributed items to sophisticated West End intimate
revues in the 1950s.

Anglia's splendid excursion into musical theatre seems to have been its
only major contribution to the genre. It is an occasion for celebration, set
around Christmas and cloaked in a tender story about a shy young immigrant
Selina Brown (the sublime Millie Small) living with her mother in their shabby
Liverpool home, where Millie longs for something better and, remembering
that 'The Lord Helps Them As Helps Themselves', goes to London in search
of her once famous second cousin Nellie Brown (equally sublime Elisabeth
Welch). Along the way, she hitches a lift from highly talkative lorry driver Dave
(Bryan Mosley giving a brilliantly inventive account of his domestic Christmas
in 'Dave's Complaint') and takes up with kindly illusionist Jasper Waxo (first-
rate Ron Moody), who promises to deliver Selina to Nellie Brown, now a figure
from the theatrical past, Miss Lillabelle Astor. Anglia's director John Jacobs
pushes the boat out for the all-white production number 'Lillibelle Astor,
We Love You', choreographed by Irving Davies. When we at last see what has
become of the great artiste Miss Astor, she is living in reduced circumstances, long forgotten, and wondering what Time has done to her in Calman and
Gould's exquisite 'A Million Years Ago':

> A million years ago, or was it yesterday,
> That each tomorrow seemed at least a million years away?
> The world belonged to us, as did each star.
> The month was May, it always is when you're in
> Shangri-La.
> How soon December comes, it's inconceivable
> To think in Spring his love was real seems unbelievable
> So unbelievable.
> You're bound to say
> Was it a million years ago, or was it yesterday?

Welch's performance displays artistry of the highest order. In her last years,
she explained, 'I have no technique. No art, no training, nothing. Just myself. I
describe myself as a singer of popular songs.'[21]

Jacobs's precision in casting extends to the minor roles: Mosley's *tour
de force* account of what his Christmas will be; Tommy Godfrey's frustrated
agent; sparrow-sized Patsy Smart in beautifully judged timidity as his harassed
secretary; Avril Fane's pianist Miss Pendleton in her all-too-brief but hilarious
audition rendition of 'Now Is the Time for Tears'. So soon after his stage
success as Fagin, Moody too is on top form, warning Selina that 'You're Going
to Be Late for Christmas', but once in London with Nellie she looks forward

expectantly in the ecstatic 'I Can Hear Bells'. In the pub, the Cliff Adams Singers celebrate in a brilliant music-hall pastiche number around the piano, 'You Can Bet Your Life', and at home Selina and Nellie duet at the piano in the jaunty 'No Better Number Than Two'. A fall of real snow (the genuine article, after Nellie and Waxo have sent shredded paper into the street to convince Selina that the weather is doing what is expected of it) completes Selina's happiness and the consolidation of her new-found life with Nellie Brown.

If only the British musical film of so many past years had opened itself up to such joy as can be found here, rather than prostituting itself to what it mistakenly considered popular taste. Without doubt, Claman, Gould, Jacobs, and their fine band of gypsies deserve to be remembered for this heartful achievement, one of which the British musical *on film* could rarely be congratulated. That world is briefly described by the novelist Dorothy Whipple on one of her rare visits to a British studio, most probably in the mid-1940s when her novels *They Were Sisters* and *The Knew Mr Knight* were being filmed, an experience that 'filled me with horror somehow – no reality there'. Whipple found 'a girl' sleeping on a property bed, her eyes closed, her hands clasped as if in prayer.

> The pillow-slips and sheets of the bed were of sateen, decidedly grubby. They were bordered with deep coarse lace, equally grubby. I suppose, on the screen, they would come out looking like sumptuous satin and the best Torchon [...] The girl lay unmoved. Calm and concentrated. She never opened her eyes, not even when a woman came with a puff full of ochre-coloured powder and pressed it here and there to her face.

When the cameras were ready, in the presence of what seemed to Whipple to be hundreds of onlookers, 'She went through a scene of a few words over and over again. Over and over again, she kissed, to order, the man she was acting with. I marvelled at her. Miss B. said her name was Anna Neagle.'[22] It must have been from such grubbiness that Wilcox and Neagle were able to weave the romanticism of their films, exulting in the over-arching artificiality of everything such endeavour demanded. There is no reason to suppose that grubbiness was just as prevalent in films before the end of the war; indeed, the conditions that war imposed on the industry ensured that it was.

1965

The songs have the ring of theatre about them, and are rather more typical of British stage musicals of the time than of British musical films

I've Gotta Horse

Pop Gear	*Catch Us If You Can*
Gonks Go Beat	*Help!*
I've Gotta Horse	*Up Jumped a Swagman*
Three Hats for Lisa	*Cuckoo Patrol*
Be My Guest	*Dateline Diamonds*

JANUARY

The intervening years have given Associated British Pathé's **Pop Gear** an archival relevance that it did not own in 1965. Despite the hastily contrived treatment these performers and groups, miming to their recordings, receive from producer Harry Field and director Frederic Goode, we at least have this depository of a slice of British pop music circa 1964. Presumably, the sole purpose of its credited writer Roger Dunton was to provide disc jockey Jimmy Savile with some bare bones linking comments between the acts. Thanks to modern technology not available in the mid-sixties, we may decide to swiftly move on from these. Anyway, Matt Monro, the most veteran of the film's guests, has already alerted us as to what we are in for in John and Joan Shakespeare's title song:

> It's been a swinging year for the groups that made the grade,
> Those discs you played and played and then played again.
> You got the music that you long to hear, It's all here,
> and it's pop gear. The Stones are crazy about it
> Dave Clark stamps his foot for it.
> The Mersey Sound became a hit and the Beatles started it.
> You were the problem child in a world where music sings
> Your emotions took on wings, the frenzy, the dreams.
> Why, you almost heard the music through the screams!
> Yes indeed, and you need,
> Oh how you need some more pop gear
> Pop, pop, pop gear: This was pop gear!

The real meat of *Pop Gear* is sandwiched between an opening sequence of The Beatles performing 'She Loves You' and a final sequence of them singing Phil Medley and Bert Berns's 'Twist and Shout', both songs being borrowed from a Pathé film. In between, this glorious celebration of the state of British pop as it approached the mid-sixties does what its highly respected senior statesman balladeer Monro has promised. He returns with Udo Jürgens and Don Black's compelling 'Walk Away' and with Charles Aznavour and Black's 'Mama', which may well be 'an almost unbelievable piece of glucose balladry'[1] but is very finely achieved. Monro's maturity is in sharp contrast to much of his surroundings, but gems, several of minor importance, are encapsulated.

The territory is overwhelmingly male, and white. The traditional 'House of the Rising Sun', arranged by Alan Price, is probably the toughest of the numbers in this retrospective. It may indeed be the film's highlight, with an insistent intensity that grips. It seems that another brilliant Animals number, Bennie Benjamin, Gloria Caldwell, and Sol Marcus's 'Don't Let Me Be Misunderstood', was filmed but unused. 'Have I the Right', written by Ken Howard and Alan Blakley, is splendidly delivered by The Honeycombs with its female drummer, and the group returns for Howard and Blakley's 'Eyes'. The Spencer Davis Group score, with Bill Medley and Bobby Hatfield's 'My Babe', was singled out by the *MFB* as 'the knockout bit' of the film in which 'Steve Winwood's vocalising is tremendous'.[2] In jollier vein, Herman's Hermits invest Gerry Goffin and Carole King's 'I'm into Something Good' with terrific teenaged hopefulness. It's apparent, too, in another pearl of the period, Lennon and McCartney's 'A World Without Love', sung simply and possibly 'apathetically'[3] by Peter and Gordon.

An air of continued innocence swirls around Mort Shuman and John McFarland's 'Little Children', with which Billy J. Kramer will be forever associated. Along the way, Kramer and The Dakotas' version of Kenny Lynch's 'It's Gotta Last for Ever' was cut. Meanwhile, The Rockin' Berries impress with Gerry Goffin and Carole King's haunting 'He's in Town' and Jimmy Wisner and Billy Jackson's falsetto-fuelled 'What in the World's Come over You?' The Nashville Teens are represented in two numbers by John D. Loudermilk, 'Tobacco Road' and 'Goggle Eye'.

The Four Pennies appear with Leadbelly's 'Black Girl', with its cry of 'Black girl, black girl, where will you go? She goes where the cold wind blows', and Lionel Morton, Fritz Fryer, and Mike Wilsh's 'Juliet'. *Films and Filming* thought 'Juliet' 'disastrous – the three guitarists perambulate endlessly round a ridiculously ornate fountain, whilst drummer Alan Buck sits unhappily on the outskirts'.[4]

The Fourmost present Russell (Russ) Alquist's 'A Little Loving', while a novelty number, 'Humpty Dumpty', offers some light relief from Tommy Quickly and The Remo Four. Dance routines choreographed by Leo Kharibian intermittently remind us of the prevailing sense of enjoyment, and Sounds Incorporated impress with David Clowney's instrumental 'Rinky Dink' and an invigorating update of Rossini's overture to his *William Tell* with its leaping musicians and heavily saxophone arrangement. Space is found for only two female performers. Billie Davis is highly impressive in Chuck Willis's 'Whatcha' Gonna Do', and Susan Maughan sings Bob Barratt's 'Make Him Mine' straight down the line. Two of the Beatles' most famous numbers may sandwich this extraordinary gathering of pop talent, but the film-makers' decision to begin and end the celebration with snatched glimpses of the Fab Four is unnecessary. Rather than frame the acts that make up *Pop Gear*, it suggests that they will forever remain in the shadow of The Beatles.

Robert Hartford-Davis, the director of Titan Film Productions' idiosyncratic ***Gonks Go Beat***, is rumoured to have left instructions that on his death all prints of his films were to be destroyed. If stated, his wishes went unfulfilled, meaning that we may still experience a work of which one critic has warned that 'It will crush you beneath a warm fuzzy blanket of dead-eyed mediocrity that will seriously damage your ability to reason coherently.'[5]

Hartford-Davis cannot be held solely responsible, although he co-produced with Peter Newbrook, and their original story was screenplayed by Jimmy Watson. Others in the creative team include art director William Constable with some atmospheric galactic settings that show the film's splendid East-mancolor to full effect despite the all-too-obvious financial restraints, while the ill-coordinated choreography is somewhat anonymously credited to Dance Groups (London).

Somewhere in space, the impressive Great Galaxian (Jerry Desmonde), in an outfit that might have belonged to Dan Dare, sends timid Wilco Roger (top-billed Kenneth Connor) on an ambassadorial mission to resolve the conflict (fought with musical instruments) between the inhabitants of rock'n'roll crazy Beatland and the more sedate Balladisle. We have been handed an allegory, for some reason involving the squat, placid, obviously friendly, and unthreatening Gonks, toys invented after World War II by Robert Benson. At the core of Watson's slim plot is a Montague–Capulet style romance between the film's Romeo and Juliet, Steve (Iain Gregory, his singing voice dubbed by Perry Ford) and Helen (Barbara Brown, Liesl in the original London production of *The Sound of Music*).

Films and Filming got the message, but saw 'a *West Side Story* for the under-twelves' that was 'nothing more than a string of mediocre pop numbers.'[6] Half a century later, Kim Newman considered the film 'At once frankly insane and mildly dull' and that 'most of the music is as bland as the jokes are flat.'[7] Fair enough, but *Gonks Go Beat* survives as a fascinating document, bravely free (with the brief exception of Lulu and Her Luvvers) from the more prominent pop performers of the time. The names and reputations of many of its singers may have slipped, among them blond Alan David, Perry Ford of the Ivy League, and The Long and the Short. Mildest of the participants are the twin brother and sister vocal duo Elaine (wrongly credited as Elain) and Derek;

he subsequently became the BBC's most highly paid actor in a long-running hospital drama series.

Mike Leander contributed 'Choc Ice' and 'The Only One' for Lulu and the Luvvers and 'Poor Boy' for The Nashville Teens, and he arranged the 'Drum Battle', one of the most interesting numbers, played by Alan Grimley, Ronny Verrell, Andy White, and Ronnie Stephenson. Robert Richards wrote the title theme and 'Burn Up' played by the Titan Sound Orchestra, as well as two duets co-written with Mike Pratt for Perry Ford and Barbara Brown, 'Loving You' and 'Takes Two to Make Love'. Al Saxon provided solos for Ford ('In Love with You Today') and Brown ('Penny for Your Thoughts'). Elaine and Derek sing Robert Hartford-Davis and William Leyland's 'Broken Pieces', while Alan David performs Richards and Dennis O'Connell's 'Love Is a Dream'. Dougie (Douglas) Robinson and the Titan Sound Orchestra appear in Ronnie Keene and Ricky Cannon's 'As Young As We Are'; 'Take This Train' is performed by The Long and The Short, and Marty Wilde's 'Harmonica' is played by The Graham Bond Organisation.

Critical reaction for ***I've Gotta Horse***, the nearest Billy Fury came to an autobiographical film, was mixed. In a kindly review that singled out the choreography for praise, the *MFB* felt that 'somehow or other the polish does not create a real shine'.[8] For *Films and Filming* 'Billy Fury's latest splits the difference between the *Summer Holiday* formula, all good-humoured, well-washed boys and girls prancing about in the fresh air, and the zanified [*sic*] star-worship of *A Hard Day's Night* – Billy plays Billy, fey and unspoiled, always late for rehearsals, but all right on the night'.[9] *Time Out* has been less charitable:

> By 1965, Fury had broadened into a lukewarm entertainer, and this effort, which desperately plugged his affection for his four-legged friends, was a misguided attempt to (a) widen his appeal to mums, and (b) to regain some of the fans that he and other solo artists had lost since the advent of group-mania in 1963. The film slipped by unnoticed.[10]

In more ways than one, *I've Gotta Horse* belongs in the stable of the pop-singer films that overran the 1960s film industry. We hope that veteran actor Leslie Dwyer was a dog-lover. He is besieged by them in the opening shots, with Fury driving his dogs (and they were his) and Dwyer onto the Acle 'straight' en route to Great Yarmouth, where Billy is playing in summer season at the Royal Aquarium. Presented by Windmill Films, the picture was produced by Larry Parnes and director Kenneth Hume, and was made in Yarmouth and at Shepperton, with a screenplay by Ronald Wolfe and Ronald Chesney based on an original storyline by Parnes and Hume. By this time, having a pop singer at the centre of a British film was a trusted formula following Tommy Steele's rise to prominence in the late 1950s and the Cliff Richard vehicles. The advent of The Beatles had a deleterious effect on such ventures, seeming to circumvent frivolity and show-bizzy elements of their predecessors. Much of *I've Gotta Horse* catches the spirit of the enjoyable *Every Day's a Holiday* of the previous year, and it remains one of the best of its type of the decade, with the bonus of the popular Irish trio The Bachelors, riding Yarmouth's dunes in 'Far Far Away' and giving it up for gospel at a barbecue with 'He's Got the Whole World in His Hands', and The Gamblers performing 'Cried All Night'. The songs have the ring of theatre about them and are rather more typical of British stage musicals of the time than of British musical films.

The casting is first-rate, gathering some of the brightest young talents of the period and experienced character actors in Dwyer, Jon Pertwee in the set piece ensemble number 'You've Got to Look Right for the Part', a glimpsed Fred Emney, and Bill Fraser as an irascible theatre producer. Amanda Barrie is a bright-eyed leading lady, surviving some clumsy sound editing in her numbers. She is joined by Sheila O'Neill, a now almost forgotten dancer and performer who two years later played the lead in London's production of *Sweet Charity* and subsequently threatened to steal the notices from Lauren Bacall in the West End version of Broadway's *Applause*. Ross Taylor's youthful choreography is generously on display. All musical numbers with the exception of 'Wonderful Day' are by David Heneker and John Taylor, proficient writers for British musical theatre. Their score is typical of their workmanlike output, pleasant, apposite, and unremarkable. Bright, zippy, and charmingly child-proof in Ann Lancaster's sweet shop for the children's 'I Like Animals', the songs carry the film along, with Fury at its centre. He does not present as an actor, and never ventured into other territory as Steele and others did, but in this company he brings an apparently natural gentleness. This quality is surely something rare in singers of his type, a sort of deep-rooted melancholy that is never far off. It finds full expression in his plaintive 'Won't Somebody Tell Me Why?', filmed on what was obviously a dismal, freezing cold day on Yarmouth's quayside. In the roundness of this performance, *I've Gotta Horse* serves as a decent memorial, almost convincing us that if it hadn't been for the presence of its animals, Fury wouldn't have put his soul into it.

The score includes several numbers for Fury: the title song; 'Stand by Me' with The Gamblers (who also perform 'Cried All Night'); 'Find Your Dream' sung to Amanda Barrie; the touching 'Won't Somebody Tell Me Why?'; 'The Old Soft Shoe' with Sheila O'Neill; and 'I Like Animals' with the children. The Bachelors are represented by 'Far Far Away' and 'He's Got the Whole World in His Hands'. Other production numbers, very much the sort of stuff that was permeating British stage musicals of the period, involve Barrie and Michael Medwin with 'Problems'; O'Neill, Barrie and dancers in the choreographic 'Dressed Up for a Man'; and the set piece 'You've Got to Look Right for the Part' for Fury, Barrie, and Jon Pertwee. It is workmanlike stuff, to which must be added Michael Leander's 'Wonderful Day'.

How to evaluate Seven Hills' production of one of the slightest, mayfly musical films of the 1960s? *Three Hats for Lisa* is such a light confection. Eric Rogers's busy orchestrations do their best to brush up Leslie Bricusse's songs, but nothing of note emerges in what is a cross between a gossamer-weight fantasy and a travelogue of London (much of it concreted). The promising opening has our hero cycling around London's industrial locations (some of the most striking images in the film) and a closing sequence that suggests the yet unfinished Post Office Tower will be one of man's most civilised achievements, with a revolving restaurant.

Talbot Rothwell's screenplay weaves the plot around cockney bright spark Johnny Howjego (Joe Brown) and his obsession with Italian film star Lisa Milan (Sophie Hardy). Their chance meeting when she arrives in London leads on to the film's *raison d'être*, light-fingered Lisa's determination to nick titfers, her ultimate trophy being a policeman's helmet. It's a fanciful theme. Nothing much else happens in a film that constantly tries to jolly us up, and it is to director Sidney Hayers's credit that he rouses his actors to the task in hand. Already noted in the 1963 *What a Crazy World*, Brown is a likeable presence. At times, his personable performance might be an audition for the stage musical *Charlie Girl*, in which he was to share top-billing with Anna Neagle at the end of the year.

Brown is accompanied throughout by Una Stubbs, by now entrenched in the minds of British filmgoers as the unrelentingly pert, romantically-undemanding girlfriend of Cliff Richard via *Summer Holiday* and *Wonderful Life*. Along with Hardy's charming Italian minx, Stubbs cannot be faulted. There are two other good reasons for sitting through *Three Hats for Lisa* – Sid James's irrepressible taxi-driver, and Gillian Lynne's choreography, for it is in the dancing that this film meets the stage musical, Lynne's troupe forever bounding and leaping into view. The dancers become as recognisable and significant as any of the players, one minute road workers draped in scaffolding, another moment balletic costermongers among the fruit and veg of Covent Garden. The film would be very much duller without their constant interruptions.

If only Bricusse's songs were better, although generally their lightness seems appropriate to the whimsicality of the concept, with retrospective whiffs of the theatrical mid-1950s, when innocence – at least in musicals – abounded. The innocent adventure of Johnny and Lisa has some of the quirkiness of such British stage musicals as Julian Slade and Dorothy Reynolds's *Salad Days* and *Follow That Girl*. Despite his great skills, Mr Bricusse is no Slade or Reynolds (and no doubt glad not to be so), but no Rodgers or Hammerstein either. We can be confident that in his hands *Carousel* would have turned out very differently. Somehow, his belief that there is nothing the British public enjoys more than a good old knees-up is never far off.

The generous quantity of music is outweighed by its lack of distinction, its emphasis on the sort of celebration generally understood to be enjoyed and practised by spirited East Enders: 'This Is a Special Day' with its lyric by Robin

Beaumont sung by Joe Brown; 'The Boy on the Corner of the Street Where I Live' (Una Stubbs, Sandra Hampton, and Beth McDonald); 'Something Tells Me' (Brown, Stubbs, Dave Nelson); 'I'm The King of the Castle' (Brown, Stubbs, Nelson); 'Bermondsey' (James, Brown, Sophie Hardy, Stubbs, Nelson); 'London Town' (Brown, Hardy, James, Stubbs, Nelson); 'Three Hats for Lisa' (Brown, Hardy, James, Stubbs, Nelson); 'Two Cockney Kids' (Brown, Stubbs); 'Have You Heard about Johnny Howjego?' (James, Stubbs, Nelson); 'That's What Makes a Girl a Girl' (Brown, Hardy, James, Stubbs, Nelson); 'I Fell in Love with an Englishman' (Hardy); 'A Man's World' (Hardy); 'Covent Garden' (Brown, Hardy, James, Stubbs, Nelson); and 'One Day in London' (ensemble). In short, too many.

FEBRUARY

Two years after his 1963 *Live It Up*, producer-director Lance Comfort reunited with screenwriter Lyn Fairhurst for Three Kings Films' ***Be My Guest***, an update on the laddish boy-band comprising Dave Martin (David Hemmings), Phil (John Pike), and Ricky (Stephen, later Steve, Marriott). Sadly missed from the follow-up is Heinz Burt; by now, his brief popularity had waned. Musically, *Be My Guest* hasn't the cohesiveness of its predecessor, where all but one of the plentiful songs are by Joe Meek. Meek, indeed, had been a good enough *raison d'être* for *Live It Up*; two years on, there doesn't seem an obvious reason for re-treading. Although it's a decent enough successor, its promotion as a 'pop' music film is much less convincing. Still restrained by the modesty of his budget, Comfort treats the musical acts as the title suggests, with politeness and as guests within his film, entitled to have their talent exhibited as effectively as can be managed.

The home-life scenes showing the Martin family at their most everyday had been one of the most successful aspects of *Live It Up*. Now, Ivor Salter and Diana King play Dave's parents, who inherit a museum-piece of a Brighton guesthouse, complete with a curmudgeonly maid-of-all-work Mrs Pucil (Avril Angers). Her presence is meant to supply the film's comedy, but Angers can do little with it. The possibilities offered by Brighton's vibrant character, at a time when social attitudes were changing so fast, play no part in the proceedings, with no imaginative use of its native atmosphere.

The showbusiness tale, wearily familiar, seems tired in comparison with what has gone before, with the focus on the boys less sure. Dave is now a cub reporter on the local Brighton newspaper, and plans with Phil and Ricky to win a song competition masterminded by the exploiting American Hilton Bass (David Healy) with his battle-cry 'The Mersey sound can move over, from here on it's the Brighton beat.' It has to be said that his ambition is unrealised by Comfort's film. While Dave and his mates are making barely a dent on the British pop scene, The Beatles are on their second American tour.

The tenuous plot emerges with difficulty, leaving us wondering if (given the nature of film-making) the cast ever quite understood what was supposed to be happening. As before, it is the 'lollipop' sequences when the pop singers take over that are guaranteed to attract us. It is, perhaps, not so extraordinary a line-up as for *Live It Up*, but its crowning glory may be Jerry Lee Lewis performing Peter Gage and Geoff Pullum's 'No One But Me'.

Otherwise, there are The Zephyrs (originally formed as Johnny Saville and the Clee-Shays) presenting Gage and Pullum's 'She Laughed'; The Nashville Teens singing John Cable and Barrie Jenkins's 'Watcha Gonna Do?'; The Plebs; Trinidadian Kenny Bernard and The Wranglers with Gage and Pullum's 'Somebody Help Me'; The Niteshades; and Dave, Phil, and Ricky with the title song written by Shel Talmy and John Burchell. It's an interesting peep into the current pop scene, mixed a little incongruously with some vague dance routines choreographed by Leo Kharibian, and Joyce Blair as Wanda pouting her way through John Barry and Mike Pratt's 'Gotta Get Away Now'. Why anyone would have considered that this belonged in a picture aimed at a younger audience is difficult to understand, although Wanda seems pleased enough: 'It's my new sound,' she explains. 'I hope the teenagers like it.'

Films and Filming applauded 'a pleasantly lively compact comedy, a slight send-up of the pop scene, innocuous, amusing [...] the screenplay displays a keen ear for youthful dialogue, warmly amusing and occasionally dangerously witty'.[11] 'Although not particularly well made', the *MFB* reassured readers, 'this tremendously good-humoured teenage frolic is kept alive by the hopefulness of its performances.'[12] It may be that the non-theatricals have the edge here, as neatly pointed out by Mr Martin's fondness for the older types of musical entertainment. Why can't Dave appreciate them instead of pop music? After all, '*The Roaming Vagabond* was very popular. We did it two years running.' As the exploiting American impresario scornfully remarks, 'The Milk Marketing Board are putting on *Miss Hook of Holland*.' Despite the show-biz types that come along and spoil the game, our interest remains with the three lads, not least when Phil and Ricky try their hand at British Rail catering, which appears to have remained remarkably consistent in the ensuing sixty years.

APRIL

The fact that nobody attempts to break into song at once distinguishes Bruton Film Productions' **Catch Us If You Can**. Late in the day – the lifespan of the British pop musical was slowly drawing to its close – this is a work that broke free of many of the understood characteristics of what had gone before. Written by Peter Nichols, and John Boorman's first directorial assignment, this is probably the most enigmatic of the sub-genre. It may have marked a sea-change in the very nature, via the most popular of the proliferating groups that peopled the charts, of pop films. It was a question of timing. By the time of *Catch Us If You Can*'s release, Richard's *amour propre* with the three Myers–Cass musicals (*The Young Ones*, *Summer Holiday*, and *Wonderful Life*) was done. Tommy Steele's association with the pop film had wound down and all but petered out with the thoroughly indifferent *It's All Happening*. Those semi-pop musicals such as the likeable *I've Gotta Horse*, with the likeable Billy Fury, and *Every Day's a Holiday*, which accommodated not only Mike Sarne and John Leyton but Freddie and the Dreamers, bore distinct echoes of the British stage musicals of the period, as did the Myers–Cass Richard films, despite the fact that Myers and Cass's attempts at writing for British musicals had not been particularly successful. In *Catch Us*, Nichols and Boorman eschewed this stagey approach, at the same time avoiding the heavy-handed signalling of the next song. Anyway, the signals in *Catch Us* are at best ethereal, never glibly obvious. It exists in a manner quite separate from anything that had previously presented as pop film.

It was the Dave Clark Five's only film. Probably the leading exponent of the Tottenham Merseybeat Sound, the group established itself at Tottenham's South Grove Youth Club, comprising Clark, Dennis Paynton, Mike Smith, Rick Huxley, and Lenny Davidson. They are always somewhere around during *Catch Us*, but they have nothing in common with Richard's Shadows or Freddie's Dreamers, existing within the fabric of the film but never obtruding. Their popularity could even outstrip that of The Beatles. They appeared on America's *The Ed Sullivan Show* eighteen times, more than any other British group, and American critics welcomed the film, renamed *Having a Wild Weekend*, as 'fresh and fetching' and 'an obvious but strangely haunting romance'.[13]

At home, the *MFB* thought it 'consistently worth looking at, and it finds intelligent expression for a genuinely youthful point of view. In fact, it doesn't deserve to be described as a teenage musical at all'; it was 'a director's film from start to finish'.[14] *Films and Filming* applauded 'One of the most interesting and thought-provoking of the British films of this year [...] a worthy achievement',[15] while Andy Medhurst has appreciated 'the liberating jolt of newness that permeates the film', which 'especially in its first startling thirty minutes, goes all out for the shiny plastic immediacy of the moment. It is, in short, where the pop film becomes the Pop film'.[16] Roger Mellor has recognised 'a film that shifts into melancholy. It becomes a critique of the vacuity of the opening images. For a "pop" film, that is radical.' Furthermore, *Catch Us* 'touches on mid-60s themes: the commodification of youth culture, the manipulative role of the "media industry", the all-pervasiveness of images and advertising, and the resulting sense of alienation'.[17]

Mr Clark shows little inclination to be an actor, but Nichols and Boorman do not require him to be one. In a film that is throughout obsessed with image, he is the right man, blunt-featured, for the job, just as Barbara Ferris is the right girl. Their twinned black and white tops as they make their hectic exit from the world they have been inhabiting are among the many striking images in a film that specialises in them. But what are we to make of their escape from the meat commercial that uses Dinah's image, brilliantly exploited by Manny Wynn's superlative cinematography? What do we make of the commune of dropouts from society who eke out an existence at what seems to be an abandoned settlement of broken buildings? What do we make of its bombing? What do we make of the middle-aged couple who threaten, in their way, to swallow our hero and heroine up? Do Guy (a svelte, unsettling Robin Bailey) and man-hungry Nan (Yootha Joyce) mean to seduce them into their world of sophisticated immorality? There's no chance of that. Steve even refuses the offer of a cigarette and glass of sherry. And why, when the chase is over (after all, *Catch Us*, as its title suggests, is basically a chase movie), does Steve drive off into yet another unknown and leave Dinah alone?

Along the way, we hear Clark and Davidson's brilliant title song 'Time', 'When', 'I Can't Stand It', and 'Sweet Memories', as well as Clark and Paynton's 'On the Move', 'Move On', and 'Ol Sol'.

JULY

'At the beginning of the sixties, the upper-echelon British movie typically offered gritty portrayals of northern life in black-and-white; even *A Hard Day's Night*, The Beatles' first film, made a slight attempt to observe reality. But by 1965, in **Help!**, you can barely see the moptops for the crazy sets, the surreal japes, and the movie parodies.[18]

Following his collaboration with The Beatles in the previous year's *A Hard Day's Night*, director Richard Lester returned with Subafilms' *Help!*, produced by Walter Shenson and written by Marc Behm and Charles Wood from a story by Behm. Dandy Nichols and Gretchen Franklin happen to be passing by just as the Fab Four (John Lennon, Ringo Starr, Paul McCartney and George Harrison) are stepping out of their sleek limousine. It's only natural that the old dears should relish this glimpse of these wholesome young men. 'Wave? Shall I? They expect it, don't they? Lovely lads and so natural. I mean, adoration hasn't gone to their heads one jot, has it? You know what I mean – success. Just so natural and still the same as they was before they was.'

Here was a pretty accurate summing-up of how a vast number of the British public saw the phenomenon that was The Beatles. George Perry identified the connection the film made between contemporary culture and Lester's treatment, noting that 'The photographic treatment was inspired by both television commercials and colour supplement advertisements, with soft filters.' This enabled the musical numbers to be 'miniature pyrotechnic exercises. But it was apparent that a measure of slickness in Lester's work was overtaking the power of the content.'[19] *Films and Filming* looked forward to The Beatles' next film (then rumoured to be an adaptation of Richard Condon's novel *A Talent for Loving*), which 'should reveal whether or not they have anything to offer the cinema apart from Goon-style humour, engaging personalities and attractive songs'.[20] The *MFB* reported 'visual virtuosity of such a lavish, and ultimately exhausting sort that for every point well taken one gets the feeling that five or six others have shot by at somewhere around the speed of light'.[21] Halliwell laconically suggested that the film 'goes to prove that some talents work better on low budgets'.[22]

The songs were the main attraction: Lennon's 'You're Going to Lose That Girl' and 'You've Got to Hide Your Love Away'; Lennon and McCartney's 'Help!', 'Ticket to Ride', and 'Tell Me What You See'; McCartney's 'The Night Before' and 'Another Girl'; and Harrison's 'I Need You'. The opening moments suggested that this might be a Hammer film as orientally inclined Clang (Leo McKern) and his handmaiden Ahme (Eleanor Bron) become obsessed with retrieving a sacred sacrificial ring which happens to be on Ringo's finger. The mystical nature of this storyline was no doubt to some degree intended to suggest a spiritual milieu in which The Beatles were to some degree interested. Possibly, but effectually the plot begins and ends there, immediately lapsing into frenzied scenes *à la* Keystone Cops, including one in the Alps as the James Bond theme thuds out on the soundtrack. The ensuing mayhem includes a vicarage tea-party, the destruction of a gentlemen's cloakroom, and a punch-up in which Lennon is clearly heard to announce 'I hit him' as he accidentally clubs a stunt man.

There is nothing much in the way of interesting conversation; even a query about whether chewing-gum should be swallowed elicits no response. Much of the intended visual comedy suffers from being carelessly edited, and goes on, although interrupted with many *longueurs*, for over ninety minutes. The numbers are smartly done, but the endless prankishness that surrounds them is tiring, and the temperature and pace drop in the more stationary moments. No shortage of ideas, and there is good work from designer Ray Simm and cinematographer David Watkin, but essentially the thing never develops satisfactorily, and the various talents of the supporting cast are not served well. Perhaps those Beatles were not fully aware of what they were involved in. Lennon subsequently said that Lester had never satisfactorily explained what the film would be. Besides, it was 'partly because we were smoking marijuana for breakfast during that period. Nobody could communicate with us, it was all glazed eyes and giggling all the time. In our own world.'[23]

SEPTEMBER

Perhaps *Up Jumped a Swagman*, Coventry-born Frank Ifield's one and only contribution to the British musical film, deserves to be better remembered. As a pop singer, forever identified as a formidable yodeller, he had a maturity, exported from Australia, that distinguishes him from Fury and Richard and Clark and Freddie, and his very gentleman-ness makes him all the more appealing. In the mid-sixties, inevitably overshadowed by The Beatles and the apparently seismic effectiveness of *A Hard Day's Night*, this was a piece that tried to combine several elements into a cohesive entertainment.

Films and Filming's verdict was that 'As a vehicle for a solo singer it doesn't compare with the better Presley films and is nothing like as good as the Cliff Richard films. It fails to *project* Ifield, submerging him in a welter of gimmicks and plot ramifications.'[24] The *Daily Worker* disagreed, finding a film that

> makes pop-film history. It's the first pop-idol vehicle in which the singer's dream of fame doesn't come true. As a matter of fact it puts its foot through much of the mythology of charts and agents and dream-girls and teenage raves in a gay comedy style that blithely mixes fiction with fantasy. It is brim-full of imaginative ideas.[25]

Unenthusiastic as the *MFB* was about Lewis Greifer's 'generally lifeless screen-play', it thought Ifield 'a likeable enough personality'.[26] The *Daily Mirror* thought that 'the story is too loose and easy-going' but that Ifield 'bounces through his first feature film with the zest of an eager young kangaroo [...] Not that this highly-coloured, comedy-fantasy does much to advance British musicals.'[27]

It was the first major project for director Christopher Miles following The Shadows' inventive *Rhythm 'n' Greens*. The original intention was that Peter Myers and Ronnie Cass would write it, but according to Miles that team had by this time broken up. In fact, Cass was credited as Miles's assistant. This did not suppress Leslie Grade's ambition to get the film made because he reckoned that Ifield had made more money from a summer season in Blackpool than Cliff Richard. Subsequently, Miles seems to have regretted his commission, recalling that 'Brunel made musicals at one time and he probably destroyed the negatives [...] Like me, he needed the money.' In 1969, Miles told the *Daily Mirror* that 'I was twenty-five when I got that film. At that age you think you can make a celluloid purse out of a sow's ear. But I didn't.'[28]

Dave Kelly (Ifield) arrives in Britain with several songs in his repertoire and a fondness for yodelling. When Richard Wattis's agent Lever hears him he's initially unimpressed: 'I think we can argue that as a marketable product that last song was 50% puerile and 50% pathetic.' 'You need a sound,' he tells him, 'get me a new sound.' He has already agreed that Dave is 'a perfect example of British manhood', but it's the yodelling that makes Lever sit up. Almost at once when he arrives in England, Dave is captivated by the image of Melissa (Suzy Kendall), but true love appears in the form of Patsy (Annette Andre). The major problem is that between them Greifer and Miles have stuffed the thing with so much irrelevance and so many bizarre ingredients, not least the (much appreciated) Cox Twins (Fred and Frank), two of the very last reminders of British music-hall. For this alone we should be thankful, but much is scuppered by a tiresome plot involving a gang of robbers masterminded by Harry King (Ronald Radd).

Most crucially, we have Ifield's theme song 'I Remember You' by Victor Schertzinger and Johnny Mercer. Hats off to Ifield and his director for not taking this seriously; indeed, everything that can be used to undermine the importance of the moment is pulled in. Ifield wrote several of the attractive numbers: 'Look Don't Touch', which found him shaving in Trafalgar Square, and 'I've Got a Hole in My Pocket' sung to a baby in a perambulator. He collaborated with Mike Conlin in writing the title song, adapted from the traditional 'Waltzing Matilda', and 'I'll Never Feel This Way Again', 'Cry Wolf', 'Lovin' on My Mind', and 'I Guess I'd Better Say Goodbye'. Also heard are Henri Salvador and William Engvick's 'Make It Soon' and Christina Macpherson and Banjo Paterson's version of 'Waltzing Matilda'.

The traditional 'Wild Rover' is enlivened with Pamela Devis's thrusting choreography, but it's 'Waltzing Matilda' that remains in the mind, beautifully exploited by Miles in the street market finale with its jostling crowd. It's a glorious tidying-up of the film's threads, reminiscent of the closing scene of *What a Crazy World* and generating a sense of communal happiness that would surely have brought a glow of contentment to John Baxter. Plans for a second Ifield film were discarded.

OCTOBER

When did a pop singer last have you rolling in the aisles? One of the fates of British pop singers was to find themselves in films that insisted on being musical comedies, i.e. films in which they were obliged to participate in comedic situations and even (unlikely as that seemed) make us laugh, but few of us have had our ribs tickled by the likes of Cliff Richard, Tommy Steele, or Billy Fury. The Richard films illustrate how potential comedy becomes unfunny when delivered by those who have not the slightest aptitude for it. The Myers–Cass scripts for Richard and his company of comedians are chock-a-block with dull dialogue, always trying to convince us that what we are seeing is modern, is youthful, is of the moment, is funny, when it is patently not so.

The films made from those scripts have an in-built unfunniness about them, a deficiency exacerbated by the fact that none of the actors create anything so interesting as character. The closer we look, the more we see that even in these pop films there are, centre screen, participants who do little more than stand about, filling the blanks in landscape with human blanks. They seem to have little purpose beyond being where they are, except in accompanying the star whose name is at the top of the film. These people are called by various names: The Shadows, The Pacemakers, and in Eternal Films's **Cuckoo Patrol**, The Dreamers. In this case, The Dreamers (Derek Quinn, Roy Crewdson, Bernie Dwyer, and, most prominently, Peter Birrell) accompany British pop's comedy relief pop singer Freddie Garrity, the domestic jack-in-the-box Peter Pan, rarely still, ever ready to leap into the air and rip off his trousers to exhibit his fondness, once expressed in song, for short shorts, a tendency already exhibited in the previous year's enjoyable holiday-camp musical *Every Day's a Holiday*. Freddie and his boys had also been a welcome feature of *What a Crazy World*.

Produced by Maurice J. Wilson and directed by Duncan Wood, *Cuckoo Patrol* describes the adventures of a Boy Scout troop managed by scoutmasters Gibbs and Wick (John Le Mesurier and Kenneth Connor). It is unlikely that Baden-Powell would have been amused. The *MFB* regretted 'A plotless and quite incredibly unfunny farce with the further embarrassment of a team of grown men [...] impersonating moronic Boy Scouts.'[29]

Scouting for boys is one thing, scouting for men quite another, but this is the dilemma for the screenplay by Les Schwarz, a writer with countless television comedy series to his credit. For those, of course, he had genuine comic performers. Here, he has Freddie and those Dreamers, most of whom amble pointlessly through the film. It is inevitable that at one point our manly scouts run into a group of nubile female scouts, a meeting that summons two of Schwarz's immortal exchanges. When the boys talk of exploring nearby woodland, one of the girls advises, 'You'd better take Marilyn then. She's pretty hot stuff in the woods at night.' 'Your girls are very clever,' Freddie tells the barking scout mistress (Peggy Ann Clifford) and, tapping his head, 'They've got it up here.' 'I know where they've got it,' she replies, 'and believe me, they're not staying here until you find it.' Arthur Mullard and Victor Maddern, indispensable as two crooks, give much-needed life to the project, but it is Garrity, unfortunately exposed at this tail-end of the British pop film, who carries the burden. He has a natural, childish charm that is sometimes compensation enough. He is endearing, and of how many British pop performers in British cinema can this be said? Sadly, we have only three numbers: a title song, 'It Wasn't Me', and 'Seems Like Things Are Turning Out Fine Again'. They are dry things compared with the friendly, zany stuff that Freddie, with or without his Dreamers, was capable of.

NOVEMBER

Having gained access to Radio London's premises and staff, it remains a mystery why Viscount Films mistakenly used it as a background to a mild crime scenario. As produced by Harry Benn, Tudor Gates's screenplay based on an idea by Harold Shampan is half drama, half pop songs; as the *MFB* explained, 'Neither element is in any way distinguished.'[30] The drama half doesn't turn out very dramatic; it is about a cashiered ex-major who steals and smuggles diamonds, blackmailing an ex-army colleague (Kenneth Cope), who happens to be the manager of a group called The Small Faces, to assist him. The police investigation moves stoically but at a snail's pace (the on-street enquiries are decidedly unprofessional), but is lightened by some comic interruptions from Patsy Rowlands. 'Not a bit like *Z Cars*, is it?' she asks, and she's right. The pop half is inoffensive and gives us an opportunity to recall some lesser figures among its stars, although The Small

Faces, the real star of the piece, cry out for better treatment from director Jeremy Summers. Nevertheless, the film (for some not immediately apparent reason called **Dateline Diamonds**) has a naïve charm.

We hear 'Small Town' by Les Reed and Barry Mason sung by Kiki Dee; 'Please Don't Kiss Me' by Rick Minas sung by the Chantelles, who were signed for the film following their debut recording success 'I Want That Boy', and appear in several scenes. They return with Keith Mansfield and Dave Gold's 'I Think of You', making way for The Small Faces performing their own 'I've Got Mine'. Their manager had high hopes of this iconic boy-band, assigning them to the film which he hoped would boost their reputation, but the release of *Dateline Diamonds* was delayed, and the record did not get into the charts. In truth, the picture did nothing to help their careers, thus missing a chance to redeem itself. It did not prevent The Small Faces from becoming one of the most iconic, and ultimately psychedelic, pop groups of the decade. The Chantelles get a reprise of 'Please Don't Kiss Me'.

American singer Mark Richardson was filmed on location at the Radio London Night Out at the Rank Ballroom in Watford singing his 'What 'Ma Gonna Do?' in front of a very youthful crowd. After The Small Faces perform their 'I Got My Baby', we have Bournemouth's ex-window-cleaner and scaffold-er Rey Anton and The Pro Form's 'First Taste of Love' sung by Anton, described by the magazine *Pop World* as 'Shortish but very muscular. A good looker whose fan club is already being swollen with fanatical enthusiasts.'[31] Indeed, the ensuing screaming carries on long after the 'dramatic' part of the film is re-introduced. Other numbers credited as performed by The Small Faces, 'It's Too Late', 'Come On Children', and 'Don't Stop What Your [*sic*] Doing', seem not to have been used (perhaps these were among the reasons for the film's delayed release) or are indistinguishable. A background score by Johnny Douglas plugs the gaps.

1966

Here was the whole of life personified by unimportant little Littlechap, enduring an unsatisfactory existence of fornication and failure before beginning to realise what kind of fool he was

Stop the World – I Want to Get Off

Stop the World – I Want to Get Off *Just Like a Woman*
Secrets of a Windmill Girl *Finders Keepers*

MARCH

In a dreary year for the British musical film, the filming of Anthony Newley and Leslie Bricusse's stage success ***Stop the World – I Want to Get Off*** probably counts as the dreariest, notwithstanding that it was assuredly the British stage musical hit of 1961; commercially, there was in that year no competitor. It was vivid with pretension, the story of one man's life in an amalgam of song, dance, and that least urgent and most unloved of theatrical forms, mime. It declared itself allegorical and of social significance, with Newley as Littlechap, a sort of cross-breed Charlie Chaplin and Norman Wisdom, the star made up to look like an escapee from *commedia dell'arte*. Here was the whole of life personified by unimportant little Littlechap, enduring an unsatisfactory existence of fornication and failure before beginning to realise what kind of fool he was.

Much of *Stop the World*'s appeal had been visual, courtesy of Sean Kenny's spectacularly ordinary set, a stark circus background with a group of female chorines doing for Littlechap what a Greek chorus had done for Euripides. The daring was that the show went back to theatrical basics while exhibiting bravery in what it set out to demonstrate. It was indeed something new in British musicals, which by 1961 were in a pretty deplorable state. The London and Broadway productions were notable successes, but Philip Saville's decision to film a stage performance destroyed the spirit of it, serving up neither fish nor fowl. We seem not to know why Newley isn't there to steer the piece into port; instead, we have his understudy and take-over Tony Tanner, a name that would have meant little to the British cinemagoer. His Evie is Millicent Martin, never associated with the stage version.

The score, representing the best of the collaborators' output (with – a rarity in British musicals – three standout numbers that have endured) included all those used in the stage production except Evie's 'Typische Deutsche': 'I Wanna Be Rich', 'Typically English', 'Lumbered', 'Gonna Build a Mountain', 'Glorious Russia', 'Meilinki Meilchick', 'Family Fugue/Nag Nag Nag', 'All-American', 'Mumbo Jumbo', 'Once in a Lifetime', 'Someone Nice Like You', 'What Kind Of Fool Am I?', and 'I Believed It All' by Al Ham, Alan Bergman, and Marilyn Bergman.

An endurance test at 100 minutes, the film had a week's airing in the West End and all but vanished. The *MFB* had it right, reporting that 'the vitality of the stage performance is quite lost in what comes over as a synthetic hotch-potch of a film' resulting in 'an awkward *mélange* of television techniques.'[1]

APRIL

By 1966 the British sexual exploitation film was fast approaching orgasm. The most virile beginnings of the British sex movie may have begun in 1958 with the supposedly informative semi-documentary *Nudist Paradise*, probably intended for those who kept their copies of the latest *Health and Efficiency* magazine hidden between the pages of *Fur and Feather*. As part of an imaginative publicity campaign, prospective patrons were promised free entry if they arrived naked at the cinema. In 1959 they had the opportunity to enjoy *Travelling Light* in which producer-director naturist Edward Craven Walker (aka Michael Keatering) ex-plained that 'many people nowadays are beginning to find that they can only keep pace with modern life by spending more of their leisure hours in natural surroundings. But those who call themselves naturists go further.'

The third British sex movie of the decade, and the first from director Arnold Louis Miller and photographer Stanley Long, was *Nudist Memories*, shot in a week and made, as they admitted, 'in complete ignorance'. Michael Winner and the Edwin J. Fancey dynasty (including Adrienne Fancey) and George Harrison Marks were others who took advantage of the new genre, while Miller and Long were among the busiest, turning out *Nudes of the World* (1961) narrated by Valerie Singleton, who in latter years denied her participation (it's on film). The following year Miller and Long produced *Take Off Your Clothes and Live*; the girls put on bikinis before dancing the Twist. Their 1964 offering *London in the Raw* ('Be shocked by the sin in the shadows!') was followed by *Primitive London*, a testosterone-inspired romp that its chronicler Simon Sheridan holds partly responsible for introducing wife-swapping to a jaded British public. The Miller–Long partnership came to its shuddering conclusion with one of their most interesting, and certainly most musical, features, **Secrets of a Windmill Girl**. It begins with an unseen Valerie Mitchell singing Sidney Filbert's lament for an age gone by as on screen we see the famous 'Fan Dance' as staged at London's Windmill Theatre:

> The Windmill Girls, they were so gay
> But now it's over, they've gone away
> Gone is the laughter, so warm and so bright

'We Never Closed', come and see us tonight
Feathers were flying as we danced the night through
Men wildly cheering, admiring the view
The Windmill Girls, lovely and gay
But now it's over, they've gone away.

Again, we are in semi-documentary territory, flashbacked from the death of fun-loving Pat Lloyd (Pauline Collins) in a reckless car crash. An unconvincing police inspector (hilariously badly acted by Derek Bond, who looks as if he wished he might be anywhere else) visits Pat's best friend and fellow Windmill Girl Linda Gray (top-billed April Wilding), who relates their story and their experiences at the theatre. Basically, we are told (and shown, graphically) how Pat goes steadily downhill, becoming, in Linda's words, 'a burnt-out husk verging on the edge of a mental breakdown'. Throughout the film, it is her misfortune to be sexually threatened by a series of seriously unappealing old geezers, including Howard Marion Crawford, who at one moment collapses on her so heavily that he obliterates her from view. In this, of course, Miller's screenplay is in danger of suggesting that the Windmill Girls were a louche bunch with mislaid morals, although what happens to Pat happens exclusively outside the theatre itself. In fact, it is an established fact, attested by the girls who over many years appeared on its stage, that the theatre was run on convent lines. Those Windmills Girls were as much postulants as scantily draped chorines. The theatre's proprietor Vivian Van Damm, and subsequently his daughter-successor Sheila Van Damm, ran the organisation along highly principled lines. Judith Bruce, who performed the Windmill's Fan Dance at the age of sixteen, was advised by her mother to look on it as an office job.

We must understand that *Secrets of a Windmill Girl* had an unusual beginning. The original idea was to produce a documentary. The footage shot at the Windmill was taken in the final weeks of 'Revudeville' before its closure in October 1964. It is this material that David McGillivray labels 'important as documentary evidence of the kind of tat that inflamed the senses of a million voyeurs during the three decades the Windmill operated non-stop revue'.[2] Those documentary elements of Miller and Long's pasted-together film exist quite separately and beyond the subsequently invented fictional scenes; it is the Windmill location that is our principal concern. We need only peel back the seedy layers of the rest to reveal a touching memorial of the little theatre, where unpretentiousness was a financial necessity. This, after all, was the theatre that boasted 'We Never Closed' during the darkest nights of war. Just as accurately, one of the girls with a lisp offered the alternative 'We Never Clothed'.

What makes this interesting to the social historian is that, although Van Damm offered so many famous British comedians their first break, it is the girls (in various stages of nudity) that fill those pages. How else would the management have sold copies of that day's programme, priced (at least for the thirty-fourth edition) five shillings, with the tantalising offer of owning their own black and white copies from the original negatives of any of the featured photographs? Despite the other, clothed, acts, the real stars at the Windmill were its famous but largely anonymous girls. They were kept busy at 'London's modern Temple of Venus' with continuous revue from 12 noon to 10.35 p.m. every day, with a complete change of programme every six or seven weeks. The heyday was probably World War II, when (so the management told us) between appearances the girls knitted for the troops. The can-can was danced at every performance, 'always arranged by a different member of the production staff to ensure that there is never any similarity in choreographic style'.[3]

It is appropriate that the dances are the real heart of the film, often straining to convey an erotic exoticism, as in the 'Corrida' and 'Borneo' routines, the music arranged and conducted by Malcolm Lockyer, with Peter Gordeno as one of the most prominent and young London choreographers of the 1960s credited with 'Special Choreography', in which he participates. Ken Roland sings and plays Carolyn Leigh and Cy Coleman's 'Witchcraft'; Dawn Maxey, or perhaps Sally Crow, performs the inevitable 'Fan Dance' (Crow was the dancer on the last night); Tony Vivian sings 'Your Business Is Love'; Ed Graham, Mark Bryant, and Elizabeth Hill perform their signature number 'We Are the Vaudeville Three'; Roland returns with a medley of Harry Barris, Ted Koehler, and Billy Moll's 'Wrap Your Troubles in Dreams', Haven Gillespie and J. Fred Coots's 'You Go to My Head', and Koehler and Harold Arlen's 'I've Got the World on a String'. It is doubtful whether the presumably almost completely male audiences took any notice of all this or of the male dancers thanklessly discharging their obligations and carrying on regardless.

Outside the theatre scenes, Rey Anton appears in a nightclub sequence performing 'Hold It Babe', backed by The Pro Form. Would anybody know the identity of the uncredited performer with his 'Stuttering Minstrel' song? Would anyone care? Perhaps not. Ultimately, it is the modest, carefully refined dance scenes that stay in the mind, and the skilful use of a tiny stage. Even Miller and Long's mistreatment cannot rob these moments of their sad magic. One of the Windmill's most celebrated choreographers, Keith Lester, requested in the last night's celebratory programme that there be 'no tears for our final curtain – let it come down tonight to end the long day of striving and glory, as it has always come down, to laughter and applause'. There is something wonderfully gallant, simple, dignified in those words. Perhaps Mr Lester was a poet as well as a dancer. *Secrets of a Windmill Girl* was Miller and Long's last film. It is unmentioned in Sheila Van Damm's affectionate autobiography *We Never Closed*.

JUNE

In a year otherwise short on charm, Dormar Films' ***Just Like a Woman*** was refreshingly welcome, even if the *MFB* was unamused: 'It's the archness of the thing that really appals.'[4] Produced by Robert Kellett at Isleworth studios, it's an appealing account of the tempestuous marriage of television director Lewis (Francis Matthews at his most relaxed and effective) and Scilla McKenzie (Wendy Craig at her scattiest). Written and directed by Robert Fuest (his directorial debut), this is a warm-hearted and witty take on an emotional relationship that we know from first frame will survive. *Films and Filming* recognised that 'Fuest is joking pointedly about a scraggy slice of modern life' in 'a film that sets out to make mock of the modish. The mock it makes, however, is often very funny, with clever colour and amusing cine-allusions.'[5]

The comedy is swift and sly, happily satirising British television's popular entertainment, with Peter Jones as the agitated BBC executive whose office is peopled by garden gnomes and who has one of the most tasteless drink cabinets imaginable. Among the splendidly written character vignettes we have Barry Fantoni as spaced-out Elijah Stark, Dennis Price's salesman, and Clive Dunn on brilliant form as a crazed Nazi architect. Fuest also makes room for a guest appearance by 'strongman' Ted Durante, one of the most enduring of 1960s variety turns, seen here without benefit of his wife and on-stage assistant Hilda, always summoned to his side by the command of 'Kraut!' Throughout, the piece is suffused with a natural warmth to which Matthews and Craig respond with total sympathy, but the casting of everyone involved (not least John Wood's performance as Scilla's discreetly gay friend, on whose shoulder she may cry) is considered. Fuest manages to move us even as Scilla walks through a field of cows to reach her Nazi-architectured home. It is a film that radiates intelligence and colour and in which music plays a modest role. Mark Murphy sings the title song and is joined by Craig in 'Let's Take a Chance', both numbers being composed by Kenny Napper with lyrics by Fuest. Unremarkable, yes, but they contribute to the light-heartedness of the enterprise.

OCTOBER

The lightness of touch that director Sidney Hayers had instilled in *Three Hats for Lisa* was lacking in Cliff Richard's follow-up to *Wonderful Life*, Inter-State Films' **Finders Keepers**, but there is little room for whimsicality in Michael Pertwee's feeble screenplay, which is based on a story by producer George H. Brown about a missing American nuclear bomb that Cliff and the always-pleased-to-meet Shadows discover when they arrive to work in Spain. The *MFB* suggested the idea was 'to say the least, a little ill-conceived', in a film that 'makes no demands on anyone involved, least of all the actors.'[6] For Robin Bean, 'the musical numbers are completely unmemorable [...] Away from the hands of Sidney Furie and Peter Yates, Cliff Richard remains definitely grounded, even in the production numbers.'[7]

The Shadows' score, performed by themselves and Richard, comprises 'Finders Keepers', 'Time Drags By', 'Washerwoman' (to accompany a scene of choreographed riverside laundering), 'La La La Song' (sung by Richard to a group of adoring children), 'My Way' (a dull moment of cabaret), 'Wonderful Life', and David Siddle and Harry Roberts's 'Paella'. Malcolm Clare struggles to provide vital choreography in musical numbers staged by Hugh Lambert. The obligatory grumpy older generation (represented by Robert Morley in *The Young Ones* and Walter Slezak in *Wonderful Life*) resurfaces as Robert Morley, with a side serving of Peggy Mount and Graham Stark. Frankly, by now The Shadows look too mature to be involved in such malarkey played out in so minor a key, and their songs are a disappointment. The all-too-obvious disparities between the Spanish locations and Pinewood's studio are unconvincing, as are the attempts at romance and comedy.

1967

By and large, critical brickbats were aimed not at Sidney's film or the performances within it, but at the musical itself

Half a Sixpence

The Mikado   *Red and Blue*
Half a Sixpence   *Two a Penny*
Smashing Time

FEBRUARY

What was it about Gilbert (W. S.) and Sullivan (A.) that held Britain in their grip from the beginning of the D'Oyly Carte Opera Company in 1879 until the company's closure in 1982? For 103 years, without pause except for a brief annual holiday, the operas of William Schwenck Gilbert and Arthur Sullivan (both became Sirs) were performed nightly (plus two matinees each week), filling forty-eight weeks of each year, in London, in the provinces, and frequently abroad. This is an unequalled achievement in theatrical history. The facts and figures and dates and locations and changes of cast and the noting of understudy replacements are painstakingly available in the extraordinarily detailed volume *Record of Productions 1875–1961*, with even more mind-boggling information in two loose-leaf supplements, respectively for 1961–66 and 1966–71.[1] This exemplary documentation is pure oxygen for the Gilbert and Sullivan geek.

In 1966, the company was still in fine fettle. *The Mikado* remained the most popular work in the repertoire (from which some of the lesser-known operas such as *Princess Ida* and *The Sorcerer* had fallen away). Much travelled and no doubt physically shabby after its tremendous journeying, Gilbert's Japanese fantasia was singled out by the management as due for refreshment: a rare decision, as many of the operas remained almost unaltered from their original productions. The new, spruced-up *Mikado* had the benefit of new décor by Disley Jones, as in his sylvan setting for Yum-Yum's 'The Sun Whose Rays' in Act II, which perfectly framed Valerie Masterson's liquid singing. In fact, Anthony Besch's new stage production in 1964 refreshed the work rather than reimagined it, and it was this version that Stuart Burge filmed for BHE Presentations' ***The Mikado***, produced by Anthony Havelock-Allan and John

Brabourne. It seems clear that Burge's intention was not to adapt Besch's production for the screen, but to film it as a 'live' performance, given 'cold', as it was re-enacted on stage at the Hippodrome, Golders Green, without benefit of an audience. It may be that, as Roberta Morrell has suggested, Besch's main contribution to the ongoing theatrical life of D'Oyly Carte's Mikado was that he was capable of creating 'a production that was a complete departure from the usual D'Oyly Carte house style'.[2]

The very idea that anything approaching realism should be introduced into the operas is questionable, but the company's on-stage movements were notoriously stuck-in-the-mud: a D'Oyly Carte performer who took a step to the left or right that was not marked in Gilbert's prompt copy could incur the management's displeasure. This abiding inflexibility was a standing joke in theatrical circles, neatly satirised by Michael Flanders and Donald Swann's 'In the D'Oyly Carte' performed in the 1948 London revue *Penny Plain* as if by a trio of tired D'Oyly Carte cast members, impersonated by Max Adrian, Rose Hill, and Diana Churchill:

All:	Why is it so admired
	This business first inspired
	By former artists long retired
	From D'Oyly Carte?
Patience:	Anything new is disallowed
All:	Turn – pace
Point:	Wait for the pause!
Yum-Yum:	Blasphemous change would shock the crowd
	Following in their scores!

Apparently, what we see in Burge's film reproduction is Savoy opera that has been partially re-dressed, as if revived by artificial respiration, at a time when the rest of the company's productions remained hidebound by established convention. We can of course take Burge's film as a completely accurate depiction of the D'Oyly Carte production of the opera that was to be recognised

> by public and connoisseurs alike, as among the best – perhaps indeed the best – of Sullivan's operettas. It is also a *tour-de-force* of Gilbert's, because the whole piece wears a kind of comic mask. Though billed as 'a Japanese opera', it does not present Japan: under the pretence of doing so it presents England.[3]

There is something about this utter Englishness that helps to explain the affectionate companionship with which the British, and amateur performers insistent on keeping the Savoy operas alive, regard these works. The on-stage antics reflect British peculiarities, prejudices, and attitudes. They are, of course,

Victorian peculiarities, prejudices, and attitudes, and remain Victorian. Until the company's demise, Gilbert's dialogue and lyrics had continued to be a balm, steady, unchanging (as pointed out by Flanders and Swann). An alarm was sounded when D'Oyly Carte's copyright on the operas expired in 1961 and the works became available to other professional companies. The company still had twenty-one years to go, 'G and S' pulsing on through the British bloodstream.

America had been a safe haven for D'Oyly Carte, perhaps persuading its inhabitants that the operas told them everything they needed to know about British life, but the *New York Times* review, headlined 'An Awkward Movie "Mikado": Copy of Staged Classic Doesn't Work Out', felt that 'the viewer gets the odd sensation that he is prompting a performance, not attending one', and that the soundtrack 'muddles the message. Those who know the transparent sound that Isidore Godfrey invariably coaxes from an orchestra will wince at the iron-string harshness of the City of Birmingham Orchestra.'[4] One might have expected a more prominent band for Malcolm Sargent to conduct, but by this time the company (and the film's producers) could not afford better. For live performances, they had long depended on Godfrey picking up itinerant players as they moved from place to place; one can only imagine some of the noises coming from the pit that the performers had to put up with each week.

They also put up with the scrimping Carte management. The company's financial stability over a century kept it afloat without a penny of public subsidy until its very last months, when the Arts Council turned its back. As money poured into the Royal Opera and other more highly regarded musical institutions, D'Oyly Carte crumpled under a blistering disregard and condemnation of its standards by the body set up to protect and support artistic endeavour. The MP Simon Hughes maintained that 'This company is the best of British and it tells us about Britain.' Mrs Thatcher was not a fan. In an unpublished report on the company's current production of *The Pirates of Penzance* the Arts Council's deputy secretary-general spoke of 'fourth rate panto stuff' with 'the worst excesses of obsessional stage symmetry I have ever seen on the professional stage; every choral gesture in clockwork motion.'[5] In fact, D'Oyly Carte had approached the Arts Council as early as 1967, aware that without financial support the company would close.

It was under this shadow that *The Mikado* was filmed. We may confidently assume that the fees paid to the players did not reach those paid to many film performers. As late as 1975, D'Oyly Carte's stern rules (for its gramophone recordings, men were expected to wear ties and suits, the women hats) seemed like leftovers from another age. Staff behaviour was conscripted, with the girls of the wardrobe department allowed to speak for only twelve minutes a day (six in the morning, one presumes, and six thereafter, or perhaps in permutations that reached the total by knock-off time). D'Oyly Carte artists were paid below Equity rates. Writing of the company's 'miserly' policies, Ian Bradley tells us that

In 1975, for example, the parts of the foreman in *Trial by Jury*, Fleta in *Iolanthe*, Go-To in *The Mikado*, and the first and second citizen in *Yeomen* attracted the paltry sum of 75 pence apiece, while those playing the four speaking ghosts in *Ruddigore* each received twenty pence for their moment of stardom, and the carpenter in *Pinafore* the princely sum of £1.25. By 1982, these payments had risen to £1.43, 44 pence and £2.20, respectively.[6]

OCTOBER

In the more than occasionally lacklustre canon of British musicals, *Half a Sixpence*, produced by Charles H. Schneer and its director George Sidney, is one of that tiny percentage that made it on film. Sidney approached it with the fervour already evident in his long list of Hollywood musicals, among them *Kiss Me Kate, Annie Get Your Gun, Show Boat, Pal Joey*, and one of the last of the Golden Age Broadway works, *Bye Bye Birdie*. Sidney was a genuine veteran of the genre, and ***Half a Sixpence***, adapted from the London stage production of 1963, marked his debut in British studios. A film version without the show's original star Tommy Steele would have been unthinkable. In the event, as Alexander Walker recalled:

> Steele's performance was charged with a robust professionalism that stood fair and square on its own two cockney feet. It was meant to possess an American energy that would commend it internationally, and a family appeal that would happily repeat the success of *The Sound of Music*. In spite of its virtues, it signally failed to achieve those aims.[7]

Based on H. G. Wells's 1905 novel *Kipps*, *Half a Sixpence*'s book was by Beverley Cross, with songs by David Heneker, whose earlier scores had been heard in musicals – among them *Expresso Bongo* and *Make Me an Offer* – that seemed to promise a new, grittier New Wave overtaking British musical theatre. Now, Dorothy Kingsley shared the credit for the film adaptation. On stage, the show's success was in no small way down to Steele's chirpy impersonation of draper assistant Arthur Kipps. On film, Cross and Heneker's play opened itself to further criticism, or faint praise as offered by *The Times*. Never mind that the film was 'a bit too long', it was 'a relief [...] to have a musical which really looks like a musical, directed by someone who obviously relishes the whole convention' and who provides 'a nice big treat for the whole family.'[8]

By and large, critical brickbats were aimed not at Sidney's film or the performances within it, but at the musical itself. We should bear in mind that in its transition to film the piece had undergone many changes, but it was the score that attracted much attention. The *New York Times* decided that 'the songs themselves, trite, gay, and thoroughly meaningless, make absolutely no concession to anything that has happened in popular music the last ten years.'[9] The *Chicago Tribune* found the numbers 'incredibly and unanimously nondescript', while Roger Ebert thought them 'ferociously standard' and went on to criticise Sidney's timing, stating that it 'tends to lag, his sight gags telegraph ahead, and his songs drag'.[10] Nevertheless, *Films and Filming* considered that 'Sidney has the ability to inject excitement into what is basically rather thin material'.[11] There was such an intense focus on Steele that others involved, including some unlikely casting, had little opportunity to shine. Julia Foster's heroine Ann had little to do except look innocent, and Cyril Ritchard brought a dash of Broadway pizzazz to the thankless role of Harry Chitterlow, but both lost numbers used in the original London production.

Items heard in the film (with London's original Ann, Marti Webb, dubbing Foster's songs) include 'All in the Cause of Economy' performed by Steele and the ensembled staff of Shelford Emporium, the title song for Steele and Foster, the set piece 'If I Had Money to Burn' with Steele and Ritchard working up what passes for a storm, and Foster's hot-blooded 'I'm Not Talking to You' and reflective 'I Know What I Am'. Steele headed the company with the kicking-up-heels 'If the Rain's Going to Fall' and with the standout 'Flash! Bang! Wallop!' Steele's mournful complaint 'She's Too Far above Me' served only to emphasise the hero's humble origins, while 'A Proper Gentleman', 'The Race Is On' (co-written by Heneker and Irwin Kostal), and 'This Is the World' didn't amount to much.

Several numbers from the 1963 West End production were unused, among them 'Long Ago' (probably the best of Heneker's bunch), Chitterlow's 'The One That's Run Away', Helen Walsingham's nostalgic 'The Oak and the Ash', and the ensemble's jaunty 'The Old Military Canal'. A major stage revival by Cameron Mackintosh and Julian Fellowes made major revisions to Heneker's original score. Their confidence in Heneker's work was hardly reflected in the fact that much of it was jettisoned in favour of seven new, patently inferior substitutes written by George Stiles and Anthony Drewe.

Ultimately, Sidney's generous, lush, and often brilliantly effective interpretation presented the piece in its Sunday best. More could not have been done to spruce things up. For many, the highlight will be that old, perhaps ageless, chestnut of a cockney knees-up, 'Flash! Bang! Wallop!' enjoyed at Kipps and Ann's wedding. For some, this raucous celebration of getting spliced sounds like something washed up from the 1930s, with a dash of George Formby and *Me and My Girl*; it is so determined in its need to cheer us up that it can only deepen our depression. It is, in fact, the sort of number the British stage musical has persisted, against critical advice, in churning out for decades. Stuff of similar sort can be found elsewhere in these pages. Listen, if you will, to Stanley Holloway and Herman's Hermits larking about in Covent Garden in *Mrs Brown You've Got a Lovely Daughter*. It's a brave British musical that doesn't make way for a good old knees-up!

'Where are all these men we're supposed not to speak to?' asks Brenda (Rita Tushingham) of her best friend Yvonne (Lynn Redgrave) when they arrive in supposedly constantly swinging London, urgently in need of Carnaby Street and determined to have a ***Smashing Time***. It's a valid question when their first experience of London male is a drunk Irishman (George A. Cooper) and a meat-cleaving café owner (Arthur Mullard). We don't need the title to tell us that the girls are out on a spree, but it isn't long before Brenda's money is stolen by a tramp. It's typical of George Melly's gently ironic screenplay that even as she discovers it's gone, the tramp is sitting behind her in the café, tucking into the lunch she has unknowingly provided.

The thrill of being in London dims. Soon enough, Brenda is plonked in a puddle (twice), and the pair are hurtled into a series of misadventures. Melly presents them obliquely, the two innocents moving dream-like through what often seems little more than a colourful travelogue of some of the back streets of London, a London fractured and begrimed two decades after the war that had so damaged it. It is to Melly's credit that the lack of any substantial plot becomes unimportant. What matters is that, in the cinema of 1967, Carlo Ponti and Roy Millichip's production *Smashing Time* defies classification.

The London scene is only for Brenda and Yvonne to observe, rather in the manner of observing wild animals at the zoo. They are birds of very different feather, both from each other and from those they bump into during the course of this charming picture. The skill of Melly and director Desmond Davis is to preserve the disconnect between the girls and the London 'influencers' they meet: the exuberantly handsome society photographer Tom Wabe (Michael York), tired but wealthy businessman-lothario Bobby Mome-Rath (Ian Carmichael), vintage clothing entrepreneur Mrs Grimble (dog-loving Irene Handl), and shop-owner Charlotte Brilling (Anna Quayle). None are given much characterisation, and throughout, the girls' association with them strikes us as fleeting; they are too extravagant and unworldly for our girls, in whose lives they are passers-by, doomed to be incidental. It is obvious, too, that for much of the playing time Melly has handed Davis a blank canvas to play with as he may. He plays, frequently creating cinematic havoc in a film that, on first showing, may strike the casual observer as resembling little more than a protracted, speeded-up Benny Hill sketch. The casual observer would be wrong, despite the ensuing custard-pie messiness of what follows.

With Davis spattering the screen and his players with vivid explosions of almost diabolic colour, slapstick becomes art form, psychedelic liquids squirting insanely from sauce bottles in Mullard's caff, and liquids of all sorts (not least bath softener and laxatives), exploited as ballistics, every now and then erupting until the mammoth custard-pie battle. Through it all, Brenda's innocence is never compromised, even when she finds herself an unwilling spectator at Yvonne's seduction by Moom-Rath, beautifully played by Carmichael when beset by hiccups.

Less innocently, we see how London itself lures Yvonne, sexually and commercially ambitious, into becoming an up-to-the-moment celebrity. It is, alas, a state for which Yvonne has had no training or talent, but Melly promotes her career as the ever-plangent Brenda, whom London will not alter, looks on. She has long ago accepted that Yvonne is a different sort of person; as she sings, 'She knows all the ploys, How to get the boys.' In her desperation for publicity, Yvonne crashes into absurdity in a dress parade of increasing ugliness and tastelessness, and makes a pop record. Incidental satirical touches include a take-off of BBC Television's *Juke Box Jury*, and Peter Jones and Amy Dalby in a wonderfully funny *Candid Camera* on-screen confrontation.

At first hearing, John Addison's score, apart from its jolly, promising title song, seems pretty insignificant, but as a musical accompaniment to what Melly and Davis have created, it may be pitch-perfect, never attempting to be a full-bodied musical, but serving as addenda and flavourings dotted throughout, appearing and vanishing as speedily as those liquid interruptions. Tushingham and Redgrave share the numbers, which include 'Carnaby Street', 'Waiting for My Friend', 'New Clothes', 'Trouble', 'It's Always Your Fault', 'While I'm Still Young', 'Day Out', 'The Morning After', 'Baby Don't Go', and 'Swinging thru' London'.

The *MFB* was unamused, complaining that 'the glossy vulgarity of *Smashing Time* becomes as irritating as the brash musical score and the discordant colours that constantly fill the screen',[12] but for *Films and Filming* it was 'undemanding and vastly entertaining [...] Davis lets the comedy play for itself, his great strength being in the way he lets his actors develop an individual character based largely on exploiting their own personalities.'[13] Roger Ebert's verdict seems pretty accurate: 'Although the attempt to cover swinging London quickly becomes tiresome, there are several scenes so funny that they redeem the movie.'[14] We can, however, hardly deny that Tushingham and Redgrave make a delightful team, throwing themselves into every predicament.

DECEMBER

Surely Andrew Martin slightly overstates the significance of **Red and Blue** by suggesting that 'If you can't get into this film at the level of what it's trying to be, just give up on musicals, because as well as the classical musicals and the Broadway musicals, this is a marvellous example of what you can do in a slightly more experimental form of the musical.'[15] Is it? Moreover, 'It's a musical that responds to the very sixties question of how do you make a modern musical that takes into account the French New Wave, the different revolutions in music and cinema and so on.'[16]

How are we to compare director Tony Richardson and Julian More's elliptical mini-musical (thirty-five minutes) with the atmosphere conjured by 'Le Tourbillon de la Vie' sung by Serge Rezvani (alias *Red and Blue*'s composer

Cyrus Bassiak) to Jeanne Moreau in the 1962 *Jules et Jim*? There is something, however fragile, memorable in that moment, that somehow eludes *Red and Blue*. Corseted in its half-hour span, how does it compare to other mini-musicals of our period? What did the little-known Jacques de Lane Lea think of Richardson's trinket? Lea deserves to be remembered for his 1956 short *Five Guineas a Week*, a work that shuns the modish and pretentiously significant. Made in a swimming pool, *Five Guineas a Week* deserves recognition not only as Britain's first mini-musical to be made widescreen and in colour. Lea would return in 1968 with another mini-musical, *Les Bicyclettes de Belsize*, a delightful fragment that eclipsed *Red and Blue* on every count, being completely accessible and boasting a vastly better, sometimes brilliant, score while suggesting itself as a cousin to the yet incomparable *Les Parapluies de Cherbourg* with its Michel Legrand score directed by Jacques Demy. The profundity of that film's tragedy finds no equivalent in *Red and Blue* in a work that generally shuns delight.

Although Richardson's film was registered as a separate item, it was conceived as one-third of the portmanteau trilogy *Red White and Zero*, which also included Peter Brook's *The Ride of the Valkyrie* and Shelagh Delaney's diverting *The White Bus*, directed by Lindsay Anderson. Most of the songs used in *Red and Blue* had already been recorded by Moreau, who had been Richardson's, and probably Bassiak's, first choice for the Parisian chanteuse Jacky as she moves from one lover to another, but the role went to Vanessa Redgrave.

The English translation of the original French lyrics was by the Francophile Julian More, a prominent contributor to British stage musicals of the 1950s; one of his composing colleagues from that period, Monty Norman, is credited as music consultant. Bassiak's songs, both in their music and in More's translated lyrics, have a lightness and elusiveness that provide a quiet atmosphere to the proceedings without becoming memorable or really establishing a style of their own, and Redgrave, no matter how skilful at suggesting the play's essential tragedy (full-stopped when she blanks one of her old lovers at a deserted airport), never quite shakes off a sort of British schoolmistress manner, although she is bohemian enough to smoke in bed. This heroine is a cross between Miss Jean Brodie and (itself a product of More and Norman) Irma la Douce.

Jacky's romantic retrospective weaves in and out of time as the men she has known appear and, one by one, fade away; circus boy Michael York, songwriter Gary Raymond, trumpeter William Sylvester, elderly millionaire Douglas Fairbanks Junior; thankfully she shakes off the crude suggestiveness of the businessman on the train (John Bird). The various episodes are imaginatively lit in cinematographer Billy Williams's wheels of incandescent colour.

Despite their various qualities and originality, neither Holly Productions and Woodfall Film productions' *Red White and Zero* nor its musical component, *Red and Blue*, drew much attention, and they were withdrawn after a brief London showing. While it was insubstantial enough for its editor

Kevin Brownlow to describe *Red and Blue* as a 'popcorn movie', there were at least kindly words in *Films and Filming*'s acknowledgement that it was 'gently melancholic by design, about a nightclub singer lamenting the transitory nature of life and love', and 'no inconsiderable part of the Richardson oeuvre'.[17]

Our Cliff as a no-good untrustworthy son, stealing from his mum, running drugs, demanding pre-marital sex? It beggars belief but for World Wide Pictures' **Two a Penny** with its publicity-campaign enthusiasm that '*Two a Penny* is a feeling!', 'a decidedly different story of love'. Gone is the Cliff we grew older with in *The Young Ones*, *Summer Holiday*, and *Wonderful Life*, when we knew that whatever character he pretended to be was Cliff by any other name, but Stella Linden and an uncredited David Winters have provided him with a dramatic turning point, in its way one of the most distinctive British musical films of the decade in which, crucially, there are no Shadows of the past, no opportunity for a Una Stubbs or Teddy Green or Richard O'Sullivan. Following on from *Two a Penny*, its director James F. Collier went on to direct the American *For Pete's Sake*, which has been called a 'classic dollop of Christploitation', a 'soapy melodrama with a leaden infomercial about Billy Graham's nearly magical power'.[18] As much might be said of *Two a Penny*.

It was around the time of *Wonderful Life* that Cliff Richard pronounced his Christian belief, which was publicly expressed in his association with America's greatest evangelist, and subsequently in the Festival of Light movement, which campaigned against Britain becoming a permissive society. In this, Richard worked alongside that redoubtable enemy of the BBC, Mary Whitehouse, and Lord Longford, Dora Bryan, and one of the country's most vocal intellectuals, Malcolm Muggeridge. By 1966 Richard had spoken publicly at one of Graham's massive London rallies, and now *Two a Penny* was set against the background and in the shade of Graham's 'Greater London Crusade', with its 2,000-voice choir and its nightly exhortation for sinners to turn to Jesus. Once inside the Crusade, any subtlety in Linden's screenplay goes to the wall, so clumsy and obviously out of synch is this documentary material with its fictional embellishments.

Beyond the Crusade, there is much to appreciate, not least how well Richard's performance as the film's anti-hero and anti-Christian art student Jamie Hopkins works. Linden has created a milieu that has nothing in common with the wholesome inventions of Myers and Cass. Richard benefits hugely from his three leading ladies. As Jamie's ingénue girlfriend, Ann Holloway treads a fine line between virginal sweetness and God-awakening awareness, imbuing Carol with pitch-perfect conviction. As Jamie's tired and disappointed mother, Dora Bryan gives another motherly performance to be remembered alongside her work in *A Taste of Honey*. Bryan's underplayed, quietly truthful characterisation is in sharp contrast to the often-under-rated Avril Angers as Carol's ex-ENSA landlady Mrs Burry. Angers gives a brilliant portrait of a clapped-out, seedy, ageing variety artiste with an eye to bedding Jamie. Reminiscing about her wartime stage career, she is at her most sexually suggestive when he makes to leave: 'I was going to show you me medal,' she tells him. 'You're just a frightened little boy, the sort that rings doorbells and runs away.' 'Yes, well,' replies Jamie, 'ding-a-ding.'

Jamie's on-off relationship with Carol is seriously fractured when, in search of a better life, she attends Graham's Crusade. Among the countless imponderables, Graham gives voice to the questions that may be nagging at his audience: 'Where did I come from?', 'Why am I here?' Although a seriously doubting Thomas, Jamie manages to get a front-row seat to observe Graham delivering an impassioned sermon that invites sinners to confess their needs. Jamie is unimpressed by what he hears, resisting Graham's promise of 'religious inoculation' ('He's flogging a dead horse').

Refreshed by what she has heard, Carol steps forward into Christianity, having been physically locked out of a church, and turned out of a service because the congregation did not reach a stipulated quorum. Feeling down and almost out in London, she even struggles to say the Lord's Prayer: 'I feel as if I've been battering on the door of the church for days.' When Jamie accompanies her to the National Gallery, she quotes Jesus and asks, 'How near is God?' Jamie replies, 'You go on about him as if he was Harold Wilson or something!'

It's an unhappy situation that Linden makes no attempt to resolve. We might have expected that by the last reel Jamie would find God and be reunited with Carol, but he turns out to be a hopeless case, leaving the film to fizzle out with his mum finally admitting her total disillusion with her wayward son. In this, *Two a Penny* is altogether puzzling. The integrity of much of Collier's direction (notably in the scenes with Bryan and Angers) is seriously marred by the documentary sequences from Graham's Crusade. As if to dampen the vigorous evangelism of Graham's preaching, Jamie's persistent pejorative comments about Graham's beliefs are unconvincing because we suspect that Richard would never endorse them. Linden seems to use Jamie (and Richard) to deflect Graham's message, in a film that reached the screen only because Graham's organisation financed it. As it is, *Two a Penny* cuts off without warning: we are no more hopeful of Jamie's conversion than when we came in.

Songs are sparingly used. When, in a smoky London pub full of elderly locals, Richard jumps up to deliver a stomping impromptu version of 'Twist and Shout', two old ladies agree that 'No one sings the old songs any more.' Richard wrote the title song, and – co-writing the lyrics with Collier - the attractive 'Love You Forever Today' and 'Questions'.

1968

The straightforwardness of what had happened on stage was to some extent sacrificed to elephantine magnification

Oliver!

Oliver!
A Little of What You Fancy
Chitty Chitty Bang Bang

Mrs Brown You've Got a Lovely
  Daughter
Les Bicyclettes de Belsize
Popdown

APRIL

Lionel Bart's stage musical *Oliver!* was in rehearsal on 28 June 1960, two days before its opening night. The show's choreographer Malcolm Clare had just departed because his routines had been altered, his place taken by Eleanor Fazan, who was mostly associated with the fast-moving, ever-fluent staging of intimate revues. It was probably reckoned that Fazan's use of movement rather than dance was what was needed to preserve the integrity of the production. Ron Moody, himself a refugee from intimate revue and now cast as Charles Dickens's arch-villain Fagin, agreed 'with the result that no conventional choreography has been used at all – it is the flow of groups on the mobile set [designed by Sean Kenny] that Peter [Coe] has aimed at'.[1] Kenny's skeletal, flexible set itself marked a sea-change in the physical presentation of musicals in the 1960s, an attempt to shift the British musical's attitude to conventional choreographed sequences. Their removal emphasised the fact that Bart's show was essentially a modest affair, its songs in the clear light of day uncomplicated and accompanied by a small orchestral ensemble. Transferred to the screen, Bart's homage to Dickens frequently exploded into what we might regard as artificial dance. The straightforwardness of what had happened on stage was to some extent sacrificed to elephantine magnification, but there is much to be grateful for in the filmed *Oliver!* produced by John Woolf, adapted by Vernon Harris from Bart's original stage adaptation, and directed by Carol Reed. George Perry, describing Reed's 'lively image of early Victorian London', reminds us that 'The film was greeted more enthusiastically in the United States than in Britain, but Ron Moody's gaunt Fagin was favourably compared with Alec Guinness's in the David Lean version of twenty years earlier'.[2] Moody retains his very special place in the history of both the stage and screen versions. His revealing autobiography barely mentions the film, but throws a sharp light on the piece itself and thus the film, supported by extracts from the diaries that he maintained at the time.

Dickens's Fagin, after all, is at the centre of things, and Moody's long struggle to 'find' the character was complicated by the various professional difficulties he encountered with Bart, with the impresario Donald Albery, with the director Peter Coe, with the show's company manager, and, enduringly, with the original stage Nancy, Georgia Brown, involving Moody in what seems to have been – at least on his part – an obsession of professional mistrust. From the start, Moody had noticed a dumbing-down in Bart's treatment of Dickens's dialogue, noting that Fagin's 'I hope I shall have the honour of your intimate acquaintance' was rewritten by Bart as 'How d'ya do?' Moody insisted that he had 'ad-libbed, protected and sustained Dickens all through rehearsal, all through performance, and seven years later, all through the film ... and nobody ever noticed!'[3]

A book could be written about Moody and Fagin – a joint biography that would illuminate our understandings of Dickens via both, and via Bart and Reed. Alec Guinness's reconstitution of Fagin in David Lean's 1948 *Oliver Twist* had principally been the conception of an actor, whereas Moody's was nuanced through the medium of revue in which he had established his reputation. It was from this long-neglected segment of British theatre that Vivienne Martin emerged. Moody acknowledges that this actress of power and integrity, herself nurtured in intimate revue, was important in helping him evolve his performance. It seems inevitable that we should see in his Fagin the techniques and skills learned and practised in revue. It is in this way that the chasm of difference between Guinness and Moody manifests itself.

Time Out's Stephen Gilbert remarked that 'Reed is craftsman enough to make an efficient family entertainment of Lionel Bart's musical, but not artist enough to put back any of Dickens' teeth which Bart had so assiduously drawn.'[4] Of course, it had never been Lean's or Guinness's intention to provide 'an efficient family entertainment'; it was, if we may borrow the title of one of those revues of which Moody was an expert exponent, 'for adults only'. Critic Jan Dawson was one of those who recognised what the film was about: although it was 'obviously intended to become everybody's favourite Christmas outing, there is a heightened discrepancy between the romping jollity with which everyone goes about his business and the actual business being gone about'.[5]

Dickens spent much of his book portraying the dark underbelly of Victorian lowlife. In comparison to the usually trite social issues mentioned in British musical films, *Oliver!* is spoilt for choice. We have murder (Sikes of Nancy), robbery with highly likely GBH (Sikes), child exploitation by sundry individuals including the Beadle and the Sowerberrys, domestic abuse (Sikes of Nancy), prostitution (unspecified but surely involving Nancy), malfeasance in public office (Beadle and Widow Corney), corruption in public office (the selling of boys by the Beadle), and most prominently Fagin's highly dubious association and living arrangements with his gang of ill-educated under-fed minors. It is an organisation that today would merit a visit from Social Services. How we balance this against Moody's perhaps off-the-cuff remark that he saw Fagin as 'a crazy old Father Christmas gone wrong'[6] is for us to decide. The *New York Times* recognised Moody's characterisation as played 'in a London music-hall style, which is very well if you insist on turning Fagin into an only slightly bent scoutmaster.'[7] Elsewhere, Reed's readjustment of Dickens and Bart's melodrama was much appreciated in 'a prancing musical film which by reason of its stagecraft and performance is more exhilarating than it was on stage, better rounded in its "free" adaptation.'[8]

Many appreciated the policy of all-star casting throughout the roles, although nothing much is gained by Harry Secombe's Beadle or the incomparable Hylda Baker's Mrs Sowerberry; indeed, our appreciation of Dickens's cast list may thus be less effective, but all are efficient. Perhaps (how can we know?) Moody's professional ups and mostly downs with his original stage Nancy in London and New York spoiled her chances of being cast for the film, but Shani Walli's Nancy never quite touches the tragedy. In the time-honoured manner of such things, none of the subsequent London Nancys (Judith Bruce, who had also played the role on Broadway, Vivienne Martin, and Nicolette Roeg – each of them big-voiced troupers who might have filled the role more effectively) were considered for the film. As was often the way of film versions of theatre musicals, several character songs that effectively painted detail into Bart's canvas on stage were dropped: the Beadle and Widow Corney's 'I Shall Scream', Sowerberry's undertaker's anthem 'That's Your Funeral', and Sikes's autobiographical threat 'My Name'.

A minor footnote to the genesis of *Oliver!* might be the recollection that as recently as 1966 Moody had announced his retirement from the stage when *Joey Joey*, the musical about Joseph Grimaldi that he had spent years writing and in which he played the great Regency clown, was served with its closing notice at the end of its first week in the West End. It was a major blow to his career, although by Christmas 1966 he was back playing Captain Hook in *Peter Pan*. Only a little way off, *Oliver!* was to ensure his place in British musical film history.

MAY

The shadow of the film-fanatical Fancey family hangs heavily over Border Film Productions' *A Little of What You Fancy*, 'produced' (i.e. cobbled together) by Ray Donn, Denis Martin (*éminence grise* of the Players' Theatre), and the no doubt dominating Olive Negus-Fancey. For a documentary, Ray Mackender's script works well enough, although it is most likely than Mackender had to fit it around the segments of film that were presented to him. Direction is credited to Robert Webb and Michael Winner, but the sense that anything happening to be close at hand has been stirred into the mix is inescapable. Nevertheless, this is an attempt to demonstrate (to a mass audience that by now was fast forgetting it) what British music-hall had once been all about, and the sad state it had fallen into by the end of the 1960s.

The past is evoked with copious extracts from acoustic recordings made by long-dead performers, and the posters and sheet music covers on which they were proclaimed. For some reason, we see and hear Helen Shapiro addressing 'The Boy in the Gallery' (once Nellie Power's signature song, later stolen by Marie Lloyd) on stage at Wilton's long disused Music Hall. For some other reason, we have Mark Eden handsomely turned out in the latest trendy gear and strolling through Carnaby Street, as an unseen Stanley Holloway chips in with 'Let's All Go Down the Strand', while the strains of 'Percy from Pimlico' remind us of earlier dandies.

Before long, we are in Villiers Street's Players' Theatre, once one of the most civilised of London's nightspots, with a programme of supposedly 'authentic' music-hall introduced by chairman Barry Cryer, encouraging his audience to join in one of the Players' anthems 'Oh! The Fairies'. Sheila Bernette, the Players' diminutive juvenile comedienne, asks 'Why Do They Always Pick on Me?' Just around the corner in Trafalgar Square, a tramp (the perfectly appropriate Sidney Bromley) shuffles into view as the still unseen Holloway explains why 'I Live in Trafalgar Square', but soon we are diverted to a chilly, cheerless Quaker social centre where elderly locals have been corralled to be forcibly entertained. It's a depressing occasion, with drag act Barri Chatt and Terri Gardner valiantly trying to whip up some enthusiasm, and soprano Irene Frederick giving an account of 'When I Take My Morning Promenade', bravely accompanied by Betty Bray and her musicians. The artistes are clearly doing charitable work, but the pointlessness of music-hall existing beyond its natural lifespan is all too obvious.

However, Messrs Mackender, Winner, and Negus-Fancey are by no means done with it, taking us to the sort of public houses that were the original breeding grounds for music-hall. Terri Day's belting-out of the autobiograph- ically relevant 'All the World Loves a Fat Girl' is followed by her cover version of Sophie Tucker's 'Some of These Days'. We can glimpse how music-hall, born of such drinking taverns, has in some ways gone back to its roots, if not gone to the dogs.

Moving on, we are reminded that posh London hotels often included a staged cabaret with performers flitting nervously around the tables as audiences, no doubt stunned into embarrassment, stared into their swiftly cooling soup. Here is another lost art. The performer is John Gordon, a very pleasant young man, accompanied by a little troupe of pretty girl dancers who are dangerously getting through a routine with twirling umbrellas as they dispense a medley of 'Tell Me, Pretty Maiden', 'While Strolling in the Park', and 'Put On Your Ta-Ta Little Girlie'.

The film's finale sends us back to the Players for one of its much-admired finale medley of songs once sung by Harry Champion, here performed by John Rutland. This is quintessentially Players' Theatre. The final credits incorrectly name Julia Sutton as one of Rutland's supporting artists; it is in fact the Players' choreographer Doreen Hermitage. It is a decent end to a film that speaks of the sort of magpie thievery on which Border Film Productions made its reputation. Its attempt to exhibit the entertainments that music-hall has given birth to is an impossible objective. When music-hall removed itself from the social conditions that spawned it, it could never be the same again; its reason no longer existed. Even today, the very reference to music-hall presents as charred remains of what once, naturally, was.

OCTOBER

As we move into the final phase of activity in the British musical film as it segued into the 1970s, we pause to look back at how the genre has shifted. As the Duke of Devonshire explains to his troops in Gilbert and Sullivan's *Patience*, 'Toffee in moderation is a capital thing. But to live on toffee – toffee for breakfast, toffee for dinner, toffee for tea – to have it supposed that you care for nothing *but* toffee [...] how would you like *that*?' The *MFB* seemed to make no concessions for the fact that this was essentially a film for children; it was 'more sickening than sweetening' and 'likely to upset the most settled of stomachs'.[9] Producer Albert R. Broccoli and those responsible for United Artists' musical adaptation of Ian Fleming's fantasy **Chitty Chitty Bang Bang** stretched it to an extreme 146 minutes; Disney's 1964 *Mary Poppins* had called it a day at 139. Co-written by Roald Dahl and director Ken Hughes, with spectacular settings and scenic effects by Rowland Emett and Ken Adam, the film retained the composers of *Mary Poppins* Richard M. and Robert B. Sherman, and *Poppins*'s chimney-sweeper Dick Van Dyke, in an otherwise mainly British cast that included Sally Ann Howes in her only musical film as Truly Scrumptious, Anna Quayle, Barbara Windsor, Lionel Jeffries, and a cast of British dependables that included Robert Helpmann as the Child Catcher. *Time* called it 'a picture for the ages – the ages between five and twelve'.[10] It was warmly welcomed in the *New York Times*' assurance that 'none of the audience's terrific eagerness to have a good time is betrayed or lost'.[11] Sherman's score included 'You Two', 'Toot Sweets', 'Hushabye Mountain', 'Me' Ol Bamboo', 'Chitty Chitty Bang Bang', 'Truly Scrumptious', 'Lovely Lonely Man', 'Posh!', 'The Roses Of Success', 'Chu-Chi Face', and 'Doll on a Music Box'.

It was almost time for game over for the British pop musical film when Ivorygate's **Mrs Brown You've Got a Lovely Daughter** reached the screen, seemingly unaware that *A Hard Day's Night* and *Help!* had long before put a stake through the heart of such trifles. In fact, Peter Noone (the Herman of Herman's Hermits) had already had a sizeable hit with the 1966 American film *Hold On!* Thankfully, *Mrs Brown* has a score that oozes charm and boasts one of the most magical songs of the sixties (Geoff Stephens and Les Reed's 'There's a Kind of Hush'), dollops of consoling sentimentality, and a dash of music-hall. Trevor Peacock's title song is a winner of a number reminding us of a composer-actor and prominent lyricist of his period, and we could not wish for a more sympathetic rendering.

Whiffs of skiffle and music-hall inhabit Lonnie Donegan, Leslie Bricusse (writing as Beverly Thorn), and Peter Buchanan's 'My Old Man's a Dustman' and the Hermits' 'Daisy Chain', with Nat Jackley and Margery Manners, two of the last standing old-timers from the halls, in attendance. Harry Champion's spirit is evoked for Holloway and the Hermits dancing (well, it's something close to dancing) through Covent Garden to the rhythms of Graham Gouldman's music-hall pastiche 'Lemon and Lime'. Gouldman also contributes 'Ooh, She's Done It Again' and 'It's Nice to Be Out in the Morning'; Kenny Young contributes 'The Most Beautiful Thing in My Life' alongside Geoff Stephens's 'Holiday Inn'.

The other main delight in Peacock and Norman Thaddeus Vane's lively screenplay, directed by Saul Swimmer, is the old codgers' contingent, which is much more welcome here than those found in earlier British pop films. We should be eternally grateful for the gorgeous few moments when Marjorie Rhodes (an actress deserving of every award; if in doubt, watch her playing John Mills's disappointed wife in *The Family Way* to see what acting can be about), Stanley Holloway, and Mona Washbourne unite with youngster Sheila White in Gouldman's 'The World Is for the Young'. It is at this point, perhaps, that we should be content to close the book on the history of the British pop musical. In its way, while never pretending to be a significant film, it catches a depth of feeling that is almost completely absent from the rest of the canon. This makes it even more regrettable that *Films and Filming* concluded that Herman, his Hermits, and his film were at the fag end of films of its type: 'watching the last death throes of a cycle is a sad and embarrassing pastime'.[12]

NOVEMBER

By 1968, Jacques de Lane Lea had enjoyed a long history of producing short films, little remembered today, many of them centred on female imagery. His 1951 51-minute *No Love from Judy* was a comedy about a model on the Riviera. Three years later he wrote and produced a documentary about mannequins, *Model Girl*, directed by his father William de Lane Lea. In 1956, Jacques de Lane Lea created one of the least-known musical films of the decade, *Five Guineas a Week*, a work quite unlike anything that was coming out of British studios.

In 1962, he produced *Four Hits and a Mister*, a fourteen-minute showcase for Acker Bilk and His Band, directed by Douglas Hickox, who again collaborated with Lea on the quirky *It's All Over Town*, made in two weeks and worked up from two small typewritten pages, and the blatantly pop music festival of the 1964 *Just for You*.

Directed by Hickox, **Les Bicyclettes de Belsize** can lay claim to being a direct descendant of these minor productions, and undoubtedly the greater achievement. In its modest, quiet way it is unique. Its title, and its dialogue-free, through-composed score may attract comparison with the 1964 *Les Parapluies de Cherbourg*. It must be said that the French film is on a much higher level of composition and execution than anything Lea or Hickox could manage. Their film lacks profundity, but it does not seek to portray it, and the tragedy that haunts the viewer after watching the deeply moving final scene at Cherbourg's snowy garage remains, for many, an image to last the years. The *MFB's* miserable response to *Les Bicyclettes* was that this 'poor substitute for the umbrellas of Cherbourg' was 'a mawkish attempt to create a musical mood piece that emerges as an over-all commercial for N.W.3'.[13]

Written by Michael Newling from Bernie Cooper and Francis Megahy's original story, the film could not have a less complex concept. Everything combines: Les Reed and Barry Mason's memorable score, with its once-heard-never-forgotten title song, 'Free As the Air', and the haunting 'Julie', all sung by the unseen Johnny Worthy, and 'All I Need Is Love' sung by the unseen Jane Marlow; the photography of Wolfgang Suschitzky as it tracks Steve (an iconic representation of 1960s gentlemanly masculinity) around Highgate Village on his colour-coordinated Raleigh; the chance meeting of Steve and the little girl (Leslie Goddard); the raspberry-blowing bad behaviour of a bus queue. But it is Steve's obsession with the giant image of Julie (made real in Judy Huxtable) that drives him and the film on, fulfilling what is probably a minor masterpiece, secure among the abundance of dross that surrounds it.

DECEMBER

Now considered lost, Fremar's musical sci-fi fantasy **Popdown** was American Fred Marshall's responsibility as producer, writer, and director. Apparently bereft of dialogue, it used an earthly visit from two aliens on a mission to understand what music teenagers in swinging London were listening to. Aries (Jane Bates) and Sagittarius (Zoot Money) are the pegs on which to hang what is basically a celebration of mod culture as represented by performers signed up to Marmalade Records. The encounter involves several individuals and groups that have thus achieved immortality, including The Blossom Toes (Jim Cregan, Brian Godding, and Brian Belshaw), Dantalian's Chariot (Colin Allen, Pat Donaldson), black singer Brenton Wood, guitarist Luiz Bonfá, the Hetty Schneider Quartet, Julie Driscoll, the Brian Auger Trinity, Treasure Chest, Don

Partridge, Tony Hicks, and Kevin and Gary. Diane Keen appeared as Miss 1970 (the year when the film was first seen). The *MFB* saw the film as 'fragmentary and undisciplined pop-culture collage, intermittently lively but consistently over-indulgent'.[14] Originally ninety-eight minutes, it seems to have resurfaced in various shortened versions, including the 25-minute *Musicorama-Popdown*.

Entirely made on location in and around London, the film has a cast list that includes illusionist Ali Bongo as a magic waiter, street dancer Jumping Jack Norris, a trick cyclist, limbo dancers, and 'a nude on a camel'. A major regret is that the absence of any print of *Popdown* denies us the opportunity to see the street singer Meg Aikman. This remarkable woman (a treasured memory for those of us who remember her singing around Leicester Square and to queuing theatregoers outside West End theatres of the 1960s and 1970s) deserves her place in folk history. Her repertoire may have been limited (for some the highlight was her moving rendition of 'Danny Boy'), but John Schlesinger's *Darling* (1965) finds her singing 'Santa Lucia' in Piccadilly Circus. It is heart-warming to know that in 1974 the London Tourist Board officially crowned this valiant lady as 'Queen of the Buskers'.

1969

Can Heironymus Merkin Ever Forget   *Oh! What a Lovely War*
Mercy Humppe and Find True Happiness?   *Goodbye Mr Chips*
What's Good for the Goose

JANUARY

Almost certainly worthy of an award for the most unmemorable title of any British musical film since the beginning of sound, *Can Heironymus Merkin Ever Forget Mercy Humppe and Find True Happiness?* is nevertheless one of the most interesting and daring. Whatever its qualities or lack of them, it cannot be criticised for its lack of originality if considered as a British musical film, but how original is it as a work *per se*? Not very. Newley's theatrical apprenticeship involved his participation in John Cranko's somewhat surrealist entertainment *Cranks* (1955), which experimented with varying degrees of success with the genre of intimate revue. An art form that has been more or less dormant since the 1960s, Cranko's distinctive material must have had its effect on Newley's development as writer and performer. Introspection featured largely in *Cranks*, and has been no inconsiderable part of Newley's subsequent work. In partnership with Leslie Bricusse, his excursions into musical theatre thrived on it. Not only was Newley the writer and sole male performer of their 1961 stage musical *Stop the World – I Want to Get Off*, he seemed to throw the mirror of life back on himself throughout it. This was musical self-flagellation at its most intense. This autobiographical formula was used again for the next on-stage Newley-Bricusse stage musical, *The Roar of the Greasepaint – The Smell of the Crowd* and subsequently for *The Good Old Bad Old Days*. It is not accidental that the central figure of each of these was in effect Newley himself, a self-obsession that continued in, and was magnified by, the adventures of Mr Merkin in the complex and sometimes baffling screenplay by Newley and Herman Raucher.

Critics threw bouquets and brickbats. In the *New York Times* Vincent Canby reported that in this debut 'as an all-purpose movie man he so over extends and overexposes himself that the movie comes to look like an act of professional suicide ... as self-indulgent as a burp'.[1] For Roger Ebert 'the film is critic-proof [...] The result may be more of a juggling feat than a directorial triumph, but it's a good act while it's on stage.'[2] The songs by Newley and lyricist Herbert Kretzmer are generally here and soon gone, but effective enough in their context, their purpose being to promote the star's aggrandisement and sexual adventures. Bruce Forsyth reminds us, with the brilliance of his show-stopping 'On the Boards', why so much of his career was wasted on the trite. It reinforces our suspicion that Merkin (and therefore Newley) is more interested in the cult of celebrity than in the doings of mankind. Taking his argument from Shakespeare, our hero sings 'If All the World's a Stage', and it is a stage that, no matter the fact that we are watching film, he never leaves. Underpinning his ambition to succeed in showbusiness, he reaches his emotional apogee in assuring himself that 'I'm All That I Need – I've Got Me, I've Got Rainbows'.

Maybe, but we also get evidence of what Merkin will become when he does a blatant impersonation of Frankie Vaughan, of whom in some ways Newley was to become a pastiche, where singing turned into the braying that divided many of Newley's admirers. Never mind: as Merkin tells us, 'I'd rather starve in make-up than wake up as a clerk'. He is accompanied by Joan Collins adding to the personal verisimilitude of the screenplay and singing 'Chalk and Cheese', while American veterans George Jessel as the god-like Presence, Stubby Kaye as the Writer, and Milton Berle as Good Time Eddie Filth comment on Merkin's efforts with portentous intent.

Richard Combs has suggested that 'There is no temptation to worry any deeper about the various turns that are shuffled on and off stage. If they carry any further meaning for such subjects as the problems of identity or the difficulties of reality and representation, it exists only on the most general and quip-providing level.' In fact, everything here is reduced to 'the same snappy pieces of vaudeville philosophy'.[3] Mr Merkin's persistent search for 'the perfect child lover' (the aforementioned Mercy Humppe) may seem less acceptable to modern audiences than it did in 1969, but, as one of the journalists recording Merkin's life observes, this is 'self-glorification of a masturbatory level'. Here, Merkin finds that child lover idly enjoying the innocence of a fairground carousel, which he celebrates by singing 'Sweet Love Child'. It is obviously only a matter of time before he ensures that the ceremony of innocence is drowned. The treatment of child death further distances Newley's concoction from its filmic cousins.

FEBRUARY

Norman Wisdom's long association with Rank ruptured in 1966 with *Press for Time*, but a sort of renaissance beckoned with the American *The Night They Raided Minsky's* (1968). Back in Britain, his next project was to play staid assistant bank manager Timothy Bartlett in Tigon's **What's Good for the Goose**. Despatched to a business conference in Stockport, Bartlett is unaware that his very own mid-life crisis, away from his hair-in-curlers wife Margaret (badly cast Sally Bazeley), is about to explode. En route, he picks up Nikki (Sally Geeson) and friend. As he drives, he shares a sandwich with Nikki as she slowly begins to undress him. These gruesome developments are a warning of equally unedifying spectacles to come. Soon, Bartlett is descending into the Screaming Apple discotheque, where he dad-dances to the music of The Pretty Things with young women considered by the film-makers to represent dolly birds. Although still in business garb, he begins his *dégringolade* into a psyche-delic world of flowered shirts and raucous music (he has preferred Sibelius, but is now moved by The Pretty Things) and wild dancing that whips him into a frenzy (i.e. the sort of falling down and hysterical antics that we recognise from so many earlier, more sedate Wisdom comedies).

Before our very eyes, his maddened romping has transmogrified our star from his loved-by-millions little gump into a flower-powered geriatric hippy, although by the film's close he returns home, a little chastened but better informed. He sings Reg Tilsley and Howard Blaikley's title song (first heard at the film's beginning sung by an uncredited performer). The Pretty Things perform their own compositions 'Blow Your Mind', 'Alexandra', 'Never Be Me', and 'Eagle's Sun'. The credits name Menahem Golan as responsible for 'direction, story and screenplay', Wisdom for 'script', and Christopher Gilmore for 'dialogue', carefully distributing any blame. The *MFB* was having none of it, labelling it 'grotesque beyond belief [...] a catalogue of disaster [...] a strong candidate for the worst British comedy for some considerable time'.[4]

MARCH

When Joan Littlewood was making her film version of Theatre Workshop's play *Sparrers Can't Sing*, with its popular title song by Lionel Bart, Gerry Raffle referred to 'The dead hand of the British film industry',[5] a phrase that with some justification might well have been repeated on several pages of this book. It is certainly appropriate in the case of **Oh! What a Lovely War**, one of the most heralded of British musical films, not least because its cast list reads like a *Who's Who* of the nation's theatrical elite. To do justice to this most extraordinary of entertainments originally fashioned by Charles Chilton, Raffles, and Littlewood, we must revert to its theatri-cal origin. Kenneth Tynan's emotional reaction to its first night at Stratford East informed readers that 'Miss Littlewood's passion has invaded one's bloodstream, and after the final scene, in which a line of reluctant heroes advance on the audience, bleating like sheep at a slaughterhouse, one is ready to storm Buckingham Palace and burn down Knightsbridge barracks'.[6] Beyond the confine of Stratford East's Littlewood milieu, the names of many of her cherished actors (she called them her 'nuts') meant little and are now seldom remembered, but a more distinctive assembly of performers would be difficult to find. Through the medium of the original cast recording of the original London West End production of this 'musical entertainment', in effect a brilliant example of that regrettably abandoned art form known as 'revue', we hear the qualities of those actors. It remains a searing, deeply moving experience.

The *MFB* argued that 'one ought to come out of the film asking the question why; instead, one is simply left admiring a worthy mosaic of bits and pieces, full of good ideas but nowhere near to being a self-contained dramatic entity', and this the stage version had unarguably been. Regrettably, 'A calculatedly Brechtian entertainment has become just an entertainment, the hard, simple anger of the original replaced by an elaborate charade.'[7] For David Parkinson, 'The huge potential of this all-star vehicle was mainly squandered through a lack of subtlety or irony.'[8] For Vincent Canby, it was 'a big, elaborate, sometimes realistic film whose elephantine physical proportions and often brilliant all-star cast simply overwhelm the material with a surfeit of good intentions.'[9]

The problem of making a unique piece of British theatrical history work on screen was never going to be easily solved, despite director Richard Attenborough's obvious commitment to make a film that served as both entertainment and homage, because fundamentally it is a work that belongs wholly to theatre in a way that almost every other British musical didn't, and capturing that quality would not be answered by simply pointing a camera at the stage show, as if a curtain was lifted at the beginning and dropped at the end. The attempt to do just that had proved disastrous for *Stop the World – I Want to Get Off* and D'Oyly Carte's filming of *The Mikado*. Many cinemagoers were understandably moved by what Attenborough and his all-stars achieved. There was no lack of respect or contemplation in its making, but, perhaps for those who had known it before cameras were involved, its new, rather grandiose aspect muted the work's original effectiveness and ability to stir us. For others, Len Deighton's screenplay rearrangement of its format in no way invalidated its powerfulness. Now, we are refocused on the misfortunes of the young men of the working-class Smith family as their lives ebb and flow in the seismic time of war. This happens a long way from anything that Raffles, Littlewood, or Chilton would recognise. Where a not-much-remembered Fanny Carby once belted out 'I'll Make a Man of You' with ice-cold coarseness on stage to tremendous effect, Maggie Smith's stellar version in the film lacks Carby's horrible potency.

Essentially, the film retained the essence of the stage show's appeal through the use of the songs that in one way or another flourished during the Great War and remain testimony to its tragedy.

AUGUST

Neither James Hilton or Terence Rattigan can be said to have had much luck when it came to musicals. Frank Capra's strictly non-singing 1937 film version of Hilton's 1934 novel *Lost Horizon* survives as a Hollywood classic. In 1956, Broadway's stage musical adaptation of the novel retitled *Shangri-La* lasted only a handful of performances. In 1972, Hilton's saga of Utopian perfection was remade in Technicolor with Peter Finch and Liv Ullmann and with songs by Burt Bacharach and Hal David. It is generally agreed that the musicalised *Lost Horizon* is unworthy to be spoken of in the same breath as Capra's masterpiece. Rattigan's association with musicals was slight and rocky. In 1960, he adapted his successful comedy *French Without Tears* into the West End musical *Joie de Vivre*. As it turned out, the show had not much *joie* and a very brief *vivre*, becoming one of the most short-lived (four performances) in West End history. Noël Coward's 1963 Broadway musical *The Girl Who Came to Supper* was based on Rattigan's 1953 play *The Sleeping Prince* but had only a short run.

Now, a British studio produced a grandiose musical version of Hilton's 1934 novel *Goodbye Mr Chips*, which had already been immortalised on film by Robert Donat in 1940. Director Herbert Ross had nursed the idea of a musical adaptation for several years before bringing Rattigan in for the screenplay, and Leslie Bricusse for the songs. The magnificence of MGM's **Goodbye Mr Chips** is evident in the quality of those considered for its leading roles. MGM's shopping list for these roles was headed by Rex Harrison and Julie Andrews, and subsequent candidates included Albert Finney, Richard Burton, and Audrey Hepburn, with Vincente Minnelli as preferred director. Ultimately, top-billing went to Peter O'Toole and Petula Clark. O'Toole confessed that the idea of it being a musical 'filled me with horror. The only reason I read the script was because Terence Rattigan had written it [...] a beautiful screenplay, elegant down to the last detail. For me, it's a marvellous role – almost Chekhovian in its range and depth.' O'Toole suggested he was no friend to the musical: 'This isn't one of your bleeding musicals where everything stops for five minutes while some bloke bellows some God-awful song.'[10]

There was not much bellowing in Bricusse's numbers, although the typically Bricusse 'London Is London' (an incessant rhyming lyric to a pedestrian but ear-worming tune) provided the ideal opportunity for the sort of pseudo-cockney knees-up that Bricusse seemed incapable of overlooking. Indeed, most of the songs are little more than a few lines of gloopy lyric and the whisper of a melody with the staying power of the average mayfly. These were whispered as much as sung. Ross used the music 'subjectively so that the songs reflected the interior personalities of his characters, making considerable use of the voice-over technique so that Chips' songs are really interior monologues. Above all, he has avoided the static, stagey quality that results when one character sings to another.'[11] These 'interior monologues' manifest themselves as the school song

Although Peter O'Toole and Petula Clark brought dignity to Leslie Bricusse's musical treatment of James Hilton's simple story *Goodbye Mr Chips* (1969), it now involved an overture, intermission, and entr'acte and 147 minutes of your attention.

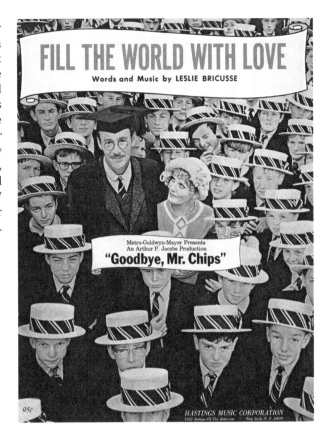

'Fill the World with Love' (surely a little florid for a private boys' school that seems to specialise in Latin?), O'Toole's pondering 'Where Did My Childhood Go?', Clark's soubrettish standout number 'London Is London', and her more intimate thoughts as expressed in 'Know Yourself', 'And the Sky Smiled', 'Apollo', 'Walk through the World', 'What Shall I Do with Today?', her reminiscences of 'School Days' shared with the boys, and 'You and I'. The internal workings of Mr Chips are revealed in 'What a Lot of Flowers' and 'When I Was Younger'.

Pauline Kael had little sympathy with 'An overblown version with songs where they are not needed (and Leslie Bricusse's songs are never needed)'.[12] Referring to the 'patched-up, sadly dated vehicle', the *MFB* noted that

> The music and songs have been discreetly withdrawn to the background, intermittently intended to deepen but not lead the dramatic content, while the traditionally stylised emotion expressed in lavish dance numbers has been abandoned in favour of a camera choreography, highly mobile cameras themselves doing their best to carry the emotions of a scene with some daringly liberated movement.[13]

Bricusse's songs 'struggle to be more than banal' and 'add nothing not already established elsewhere'.[14] For *Newsweek*, musicalising Mr Chips's adventure was 'a good example of how the old guard of the movie industry has lost track of itself, misplaced its magic wand [and] muddled old and new as woefully as poor Chips'.[15] Dilys Powell recognised the problem that 'The sentiment of the nineteen-thirties, even with the love story taking precedence over the school story, won't work in the late nineteen-sixties.'[16]

The air of enforced gravity prevents wit from breaking in. We must be grateful for the fragment of Alison Leggatt as the sour-faced wife of Mr Chips's headmaster (not much of a part for Michael Redgrave). In providing only a little vinegar, she reminds us that this is a film that for much of its time takes itself much too seriously. It even has an Overture (pretty well tuneless) through which the audience is obliged to sit, an Intermission (necessary in a film that lasts well over two hours), and an Entr'acte. It also kills off Clark's character in an off-hand manner.

1970

Finney's transition to the cheerful lover of carol singers and all mankind has none of the natural joyfulness of either of his predecessors. Hicks and Sim are able to fall back on a natural charm not available to their 1970 descendant

Scrooge

Toomorrow   *Scrooge*

AUGUST

The Shadows' Bruce Welch considered *Toomorrow* 'a disgrace. It was reminiscent of so many of the low-budget pop pictures that were made during the early sixties, and the biggest let-down of all was the music. It was all so lightweight. There were no hit songs – the numbers were jive and instantly forgettable.'[1] The *MFB* was equally unimpressed with

> a glossy and empty-headed pop fantasy, as computerised as the Alphoids' soulless music [...] If this antiseptic crew had really decided to set foot on the stage of the Round House during a pop festival, dressed like canaries and singing their cute songs of love and tears, they would have been booed, quite deservedly, off it again.[2]

The blandness of *Toomorrow*'s songs, all by Ritchie Adams and Mark Barkan, who had written much of the Monkees' material, is a blatant handicap. The numbers in *Gonks Go Beat*, a much more audacious other-worldly enterprise, knock *Toomorrow*'s into a cocked hat. The discernible items include the title song, 'Taking Our Own Sweet Time', 'Happiness Valley', 'Goin' Back', and 'If You Can't Be Hurt', but lack character or context. Some sources credit other Adams and Barkan songs, 'You're My Baby Now', 'Let's Move On', and 'Walkin' on Air', which some may identify within the film.

What *Toomorrow* succeeds in is firmly embedding itself in its time capsule: this is 1970, and the students at London College of Art are sitting in, protesting, wanting to be taken notice of, much to the annoyance of the film's very own old codger college principal (Robert Raglan). In fact, the generation gap plays little part in Guest's play; there is already the very considerable gap between earth and space, nicely accentuated in John Spears's special effects. For some reason, thousands-of-years-old anthropologist John Williams (Roy Dotrice), who has barely introduced himself to us before he peels off his face, has been sent to earth to investigate the vibrations created by the pop music of 1970, specifically the sounds made by the student pop group Toomorrow, comprising Olivia (Olivia Newton-John), Benny (Benny Thomas), and Karl (Karl Chambers). All bright and attractive young individuals, and certainly worthy of a better project.

As if *Gonks Go Beat* hadn't already blazed its trail in inter-galactic poppery, outer space returns to confront the mystery of British pop music. At the back of *Toomorrow* were producers Don Kirshner, creator of the Monkees, and Harry Saltzman of the James Bond franchise, although Kirshner subsequently claimed that he had abandoned the project before filming was completed two years later. A conflict ensued when director Val Guest decided that the commissioned screenplay by David Benedictus was unsatisfactory. Without informing Benedictus of this rejection, Guest substituted his own. This displeased Benedictus. It must be said that Guest's screenplay is so feeble that we may only wonder at the desperate quality of Benedictus's original.

Unaccountably, the film lasted two weeks at the London Palladium Cinema before an injunction served by Guest removed it from public view. Williams invites the group to use his conservatory for rehearsals, luring them with the promise 'I have a Revox!' They are fascinated by his surroundings, which include the remains of Rameses and a petrified Claudius excavated from the ruins of Pompeii, but are transported into the empyrean ('This sort of thing doesn't happen!'). When cleansed of earth germs, the group's galactic hosts investigate the group's vibrations, furthering Williams's research into 'a new form of electric harmony'; as a disciple of Project Earth, he has already condemned it as 'an abortive attempt at evolution'. Even the excitement of Dotrice being beamed up in his pyjamas falls flat.

OCTOBER

It is not only the ghosts of Christmas manufactured by Dickens that haunt Waterbury Films' ebullient **Scrooge**. British cinema has showed a consistent fascination with this 1843 seasonal tale and the reforming of the curmudgeonly miser, first played by Daniel Smith in R. W. Paul's Animatograph Works' eleven-minute silent (only four minutes have survived) *Scrooge or Marley's Ghost* of 1901, directed by Walter R. Booth. Appropriately, Booth's other day job was as a magician adept at visual trickery in film (useful when needing to conjure up ghosts of bygone Christmases). The great Edwardian actor Seymour Hicks was the shuddering Scrooge of 1913, followed by the still unspeaking Charles Rock in *A Christmas Carol* (1914). Two more silents appeared in the twenties, with Scrooge played by Henry V. Esmond in 1922 and Russell Thorndike in 1923. In 1928, the first sound version of *Scrooge* headlined Bransby Williams. Hicks returned to the role (one he had played countless times on stage) for the 1935 adaptation directed by the once leading romantic star of British silents, Henry Edwards. It remains a fascinating document, alternately frugal and extravagant, with sudden scenes at sea and at lush London banquets, but always with Hicks at its heart, supported by a first-class company. For those willing to overlook its technical deficiencies, it's an exhilarating experience. It is not that in Brian Desmond Hurst's 1951 version Alastair Sim eclipsed Hicks's interpretation, simply that, in Scrooge, Sim found a role that might have been made for him. The picture is a constant delight, with Sim's ability to travel from deep sadness to unmitigated glee obvious to behold. No one took much notice of a half-hour version of *A Christmas Carol* in 1960 starring John Hayter.

In the main, the 1970 performances do not compare well with what has gone before. Finney's Scrooge is hunched, crabbed, pinched in manner and speech, but – not the case with either Hicks or Sim – these are mannerisms. Finney's transition to the cheerful lover of carol singers and all mankind has none of the natural joyfulness of either of his predecessors. Hicks and Sim are able to fall back on a natural charm not available to their 1970 descendant. The whole film, in fact, suffers from the lack of persuasive performers, although Alec Guinness is a creditable Jacob Marley until the special effects send him hurtling towards hell. David Collings's Bob Cratchit cannot begin to compare with Hick's Cratchit (Donald Calthrop), never mind the fact that Calthrop is a clerk who has clearly conquered received pronunciation.

Hidden in a beard, Kenneth More's Christmas Present is a positive presence, but why, if the film needed star performers, not hire one with more currency? Edith Evans as Christmas Past is a static structure around whom her scenes circulate; it closely resembles acting. The angelically frail Tiny Tim is coated with excessive sugariness, made the more indigestible when he is obliged to deliver one of Mr Bricusse's more treacly numbers. His solid stage successes in the 1960s with three musicals co-written with Anthony Newley were a notable achievement in British theatre. More prolific than any other British writer in musical theatre of his period, Bricusse followed the first, *Stop the World – I Want to Get Off*, with scores for the American *Doctor Dolittle* (1967) and *Goodbye Mr Chips* (1969); his later works included a provincial stage production of *Goodbye Mr Chips*, *Kings and Clowns*, and *Sherlock Holmes* (Conan Doyle's Holmes was Ron Moody). Bricusse's hugely commercially successful career was to some extent sustained by the low bar the British public set when it came to its musical entertainment.

Naturally, and deservedly, *Scrooge* has its many admirers, but need it be such undemanding fare? Ronald Neame's Christmas card of a production wrapped up in several bows. It has all the fake snow and fabulously bright shop windows aglow with goods presumably inaccessible to the Cockney waifs peering at them hopelessly from the pavement. All is served up with sub-Lionel Bart jollity, all too evident in Paddy Stone's choreography, which is strangely lacking in style and clarity, a sort of amorphous jumping about that is never clarified or captured by Neame's camera. Was the brilliant Stone simply overcome by the impossible forces he was supposed to control as 'Thank You Very Much' goes wildly out of control?

John Russell Taylor conceded that 'Not that much of it is actually bad', although the film was 'not, be sure, anything like the best screen adaptation we have seen, but it is streets ahead of *Oliver!* and its pleasures should prove more than merely seasonal.'[3] Taylor's assertion that the film would be acceptable viewing all year round seems strangely out of focus; surely, only the accentuated sentimentality demanded by Christmas could make room for such as this *Scrooge*.

Critically, those in search of decent music and lyrics were warned to look elsewhere. For Roger Ebert, 'Bricusse's songs fall so far below the level of good musical comedy that you wish Albert Finney would stop singing them [...] Meanwhile, countless dancers and a children's choir keep up the pretence that music is happening.'[4] Pauline Kael regretted that 'The Leslie Bricusse music is so forgettable that your mind flushes it away while you're hearing it.'[5] The *MFB* admitted that

> The recitative numbers have reasonably adept lyrics – there is some pleasing triple-rhyming in Scrooge's lament 'I Hate People' – but the more sentimental songs, which include a maudlin dirge sung by a winsome Tiny Tim (Richard Beaumont), are consistently banal. The script, which closely follows the original story, is a little better, but Ronald Neame's direction is generally pedestrian.[6]

That 'a little better' script has some odd turns of phrase for a Victorian piece: one of the characters hails a 'fantastic coup'. There is, however, no doubt that Bricusse is a master of rhyme; his rhyming is endless and of the most basic metal.

We should dig deeper than some of these criticisms. The assertion that Bricusse's script 'closely follows the original story' is questionable. Anything in Dickens's novella that touches on darker aspects of the story is expunged. When Dickens digs deeper, Bricusse red-pencils it, steps away from the work's shadows, the very quality that is surely an essential reason why the book has lasted throughout history. Where are the mean, grasping actions after Scrooge's death (the taking-down of his bed curtains, the stealing of the shift off his body), events that strike at the heart of what Dickens was about? Where are Ignorance and Want, the starveling urchins huddled beneath the cloak of the Ghost of Christmas Present and revealed to Dickens in all their phantasmagorical tragedy? This, in essence, is Dickens's distillation of the message of *A Christmas Carol*, novel turning to polemic. All gone, red-pencilled by Bricusse's urgency to reduce Dickens's anguished cry to featherweight. No, what we have here is Scrooge's sudden profligate distribution of presents to all and sundry, as if he's just bought up the complete stock of Hamleys. From cold-grey gruel-fuelled skinflintiness to tasteless consumerism on an almost global scale was surely never Dickens's intended route. No wonder we are subjected to such an onslaught of 'thank yous' in the film's most popular song. Excessive gifting solves the problem.

As *Time* succinctly regretted, 'It is hard to imagine how men of supposed good will and talent could invest their time, their money and their skill in such a spectacularly shoddy enterprise.'[7]

1972

The delicacy of Wilson's work and the vivid affection for period nuance that Vida Hope's direction instilled into it suggested that turning it into any sort of film might be like putting a butterfly into a killing bottle

The Boy Friend

The Boy Friend

FEBRUARY

And so to Ken Russell's reworking of Sandy Wilson's pastiche musical of the 1920s *The Boy Friend*. One of the most successful British stage musicals of the 1950s, this most modest and delicate of confections began life at the tiny Players' Theatre in 1953. The delicacy of Wilson's work and the vivid affection for period nuance that Vida Hope's direction instilled into it suggested that turning it into any sort of film might be like putting a butterfly into a killing bottle.

There was general agreement that Twiggy made for a delightful Polly Browne, the heroine pupil at a school for young ladies in Nice. Those considered for the film through the years were Liza Minnelli (patently unsuitable), Julie Andrews (who had played Polly in the original Broadway production), and (surely not?) Debbie Reynolds. Twiggy, at the very least, breathed fresh air into the endeavour. She and Christopher Gable as boyfriend Tony Brocklehurst brought charm and lightness to their roles, alongside others often associated with West End revues, notably Max Adrian as Max Mandeville and Moyra Fraser as Mme Dubonnet. In fact, Wilson's translation from stage to film set Wilson's story at an uncomfortable adjunct as a show within a show in which two of Dubonnet's girls, madcap Maisie (Antonia Ellis) and Fay (Georgina Hale), were now revealed as lesbians, although this relationship does not materialise in the finished film.

It was punctilious of Russell to use so much of Wilson's theatre score, now rearranged by Peter Maxwell Davies and incorporating the title song and 'Perfect Young Ladies' introducing the students of Mme Dubonnet, 'Won't You Charleston with Me?' performed by Tommy Tune and Ellis, and 'Fancy Forgetting' performed by Fraser and Bryan Pringle. There were two duets for Twiggy and Gable: 'I Could Be Happy with You', clearly reminiscent of Vincent Youman's 'I Want to Be Happy', and 'A Room in Bloomsbury'. Also retained

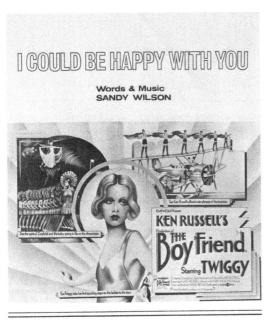

I COULD BE HAPPY WITH YOU

Words & Music
SANDY WILSON

EMI/MGM Present

KEN RUSSELL'S
Production of
The
Boy friend
Starring **TWIGGY**

20p
Made in England

1 42477

CHAPPELL

Sandy Wilson, author-composer of *The Boy Friend*, considered Ken Russell's 1972 film adaptation 'nothing but a mess' and 'what I already knew to be an impossible task'.

from the stage version were 'Sur le Plage', 'It's Nicer in Nice' (its title was the only contribution by composer Geoffrey Wright, with whom Wilson originally intended to collaborate), 'The You-Don't-Want-to-Play-with-Me-Blues', 'Safety in Numbers', 'It's Never Too Late to Fall in Love' for Adrian and Hale, 'Poor Little Pierrette', and 'The Riviera'.

To these, Wilson added Harry Champion's 1911 music-hall rouser 'Any Old Iron' by Charles Collins, E. A. Sheppard, and Fred E. Terry, now performed by Twiggy and Pringle. The inclusion of two numbers by Nacio Herb Brown and Arthur Freed also muddied the waters. 'All I Do Is Dream of You' had been heard in the Joan Crawford movie *Sadie McKee* (1934) when Gene Raymond got to sing it three times. A Hollywood musical film that featured alcoholism, it also had a number called 'How Dry I Am'. Brown and Freed's 'You Are My Lucky Star' had been heard in MGM's exuberant *Broadway Melody of 1936*. Stylistically, these numbers from the 1930s were at odds with what Wilson had composed and seriously out of time with a work that belonged (or seemed to belong) to the 1920s. It was only in 1965 that Wilson himself turned to the 1930s, hoping that his sequel to *The Boy Friend* (*Divorce Me, Darling!*) would exemplify British musicals of that decade.

The reception of Russell's film was mixed. For Roger Ebert, Russell's 'camera is so joyless that it undermines every scene'. [1] The *MFB* pondered that 'from the exaggerated parody of most of the on-stage doings, and the alacrity with which the film abandons them for its range of 1930s movies imitations, one wonders just how much feeling anyone had for *The Boy Friend* itself as more than a launching platform.[2] George Perry referred to 'the inoffensive pastiche of a twenties musical' in which Russell offered 'his second-hand impressions of Busby Berkeley' (created for Russell by choreographer Terry Gilbert).[3] The *New York Times* thought it 'often as witty as it is elaborate',[4] while Richard Schickel detected profundity in a film that far from being an exercise in nostalgia was 'a sneak attack on our most fashionable form of escapism. It is an acute, duplicitous, discomfiting movie whose message, finally, is that all times are tough for the people who must live through them, and glow golden only for those who survive them, or imagine them.'[5]

Wilson subsequently wrote that Russell, long a prominent *enfant terrible* of British cinema, 'had taken on what I already knew to be an impossible task', because

> *The Boy Friend* is essentially Theatre, relying for its effect on a style of production and performance that relates totally to a live audience. On reflection, I felt that he must have panicked in the final stages and thrown in every cinematic trick he could think of in an effort to produce something that was at least sensational.[6]

Although he appreciated the picture's 'technical expertise', Wilson considered the adaptation, written, produced and directed by Russell 'nothing but a mess; a wilful and at times incomprehensible confusion of Twenties and Thirties camp, through which poor Twiggy bravely twittered and pranced, almost suffocated by the welter of grotesquerie and surrounded by a cast whose unattractiveness was only rivalled by their incompetence.' Wilson felt sorry for Twiggy, who was revealed in the film as 'a tiny beam of pathos in a walpurgisnacht of self-indulgence'.[7]

Ultimately, who will remember Hattie Jacques and Dandy Nichols standing in for a chorus line when Arthur Lucan sings 'I Lift Up My Finger and I Say Tweet Tweet' in *Mother Riley Meets the Vampire*; the dash of Broadway that Ray Bolger brings to his 'Once in Love with Amy' in *Where's Charley?*; the touching reunion of old chums from underneath the arches of bygone years Bud Flanagan and Chesney Allen in *Here Comes the Sun*; the flickering pages of Arthur Sullivan's final diary entry ('I am sorry to leave such a lovely day') in *The Story of Gilbert and Sullivan*; Jean Kent glowingly photographed by Harry Waxman as she looks from an upstairs window into the street in *Trottie True*; Carol Raye and Peter Graves jogging through the English countryside singing their spring song, and Raye's scintillating dance routine with Jack Billings, in *Spring Song*; Sid Field skipping around his photographer's studio in *London Town*; John Baxter celebrating the down-and-outs of London in *Judgment Deferred*; Fred Emney tickling the ivories and dusting the keyboard and modelling sensational beach-wear in *Fun at St Fanny's*; Billy Fury braving murky weather on Yarmouth quay while contemplating the difficulties of love in *I've Gotta Horse*; duettists Anne Ziegler and Webster Booth in a rocky landscape enduring 'Magical Moonlight' in *The Laughing Lady*; elderly Mona Washbourne, Stanley Holloway, and Marjorie Rhodes realising 'The World Is for the Young' in *Mrs Brown, You've Got a Lovely Daughter*; Tessie O'Shea falling into the sea in Blackpool in *Holidays with Pay* and dropped from a great height into a studio pool in *London Town*; Frank Randle at the end of his comic tether, and Fred Conyngham and Diana Decker singing and dancing their way through 'Take A Step' in *When You Come Home*; the ravishing artwork of Hein Heckroth for Powell and Pressburger's *The Tales of Hoffmann*; John Rutland's tribute to music-hall star Harry Champion in what also serves as a tribute to the Players' Theatre, *A Little of What You Fancy*; the sheer quaintness and choreographic moodiness apparent in *Five Guineas a Week*; veteran leading lady of British silents Alma Taylor and music-hall veteran Hetty King glimpsed momentarily in the otherwise flatulent *Lilacs in the Spring*; Flora Robson climbing the steps up to where the man she once loved and lost is making public announcements in *Holiday Camp*; Rachel Thomas's moving apology at the end of *Valley of Song*; the fact that the real-life sailors of *Meet the Navy* do wonders for geometrical choreography while bell-bottomed: and, last but never least, Anglia Television's minor musical miracle *The Rise and Fall of Nellie Brown*, a thing that comprises all manner of joyousness including Elisabeth Welch, Ron Moody as a kindly magician, Avril Fane hilariously present for a few moments at the piano, a winning score by Dolores Claman and her librettist Robert Gould, and Millie Small singing her way into history with her ecstatic welcome to Christmas?

If, after trying to convey the essence and history of the British musical film in two volumes, I may be allowed to take only one to a restful desert island, it will be Anglia Television's *The Rise and Fall of Nellie Brown*, for its sheer happiness, its sense of togetherness, its goodness, its immediacy, its ability to enchant us still. No wonder that, as Millie sings,

> I can hear bells! I can hear bells!
> Maybe nobody else can hear them but I can hear bells
> Everything tastes like apple pie
> There's even a rainbow in the sky
> I don't know how and I don't know why
> But I can hear bells!

Notes to the Text

1945 notes

1 Robert V. Kenny, *The Man Who Was Old Mother Riley: The Lives and Films of Arthur Lucan and Kitty McShane* (Albany, GA: BearManor Media, 2014), p. 91.
2 *Monthly Film Bulletin (MFB)*, 31 May 1945, p. 59.
3 Steve Chibnall and Brian McFarlane, *The British 'B' Film (London: BFI/Palgrave Macmillan, 2009)*, p. 102.
4 Geoff Brown and Tony Aldgate, *The Common Touch: The Films of John Baxter* (London: BFI, 1989), p. 31.
5 *The Times*, 7 January 1946.
6 *Kinematograph Weekly*, 2 August 1945, p. 38.
7 *MFB*, 1946, p. 3.
8 *Kinematograph Weekly*, 17 January 1946, p. 26.

1946 notes

1 Philip Martin Williams and David L. Williams, *Hooray for Jollywood: The Life of John E. Blakeley and the Mancunian Film Corporation* (Ashton-under-Lyne: History on Your Doorstep, 2001), p. 15.
2 *Kinematograph Weekly*, 28 February 1946, p. 24.
3 *MFB*, 1946, p. 31.
4 *Sydney Daily Telegraph*, 15 June 1947, p. 32.
5 *Daily Telegraph*, quoted in Kurt Ganzl, *The British Musical Theatre* (London: Macmillan, 1986), p. 529.
6 *MFB*, 1946, p. 45.
7 *Kinematograph Weekly*, 24 February 1944.
8 *The Times*, 1 July 1946.
9 *Observer*, 30 June 1946, p. 2.
10 *MFB*, 1946, p. 45.
11 Quoted in David Kynaston, *Austerity Britain 1945–51* (London: Bloomsbury, 2007), p. 101.
12 *MFB*, March 1946, p. 61.
13 *Kinematograph Weekly*, 23 May 1946, p. 28.
14 *MFB*, 1946, p. 94.
15 *Kinematograph Weekly*, 18 July 1946, p. 26.
16 Herbert Wilcox, *Twenty-Five Thousand Sunsets* (London: Bodley Head, 1967), p. 145.
17 *Observer*, 25 August 1946.
18 *The Times*, 26 August 1946.

19 *New York Times*, 5 August 1948.
20 Quoted by Roger Philip Mellor, *BFI Screenline*, screenline.org.uk [accessed 10 December 2021].
21 Ibid.
22 Robert Murphy, *Realism and Tinsel: Cinema and Society in Britain 1939–49* (London: Routledge, 1989), p. 114.
23 Vivian Ellis, *I'm on a See-Saw* (Bath: Cedric Chivers, 1974), p. 204.
24 *MFB*, 1946, p. 122.
25 Roger Philip Mellor, *BFI Screenline*, screenline.org.uk [accessed 10 December 2021].
26 Ellis, *I'm on a See-Saw*, p. 204.
27 *MFB*, 1946, p. 134.
28 *Kinematograph*, 19 September 1946, p. 8.
29 *The Times*, 28 August 1946, p. 6.
30 Quoted in Derek Threadgall, *Shepperton* (London: BFI, 1994), p. 32.
31 Peter Noble (editor), *British Film Yearbook 1947–8* (London: Skelton Robinson, 1947).
32 John Fisher, *Funny Way to Be a Hero* (London: Frederick Muller, 1973), p. 162.
33 *Observer*, 1 September 1946, p. 2.
34 *Variety*, 4 September 1946, p. 10.
35 *Observer*, 24 November 1946, p. 2.
36 *Kinematograph Weekly*, 17 October 1946, p. 26.
37 *Variety*, 2 October 1946.
38 *MFB*, 1946, p. 149.
39 *Variety*, 2 October 1946.
40 *MFB*, 1946, p. 148.
41 *Kinematograph Weekly*, 7 November 1946, p. 25.
42 *MFB*, 1946, p. 149.

1947 notes

1 Quoted in Jeff Nuttall, *King Twist* (London: Routledge and Kegan Paul, 1978), p. 67.
2 *MFB*, 1947, p. 47.
3 radiotimes.com [accessed 9 May 2022].
4 *Kinematograph Weekly*, 27 March 1947, p. 20.
5 Fisher, *Funny Way to Be a Hero*, p. 167.
6 *MFB*, 1947, p. 76.
7 *The Times*, 9 May 1947.
8 *Observer*, 11 May 1947, p. 2.
9 *Guardian*, 21 July 1990, p. 67.
10 Kynaston, *Austerity Britain*, p. 218.
11 Ibid.
12 *MFB*, 1947, p. 127.
13 *Kinematograph Weekly*, 28 August 1947, p. 22.
14 *Kinematograph Weekly*, 19 June 1947, p. 36.

1948 notes

1 *Kinematograph Weekly*, 23 January 1947, p. 6.
2 *MFB*, 1948, p. 30.
3 *Observer*, 25 April 1948.
4 *MFB*, 1948, pp. 60–1.
5 *New York Times*, 21 February 1949.
6 *The Times*, 26 April 1948.
7 *MFB*, 1948, pp. 60–1.
8 *Guardian*, 24 April 1948.
9 *Observer*, 28 March 1948, p. 2.
10 *Guardian*, 27 March 1948, p. 3.
11 Quoted in Charles Barr (editor), *All Our Yesterdays: 90 Years of British Cinema* (London: BFI, 1986), pp. 108–9.
12 Ibid., p. 295.
13 Wilcox, *Twenty-Five Thousand Sunsets*, p. 161.
14 *MFB*, 1948, p. 108.
15 Quoted in Williams and Williams, *Hooray for Jollywood*, p. 83.
16 Dilys Powell, *The Golden Screen: Fifty Years of Films* (London: Headline, 1989), p. 25.
17 Ian Christie, *Arrows of Desire: The Films of Michael Powell and Emeric Pressburger* (London: Waterstone, 1985), p. 111.
18 *Stage*, 31 August 2006, p. 53.
19 *MFB*, 1949, p. 2.

1949 notes

1 *MFB*, 1949, pp. 58–9.
2 Mary Guillermin (editor), *John Guillermin: The Man, the Myth, the Movies* (Los Angeles: Precocity Press, 2020), pp. 29–30.
3 *Kinematograph Weekly*, 10 March 1949.
4 Guillermin, *John Guillermin*, p. 30.
5 Murphy, *Realism and Tinsel*, p. 215.
6 *MFB*, 1949, pp. 114–15.
7 Sheila Van Damm, *We Never Closed* (London: Robert Hale, 1967), p. 107.
8 *MFB*, 1949, p. 115.
9 Leslie Halliwell, *Leslie Halliwell's Film Guide*, 6th ed. (London Paladin, 1988), p. 670.
10 *MFB*, 1950, p. 101.
11 *Guardian*, 28 May 1949.
12 *The Times*, 13 August 1949.
13 *MFB*, 1949, p. 160.
14 *New York Times*, 16 April 1951.
15 *MFB*, 1949, p. 164.
16 Williams and Williams, *Hooray for Jollywood*, pp. 95–6.
17 *Kinematograph Weekly*, 25 May 1950, p. 2.
18 *MFB*, 1949, p. 60.

19 David Quinlan, *British Sound Films: The Studio Years 1928–1959* (London: B. T. Batsford, 1984), p. 217.
20 Chibnall and McFarlane, *The British 'B' Film*, p. 102.
21 Ibid.
22 Guillermin, *John Guillermin*, p. 33.
23 *MFB*, 1949, p. 60.

1950 notes

1 *Kinematograph Weekly*, 16 March 1950, p. 10.
2 Richard Traubner, *Operetta: A Theatrical History* (London: Victor Gollancz, 1984), pp. 350–1.
3 Quoted in Tony Staveacre, *The Songwriters* (London: BBC, 1960), p. 111.
4 *The Times*, 10 April 1950.
5 *MFB*, 1950, p. 66.
6 *Observer*, quoted in Sandy Wilson, *Ivor* (London: Michael Joseph, 1975), p. 231.
7 *Kinematograph Weekly*, 13 April 1950, p. 13.
8 There is currently no mention of him on the 'Novello Awards' website.
9 Traubner, *Operetta*, p. 353.
10 Letter to the author from Ken Behrens, 14 September 1988.
11 *Kinematograph Weekly*, 3 August 1950, p. 22.
12 *MFB*, 1950, p. 140.
13 Chibnall and McFarlane, *The British 'B' Film*, p. 118.
14 *Kinematograph Weekly*, 9 November 1950, p. 22.
15 Ibid.
16 *MFB*, 1950, p. 205.

1951 notes

1 *Kinematograph Weekly*, 31 May 1951.
2 Ibid.
3 *MFB*, 1951, p. 246.
4 David Shipman, *The Great Movie Stars: The International Years* (London: Angus and Robertson, 1972), p. 528.
5 Halliwell, *Leslie Halliwell's Film Guide*, p. 444.
6 *Kinematograph Weekly*, 1 November 1923, p. 32.
7 Quoted in *Kinematograph Weekly*, 8 November 1923.
8 *MFB*, 1951, p. 277.
9 Christie, *Arrows of Desire*, p. 86.
10 Bruce Babington, *Launder and Gilliat* (Manchester: Manchester University Press, 2002), p. 199.
11 Chibnall and McFarlane, *The British 'B' Film*, p. 119.
12 Kynaston, *Austerity Britain*, p. 623.

1952 notes

1 Guillermin, *John Guillermin*, p. 41.
2 *MFB*, 1952, p. 27.

3   *Kinematograph Weekly*, 12 June 1952, p. 34.
4   *Kinematograph Weekly*, 28 February 1952, p. 27.
5   Donald Peers, *Pathway* (London: Werner Laurie, 1951)
6   Michael Kilgarriff, *Grace, Beauty and Banjos: Peculiar Lives and Strange Times of Music Hall and Variety Artistes* (London: Oberon Books, 1999), p. 212.
7   *Kinematograph Weekly*, 21 May 1953.
8   *MFB*, 1952, p. 53.
9   Brown and Aldgate, *The Common Touch*, pp. 115–16.
10 *MFB*, 1952, p. 46.
11 David Parkinson, radiotimes.com [accessed 9 May 2022].
12 Brown and Aldgate, *The Common Touch*, p. 115.
13 Ibid., p. 30.
14 *Kinematograph Weekly*, 28 February 1952, p. 27.
15 Brown and Aldgate, *The Common Touch*, p. 115.
16 *The Times*, 4 August 1952.
17 *Kinematograph Weekly*, 21 May 1953, p. 31.
18 Bosley Crowther, *New York Times*, 27 June 1952.
19 *MFB*, 1952, p. 114.
20 Clive Hirschhorn, *The Warner Bros. Story* (London: Octopus, 1979), p. 302.
21 *Plays and Players*, April 1958, p. 15.
22 Tom Weaver, *Science Fiction Confidential: Interviews with 23 Monster Stars and Filmmakers* (Jefferson, NC: McFarland, 2002), pp. 150–1.
23 Ibid.
24 *Kinematograph Weekly*, 20 May 1954.
25 *MFB*, 1952, p. 112.
26 Ibid., p. 139.
27 *Observer*, 14 September 1952, p. 6.
28 *Kinematograph Weekly*, 9 October 1952, p. 27.
29 *MFB*, 1952, p. 157.
30 *Kinematograph Weekly*, 27 November 1952, pp. 22–3.
31 Scott Palmer, *British Film Actors' Credits, 1895–1987* (Jefferson, NC: McFarland, 1988), p. 588.

1953 notes

1   *Kinematograph Weekly*, 5 March 1953, p. 29.
2   *MFB*, 1953, p. 57.
3   Ibid., p. 77.
4   'Modified rapture' is a line from *The Mikado*.
5   *The Times*, 7 May 1953, p. 12.
6   *Kinematograph Weekly*, 14 May 1953, p. 17.
7   *MFB*, 1953, p. 86.
8   *Sight and Sound*, Summer 1953, p. 32.
9   *Variety*, 31 December 1952.
10 Wilcox, *Twenty-Five Thousand Sunsets*, p. 163.
11 Ibid, p. 167.
12 *MFB*, 1953, p. 100.
13 Wilcox *Twenty-Five Thousand Sunsets*, p. 164.

14 *Observer*, 7 June 1953.
15 *Kinematograph Weekly*, 11 June 1953, p. 22.
16 Notes for Decca recording of the opera, 1981.
17 *MFB*, 1953, p. 100.
18 Ibid., p. 133.
19 *Kinematograph Weekly*, 30 July 1953.
20 *Observer*, 30 August 1953.
21 *Kinematograph Weekly*, 27 August, 1953.
22 *MFB*, 1953, p. 144.
23 *New York Times*, 25 June 1953.
24 *Sketch*, 23 September 1953, p. 30.
25 John Montgomery, *Comedy Films 1894–1954* (London: George Allen and Unwin, 1968), p. 236.
26 Williams and Williams, *Hooray for Jollywood*, p. 118.
27 Ibid.
28 Ibid.
29 prideofmanchester.com [accessed 9 May 2022].
30 *Sight and Sound*, Spring 1954, p. 213.
31 *MFB*, 1954, p. 13.
32 *Kinematograph Weekly*, 3 December 1953, p. 14.

1954 notes

1   *MFB*, 1954, p. 121.
2   *Theatre World Annual No. 4* (London: Rockliff, 1953), p. 110.
3   Philip Hope-Wallace, *Guardian*, 2 March 1953, p. 2.
4   *MFB*, 1955, p. 4.
5   Stephen Vagg, *The Films of Errol Flynn Part 5*, FilmLink.com.au [accessed 9 May 2022].
6   *Films and Filming*, February 1955, p. 19.
7   Fisher, *Funny Way to Be a Hero*, p. 262.
8   *Guardian*, 18 December 1954, p. 3.
9   *MFB*, 1956, p. 26.
10 *Kinematograph Weekly*, 30 December 1954, p. 9.

1955 notes

1   Halliwell, *Leslie Halliwell's Film Guide*, p. 52.
2   David Shipman, *The Great Movie Stars: The Golden Years* (London: Hamlyn, 1970), p. 85.
3   *Kinematograph Weekly*, 10 March 1955, p. 23.
4   *MFB*, 1955, p. 56.
5   *Variety*, 6 April 1955, p. 6.
6   *Kinematograph Weekly*, 10 March 1955, p. 23.
7   *Bye Bye Birdie* (New York, 1960) had music by Charles Strouse, lyrics by Lee Adams, and book by Michael Stewart. The London production of 1961 was followed by the 1963 film version.
8   *You Lucky People*, DVD (2011), booklet notes by Vic Pratt.

9   *MFB*, 1955, p. 156.
10 Ibid.
11 Ibid., p. 149.
12 *Variety*, 28 September 1955, p. 9.
13 *Mirror* (Perth), 24 September 1955, p. 12.
14 *Observer*, 8 December 1957, p. 15.
15 Traubner, *Operetta*, p. 118.
16 Christie, *Arrows of Desire*, p. 90.
17 *The Times*, 21 November 1955.
18 *Films and Filming*, January 1956.
19 *MFB*, 1956, p. 4.
20 *Sketch*, 30 November 1955, p. 28.
21 Christie, *Arrows of Desire*, p. 90.
22 *Illustrated London News*, 10 December 1955, p. 42.
23 *The Times*, 11 October 1980, p. 9.
24 *Picture Post*, 6 November 1954, p. 26.
25 Ibid.
26 *The Times*, 20 July 1953, p. 11.
27 Quoted in Wilson, *Ivor*, p. 254.
28 *MFB*, 1955, p. 176.
29 Quoted in Wilson, *Ivor*, p. 259.
30 Ibid.
31 *The Times*, 27 October 1955, p. 3.
32 *Kinematograph Weekly*, 25 June 1953, p. 15.
33 *MFB*, 1955, p. 168.
34 A. H. Weiler, *New York Times*, 31 October 1955.
35 *The Times*, 5 December 1955.
36 *Films and Filming*, January 1956.
37 *Observer*, 4 December 1955.
38 *MFB*, 1956, p. 6.
39 *Variety*, 7 October 1957.
40 *Stage*, 16 September 1954, p. 9.

1956 notes

1   *MFB*, 1956, p. 19.
2   *Fun at St Fanny's*, DVD (2011), booklet notes.
3   *Stage*, 9 October 1952, p. 3.
4   *Stage*, 9 May 1957, p. 13.
5   *Kinematograph Weekly*, 5 April 1956, p. 17.
6   Alan Dent, *Illustrated London News*, 19 May 1956.
7   *MFB*, 1956, p. 42.
8   Andy Medhurst, 'It Sort of Happened Here', in Jonathan Romney and Adrian Wootton (editors), *Celluloid Jukebox* (London: BFI, 1995), p. 62.
9   Rodney Giesler, *Films and Filming*, June 1956, p. 23.
10 *MFB*, 1956, p. 91.
11 Roger Mellor, *Journal into Melody*, September 2009, pp. 67–73.
12 Peter Burnup, *News of the World*, 29 July 1956.

13 *MFB*, 1956, p. 78.
14 David Vaughan, 'After the Ball', *Sight and Sound*, Autumn 1956, p. 90.
15 *Observer*, 26 August 1956.
16 *MFB*, 1956, p. 126.
17 Halliwell, *Leslie Halliwell's Film Guide*, p. 522.
18 *Kinematograph Weekly*, 6 September 1956, p. 14.
19 *Guardian*, 1 September 1956, p. 3.
20 Ibid.
21 P. L. Mannock, *Films and Filming*, September 1956.
22 *Kinematograph Weekly*, 26 July 1956, p. 16.
23 Robert Ross, *The Complete Frankie Howerd* (London: Reynolds and Hearn, 2001), p. 108.
24 *MFB*, 1956, p. 157.
25 Graham McCann, *Frankie Howerd* (London: Fourth Estate, 2004), p. 213.
26 *Kinematograph Weekly*, 2 August 1956, p. 25.
27 Adrian Wright, *The Innumerable Dance: The Life and Work of William Alwyn* (Woodbridge: The Boydell Press, 2008), p. 111.
28 *Kinematograph Weekly*, 20 December 1956, p. 18.
29 *Kinematograph Weekly*, 29 November 1956.
30 *MFB*, 1957, p. 9.
31 Fisher, *Funny Way to Be a Hero*, p. 239.
32 Hubert Gregg, *Agatha Christie and all that Mousetrap* (London: William Kimber, 1980), p. 134.
33 Ibid., p. 135.
34 *Melody Maker*, 5 May 1956.
35 *Kinematograph Weekly*, 14 February 1957.
36 *Londonderry Sentinel*, 27 September 1956.
37 *West London Observer*, 2 November 1956, p. 8.
38 *Halifax Evening Courier*, 8 September 1956, p. 3.
39 *Daily Herald*, 3 September 1956, p. 1.
40 J. P. Wearing, *The London Stage: 1950–1959* (Lanham, MD: Rowman and Littlefield, 2014), p. 378.

1957 notes

1 Quoted in Carol Ann Lee, *A Fine Day for Hanging: The Ruth Ellis Story* (Edinburgh: Mainstream, 2012), p. 369.
2 *Financial Times*, 5 December 2009.
3 Matthew Partington, 'The London Coffee Bar of the 1950s – Teenage Occupants of an Amateur Space?', arts.brighton.ac.uk [accessed 20 October 2021].
4 *Financial Times*, 5 December 2009.
5 Letter to the author from Roger Philip Mellor dated 28 July 2022 containing the text of his essay 'Renewing Acquaintance with The Good Companions', originally published in the *Journal of the J. B Priestley Society*, vol. 1 (2000).
6 *Guardian*, 4 June 1957, p. 5.
7 *Variety*, 31 December 1956.
8 *MFB*, 1957, p. 43.
9 *Films and Filming*, April 1957, p. 25.

10 *Evening Standard*, 7 March 1957.
11 *Kinematograph Weekly*, 9 August 1956, p. 19.
12 Shipman, *The Great Movie Stars: The International Years*, p. 527.
13 Ibid., p. 528.
14 *MFB*, 1957, p. 72.
15 *The Times*, 29 June 1957, p. 34.
16 Medhurst, 'It Sort of Happened Here', in Romney and Wootton (editors), *Celluloid Jukebox*, p. 62.
17 Colin MacInnes, *England, Half English* (London: Hogarth Press, 1986), p. 12.
18 radiotimes.com [accessed 9 May 2022].
19 *MFB*, 1957, p. 90.
20 MacInnes, *England, Half English* (1986), p. 13.
21 *Sight and Sound*, Summer 1957, p. 43.
22 Obituary, *Guardian*, 22 October 1999.
23 *Sunday Mirror*, 26 May 1957, p. 17.
24 Roger Philip Mellor, *BFI Screenline*, screenline.org.uk [accessed 10 December 2021].
25 *Kinematograph Weekly*, 23 May 1957, p. 5.
26 *MFB*, July 1957, p. 89.
27 Chibnall and McFarlane, *The British 'B' Film*, p. 205.
28 Ernest Short, *Fifty Years of Vaudeville 1895–1945* (London: Eyre and Spottiswoode, 1946), pp. 227–8.
29 *The Times*, 12 August 1957.
30 *Films and Filming*, October 1957, p. 22.
31 Pat Kirkwood, *The Time of my Life* (London: Robert Hale, 1999), p. 202.
32 *MFB*, 1957, pp. 99–100.
33 *Kinematograph Weekly*, 13 December 1956, p. 100.
34 *Kinematograph Weekly*, 4 July 1957, p. 18.
35 *MFB*, 1957, p. 105.
36 *Kinematograph Weekly*, 5 September 1957.

1958 notes

1   *Kinematograph Weekly*, 20 February 1958, p. 16.
2   Roger Mellor, *British Musical Movies*, 24 June 1999 [website no longer available].
3   *Hartlepool Northern Daily Mail*, 21 February 1958, p. 15.
4   *MFB*, 1958, p. 46.
5   *Variety*, 12 March 1958.
6   *6-5 Special: The Whole Fabulous Story in Pictures*, *Daily Mirror* publication (no date).
7   *Independent*, 17 October 2008.
8   *6-5 Special*, *Daily Mail* publication, 1958.
9   *MFB*, 1958, p. 63.
10 *6-5 Special: The Whole Fabulous Story in Pictures*, *Daily Mirror* publication.
11 Ibid., p. 17.
12 *The Times*, 24 March 1958, p. 3.
13 *MFB*, 1958, p. 61.

14   *Variety*, 31 December 1957.
15   Letterboxd.com [accessed 9 May 2022].
16   David Parkinson, radiotimes.com [accessed 9 May 2022].
17   *Kinematograph Weekly*, 14 August 1958, p. 5.
18   *Kinematograph Weekly*, 3 July 1958, p. 7.
19   *MFB*, 1958, p. 92.
20   *Kinematograph Weekly*, 14 August 1958, p. 15.
21   Halliwell, *Leslie Halliwell's Film Guide*, p. 229.
22   Alan Dent, *Illustrated London News*, 6 September 1958.
23   *Films and Filming*, December 1958.
24   *Observer*, 9 November 1958, p. 19.
25   *MFB*, 1958, p. 151.
26   *The Times*, 1 December 2007.
27   *Time*, 5 January 1959.
28   Fisher, *Funny Way to Be a Hero*, p. 46.
29   *Kinematograph Weekly*, 4 February 1960, p. 17.
30   *MFB*,1960, p. 38.

1959 notes

1   *The Times*, 2 February 1959, p. 12.
2   Shipman, *The Great Movie Stars: The Golden Years*, p. 409.
3   *The Times*, 31 March 1959, p. 11.
4   *Films and Filming*, March 1959.
5   *MFB*, 1959, p. 34.
6   *Films and Filming*, March 1959.
7   *Daily Cinema*, 11 February 1959, p. 8.
8   Brian McFarlane, *Lance Comfort* (Manchester: Manchester University Press, 1999), p. 153.
9   Quoted in Brown and Aldgate, *The Common Touch*, p. 122.
10   Garth Bardsley, *Stop the World: The Biography of Anthony Newley* (London: Oberon Books, 2003), p. 66.
11   *MFB*, 1959, p. 59.
12   *Bye Bye Birdie* was a musical by Michael Stewart, Charles Strouse, and Lee Adams, seen in New York in 1960, and London in 1961. It was filmed in 1963.
13   Bardsley, *Stop the World*, p. 66.
14   *Films and Filming*, June 1959.
15   Ronald Barker, *Plays and Players*, April 1955, p. 19.
16   *MFB*, 1959, p. 62.
17   *Films and Filming*, June 1959.
18   *Guardian*, 8 August 1959.
19   *MFB*, 1959, p. 82.
20   *Kinematograph Weekly*, 11 June 1959.
21   *MFB*, 1959, p. 160.
22   *MFB*, 1960, p. 11.
23   *The Times*, 23 December 1959.
24   *MFB*, 1960, p. 6.
25   *Kinematograph Weekly*, 3 December 1959, p. 17.

26 *Kinematograph Weekly*, 19 May 1960, p. 27.
27 *MFB*, 1960, p. 7.
28 *Guardian*, 28 November 1959, p. 5.
29 radiotimes.com [accessed 9 May 2022].
30 *Sight and Sound*, Winter 1959–60, p. 40.

1960 notes

1 *MFB*, 1960, p. 32.
2 Bardsley, *Stop the World*, p. 72.
3 *Kinematograph Weekly*, 18 February 1960, p. 9.
4 Bardsley, *Stop the World*, p. 73.
5 Quoted in ibid.
6 *Kinematograph Weekly*, 11 February 1960, p. 10.
7 *MFB*,1960, p. 37.
8 Ibid., p. 68.
9 Ibid., p. 114.
10 *Guardian*, 24 December 2014.
11 John Cutts, *Films and Filming*, November 1960, pp. 31–2.
12 *The Times*, 22 September 1960, p. 16.
13 *Kinematograph Weekly*, 22 September 1960, p. 14.
14 *MFB*, 1960, p. 153.
15 Halliwell, *Leslie Halliwell's Film Guide*, p. 1063.
16 Shipman, *The Great Movie Stars: The International Years*, p. 311.
17 *Kinematograph Weekly*, 6 October 1960, p. 19.
18 *MFB*, 1960, p. 154.
19 Alan Dent, *Illustrated London News*, 12 November 1960.
20 Quoted in ibid.
21 Stephen Glynn, *The British Pop Music Film: The Beatles and Beyond* (London: Palgrave Macmillan, 2013), p. 42.

1961 notes

1 McFarlane, *Lance Comfort*, p. 132.
2 Ibid., p. 129.
3 *MFB*, 1961, p. 67.
4 *MFB*, 1962, p. 15.
5 Andrew Roberts, *BFI Screenline*, screenline.org.uk [accessed 10 December 2021].
6 *Variety*, 31 December 1962.
7 'Pop Culture Obsessive Writing for the Pop Culture Obsessed', avclub.com [accessed 9 May 2022].
8 Medhurst, 'It Sort of Happened Here', in Romney and Wootton (editors), *Celluloid Jukebox*, p. 67.

1962 notes

1   Raymond Durgnat, *Films and Filming*, July 1962, p. 29.
2   *MFB*, 1962, p. 95.
3   McFarlane, *Lance Comfort*, p. 131.
4   *MFB*, 1962, p. 68.
5   *Films and Filming*, May 1962, p. 36.
6   K. J. Donnelly, *Pop Music in British Cinema* (London: BFI, 2001), p. 5.
7   George Perry, *The Great British Picture Show* (London: HarperCollins, 1974), p. 241.
8   Halliwell, *Leslie Halliwell's Film Guide*, p. 874.
9   *Films and Filming*, June 1962.
10 *MFB*, 1962, p. 69.
11 www.thequietus.com [accessed 9 May 2022].
12 Alan Dent, *Illustrated London News*, 4 August 1962.
13 *Films and Filming*, September 1962, p. 32.
14 *MFB*, 1962, p. 128.
15 Ibid., p. 139.
16 *Variety*, 31 December 1962.
17 Richard Whitehall, *Films and Filming*, March 1963, p. 34.
18 *MFB*, 1963, p. 48.
19 Penelope Houston, *Sight and Sound*, Spring 1963, p. 94.

1963 notes

1   Ross, *The Complete Frankie Howerd*, p. 116.
2   McCann, *Frankie Howerd*, p. 213.
3   Raymond Durgnat, *Films and Filming*, March 1963, p. 37.
4   James Oliver, in Julian Upton (editor), *Offbeat: British Cinema's Curiosities, Obscurities and Forgotten Gems* (London: Headpress, 2012), p. 219.
5   *MFB*, 1963, p. 19.
6   Ibid., p. 66.
7   Tony Mallerman, *Films and Filming*, May 1963.
8   *Variety*, 31 December 1962.
9   MacInnes, *England, Half English* (London: Hogarth Press, 1986), p. 50.
10 Ibid., p. 52.
11 *MFB*, 1963, p. 104.
12 Medhurst, 'It Sort of Happened Here', in Romney and Wootton (editors), *Celluloid Jukebox*, p. 67.
13 David Flint, reprobatepress.com [accessed 9 May 2022].
14 http://sweetwordsofpismotality.blogspot [accessed 9 May 2022].
15 David Parkinson, radiotimes.com [accessed 9 May].
16 http://sweetwordsofpismotality.blogspot.com [accessed 9 May 2022].
17 McFarlane, *Lance Comfort*, p. 154.
18 *MFB*, 1964, p. 10.
19 radiotimes.com [accessed 9 May 2022].
20 *Guardian*, 11 April 2000.

21 Medhurst, 'It Sort of Happened Here', in Romney and Wootton (editors), *Celluloid Jukebox*, p. 68.
22 *MFB*, 1964, p. 26.

1964 notes

1 PGB, *Films and Filming*, August 1964, p. 26.
2 Mark Beaumont, *New Musical Express*, 31 July 2015.
3 *MFB*, 1964, p. 121.
4 *Sight and Sound*, Autumn 1964, p. 196.
5 Roger Mellor, screenonline.org.uk [accessed 9 May 2022].
6 *PGB, Films and Filming*, August 1964, p. 26.
7 *MFB*, 1964, p. 119.
8 Donnelly, *Pop Music in British Cinema*, p. 16.
9 *MFB*, 1964, p. 122.
10 Ibid., p. 175.
11 radiotimes.com [accessed 9 May 2022].
12 *Films and Filming*, January 1965, pp. 31–2.
13 Medhurst, 'It Sort of Happened Here', in Romney and Wootton (editors), *Celluloid Jukebox*, p. 67.
14 *MFB*, 1965, p. 38.
15 *Films and Filming*, February 1965, pp. 34–5.
16 Bill Harry, 'The Merseyside Movie: Gerry on the Mersey', the-shortlisted.co.uk [accessed 8 February 2022].
17 Ibid.
18 *New York Times*, 20 February 1965.
19 Ibid.
20 *MFB*, 1965, p. 7.
21 Stephen Bourne, *Soft Lights and Sweet Music* (Oxford: Scarecrow Press, 2005), p. xvii.
22 Dorothy Whipple, *Random Commentary* (London: Michael Joseph, 1966), p. 31.

1965 notes

1 *MFB*, 1965, p. 58.
2 *Films and Filming*, October 1965, p. 31.
3 Ibid.
4 Ibid.
5 MarkDavidWalsh.wordpress.com [accessed 9 May 2022].
6 Kevin Gough-Yates, *Films and Filming*, September 1965.
7 Johnnyalucard.com [accessed 18. November 2020].
8 *MFB*, 1965, p. 75.
9 Raymond Durgnat, *Films and Filming*, May 1965, p. 32.
10 *Time Out*, 10 September 2012.
11 *Films and Filming*, June 1965, pp. 33–4.
12 *MFB*, 1965, p. 74.
13 Bosley Crowther, *New York Times*, 19 August 1965.

14 *MFB*, 1965, p. 118.
15 *Films and Filming*, August 1965, pp. 27–8.
16 Medhurst, 'It Sort of Happened Here', in Romney and Wootton (editors), *Celluloid Jukebox*, p. 68.
17 Roger Philip Mellor, *BFI Screenline*, screenline.org.uk [accessed 10 December 2021].
18 *The Times*, 27 April 1993, p. 35.
19 Perry, *The Great British Picture Show*, p. 242.
20 David Rider, *Films and Filming*, October 1965, p. 27.
21 *MFB*, 1965, p. 133.
22 Halliwell, *Leslie Halliwell's Film Guide*, p. 458.
23 David Sheff, *All We Are Saying* (New York: St Martin's Press, 2000), p. 176.
24 David Rider, *Films and Filming*, April 1966, pp. 54–5.
25 Quoted in christophermiles.info [accessed 9 May 2022].
26 *MFB*, 1966, p. 4.
27 Dick Richards, *Daily Mirror*, 15 December 1965, p. 5.
28 *Daily Mirror*, 8 August 1969, p. 9.
29 *MFB*, 1967, p. 74.
30 *MFB*, 1966, p. 22.
31 *Pop World*, 20 July 1963.

1966 notes

1 *MFB*, 1966, p. 73.
2 David McGillivray, *Doing Rude Things* (London: Sun Tavern Fields, 1992), p. 35.
3 Windmill Theatre, programme for *Secrets of a Windmill Girl*, 34th edition.
4 *MFB*, 1967, p. 45.
5 Gordon Gow, *Films and Filming*, May 1967.
6 *MFB*, 1967, p. 27.
7 *Films and Filming*, February 1967, p. 37.

1967 notes

1 Cyril Rollins and R. John Witts, *The D'Oyly Carte Opera Company in Gilbert and Sullivan Operas: A Record of Productions 1875–1961* (London: Michael Joseph, 1962).
2 Roberta Morrell, *D'Oyly Carte: The Inside Story* (Leicestershire: Matador, 2016), p. 38.
3 Arthur Jacobs, *Arthur Sullivan* (Oxford: Oxford University Press, 1984), p. 205.
4 *New York Times*, 15 March 1967.
5 Quoted in Ian Bradley, *Oh Joy! Oh Rapture!: The Enduring Phenomenon of Gilbert and Sullivan* (Oxford: Oxford University Press, 2005), p. 44.
6 Ibid., pp. 34–5.
7 Alexander Walker, *Hollywood England* (London: Michael Joseph, 1974), p. 394.
8 John Russell Taylor, *The Times*, 21 December 1967, p. 4.
9 Renata Adler, *New York Times*.
10 rogerebert.com [accessed 9 May 2022].

11 David Austen, *Films and Filming*, February 1968, p. 25.
12 *MFB*, 1968, p. 11.
13 Robin Bean, *Films and Filming*, February 1968, p. 21.
14 rogerebert.com [accessed 6 May 2022].
15 *Red and Blue*, DVD (2014), booklet notes.
16 Ibid.
17 Gordon Gow, *Films and Filming*, October 1968, p. 48.
18 Steven Puchalski, shockcinemamagazine.com [accessed 9 May 2022].

1968 notes

1   Ron Moody, *A Still Untitled (Not Quite) Autobiography* (London: JR Books, 2010), p. 184.
2   Perry, *The Great British Picture Show*, p. 229.
3   Ibid., p. 158.
4   *Time Out*, 26 January 2006.
5   *MFB*, 1968, pp. 172–3.
6   Obituary by Dennis Barker, *Guardian*, 11 June 2015.
7   Vincent Canby, *New York Times*, 12 December 1968.
8   Henry T. Murdock, *Philadelphia Inquirer*, 20 December 1968.
9   *MFB*, 1969, pp. 24–5.
10 *Time*, 27 December 1968.
11 Renata Adler, *New York Times*, 19 December 1968.
12 Richard Davis, *Films and Filming*, November 1969, p. 54.
13 *MFB*, 1969, p. 38.
14 *MFB*, 1970, p. 232.

1969 notes

1   *New York Times*, 20 March 1969.
2   *Chicago Sun-Times*, 28 May 1969.
3   *MFB*, 1969, p. 157.
4   Ibid., p. 108.
5   Peter Rankin, *Joan Littlewood: Dreams and Realities* (London: Oberon Books, 2014), p. 145.
6   Quoted in ibid., p. 151.
7   *MFB*, 1969, p. 94.
8   *Empire*, 2 August 2014.
9   *New York Times*, 25 August 2014.
10 *Films and Filming*, September 1969, pp. 48–50.
11 Ibid.
12 *New Yorker*, quoted in Halliwell, *Leslie Halliwell's Film Guide*, p. 417.
13 *MFB*, 1970, p. 4.
14 Ibid.
15 Quoted in Geoffrey Wansell, *Terence Rattigan* (London: Fourth Estate, 1995), p. 360.
16 Ibid.

1970 notes

1 Bruce Welch, *Rock'n'Roll: I Gave You the Best Years of My Life* (London: Viking, 1989).
2 *MFB*, 1970, p. 190.
3 John Russell Taylor, *The Times*, 27 November 1970.
4 rogerebert.com [accessed 6 May 2022].
5 *New Yorker*, November 1970.
6 *MFB*, 1971, p. 13.
7 *Time*, 7 December 1970.

1972 notes

1   rogerebert.com [accessed 9 May 2022].
2 *MFB*, 1972, p. 48.
3 Perry, *The Great British Picture Show*, p. 276.
4 *New York Times*, 17 December 1971.
5 *Life*, 21 January 1972, p. 16.
6 Sandy Wilson, *I Could Be Happy with You* (London: Michael Joseph, 1975), p. 270.
7 Ibid.

Select Bibliography

Babington, Bruce, *Launder and Gilliat* (Manchester: Manchester University Press, 2002)

Bardsley, Garth, *Stop the World: The Biography of Anthony Newley* (London: Oberon Books, 2003)

Barr, Charles (editor), *All Our Yesterdays: 90 Years of British Cinema* (London: BFI, 1986)

Barr, Charles, *Ealing Studios* (Berkeley and Los Angeles: University of California Press, 1998)

Bourne, Stephen, *Soft Lights and Sweet Music* (Oxford: Scarecrow Press, 2005)

Bradley, Ian, *Oh Joy! Oh Rapture!: The Enduring Phenomenon of Gilbert and Sullivan* (Oxford: Oxford University Press, 2005)

Brown, Geoff, and Aldgate, Tony, *The Common Touch: The Films of John Baxter* (London: BFI, 1989)

Chibnall, Steve, *Quota Quickies: The Birth of the British 'B' Film* (London: BFI, 2007)

Chibnall, Steve, and McFarlane, Brian, *The British 'B' Film* (London: Palgrave Macmillan, 2009)

Christie, Ian, *Arrows of Desire: The Films of Michael Powell and Emeric Pressburger* (London: Waterstone, 1985)

Donnelly, K. J., *Pop Music in British Cinema* (London: BFI, 2001)

Ellis, Vivian, *I'm on a See-Saw* (Bath: Cedric Chivers, 1974).

Fisher, John, *Funny Way to Be a Hero* (London: Frederick Muller, 1973)

Ganzl, Kurt, *The British Musical Theatre* (London: Macmillan, 1986)

Gardiner, Juliet, *Wartime: Britain 1939–45* (London: Review, 2005)

Gifford, Denis, *Entertainers in British Films: A Century of Showbiz in the Cinema* (Westport, CT: Greenwood Press, 1998)

Gifford, Denis, *The British Film Catalogue 1895–1985* (London: David and Charles, 1986)

Gifford, Denis, *The Golden Age of Radio: An Illustrated Companion* (London: B. T. Batsford, 1985)

Gifford, Denis, *The Illustrated Who's Who in British Films* (London: B. T. Batsford, 1979)

Glynn, Stephen, *The British Pop Music Film: The Beatles and Beyond* (London: Palgrave Macmillan, 2013)

Gregg, Hubert, *Agatha Christie and all that Mousetrap* (London: William Kimber, 1980)

Guillermin, Mary (editor), *John Guillermin: The Man, the Myth, the Movies* (Los Angeles: Precocity Press, 2020)

Halliwell, Leslie, *Leslie Halliwell's Film Guide*, 6th edn (London: Paladin, 1988)

Harding, James, *Ivor Novello* (London: W. H. Allen, 1987)

Hirschhorn, Clive, *The Warner Bros. Story* (London: Octopus, 1979)

Hughes, Gervase, *Composers of Operetta* (London: Macmillan, 1962)

Jacobs, Arthur, *Arthur Sullivan: A Victorian Musician* (Oxford: Oxford University Press, 1984)

Kenny, Robert V., *The Man Who Was Old Mother Riley: The Lives and Films of Arthur Lucan and Kitty McShane* (Albany, GA: Bear Manor Media, 2014)

Kilgarriff, Michael, *Grace, Beauty and Banjos: Peculiar Lives and Strange Times of Music Hall and Variety Artistes* (London: Oberon Books, 1999)

Kilgarriff, Michael, *Sing Us One of the Old Songs: A Guide to Popular Song 1860–1920* (Oxford University Press, 1998)

Kirkwood, Pat, *The Time of my Life* (London: Robert Hale, 1999)

Kynaston, David, *Austerity Britain 1945–51* (London: Bloomsbury, 2007)

MacInnes, Colin, *England, Half English* (London: MacGibbon and Kee, 1961)

McCann, Graham, *Frankie Howerd* (London: Fourth Estate, 2004)

McFarlane, Brian, *Lance Comfort* (Manchester: Manchester University Press, 1999)

McGillivray, David, *Doing Rude Things* (London: Sun Tavern Fields, 1992)

Montgomery, John, *Comedy Films 1894–1954* (London: George Allen and Unwin, 1968)

Monthly Film Bulletin (*MFB*)

Moody, Ron, *A Still Untitled (Not Quite) Autobiography* (London: JR Books, 2010)

Morrell, Roberta, *D'Oyly Carte: The Inside Story* (Leicestershire: Matador, 2016)

Murphy, Robert, *Realism and Tinsel: Cinema and Society in Britain 1939–49* (London: Routledge, 1989)

Noble, Peter (editor), *British Film Yearbook 1947–8* (London: Skelton Robinson, 1947)

Nuttall, Jeff. *King Twist* (London: Routledge and Kegan Paul, 1978)

Overy, Richard, *The Morbid Age: Britain and the Crisis of Civilization* (London: Penguin Books, 2010)

Palmer, Scott, *British Film Actors' Credits, 1895–1987* (Jefferson, NC, and London: McFarland, 1988)

Perry, George, *The Great British Picture Show* (London: HarperCollins, 1974)

Powell, Dilys, *The Golden Screen: Fifty Years of Films* (London: Headline, 1989)

Quinlan, David, *British Sound Films: The Studio Years 1928-1959* (London: B. T. Batsford, 1984)

Rankin, Peter, *Joan Littlewood: Dreams and Realities* (London: Oberon Books, 2014)

Romney, Jonathan, and Wootton, Adrian (editors), *Celluloid Jukebox* (London: BFI, 1995)

Roper, David, *Bart!: The Authorised Life and Times* (London: Pavilion, 1994)

Ross, Robert, *The Complete Frankie Howerd* (London: Reynolds and Hearn, 2001)

Sandbrook, Dominic, *Never Had It So Good* (London: Little, Brown, 2005)

Sandbrook, Dominic, *State of Emergency* (London: Allen Lane, 2010)

Shipman, David, *The Great Movie Stars: The Golden Years* (London: Hamlyn, 1970)

Shipman, David, *The Great Movie Stars: The International Years* (London: Angus and Robertson, 1972)

Short, Ernest, *Fifty Years of Vaudeville 1895–1945* (London: Eyre and Spottiswoode, 1946)

Staveacre, Tony, *The Songwriters* (London: BBC, 1960)

Thornton, Michael, *Jessie Matthews* (London: Hart-Davis, MacGibbon, 1974)

Threadgall, Derek, *Shepperton* (London: BFI, 1994).

Traubner, Richard, *Operetta: A Theatrical History* (London: Victor Gollancz, 1984)

Upton, Julian (editor), *Offbeat: British Cinema's Curiosities, Obscurities and Forgotten Gems* (London: Headpress, 2012)

Vahimagi, Tise (compiler), *British Television: An illustrated guide* (Oxford: Oxford University Press, 1994)

Van Damm, Sheila, *We Never Closed* (London: Robert Hale, 1967)

Walker, Alexander, *Hollywood England* (London: Michael Joseph, 1974)

Wansell, Geoffrey, *Terence Rattigan* (London: Fourth Estate, 1995)

Warren, Patricia, *British Film Studios: An Illustrated History* (London: B. T. Batsford, 1995)

Wearing, J. P., *The London Stage: 1950–1959* (Lanham, MD: Rowman and Littlefield, 2014)

Weaver, Tom, *Science Fiction Confidential: Interviews with 23 Monster Stars and Filmmakers* (Jefferson, NC: McFarland, 2002)

Welch, Bruce, *Rock'n'Roll: I Gave You the Best Years of My Life* (London: Viking, 1989)

Whipple, Dorothy, *Random Commentary* (London: Michael Joseph, 1966)

Wilcox, Herbert, *Twenty-Five Thousand Sunsets* (London: Bodley Head, 1967)

Williams, Philip Martin, and Williams, David L., *Hooray for Jollywood: The Life of John E. Blakeley and the Mancunian Film Corporation* (Ashton-under-Lyne: History on Your Doorstep, 2001)

Wilson, Sandy, *Ivor* (London: Michael Joseph, 1975)

Wright, Adrian, *Cheer Up!* (Woodbridge: The Boydell Press, 2020)

Wright, Adrian, *The Innumerable Dance: The Life and Work of William Alwyn* (Woodbridge: The Boydell Press, 2008)

Index of Film Titles

General Index

Brothers Grimm   181
Brown, Barbara   261, 262
Brown, Burton   4
Brown, George H.   197, 278
Brown, Georgia   148, 291
Brown, Janet   67
Brown, Joe   233, 238, 240, 248, 264, 265
Brown, Lew   243
Brown, Nacio Herb   311
Browne, George   161, 207
Browne, Irene   192
Browne, Wynyard   151, 209
Browning, Maurice   228
Bruce, Judith   52, 276, 292
Brune, Gabrielle   92, 130, 146
Brunn, George Le   235
Bryan, Dora   107, 112, 116, 183, 198, 288
Bryant, Gerard   51, 158
Bryant, Margot   213
Bryant, Mark   277
Buchel, Philip and Betty   39, 54, 109
Buck, Alan   260
Buckland, Robert   46
Bunnage, Avis   238, 239
Burge, Stuart   280
Burke, Aileen   49, 59, 241
Burke, Brian   148
Burke, Johnny   19, 223
Burke, Patricia   7
Burnett, Al   196
Burns, Robert   35–6
Burns, Wilfred   23, 101
Burt, Heinz   240, 241, 242, 265
Burton, Richard   302
Busby, Bob   30
Butler, Joan   1
Butlin, Billy   32, 251
Butt, Clara   61
Butterworth, Peter   130, 181
Buxton, Sheila   171
Bye Bye Birdie   114, 191, 238, 283
Bygraves, Max   49, 50, 59, 107, 116, 131, 132, 133, 167, 173, 178, 179

Cabaret   2
Cable, John   266
Cadell, Jean   193
Cahn, Sammy   223

Calamity Jane   179
Caldwell, Gloria   260
Calthrop, Donald   307
Cameron, John   98
Camp, William   191
Campbell, Keith   51
Campbell, Murray   171
Campbell, Colin   46
Campion, Gerald   131
Candles at Nine   30
Cannan, Denis   30
Cannon, Esma   33
Cannon, Freddy   233
Cannon, Ricky   262
Canterbury Tale, A   119
Capra, Frank   38, 80, 302
Carby, Fanny   238, 301
Cardboard Cavalier   23
Carden, George   157, 181
Carey, Dave   243, 247, 248
Carey, Joyce   71
Carlisle, Carl   2, 16, 50
Carmichael, Ian   285
Carney, Kate   234
Carousel   201, 264
Carpenter, Freddie   12, 19, 87
Carr, Carole   87
Carr, Leon   196
Carr, Michael   8, 137, 182, 183, 220, 243, 248
Carroll, Peter   118
Carson, Jean   43, 114, 115, 127
Carstairs, John Paddy   104, 110, 118, 147, 197, 199
Carwithen, Doreen   141–2
Cass, Ronnie   117, 177, 245, 270
Castle, Helénè   102
Castle, Roy   182, 183
Castling, Harry   210, 234
Caton, Lauderic   27
Cavalcanti, Alberto   30, 40
Cavell, Andy   241
Cavell, Edith   186
Chadwick, Les   256
Chagrin, Francis   131
Chalmers, W. G.   171
Chambers, Karl   306
Champagne Charlie   10, 55, 115